A Documentary History *of* Nepalese Quinquennial Missions to China 1792-1906

Vijay Kumar Manandhar

M.A.(T.U.), M.A. (Wisconsin), Ph.D. (T.U.)
Associate Professor
Central Department of History
Tribhuvan University, Kirtipur
Kathmandu, Nepal

ADROIT PUBLISHERS
DELHI-110 053

Published by
ADROIT PUBLISHERS
C-8/2, Yamuna Vihar, Delhi-110 053
e-mail: akhilbooks@yahoo.com
Phone: 3266030

ISBN : 81-87392-21-5

Laser Typeset by
Krishna Kumar Thapa
Kirtipur, Kathmandu, Nepal

Printed in India by
Nice Printing Press, New Delhi

For Rupa
and our daughters
Pratibha, Prerana and Pragya

Foreword

Conducting the foreign policy and relations of a small state situated between two big powers with different political ideologies is rather a difficult task. Nepal, situated between two powers like India and China, has to conduct its foreign policy and relations in the most tactful and diplomatic way. The Nepalese statesmen had maintained good relations with both neighbours in the most diplomatic way befitting the situation (national and international) as well as for the benefit of the nation. Such handling of foreign policy does not mean that the Nepalese rulers had become tools of any power. At times they had shown their national interests without yielding to anyone. The friendly gestures like helping the next door neighbour in time of crisis or sending missions with presents (which were in reality reciprocated) should not be interpreted otherwise. Foreign writers have seldom presented Nepal as a state dominated by either by north or by south. But Nepal has always remained a sovereign independent state.

Writing a book about Nepal's foreign policy is also a difficult task because of the inaccessibility of the primary sources. Foreign Ministry Archives/Nepal is now not accessible to any scholar. Indian National Archives also does not allow foreign scholars to consult post-1914 documents.

Under such circumstances Dr. Vijay Kumar Manandhar has written a scholarly book on the Nepalese quinquennial missions to China (1792 to 1906). This is not the first book on the subject as Dr. Tri Ratna Manandhar and Dr. Tirtha Prasad Mishra had written the first book in 1986 A.D. Fortunately all the three scholarly teachers had opportunity to consult the unpublished official documents of the Foreign Ministry Archives of Nepal when it was open two decades back. On the basis of the documents of the Foreign Ministry Archives/Nepal and Indian National Archives/New Delhi and other standard books, Nepalese scholars started writing books on Nepal's foreign relations. Leo E. Rose has also written a standard book on Nepal's foreign policy entitled *Nepal: Strategy for Survival.* He had the opportunity to consult first hand information about China and Tibet also.

Dr. Vijay Manandhar is one of my most intelligent and scholarly student-cum-colleagues who has worked on Nepal-China relations for the last several years. He has the opportunity to consult most authentic books with documents relating to Chinese foreign policy, when he was in the United States. Nothing would be happier to me than to see my own student-cum-colleague come forward with standard academic contributions. Dr. Manandhar's present work is his second contribution on Nepal-China relations.

Dr. Manandhar has dealt with all the quinquennial missions (18 in number) describing all the details i.e. the composition, details of the presents, meeting with different foreigners *en route*, hardship and details of the travels, audience with the Chinese Emperors, return etc. The achievements of all the missions are most critically assessed, which bear testimony to the scholarship of the writer.

The scholar has rightly presented that the missions of the pre-Rana period were political motivated to maintain cordial relations between the two countries. Chinese Emperors also wished for Nepal's prosperity and happiness. The then Nepalese rulers had their political purpose in sending the missions within the country and abroad. But the missions were misused by the Ranas, who exploited the system for the monetary benefit. The missions were sent to smuggle opium and other goods in Chinese market which had rather defamed them. Later when opium trade was found impossible in China due to the declaration of opium as contraband product, the Ranas lost their interest in sending the mission. Later the Ranas discontinued the system taking advantage of changed political scenario in China.

All the details of the missions are very analytically assessed. The present work is a testimony of standard scholarship of the writer who has not only consulted Chinese sources and standard books but has also consulted and produced all the mission related unpublished documents available in Royal Nepal Army Head-quarters, National Archives of Nepal, Foreign Ministry Archives/Kathmandu and Indian National Archives, New Delhi. By the publication of these more than two hundred relevant unpublished documents, the other scholars are given an opportunity to undertake further research work on the subject.

I wish Dr. Manandhar would come forward with more books in future.

Prof. Dr. Tulasi Ram Vaidya
Head, Central Department of History
Tribhuvan University
Kirtipur, Kathmandu, Nepal

Preface

The Quinquennial mission system, originated from the peace agreement between Nepal and China in 1792, formed an integral part of Nepal-China relations. A pioneering research work on the subject has been made by Tri Ratna Manandhar and Tirtha Prasad Mishra. In that excellent research work, the writers have not only dealt with the complete history of Nepalese quinquennial missions to China from 1792 to 1906, but have also analysed the different aspects of the Nepalese five-yearly missions to China using primarily unpublished, original sources derived from different government offices and archives of Nepal and India. This work was indeed the first of its kind in the field of Nepal-China relations, and thus a great contribution for studying the important aspects of Nepal-China relations. Despite these merits, the writers have very briefly traced the history of Nepalese missions to China and have not used Chinese sources. Nevertheless they have been a great source of inspiration to me to undertake this research work..

The main objective of this book is to trace the detailed history of the Nepalese quinquennial missions to China and to bring out all the available mission related unpublished documents of Ministry of Foreign Affairs, Kathmandu; Royal Nepal Army Head-quarters, Kathmandu; National Archives of Nepal, Kathmandu and National Archives of India, New Delhi. Thus this work is mainly based on these unpublished original documents. The Chinese sources have also been used. Besides that, relevant books, articles and published documents are utilised at proper places.

In this book, the history of Nepalese five-yearly missions to China has been divided into two parts. The first part deals with the Pre-Rana period, i.e. the eleven missions from 1792 to 1842. The second part discusses the Rana-period, i.e. seven missions from 1847 to 1906.

I like to take this opportunity to express my deep gratitude to my esteemed teacher Prof. Dr. Tulasi Ram Vaidya, Head, Central Department of History, Tribhuvan University, Kirtipur, Nepal, whom I regard as my chief mentor and the great source of inspiration to me interested in the subject. I am also obliged to him for contributing scholarly foreword as well. I am profoundly grateful to Prof. Dr. Tirtha Prasad Mishra, Executive Director, CNAS, T.U. for his generous help of providing the unpublished documents of Ministry of Foreign Affairs, Kathmandu and to Historian Hari Ram Joshi and my colleague Dr. Shanker Thapa for their constant help and encouragement. I do wish to express my special thanks to my colleague Mr. Bhaveshwar Pangeni, Lecturer, Central Department of History, T.U., Kirtipur who has been good enough to read through the manuscript and give me many valuable suggestions and corrections. I would also like to thank Brigadier General (Retd.) Keshar Bahadur Gadhatola for making available to me the historic photos of his family. I owe a particular debt of gratitude to Mr. Krishna Kumar Thapa for all the computer related work. I also wish to express my thanks to the concerned staff of the National Archives of Nepal, Kathmandu; the Royal Nepal Army Head-quarters, Kathmandu and the National Archives of India, New Delhi. I also express my profound thanks to Adroit Publishers for taking great pains to publish this book.

Finally, I wish to express my special appreciation to my wife Rupa Manandhar for her untiring efforts and inspiration in writing this book.

Needless to say, the individuals mentioned above are not responsible for the views, interpretations, and misinterpretations that appear in the following pages. All errors of fact and judgement are my own. Healthy criticism and suggestions are always welcome.

Central Department of History
Tribhuvan University
Kirtipur, Kathmandu
Nepal

Vijay Kumar Manandhar

Background

Nepal and China have a long history of political, social, economic and cultural relations. In the absence of contemporary evidences it cannot be said when the Nepal-China relation began. But due to geo-political location of Nepal, the socio-economic, cultural and political relations between the two must have been in existence since long. However, the epigraphic evidences refer to the contact between the two from the fifth century. Historically, political relations between the two countries go back to the seventh century A.D. During this period, official contacts between the Nepalese court and the T'ang dynasty were maintained through the exchange of political missions. However, unofficial contacts between the two countries began in the fifth century A.D. with the visit of Chinese monks to Nepal and a Nepalese Buddhist teacher to China; thus Buddhism became the chief source of links between the two countries. With the collapse of the T'ang dynasty (618-907 A.D.), relations between the two countries were suspended for about two hundred and fifty years. During the Yuan dynasty (1271-1368 A.D.), Sino-Nepalese relations were revived through A-ni-ka (Arniko), the gifted Nepalese artist who established his artistic glory in China by demonstrating his skill at the court of the Mongol Emperor of China, Kublai Khan. In the Ming dynasty (1368-1644 A.D.), there was a reestablishment of diplomatic relations between the two countries, but this time, the Ming rulers established relations with Nepal's powerful Ramavardhan family through exchange of missions, ignoring the Malla rulers of the Nepal Mandala. After the suppression of the Ramavardhan family, the Malla rulers of the Nepal Mandala terminated Nepal's relations with the Ming court, and later on they tried to establish relations with the Ch'ing court.

It was only after the creation of modern Nepal by King Prithvi Narayan Shah in 1769 that Sino-Nepalese relations entered into a new, but somewhat controversial phase, with Tibetan affairs dominating the situation. Nepal's commercial disputes with Tibet led it into direct conflict with China in 1791-1792. The system of sending Nepalese complimentary quinquennial missions to China had its origin in the peace agreement of September 1792 between Nepalese and Chinese officials following the end of the Sino-Nepalese war. There were several instances of Nepalese missions visiting China in the past, but the new arrangement in accordance with the peace agreement of 1792 made it obligatory for Nepal to send a complimentary diplomatic mission with presents to the "Son of Heaven" (the Chinese Emperor) every five years. Thus it is a known fact that Nepal sent her five-yearly missions to China as an obligation due to the outcome of the peace agreement.

Here it will not be out of context to mention why this new arrangement for quinquennial missions was made as part of the peace agreement of 1792. Several Nepalese missions visited China during the ancient and medieval periods. In 1789 also, Nepal herself took the initiative of sending a mission to China in order to please the Ch'ing court. But in accordance with the agreement of 1792, the new arrangement made it obligatory for Nepal to send a diplomatic cum complimentary mission with gifts and an *arji* (special letter) to the Chinese Emperor every five years. In return, the Nepalese delegation received awards, presents and a golden *Parwana* (letter) to give to the Nepalese king on behalf of the Ch'ing Emperor. It seems that the new arrangement of the mission system though had nothing to do with Nepal-Tibet relations and was a way of degrading Nepal's status, at least in Chinese eyes.[1] From the traditional Chinese point of view, any foreign state having any relation or intercourse with China was a tributary. That is why China wanted to maintain "tributary" relations with Nepal -- in order to follow the ancient Chinese maxim : "The Chinese rulers exercised power over all peoples of the World through the will of the Devine Overlord."[2] Here it should be mentioned that China wanted to check the dominant position of Nepal in Tibet. Furthermore, the mission system

---

1. Tri Ratna Manandhar and Tirtha Prasad Mishra, *Nepal's Quinquennial Missions to China*, Kathmandu: Purna Devi Manandhar and Puspa Mishra, 1986, p. 15.
   Regarding the new arrangement of the mission system following the peace agreement of 1792, Tucci and Pande have wrongly stated that Nepal sent missions to China with gifts in every three years and ten years respectively.
   Giuseppe Tucci, *Nepal: The Discovery of the Malla*, London: George Allen and Unwin, 1962, and Bhim Bahadur Pande Chhetri, *Rastra Bhakti Ko Jhalak : Pande Bamsa Ko Bhumika, 1594-1904* (A Glimpse of Loyalty to the Nation : Role of the Pande Dynasty, 1539-1847), Kathmandu : Ratna Pustak Bhandar, 2034 B.S., p. 156.
2. L.I. Duman, "Ancient Chinese Foreign Policy and the Origins of the Tribute System", *China and Her Neighbours*, S.L. Tikhvinsky (ed.), Moscow: Progress Publishers, 1981, p. 27.

placed Nepal under an obligation to accept Chinese decisions on all her relations, especially with Tibet. The Chinese *Ambans* (Imperial Residents) at Lhasa controlled Tibet's foreign relations, trade and defence. In spite of all these measures, the Ch'ing court could gather information about Nepal only through its *Ambans* at Tibet. The Ch'ing court realized that some sort of direct communication should be made with Nepal. This new arrangement of five-yearly missions presented an opportunity (a favourable occasion) to the Ch'ing court to have direct communication with the Nepalese court at higher level. For this reason, Chinese officials always insisted that the Nepalese quinquennial mission to China should be led at least by a person of *Kazi* rank.[3]

Regarding the origin of the new system of sending Nepalese quinquennial missions to China, Prem Raman Uprety opined that the sending of quinquennial mission had started after Nepal defeated Tibet in 1788[4], but his view cannot be justified due to three reasons. Firstly, the Nepalese, Tibetan and Chinese versions of the treaty of 1789 do not mention anything at all about the sending of the five-yearly missions as a part of the treaty. On the otherhand, each and every so far available copy of the treaty of 1792 clearly mentions the quinquennial mission in detail[5]. Furthermore, Tibetan and Chinese sources[6] suggest that the treaty of 1789 was signed by both Nepal and Tibet without the approval or even knowledge of China. The question thus naturally arises as to how is it possible to include the quinquennial mission provision in the treaty of 1789, in which China had not participated. Secondly, the Nepalese mission sent to Peking in September 1789 under the leadership of Hari Shah was a special mission and not a five-yearly mission. Such special Nepalese missions were sent to China even during the ancient and medieval periods. Furthermore, the Nepalese decision to send a special mission to the Ch'ing court

---

3. Manandhar and Mishra, f.n.no. 1, p. 16.
4. Prem R. Uprety, *Nepal-Tibet Relations, 1850-1930*, Kathmandu: Puga Nara, 1980, p. 191.
5. Leo E. Rose, *Nepal: Strategy For Survival,* Berkeley: University of California Press, 1971, p. 65.
   Pudma Jung Bahadur Rana, *Life of Maharaja Sir Jung Bahadur,* Kathmandu: Ratna Pustak Bhandar, Reprint, 1980, p. 8.
6. For the Tibetan source, see Tsepon W.D. Shakabpa, *Tibet: A Political History,* New Haven: Yale University Press, 1967, p. 161.
   For the Chinese source, see Rose, f.n.no. 5, pp. 43-44.

was made only after a treaty had been signed between Nepal and Tibet in 1789, thus clearly indicating that the topic of the mission was not connected with the Nepal-Tibet treaty of 1789. The Chinese sources state that the Chinese officials approved the treaty of 1789, possibly without examining its provisions once Nepal consented to send a mission to Peking in order to pay respect to the "Son of Heaven", the Chinese Emperor. Thirdly, the Chinese patents conferred to the Nepalese King Ran Bahadur Shah in 1790 did not mention anything about the five-yearly mission[7], whereas in his letter to the Ch'ing Emperor, Ch'ien Lung, the Nepalese King Ran Bahadur Shah had distinctly mentioned that *Kazi* Dev Datta Thapa (the leader of the 1792 Nepalese mission to China) was the first Nepalese official to lead a five-yearly mission to China.[8]

In this way, one can conclude that the quinquennial missions to China were sent only after 1792, and not in 1789, and that new arrangement of the mission system was the outcome of the peace agreement between Nepal and China in 1792. Certainly the Nepalese mission of 1789 was the first one to go to China in modern times, but that was definitely not a five-yearly mission. In fact, the new arrangement of sending Nepalese quinquennial missions to China began only in 1792. With this, Nepal's relations with China entered into a new phase.

Remarkably enough, even though the journey from Kathmandu to Peking was quite difficult, long and hazardous, Nepal continued to send missions to Ch'ing Court from 1792 to 1906. During this period, Nepal dispatched altogether eighteen missions to China. The details of these missions are to be discussed in the following pages.

* * *

---

7. Patent of 5 March 1790, Foreign Dept. Secret (Sec.) E. July 1911, No. 264, National Archives of India, New Delhi (hereafter referred as NAI). See also Vijay Kumar Manandhar, *Cultural and Political Aspects of Nepal-China Relations*, Delhi: Adroit Publishers, 1990., pp. 22-25.
8. Nepalese King to Chinese Emperor, 1899 B.S. Ashad 8 Roj 6 (23 June 1842), Ministry of Foreign Affairs, Kathmandu (hereafter mentioned as MFA), Unnumbered *Poka.*
   Nepal Government to Government of China, 1899 B.S., Ashad Badi 8 Roj 6 (23 June 1842), National Archives of Nepal, Kathmandu (hereafter referred as NAN), *Poka* No.5, Letter No. 44. But Manandhar and Mishra have given the date of the aforementioned letter as 1899 B.S. Ashad 2 Gate Roj 6, see Manandhar and Mishra, f.n.no. 1, pp. 79-81.

Contents

Foreword
Preface
Background

Part One
Pre-Rana Period 1792-1842

1.	*Kazi* Dev Dutta Thapa's Mission of 1792	1
2.	*Kazi* Narsingh Gurung's Mission of 1795	6
3.	*Kazi* Sarvajit Pande's Mission of 1802	22
4.	*Kazi* Bhaktabir Thapa's Mission of 1807	31
5.	*Kazi* Bhaktabir Thapa's Mission of 1812	37
6.	*Kazi* Ranajoor Thapa's Mission of 1817	46
7.	*Kazi* Dalbhanjan Pande's Mission of 1822	48
8.	*Kazi* Bir Keshar Pande's Mission of 1827	60
9.	*Kazi* Bir Keshar Pande's Mission of 1832	65
10.	*Chautariya Kazi* Pushkar Shah's Mission of 1837	76
11.	*Kazi* Jagat Bam Pande's Mission of 1842	85

Part Two
Rana Period 1847-1906

12.	*Kazi* Surath Singh Pantha's Mission of 1847	105
13.	*Kazi* Gambhir Singh Adhikari's Mission of 1852	119
14.	*Kazi* Jagat Sher Sijapati's Mission of 1866	137
15.	*Kazi* Tej Bahadur Rana's Mission of 1877	161
16.	*Kazi* Ran Bikram Rana's Mission of 1886	180
17.	*Kazi* Indra Bikram Rana's Mission of 1894	189
18.	*Kazi* Bhairab Bahadur Gadhatola's Mission of 1906	200
	Conclusion	235
	Chronology of Nepalese Quinquennial Missions to China 1792-1906	238
	Selected Bibliography	241
	Index	248

Part One

Pre-Rana Period 1792-1842

1

Kazi Dev Dutta Thapa's Mission of 1792

In accordance with the peace agreement between Nepal and China in September 1792, Nepal soon sent her first five-yearly mission to the Ch'ing court in October 1792 under the leadership of *Kazi* Dev Dutta Thapa.[1] The Chinese Imperial records have also mentioned about the 1792 Nepalese quinquennial mission to China.[2] The other members of the 1792 Nepalese five-yearly mission were *Subba* Pratiman Rana, deputy leader of the mission, Jayanta Sahi (Gurung), son of *Jetha Budha* Narsingh (Gurung) *Taksari*, and Balbhadra, son of *Khardar* Vishnu Shankar.[3] There were some *Jamadars* (junior military personnel), and two Kashmiri interpreters in the mission.[4] The delegates carried an *arji*[5], a letter[6] and huge gifts from the Nepalese King Ran Bahadur Shah to the Ch'ing Emperor Ch'ien Lung. On 6 October, 1792, along with Chinese Commander Fu K'ang-an, the Nepalese mission left Dhaibung for Lhasa *en route* to Peking.[7] There is also the reference of the Chinese Commander asking King Ran Bahadur Shah to send the Nepalese mission to China soon.[8] Another Nepalese document

---

1. *Arji* to the Emperor, dated 1849 B.S. Ashwin Sukla 1 Roj 2 (1792), Ministry of Foreign Affairs, Kathmandu (hereafter mentioned as MFA), *Poka* No. Pa. 64. See Appendix B.
2. J.K. Fairbank and S.Y. Teng, "On the Ch'ing Tributary System", *Harvard Journal of Asiatic Studies*, Vol. VI, 1941, pp. 195-198.
3. Dhanavajra Vajracharya (ed.), *Tri-Ratna Saundarya Gatha* (An Account of the Beauty of the Three Jewels), Kathmandu: Nepal Sanskritik Parishad, 2019 B.S., p. 281.
4. D.R. Regmi, *Modern Nepal*, Vol. I, Calcutta: Firma K.L. Mukhopadhyay, Second Edition, 1975, p. 482.
5. *Arji* to the Chinese Emperor, dated 1849 B.S. Ashwin Sukla 1 Roj 2 (1792), MFA, *Poka* No. Pa 64. See Appendix B.
6. Nepalese King to Chinese Emperor, 1849 B.S., Ashwin Sudi Roj 3 (1792), MFA, *Poka* No. Pa 64. See Appendix C.
7. Dhanavajra Vajracharya and Jnanmani Nepal (eds.), *Aitihasik Patra Sangraha* (Collection of Historical Letters), Vol. I, Kathmandu: Nepal Sanskritik Parishad, 2014 B.S., p. 61.
8. Thung thang Chang-Chun to King Ran Bahadur Shah, 1849 B.S. Ashwin Badi 10 Roj 2 (1792), MFA, *Poka* No. Pa 64. See Appendix A.

has mentioned about the Chinese *Amban's* pardoning of Nepal's wrong doings and recommending the Chinese Emperor to confer titles and honours to the Nepalese party.[9] The mission took nearly a year to make a round-trip from Nepal to China and back. This Nepalese mission remained in Peking for about five months. Like the earlier special Nepalese mission of 1789[10], the first Nepalese complimentary quinquennial mission of 1792 carried some elephants and horses from Nepal's Tarai area as presents for the Ch'ing Emperor Ch'ien Lung. However, due to certain difficulties on the way to Lhasa, the elephants had to be returned from Kuti to Nepal and there was the report of the death of *Mahout* (the keeper and driver of an elephant).[11] The Chinese sources also indicate that an orchestra was also included in the first Nepalese mission of 1792. The orchestra was composed of two female dancers, five singers and six musicians (instrument players). Those two female dancers wore red and green silk clothes. They also wore red hats made of wool. Their shoes were made of red silk. The dancers had tied *Ghungaroo* (ringing bells) around both of their legs with red cords. As for the singers, they wore red and green clothes and red shoes. This orchestra had left a book entitled *Gorkha Ko Geet* (Songs of Gorkha) in China.[12] This delegation of 1792 brought a letter and various valuable presents from the Ch'ing Emperor Ch'ien Lung to the Nepalese King Ran Bahadur Shah and Regent Bahadur Shah.

The importance of this mission of 1792 lies in the fact that it inaugurated the system of complimentary quinquennial missions to China, thereby regularising Nepal's direct contact with the Peking government. With this, Nepal's relations with China entered into a new phase. This quinquennial mission system continued till 1906.

---

9. Chinese *Amban* to Nepalese King, 1850 B.S. Chaitra Sudi 8 Roj 4 (1793), MFA, *Poka* No. Pa 64. See Appendix F.
10. For the details of the special Nepalese mission of 1789, see Vijay Kumar Manandhar, *Cultural And Political Aspects of Nepal-China Relations*, Delhi: Adroit Publishers, 1999, pp. 11-26.
11. Chinese *Amban* to Ran Bahadur Shah, 1851 B.S. Chaitra (1794), MFA, *Poka* No. Pa 64. See Appendix D.
12. Niranjan Bhattarai, *Chin Ra Tyas Sita Nepal Ko Sambandha* (China and Nepal's Relations with her), Kathmandu: Nepal Academy, 2018 B.S., pp. 171-172.

Moreover, the mission of 1792 was the first ever five-yearly mission which completed the round-trip journey from Nepal to China in the shortest period, that is, within one year. Afterwards from 1795 to 1852, the journey of the each Nepalese mission to China was completed in less than two years. Later on with the involvement of Nepalese quinquennial missions in trading activities, their journey became quite longer. Lastly, while discussing the mission of 1792, D.R. Regmi and Shakabpa have mentioned that through this very mission of 1792 the Ch'ing Emperor conferred the title of *Wang* and plumes for their crowns on King Ran Bahadur Shah and Regent Bahadur Shah.[13] This is, however, far from the truth. In fact, it was through the special mission of 1789 that King Ran Bahadur Shah and Regent Bahadur Shah received the Ch'ing Emperor's titles of *Wang* and *Kung* (*Ghung*) respectively in 1790.[14]

Appendix A

सम्वत १८४९ साल आश्वीन वदी १० रोज २ मा धैवुङ काम्पा वाट टुंथ्वाङ च्यांचुनले श्री ५ रण वहादुर साहलाई पठाएको पत्रमा- डीगर्चामा लुटको धनमाल र स्यामराको हाल धनमाल गरी भारी ७ आइ पुग्यो– लुटको धनमाल राख्नु नराम्रो हुनाले सवै धनमाल फर्काइ दिनु– चिन पठाउने काजी भारदार सरसौगाद स्मेत चाडो पठाउनु ....

(Thung thang Chan–Chun to King Ran Bahadur Shah instructing to return all the plunderings of Digarcha and to send the Nepalese mission to China soon.)

Source : Ministry of Foreign Affairs, Kathmandu (MFA), *Poka* No. Pa. 64.

13. Regmi, f.n.no. 3, p. 483, and Tsepon W. D. Shakabpa, *Tibet: A Political History,* New Haven: Yale University Press, 1976, p. 169. Chinese *Amban* to Nepalese King, 1850 B.S. Shrawan Badi Roj 1 (1793), MFA, *Poka* No. Pa 64. See Appendix E.
14. Patent of 5 March 1790, Foreign Dept. Sec. E, July 1911, No. 264, National Archives of India, New Delhi (hereafter referred as NAI), and Chinese Emperor to King Ran Bahadur Shah, dated Chhayalun 55th year 1st month (1790), MFA, *Poka* No. Pa 64. See Manandhar, f.n. no. 9, p. 26. See also Leo E. Rose, *Nepal: Strategy For Survival*, Berkeley: University of California Press, 1971, pp. 45-46, and Chitta Ranjan Nepali, *Shree Panch Ran Bahadur Shah* (King Ran Bahadur Shah), Kathmandu: Ratna Pustak Bhandar, Second Edition, 2044 B.S., p. 90.

Appendix B

काजी देवदत्त थापा (मामुलि सौगाद लि चीन) जादाको लेषी गयाको ....
स्यामरपाले गर्दा भोटमा लस्कर गयाको हो - दीगर्चा लुटी फर्कदा १०००/१२०० नोक्सान भएको - तुङ थ्याङको आक्रमण ३।४ हज्जार फौज हाम्रो नेपालको नोक्सान भएको - स्यामरपाको हाड खोड, स्वास्नी दीगर्चाको माल पठाएको . हिजो पनि भोटसंग मिलेकै. अव झगडा हुनन. म वालक र काका वावा मुलुकको काम काज गर्ने हुनाले दर्सन गर्न आउन पठाउन सकीन. काजी देवदत्त थापा सुव्वा प्रतिमनहरु लाई पठाएको छ. प्रति वर्ष दर्सन गर्न पठाउं भन्या ञाहादेखि चीन टाढा छ ५ वर्षमा ससौगाद दिइ काजलिाइ पठाउला भंन्या १८४९ साल आश्वीन शुक्ल १ रोज २ श्री ५ चीन वादशाहका हर्जुमा लेषी पठाउनलाई लेषी गयाको अर्जी ....
(In this *arji* to the Chinese Emperor, King Ran Bahadur Shah has mentioned the sending of the Nepalese mission to China under the leadership of *Kazi* Dev Dutta Thapa.)

Source : MFA, *Poka* No. Pa. 64.

Appendix C

काजी देवदत्त थापा जादाको लेषी गयाको ....
१८४९ साल आश्वीन सुदी रोज ३. श्री ५ चीन वादसाहलाई पठाएको चीट्ठीमा- स्यामर्पा ले गर्दा झगडा भएको हो. ल्हासामा षोटो टक र चोषो टक वरावर चलेको छ. षोटो चलन नगर्नु चोषो मात्र चलन गर्नु भन्न ल्हासालाई हुकुं हुनु पर्ने हो आदि कुरा चीन वादशाह गर्ने भनी काजी देवदत्त थापालाई निर्देशन दिने चीट्ठी तयार भएको
(In this letter to the Chinese Emperor, King Ran Bahadur Shah has mentioned Symarpa Lama as the main cause of the conflict and requested the circulation of pure coins in Tibet.)

Source : MFA, *Poka* No. Pa. 64.

Appendix D

हाती ली जाने माहुते विरामी भै औषधी खुवाउदा पनि निको नभै मरेको हुनाले ५९ सम्वत १८५१ मा चैत्रमा कंयुस्यान सुहोतारिन अंवाले श्री ५ रण वहादुर साहलाई पठाएको..

(Chinese *Amban* to King Ran Bahadur Shah informing about the death of *Mahout* (the keeper and driver of an elephant).)

Source : MFA, *Poka* No. Pa. 64.

Appendix E

आफुलाई वाङ को र काकालाई घुङको षिताव पेचिन जाने काजी देवीदत्त थापा गजुर, रण सिं थापा स्मेत ४ जनालाई टुङ थ्वाङले गजुर वक्साई दिनु भयो शक्ती साहीहरु १२ जवानले पनि पहलो गजुर पाये– यति ठूलो मान पहिले नपाएको पछि पाउन पनि कठिन श्री ५ वादशाहलाई मानी रहनु भंन्या र चिनिया अक्षर सिक्नलाई मानिस पठाउने वारेमा. श्री ५ वादसाहका हजुरमा नसाधी हुँदैन भंन्या स्मेत वेहोराको १८५० साल श्रावण वदी रोज १ कंपुस्यान अम्वाले श्री ५ का हर्जुरको लेषेको १

(Chinese *Amban* to Nepalese King informing about the Chinese Emperor awarding the titles of *Wang* and *Kung* to King Ran Bahadur Shah and Regent Bahadur Shah respectively as well as the Chinese Emperor honouring *Kazi* Dev Dutta Thapa and other Nepalese members.)

Source : MFA, *Poka* No. Pa. 64.

Appendix F

१८५० साल चैत्र सुदि ८ रोज ४ मा थ्वाङ च्यांचुन अम्वाले श्री ५ लाई पत्र– नेपालले विराएको सम्वन्धमा सव माफ गरी चीन वादशाह लाई चीट्ठी पठायौ. हामी पेचीन पुगे पछि विंती गरी मान दर्जा वक्साई दिउला ताहावाट काजी देवदत्त थापालाई पठाएको चीट्ठी पेचिन पठाई दिउँ चीन चिट्ठी पठाउदा ल्हासाका अंवा मार्फत पठाउनु ....

(Chinese *Amban* to Nepalese King mentioning about pardoning of Nepal's wrong doings and requesting the Chinese Emperor to confer titles and honours to the Nepalese party.)

Source : MFA, *Poka* No. Pa. 64.

* * *

2

Kazi Narsingh Gurung's Mission of 1795

According to the new arrangement of the mission system, Nepal was to send the next five-yearly mission in 1797, but Nepal dispatched the second mission in 1795, two years before the scheduled period. It was due to the abdication of Ch'ing Emperor Ch'ien Lung in 1795 in favour of his son Chia Ch'ing that Nepal sent her second mission in 1795. Here it should be pointed out that the Chinese Imperial records have mentioned Nepal's sending missions to China in 1794 and 1795.[1] But the Nepalese archival documents state of Nepal's dispatching of mission to China in 1795 only. It was reported that the Chinese authorities insisted on Nepal's sending a special mission to pay respect to the new Emperor with special presents[2], whereas Nepal requested to send a single mission with presents to the new Chinese Emperor along with the usual five-yearly presents[3]. With the acceptance of the Nepalese request by the Chinese authorities, the second Nepalese mission, consisting forty-five members, led by *Kazi* Narsingh Gurung,[4] left for China in 1795.[5] The other members of the mission were *Jetha Budha*

---

1. J.K. Fairbank and S.Y. Teng, "On the Ch'ing Tributary System", *Harvard Journal of Asiatic Studies*, Vol. VI, 1941, pp. 195-198.
2. Chinese *Amban* to King Ran Behadur Shah, 1852 B.S. Jestha Sudi (1795), MFA, *Poka* No. Pa 64. See Appendix A.
3. Tri Ratna Manandhar and Tirtha Prasad Mishra, *Nepal's Quinquennial Missions to China*, Kathmandu: Purna Devi Manandhar and Puspa Mishra, 1986, p. 23.
4. Chinese *Amban* to King Ran Bahadur Shah, 1852 B.S. Shrawan Sudi 11 Roj 2 (1795), MFA *Poka* No. Pa 64. See Appendix B. Fisher and Rose have mistakenly referred to Narsingh Gurung as Narsingh Sah. See Margaret W. Fisher and Leo E. Rose, *England, India, Nepal, Tibet, China, 1765-1958*, Berkeley: University of California Press, 1959, pp. 2-12.
5. The details of the 1795 Nepalese mission have been recorded in MFA, *Poka* No. Pa 64. See also Jnanmani Nepal, *Nepal-Bhot Chin Sambandha Ka Kehi Sanskritik Paksha* (Some Cultural Aspect of Nepal-Tibet China Relations), Kathmandu: Royal Nepal Academy, 2045 B.S.; pp. 66-68, and Jagman Gurung, *Nepalko Ekikaranma Gurungharuko Bhumika* (Role of The Gurungs in the Unification of Nepal), Pokhara: Sri Bauddha Arghaun Sadana, 2041 B.S., pp. 70-72.

Madho Sahi, the deputy leader of the mission, interpreters Satar Miya, Mani Ram Lama and Narayan Tewari, letter writer Khadananda Padhya, *Omrao* Kashi Gurung, *Talabdar* Mahamad Ali, *Dhakre* (unemployed) Kishun Karki and Narendra Karki, and twenty soldiers.[6] Here it should be mentioned that by 1795, King Ran Bahadur Shah had already assumed full power himself and had dismissed Regent Bahadur Shah from all offices. In order to impress upon the Ch'ing Emperor that he had assumed full power himself from Regent Bahadur Shah, King Ran Bahadur Shah collected several things to present to the new Ch'ing Emperor Chia Ch'ing from various parts of Nepal as well as from different parts of India such as Patna, Banaras and Calcutta. The mission of 1795, which carried five-yearly presents and special presents to the new Ch'ing Emperor Chia Ch'ing on the occasion of his ascent to the throne, left for Peking bearing various types of presents, including different types of palanquins, such as *Khadkhadiya*, *Myana* and *Palaki,* of extraordinary fineness. Four elephants and four horses from Nepal's Tarai area were also sent to Lhasa *via* Bhutan *en route* to Peking.[7]

Kazi Narsingh Gurung reached Lhasa on Bhadra Sudi 6, 1852 B.S. (1795) and the Nepalese mission left Lhasa for Peking on Bhadra Sudi 15, 1852 B.S. (1795)[8]. The Nepalese mission, which handed over an *arji*[9] and presents to the new Ch'ing Emperor[10], remained at Peking for thirty-five days[11]. The 1795

6. The records deposited in the Royal Nepal Army Head-quarters mention the names of the leading members of the Nepalese quinquennial missions to China as well as the detailed list of the presents sent along with the Nepalese missions to China from 1795 to 1852. See Royal Nepal Army Head-quarters (hereafter mentioned as RNAH) Part 3, Serial No. 63 (53).
7. Nepal, f.n. no. 5, pp. 67-68. See also Chinese *Amban* to King Ran Bahadur Shah, 1852 B.S. (1795). National Archives of Nepal, Kathmandu (hereafter referred as NAN), *Poka* No. 2, Letter No. 81. See Appendix J.
8. For the details of the Nepalese mission's arrival at Lhasa and its departure to Peking, see Appendices E, F, G, H and I.
9. Chinese *Amban* to King Ran Bahadur Shah, Chyachhin 1st Year, 1852 B.S. (1795), MFA, *Poka* No. Pa 64. See Appendix L.
10. *Kazi* Narsingh's *arji*, dated 1853 B.S. Baisakh Badi Roj 4 (1796), MFA, *Poka* No. Pa 64. See Appendix N.
11. Gurung, f.n. no. 5, p. 70.

Nepalese mission had carried nineteen items as ordinary presents and thirty one items as special presents to the new Ch'ing Emperor[12]. It was given a very warm welcome in Peking. The mission members were entertained through the Chinese plays and dances[13]. Being happy with the Nepalese mission, the Ch'ing Emperor awarded *Tog* (Crown) of the first rank and a *Parwana* to King Ran Bahadur Shah. The Ch'ing Emperor also awarded red *Tog* of the second rank and plume of peacock feathers to *Kazi* Narsingh Gurung. Besides that the Nepalese *Kazi* received five pieces of *Khaki*, five pieces of *Sijyapurima*, five pieces of *Shashi*, five pieces of *Nusi*, 100 *taks* of silver, four pieces of glass utensils, four pieces of porcelain utensils and eight thermos flasks[14]. Along with the other members of Nepalese mission, *Kazi* Narsingh had also received tea as presents from the Ch'ing Emperor[15].

While returning from Peking, *Kazi* Narsingh Gurung halted at Tarchindeo due to illness. He halted at Lhasa for one week only[16] and seemed to have reached Kerung by Bhadra, 1853 B.S. (1796)[17]. The Chinese and Tibetan officials escorting the Nepalese delegation returned from Kerung, and they were given some presents by the Nepalese mission[18]. Interestingly the Chinese *Ambans* had stated King Ran Bahadur Shah to be kind enough towards *Kazi* Narsingh Gurung for he had worked hard for the promotion of Nepal-China relations. *Kazi* Narsingh had maintained good rapport with the Chinese *Ambans* at Tibet even in future. He seemed to have made great efforts at Peking for promoting and strengthening Nepal-China relations[19]. Here it should be mentioned that *Kazi* Narsingh had played an important role in the signing of the peace agreement between Nepal and China in 1792. As such he was duly recognized by King Ran Bahadur Shah as well as by the

12. RNAH, Part 3, Serial No. 63 (53). See Appendix C.
13. Chinese Emperor's *Parwana* dated 1853 B.S. (1796), MFA, *Poka* No. Pa 64. See Appendix N.
14. Gurung, f.n. no. 5, p. 71.
15. Nepal, f.n. no. 5, p. 111.
16. Gurung, f.n. no. 5, pp. 71-72.
17. *Kazi* Narsingh to *Kazi* Damodar Pande, 1853 B.S. Bhadra Badi 9 Roj 7 (1796), MFA, *Poka* No. Pa 64. See Appendix O.
18. RNAH, Part 3, Serial No. 63 (53). See Appendix P.
19. Gurung, f.n. no. 5, p. 72.

Chinese Commander Fu-k'ang-an[20].

According to the Royal Nepal Army Head-quarters' documents, it seems that the total cost of the mission of 1795 was Rupees 39,220/2[21] and not 29,220.2 as was mentioned by Manandhar and Mishra,[22] and the regular five-yearly presents were valued at Rs. 4,829 while the value of special presents was fixed at Rs. 14,902III [23]. At the time of sending 1795 quinquennial mission to China, Nepal also sent presents to the Chinese and Tibetan authorities, such as the Chinese *Ambans*, the *Potala* (Dalai) Lama, Lama of Digarcha (Shigatse), *Chuii* of Digarcha, *Talloye* (Chinese officials) of Tingri, *Dhewas* (Tibetan officials) of Kuti, *Chundu* (Governor or Viceroy) of *Sinthaya* (Sindafu ?), the four *Kajis* of Lhasa, Lama of Sakya, *Chundu* of Chindafu[24]. Interestingly, in spite of his dismissal from all offices, through this mission of 1795 ex-Regent Bahadur Shah sent presents to the Chinese *Amban*[25] and Ch'ing Emperor[26], perhaps with the hope of gaining the Emperor's sympathy. The Ch'ing Emperor did not accept Bahadur Shah's presents though, on the grounds that it was against the Ch'ing court's custom to receive presents from persons not holding any government posts. Although the Ch'ing Emperor returned the presents sent by Bahadur Shah with thanks, in the meantime, he sent presents to ex-Regent Bahadur Shah and King Ran Bahadur Shah through this mission of 1795[27]. Besides other items as presents, the Ch'ing Emperor had also sent eight and four jars of tea to King Ran Bahadur Shah and ex-Regent Bahadur Shah respectively[28]

---

20. *Ibid.*, p. 65.
21. RNAH, Part 3, Serial No. 63 (53). See Appendix C.
22. Manandhar and Mishra, f.n.no. 3, p. 73.
23. RNAH, Part 3, Serial No. 63 (53). See Appendix C.
24. *Ibid.*
25. Chinese *Amban* to Bahadur Shah, 1852 B.S. (1795), MFA, *Poka* No. Pa 64. See Appendices D and E.
26. Chinese *Amban* to Bahadur Shah, 1852 B.S. (1795), MFA, *Poka* No. Pa 64. See Appendix E
27. Chinese Emperor's *Parwana* dated 1853 B.S. (1796), MFA, *Poka* No. Pa 64. See Appendix M.
28. Nepal, f.n. no. 5, p. 111.

The importance of the mission of 1795 lies in the fact that it was not only the first Nepalese quinquennial mission to go to Peking two years before the scheduled time, but also that it was the first Nepalese mission to carry at one time the usual five-yearly presents as well as special presents on the occasion of the Ch'ing Emperor's ascent to the throne. Significantly enough, the members of 1795 mission had an audience with the Ch'ing Emperor Chia Ch'ing twenty five times[29], the highest number of such audiences ever granted to any Nepalese complimentary five-yearly mission. It was also the last Nepalese mission to carry elephants and horses as presents to the Ch'ing Emperor. Afterwards Nepal stopped sending elephants and horses as presents to the Ch'ing Emperor as per the Chinese *Ambans'* instructions of not sending those animals as presents to the Ch'ing Emperor[30] realizing the difficulty of sending them to China.

Appendix A

१८५२ साल ज्येष्ठ सुदीमा कुंपुस्यान अम्वाले श्री ५ को हजुरमा पठाएको चिट्ठीमा गादि ममारषको दस्तुर अर्जि सौगाद र ५ वर्षको मामुलीको अर्जि भिन्न भिन्नै पठाउनु ......

(Chinese *Amban* to Nepalese King instructing to send mission to pay respect to the new Emperor with special presents and the usual five-yearly presents separately.)

Source : Ministry of Foreign Affairs, Kathmandu (MFA), *Poka* No. Pa. 64.

Appendix B

१८५२ छयालुं ६० साल श्रावण सुदी ११ रोज २ मा कुंपुस्यान्सु अम्वाले रणवहादुर साहलाई लेषेको चिट्ठीमा काजी नरसिंहलाई पेचीन पठाउने वन्दोवस्त भयाको ....

(Chinese *Amban* to King Ran Bahadur Shah mentioning about the deputing of *Kazi* Narsingh as the leader of the Nepalese mission to Peking.)

Source : MFA, *Poka* No. Pa. 64.

29. Manandhar and Mishra, f.n. no. 3, p. 23.
30. Chinese *Amban* to King Ran Bahadur Shah, Chyachhin 1st Year, 1853 B.S. Ashwin Sudi 8 Roj 1 (1795). See Appendix L.

Appendix C

५२ साल

चीन श्री वादसाहुलाई सौगात गयाको गादि ममारष स्मेत मार्फत काजि नरसिं जेठावुढा माधौ साहि. मिति श्रावरावदि ४ रोज. ३९२२०/12

श्री वादसाहुके ....१९७३१॥।२

सौगात...४८२९२

मुगा माला......१ के तोला २६।५। के १९८ ॥।.	
रुपौला तास थान २ के तोला के	१४४॥२
किषाप थान. ....२० के	१७५०
सुलतानि वनात ताषा.......७ के	१०५०
वुटेदार अतलस थान. ....४ के	३९
संदुकी वन्दुक..............१ के	२००
हाती दात.............४ के	१६०
लवाग धार्नि.............६ के	२६४
जायफल गोटा..............1000के	१२०
षाग गोटा..............२ के	१०
दालचिनी संदुस १ के धार्नि के	३२॥.
वनात ताषा..............५ के	५५५
तरोवार.....................४ के	१२०
कटार.....................२ के	३५
दक्षिरिाा सुपारि धार्नि.......६ के	१५
सुपारि धार्नि.............१० के	११।.
षुडा....................२ क	२०
षुकुरि....................२ के	१४
तोडेवाल वन्दुक.............२ के	९०

गादि ममारषको...१४९०२॥।.

मुगामाला १ के तोला २७ के	२०२॥.
धुकधुकी स्मेत मोतिका माला १ के	५००
रुपौला तास थान.............१ के	७३।३
ठुलो मुगा दाना ५ के तोला ७।३।के	२१०
सुनौला तास थान.............२ के	अं८५
किंषाप थान............२० के	१७५०
दोरुषा १ सुलतानी ७ ज्मां वनात थां ८ के	२१००
मैसराजाम स्मेत पाल्कि........१ के	१५००
मैसराजाम स्मेत म्याना.......१ के	२५०
कार्चोपि पंषा..............१ के	५००

चार नाल्या संदुकी वन्दुक........१ के ३००
संदुकी पेस्तवल जोडा........१ के १००
दोनाल्या संदुकी वन्दुक........१ के २५०
हाति दात..............१० के ४००
तोडेवाल वन्दुक.............२ के ९०
तरोवार.....................४ के १९०
कटार.....................२ के ३५
षुकुरि.....................२ के १४
पेस्कवुज..............२ के ६५
दुर्वेन.....................२ के १८०
हाति.....................५ के ३५००
घोडा.....................५ के १५००
लवाग धार्नि.............१२ के ५२८
केसर तोला.............१०० के ११२॥.
जायफल गोटा.............५००के ६०
षाग गोटा..............२ के १०
अतर तोला.............७२ के १९०॥.
वदाम धार्नि.............६ के १२
नरिवल गोटा.............१०० के २०।
वुट्टेदार चिहुलि थान.......४ के ७६
लषनौ छीट् थान.............६ के ६६

षोटं थ्वाङ् के..४८१
सुलतानी वनात ताषा १ के १११ किंषाप थान... २ के १६०
तरोवार...................२ के ३० मुगाको माला.......१ के ५६
हातिदात..................२ के ८० लवाग धानि (धार्नि?) १ के ४४

ल्युतरीन के...१६६
वनात ताषा.............१ के १११ किंषाप थान......१ के ५५

चुंडु ताजीन के किंषाप थान.............१ के........................५५
हैकइका छोरा के. किंषाप थान.............१ के...................४०
छिंधाफुका चंदु के..४२।.
किंषाप थान.............१ के ४० सुपारि धानि(धार्नि ?)..२ के २।.

डिगर्चाका चुइ के...११२
गलेता थान १ के १० सुपारि धार्नि........१ के १२

टिगरि का तालोयके..१०॥।२
वुट्टेदार अतलस थान १ के ९॥. सुपारि धार्नि.......१ के १२

कुटिका ढेवा २ के अतलस थान.............२ के.......१६॥.
डिगर्चाका लामाज्यूके...२५८
वनात वस्ता १ के १११ किंषाप थान १ के १२०
सहन थान २ के ७ हातिदातका कटौरा २ के अं १६
अलैचि दाना संदुस....................१ के अ ४

टुंथ्वाङ् के...४०१
वनात तोषा १ के १११ किंषाप थान..२ के १६०
तरोवार.........२ के ३० मुगा माला.......१ के ५६
लवांग धार्नि.......................................१ के ४४

सिंथ्या चुंडुके..५७५॥।
वनात वस्ता....२ के २२२ तरोवार......२ के ३०
तोडेवाल वन्दुक..२ के ९० हाति दात.......२ के ८०
षुकुरि.............२ के १४ किंषाप थान.......२ के ११०
सुपारि धार्नि.......४ के ४॥ दक्षिरिा सुपारि धा २ के ५
दालचिनि धार्नि.......१ के ५ वदाम धार्नि.......२ के ४
गरि गोटा.......३० के ६।। छोहारा धार्नि.......४ के ५

पोतला लामाज्यू के..१८०।.
वनात वस्ता.....१ के १११ किंषाप थान १ के ४०
सहन थान.......२ के ७ सुपारि धार्नि २ के २।.
हातिदातका कटौरा २ के अं १६ अलैचि दाना संदुस १ के अ ४

ताचा चितुङ् के..१७४
वनात वस्ता......१ के १११ किंषाप थान.......१ के ४०
सहन थान.......२ के ७ हाती दात कटौरा २ के अं १६

ल्हासाका चार काजी के....................................१६४॥
किंषाप थान.......४ के १६० सुपारि धार्नि......४ के ४॥.

साक्या लामा के..११४॥.
वनात वस्ता.......१ के १११ सहन थान.......१ के ३॥.

२७८५॥।।

अैजन सौगात पुऱ्याउन जान्या मानीसहरु के............१४१७४॥।

काजि नरसिं के..३४९०॥

नगद मोरु...३०००

जिन्सि...४९०॥

चदेलि पगरि १ के १७ किंषाप थान २ के २२०

साल जोडा १ के १३० सालका रुमाल १ के ७०

पो.माल्दहि थां १ के २२ चस्मा थान १ के १८

ला.माझा पगरिहा ९ के ॥ ह.तास तोला ५।.। के १२॥.

षासाका रुमाल...............................१ के ॥।.

जेठा वुढा माधौ साहि के...१३१४।

नगद.मानीस. जना ४ स्मेत के...१०००

जिन्सी...३१४।

चिरा पगरि १ के ८॥ किंषाप थान २ के ११०

साल जोडा १ के १३० माल्दहि थान १ के ११

चौविसा थान १ के ३॥ साल्का रुमाल १ के ५१

पिटाका रुमाल...............................१ के ।

दोभास्या सतार मिञा के..९५१।।

तलव मैन्हा १४ को..८४०

जिन्सी...१११।।

२५ गजी पगरि १ के ४ ॥।. किंषाप थान १ के ५५

साल फर्द.......१ के ४० कासिवालहा ९ के ९

चौविसा थान...१ के २॥. पिटाका रुमाल १ के ।

अै का साथमा जान्या जना.........................२ के ४३८।।

त्लव रु...२००

जिन्सी रु...२३८।।

पदुम् काफल्या के..१२७

२२ गजि पगरि १ के ५ किंषा थान १ के ५५

चौविसा थान १ के ३ कासिवाल थान १ के ९

साल फर्द...............................१ के ५५

सतार मिञा दोभास्या के..१११।।

२५ गजि पगरि १ के ४॥। किंषाप थान १ के ५५

साल फर्द १ के ४० कासिवाल्हा ९ के ९

चौविसा थान १ के २॥ पिटाका रुमाल १ के ।

मनिराम लामा दोभास्या के..३४०।

नगद मानीस स्मेत जना ३ के...२५०

जिन्सी...९०।

साल फर्द १ के ५० किंषाप थान १ के ४०

पिटाका रुमाल............................१ के ।

नाारान तेवारि दोभास्या के ....२८७।
नगद आफु स्मेत जना २ के २५०
जिन्सी ....३७।
२५ गजी पगरि १ के ४॥. गलेता थान १ के १५
कासिवाल थान १ के ७ तोस फर्द १ के ८
चौविसा थान १ के २॥. पिटाका रुमाल १ के ।

काजि का साथमा चिठिपत्र लेषन्या षडानन्द पाध्याके ५२१।।
नगद रु...४००
जिन्सी...१२१।।
२५ गजि पगरि १ के ४॥ किषाप थान १ के ५५
साल फर्द १ के ५० कासिवाल थान १ के ९
चौविसा थान १ के २॥ पिटाका रुमाल १ के ।

कासि गुरुं उम्राव ढाक्र्या स्मेत जना ३ के नगद.........३००
किसुन कार्कि ढाक्र्या स्मेत जना ३ के नगद.............३००
महमद अल्लि तलवदार के वर्ष १ को नगद..............५४०
नरेन्द्र कार्कि ढाक्र्या स्मेत जना ३ के नगद रु...........३००
महमद अल्लिका साथका मानीस के नगद रु.............१००
काजि नरसिं का साथका सिपाहि जना २० के नगद.....३६००
वकील के जिन्सी...७५
किंषाप थान.......१ के ६५ माल्दहि थान १ के १०

हाति ५ लि जान्या फनैत माहुत गैह्न के तलव वर्ष १ के १३०५
मोह कदम फनैत के ७२ श्रीकृष्न फनैत के ७२
सुषर्षां फनैत के ७२ हिरामनि फनैत के ७२
चेतराम फनैत के ७२ माहुत जना १५ के ९००
फनैत जना ५ के थप...४५

चिरुवादार जना ७ के दर्माहा...............................१३२
लछु कसर वानिञा के १८ जिउ नरसिं के १८
पालु सिं के...........१८ लक्ष्मी धर के १८
देहाय के..............१८ जिम्मा वारि जग्या गुरुं के ४२

हाति ५ घोडा ५ लि जान्या डिठा जग्या जग्या (?) गुरुं के ल्हासा सम्म को षर्च..१४०
जागीर षेत ३ मान पुग्याको वालि..........................७५
वाटो षर्च दोभास्या स्मेत के.................................६५

हाति घोडा लि जादा वाट धाट् उजार जंगलमा दाना घास देव देवताका पुजा गैह्रके..............................४०

वाजे षर्च गयाको जिम्मा काजि........................२०१३[२]

नगद रु...१000

जिन्सी..१०१३[२]

वनात वस्ता ३ के ३३३ किंषाप थान ९ के ३६०

कासिवाल्थान १५ के १२३॥। अधर्सा थान २० के ४७॥

षारुवा थान १५ के २४।[२] पिटा थान ३० के २२॥

वन्दरि छीट् थान ६ के..................................१०२

अरु काम काममा खर्च....................................५९९॥/॥।२

हाति दात वेह्रना के. षारुवा हात................४ के ॥/

सौगाति घोडा ४ का झुलर गदि के........................२१॥[३]/।

मोटा सफा थान ८ के ९ चागा थान १० के ७॥

षारुवा हात १६ के २।[२] क्षारुवा थान १ के ॥।.

षादि थान ४ के २ धागो लडी १ के /।

सौगाति हाति ५ लैजान्या माहुत जना ५ के सिरोपाव..२३७॥[३]/॥

चौविसा थान ५ के १७॥ पटुका के चोविसा थां ५ के १५

१८ गजी पगरि थान ५ के १२॥. मौअतलस थान ५ के ७॥

साल फर्द.......५ के १८५ पिटाका रुमाल ३ के[३]/।

तरोवार कंवुजा का मोल्मा के ....५९॥/।

सुना मासा ३६ के ५७॥/। पारो मोल..........२

सौगाति पलग् के कोर मोल ....५॥।/

अै. पाल्की का छाजन वेहना के..............................१।.

षादि थान...........१ के ॥. मैन कपडा थान १ के ॥।.

भारि मा लाउना के सिदुर पाव..................१ के २/॥।

पाल्की का वास वाधनाके. धागो र कपडा १२ के १॥।.॥

चिन सौगातमा जान्या हाति.धर्मालाइ सभार सित लै

जानु भनि.चिठ्ठि लैजान्या के राह षर्च..................... १॥.

केरुं सम्म पुऱ्याउन जान्या भरिया के षर्च............... २४५॥

पाल्कि म्याना वोकि जान्या जना............२६ के ५२

पुतवार का मुषिया............................१ के ३

हिटि चोक्या मार्फत सेराका भरिया ११५ के १७२॥.

दफे भारि ५ वोकन्या भरिया १२ के १८

षलिता के..४।२॥

ढाका मलमल षगाम....................२ के २

मैन कपडाका रुमाल......................१ के /॥।

सौगाति सराजाम ढाकनाके मैन कपडा थान २के...... १

भारि मोह्रना के छाला मोल.............................. ५

माधौ साहि का चिल्ठामा लाउनाके लैस तोला ६ के... ११॥.

तेरीज

श्री वादसाह के..१९६४६॥।२

सौगात..४८२९३

गादि ममारष..१४८१७॥।.

टुंथ्वां गैह्रके सौगात...२७८५॥/।

वाजे षर्च...१०१३२

सौगात लैजान्याहरु के षर्च र सिरोपाव १५१७४॥।/

षर्च नगद रु...१३६९७

जिन्सी सिरोपाव स्मेत के..१४७७॥।/

काम कामका षर्चके..५९९॥/॥।२

३९२२०/२

वेकिमती

सुनौला तास थान........................२ के अं ८

हाति दातका कटौरा........................६ के अं ४८

अलैचिदानका सदुस्.........................२ के अं ८

६४

३९२८४/२

(The detailed list of ordinary and special presents sent along with the 1795 Nepalese quinquennial mission to China under the leadership of *Kazi* Narsingh Gurung.)

Source : Royal Nepal Army Head-quarters (RNAH), Part 3, Serial No. 63 (53).

Appendix D

१८५२ साल (छयालुं ६० साल) सुंतारी अम्वाले श्री घुङ वहादुर साहलाई पठाएको पत्रमा घुङले पठाएको रीषी पाद्यालाई माल सहित पठाएको - चीन जाने काजीहरु फर्कदा पनी पठाउला ....

(Chinese *Amban* to *Kung* Bahadur Shah mentioning receiving his presents through Rishi Padhya and promising to send presents to Bahadur Shah at the time of returning of the Nepalese mission from China.)

Source : MFA, *Poka* No. Pa. 64.

Appendix E

१८५२ छयालुं (६० साल र मैन्हा) १८ दिन जादा होतारिन अंवाले श्री वहादुर शाहलाई पठाएको पत्र– चीनमा अर्जी सौगाद चढाउने जान आउने काजी नरसिं ञाहा पुगेको– भतिजा राजाले अव रजाइको काम काज म आफै गर्छु भनि भनेको हुनाले काम काज सौंपि ध्यान धर्ममा लागे सो हाल श्री ५ वादशाहका हजुरमा जाहेर गरिदिनु होला भनी लेषनु भयाकालाई राजा आफै जांन्या भयो र आफुले रजाइ सौप्या होला भंन्या र आफुले श्री ५ वादसाहका हजुर्मा चढाई पठायाको मालहरु आफुका भतिजा वाङको अर्जि सौगाद संगै चढाई पठान्यूं हामीहरुलाई पठाउनु भयाको पनि षुसी साथ वुझि लियूं आफुलाई पनि सौगाद पठाई दियाको छ. वुझि लिनु होला ....

(Chinese *Amban* to Bahadur Shah mentioning about the arrival of *Kazi* Narsingh at Lhasa, dispatching of Bahadur Shah's presents to the Ch'ing Emperor and Chinese *Amban's* sending of presents to Bahadur Shah.)

Source : MFA, *Poka* No. Pa. 64.

Appendix F

छयालुं ६० साल भाद्र सुदी २ रोज १ मा कंपुस्यान अम्वाले श्री ५ रण वहादुर साहलाई पठाएको पत्रमा चीन जाने काजी आई पुगे पछि संभार संग पैचिन पठाई दिन्या छौं - सौगाद जाने हाती ५ घोडा धर्माको वाटोमा लिनलाई मानिस पठाउने ....

(Chinese *Amban* to King Ran Bahadur Shah assuring to send the Nepalese mission to China safely from Lhasa.)

Source : MFA, *Poka* No. Pa. 64.

Appendix G

१८५२ छयालु ६० साल असोज वदि ४ रोजमा सुतारीन होत्तारिन अम्वाले नरसिं काजीलाई चिनिञा भारदारको साथ लगाइ चिन पठाइ दिएको.....

(Chinese *Ambans'* letter referring to sending of Nepalese mission to China escorted by Chinese officers.)

Source : MFA, *Poka* No. Pa. 64.

Appendix H

१८५२ साल भाद्र सुदी १३ रोजमा ल्हासावाट काजी नरसिं ले श्री ५ रण वहादुर साहलाई पत्र- अम्वा संग भेटी सौगात दिएको . आश्वीनका १४ जादा चीन तर्फ जाने ....

(*Kazi* Narsingh to King Ran Bahadur Shah mentioning about his meeting with the Chinese *Amban* at Lhasa and the date of his departure for China.)

Source : MFA, *Poka* No. Pa. 64

Appendix I

काजी नर सिं माधो साहीले ल्हासा पुगेको र चीनीया अक्षर पढाउन पठायेका ४ जनालाई अरु ३ वर्ष लाग्ने आदि वेहोराको पत्र काजी दामोदर पाण्डेलाई १८५२ साल भाद्र सुदी १३ रोजको पत्र ....

(*Kazi* Narsingh and Madho Sahi's letter to *Kazi* Damodar Pande informing about their arrival at Lhasa and about four Nepalese being sent to Lhasa to learn Chinese language.)

Source : MFA, *Poka* No. Pa. 64

Appendix J

१८५२ छयालुं ६० सालमा ल्हासाका अम्वाले श्री ५ रण वहादुर शाहलाई पत्र-सौगाद जाने हाती घोडा आइ पुग्यो अलि दिन पछि पैचिन पठाई दिने छौं...........................

(Chinese *Amban* to King Ran Bahadur Shah informing about the arrival of the elephants and horses at Lhasa and sending them to Peking soon.)

Source : National Archives of Nepal, Kathmandu (NAN), *Poka* No. 2, Letter No. 81.

Appendix K

सम्वत १८५२ च्याछिन १ साल २९ दिनमा जादा रोज ३ मा कुंपुस्यान सुंतारीन अम्वाले श्री ५ रण वहादुर साहलाई पत्र-अर्जि देखी चिनीया वादसाह प्रसन्न भएको.............................

(Chinese *Amban* to King Ran Bahadur Shah stating the Ch'ing Emperor's happiness at the Nepalese King's *arji.*)

Source : MFA, *Poka* No. Pa. 64

Appendix L

१८५३ च्याछिन १ साल आश्वीन सुदि ८ रोज १ मा कंपुस्यान अम्वाले श्री ५ रण वहादुर साहलाई – हाती घोडा सौगात पठाउनु पर्दैन – श्री चीन वादशाहलाई लेषने अर्जिको मसौदा गरी पठाई दिएको. सोही वमोजिम लेखी पठाउने ....

(Chinese *Amban* to King Ran Bahadur Shah instructing not to send elephants and horses as presents.)

Source : MFA, *Poka* No. Pa. 64

Appendix M

१८५३ सालमा श्री ५ (चीन) वादशाहवाट आयाको सुनको प्रमानाको नक्कलमा वहादुर साहले छुट्टै अर्जि सौगाद पठाएकोमा फीर्ता पठाएको. तिमीलाई साविक वमोजिम सौगाद पठाएको. काजीहरुलाई इनाम वकसी तमासाहरु देषाई तम्रो मुलुक टाढा छ हाती घोडा पठाउनु पर्दैन ....

(Chinese Emperor's *Parwana* mentioning returning the presents sent by Bahadur Shah, honouring and entertaining the members of the Nepalese mission and instructing not to send elephants and horses as presents realizing the difficulty of sending them.)

Source : MFA, *Poka* No. Pa. 64

Appendix N

१८५३ सालमा वैसाष वदि रोज ४ लेषेको अर्जी नरसिं काजीहरुले पठाएको पत्रमा – पेचीन पुगी श्री ५ चीन वादशाह दर्शन गरी सौगात चढायाको. सोधेको कुरा जवाफ दिएको.......................................

(*Kazi* Narsingh's *arji* referring to meeting and handing over the presents to the Ch'ing Emperor at Peking.)

Source : MFA, *Poka* No. Pa. 64

Appendix O

१८५३ साल भाद्र वदि ९ रोज ७ मा नरसिं काजीले दामोदर पाण्डेलाई पठाएको–घोडा १०, ११ जवान मानिस केरुङ्गको वाटो पठाउने १६ दिन जादा आफुहरु आउने ....

(*Kazi* Narsingh to Damodar Pande informing about the date of his arrival at Kerung and requesting to send men and horses at Kerung.)

Source : MFA, *Poka* No. Pa. 64

Appendix P

<u>५३ साल</u>

नरसिं काजि चीनबाट आउदा. साथ आउन्या चिनिञा जना २ के

मेजमानी भाद्र सुदि १५ रोज.................................. ४९४/॥।

कुती तिरका चिनिञाके... २०८॥.॥।

नगद.. ११४
रक्सी कुशुरा गैह्र के २७ डोल्या ४१ के ८४
षुकुरि १ का कोथीके.. ३

जिन्सी.. ९४॥.।।।
मरीच पाव ३ के ।।।३ लवाग तोला २५ के ४ ।।।३।।।
सुपारि धार्नि १ के १२ किंषाप थान......१ के अं ४०
जिरा माना ४ के ।. वनात हात १४ के अं २८
चिनी धार्नि ४ के ४। तरोवार १ के अं १०
षुकुरि...........................१ के अं ५

केरुं पट्टी गयाको...१५२
नगद..६२।।।
रक्सी कुषुरा गैह्र के १३। भरिया....३० के ४६
तरोवार षुकुरीका कोथि को...................................४॥

जिन्सी..८९।
मरीच पाव १॥ के ।३।।किंषाप थान १ के.......... ३२
लवाग तोला २४ के ४।।।.॥ जिरा माना २ के......... २
मैन कपडा थां ४ के ३ चिनी धार्नि......२ के.... २
हिग तोला ३ के३ तरोवार.............१ के...... १३
सुपारि धार्नि ॥ के ॥ षुकुरि..........१ के अं....... ५
वनात हात...................................१४ के अं २८

काजि का साथ आउन्या फुए जना..............५ के......१३३॥
कासीवाल थान १ के ९ अतलस थान ४ के ४८
वंदुक गोटा ३ के अं ७५ षारुवा हात ८ के ११२
पिटा हात...........................४ के २

(The detailed expenses and list of the presents given to the Chinese officials escorting the Nepalese mission of 1795 up to Kerung.)

Source : RNAH, Part 3, Serial No. 63 (53).

* * *

3

Kazi Sarvajit Pande's Mission of 1802

In accordance with the peace agreement between Nepal and China in September 1792, Nepal sent her first five-yearly mission to the Ch'ing court in October 1792 under the leadership of *Kazi* Dev Dutta Thapa. Due to the abdication of Ch'ing Emperor Ch'ien Lung in 1795 in favour of his son Chia Ch'ing that Nepal dispatched the second mission in 1795, two years before the scheduled period under the leadership of *Kazi* Narsingh Gurung. The third Nepalese complimentary quinquennial mission was scheduled for the year 1800, but in view of the political confusion caused by the enthronement of the seventeen month old King Girwan Yuddha Bikram Shah, and by the self-exile of the ex-King Ran Bahadur Shah, the Chinese *Ambans*, on behalf of the Ch'ing Emperor, allowed the Nepalese government to send the scheduled mission a year later[1]. Nonetheless, the political situation did not improve the following year either, instead it became more complicated, due to the activities of the ex-King Ran Bahadur Shah at Banaras. Thus, perhaps on Nepal's request, the Chinese *Ambans* permitted the Nepalese government to send a high-level official with the usual five-yearly presents, which were intended for the Ch'ing Emperor Chia Ch'ing, to the Nepal-Tibet border area, from whence the Chinese officials were to carry the presents to Peking[2]. Here it should be pointed out that the 1802 Nepalese quinquennial mission has not been mentioned in the Chinese Imperial records[3]. But the Nepalese archival documents clearly state of Nepal's sending of five-yearly mission to China in 1802. The Nepalese documents mention that a mission led by *Kazi* Sarvajit Pande left for the

---

1. Chinese *Amban* to King (Girwan Yuddha), 1859 B.S. Baisakh Badi 10 Roj 3 (27 April, 1802), Ministry of Foreign Affairs, Kathmandu (hereafter mentioned as MFA), *Poka* No. Pa 64. See Appendix H. For the correspondence between the Chinese and the Nepalese government regarding the sending of the scheduled Nepalese mission a year later, see Appendices B, C and D.
2. See Appendix H.
3. J.K. Fairbank and S.Y. Teng, "On the Ch'ing Tributary System", *Harvard Journal of Asiatic Studies*, Vol. VI, 1941, pp. 195-198.

Nepal-Tibet border area in Bhadra, 1859 B.S. (1802)[4]. The other members of the 1802 mission were *Sardar* Chamu Bhandari, deputy leader of the mission, interpreter Narayan Tewari, Machhindra, Padmanav Kafle, Bhajuman Jaisi, Indra Singh Khadka, Jabar Thapa, Ali Bakta, Sarvajit Karki, Jasiwant Khatri and Vansaraj.[5] In the Nepal-Tibet border area, the presents and *arji* to the Ch'ing Emperor were delivered to the Chinese officials. This time Nepal did not send elephants and horses as presents to the Ch'ing Emperor, for realizing the difficulty of sending them to China, the *Ambans*, even in 1796[6] and 1800[7] had informed the Nepalese King not to send elephants and horses in the future. On this occasion, the Nepalese presents to the Ch'ing Emperor were valued at Rs. 5,330|||[8] The 1802 Nepalese mission had carried twenty items as prescnts to the Ch'ing Emperor. Interestingly enough, Queen Subarna Prabha (King Ran Bahadur Shah's consort) had also sent presents to the Chinese Emperor and the Chinese *Ambans* through the Nepalese mission of 1802.[9] At the time of sending of the 1802 quinquennial mission, Nepal also sent eleven items as presents (which were valued at Rs. 890|||.) to the Chinese *Ambans.* According to custom, the Ch'ing Emperor Chia Ch'ing sent return presents to King Girwan, Queen Subarna Prabha[10] and the mission members along with a *Parwana*[11] to the

---

4. Royal Nepal Army Head-quarters (hereafter referred as RNAH), Part 3, Serial No. 63 (53). For the dispatching of *Kazi* Sarvajit Pande's mission of 1802 and the Chinese official welcoming the mission at Kerung, see Appendices E and F. Fisher and Rose have made a mistake by stating that Sarvajit Pande led the misison of 1801. See Margaret W. Fisher and Leo. E. Rose, *England, India, Nepal, Tibet, China, 1765-1958*, Berkeley: University of California Press, 1959, pp. 2-12.
5. RNAH, Part 3, Serial No. 63 (53).
6. Chinese *Amban* to King Ran Bahadur Shah, 1853 B.S., Ashwin Sudi 8 Roj 1 (9 October, 1796), MFA, *Poka* No. Pa 64.
7. Chinese *Ambans* to King Girwan Yuddha, Chyachhin 5th year 5th month 15th day (July 1800), MFA, *Poka* No. Pa 64. See Appendix A.
8. RNAH, Part 3, Serial No. 63 (53). See Appendix I.
9. *Ibid.*, Chinese *Ambans* to Four *Kazis* of Nepal, Chyachhin 7th year 10th month 19th day (1802), MFA, *Poka* No. Pa 64. See Appendix G.
10. Chinese *Ambans* to King (Girwan Yuddha), Chyachhin 8th year 7th month 12th day (1804), MFA, *Poka* No. Pa 64. See Appendix J; Chinese *Amban* to King Girwan Yuddha, Chyachhin 8th year 1st month 2nd day (1804), MFA, *Poka* No. Pa 64. See Appendix N.

King of Nepal. *Kazi* Sarvajit Pande and his party went to Tingri Maidan, near the Nepal-Tibet border, to receive the presents sent by the Emperor of China.[12] The Chinese officials, who handed over the Chinese Emperor's presents to *Kazi* Sarvajit Pande in 1804, were also given presents by the Nepalese government.[13] According to the custom, the Nepalese King sent an *arji* to the Ch'ing Emperor after receiving the Emperor's *Parwana.*[14]

The importance of the mission of 1802 lies in the fact that it was the first Nepalese quinquennial mission that did not go to Peking itself, but only went up to the Nepal-Tibet border to hand over the usual five-yearly presents meant for the Chinese Emperor to the Chinese officials, on the grounds that the King of Nepal was very young. Besides that it was also the first Nepalese mission which had carried presents from the Nepalese Queen to the Emperor of China.

Appendix A

च्याछीं ५ साल ५ मैन्हा १५ दिन जादा १८५७ सालमा श्री ५ गीर्वाणलाई होतारीन इंतारीन अंबाले पठायाको पत्रमा – सौगातमा हात्ती घोडा मियाना पालकी पठाउनु पर्दैन अरु चीजवीज तयार गरी आउदो साल चर्तुमासा भीत्र ल्हासा पुग्ने गरी सौगात मण्डल पठाउनु ....

(Chinese *Ambans* to King Girwan reminding to send the mission in the forthcoming year and not to send elephants, horses, *Myana* and *Palaki* as presents.)

Source : Ministry of Foreign Affairs, Kathmandu (MFA), *Poka* No. Pa 64.

Appendix B

च्याछिन ६ वर्ष २ मैन्हा १३ दिन जादा १८५८ सालमा श्री ५ गीर्वाणलाई होतारिन इन्तारीन अम्वाले सौगाद चढाई पठाउन ढिलो होला भनी हामी २ अंवाले मतो गरी यस साल पेचिन आउन माफ होला भनी वकसाई पठाएको

11. Chinese Emperor's *Parwana,* Chyachhin 8th year 1st month 24th day (February 1804), MFA, *Poka* No. Pa 64. See Appendix L.
12. Chinese *Amban* to King of Gorkha and his *Bhardars* and Four *Kazis,* Chyachhin 8th year 8th month 2nd day, MFA, *Poka* No. Pa 64. See Appendix K.
13. See Appendix M.
14. Chinese *Amban* to *Kazi* Damodar Pande, Chyachhin 8th year 12th month 2nd day (1804), MFA, *Poka* No. Pa 64. See Appendix O.

उल्लेख ....
(Chinese *Ambans* to King Girwan mentioning to allow the Nepalese government to send the scheduled mission a year later.)

Source : MFA, *Poka* No. Pa 64.

Appendix C

च्याछिन ६ साल २ मैन्हा १४ दिन जादा १८५८ सालमा चार काजीलाई होत्तारीन अम्वाले लेषेको – स्वामी माहाराज वनारस गएको, राजा वालकै छन्, १ सालको मामुली माफ वक्से आउदो साल ससौगात ली काजीहरु (लाई) चढाउन आउने छन् ....
(Chinese *Ambans* to Four *Kazis* of Nepal referring to the Nepalese request of allowing to send the scheduled mission a year later due to the self-exile of the ex-King, Ran Bahadur Shah and the minority age of King Girwan.)

Source : MFA, *Poka* No. Pa 64.

Appendix D

१८५८ सालमा चारकाजीलाई इन्तारीन अम्वाले लेषेको – मामुली सौगात चीन वादशाहबाट माफ वक्सेको ....
(Chinese *Amban* to Four *Kazis* of Nepal informing the Ch'ing Emperor's approval of allowing the Nepalese government to send the scheduled mission a year later.)

Source : MFA, *Poka* No. Pa 64.

Appendix E

१८५९ सालमा गोर्षाका काजीलाई श्री ताइ तालोयेले पठायाको मा पेचीन जान मामुली सौगाद लि काजी सर्वजीत पाण्डे आउन्या छन् भनी अम्वालाई लेषी पठाएकोमा काजीलाई लिन जौषमा आइ वसेको छु चाडो गरी पठाई दिनु होला...........................
(Tai *Talloye* to *Kazi* of Gorkha informing to send the Nepalese mission soon under the leadership of *Kazi* Sarvajit Pande.)

Source : MFA, *Poka* No. Pa 64.

Appendix F

चिन जाने काजीहरुलाई भदौको २७ दिन जादा पठाउछौ भनी लेषेकोमा ञाहावाट तै तालोयेलाई केरौं सम्म लिन पठाएको छु भंने च्याछी ७ वर्ष ८ मैन्हा ७ दिन जादा इन्तारीन फुतारीन अम्वाले श्री ५ को सर्कारमा हर्जुमा लेषेको...

(Chinese *Ambans* to Nepalese government referring to the sending of Tai *Talloye* to Kerung to receive the Nepalese mission.)

Source : MFA, *Poka* No. Pa 64.

Appendix G

५।५ वर्षमा पठाउनु पर्ने मामुलि अर्जिका चिठिमा केही कुराको नफावत पर्ला भनी मसौदा गरी पठायाको छ. सो वमोजिं नफावत नपारी चीठी पठाई दिनु होला भंन्या र आफु महाराज महारानीवाट चढाई पठायाको अर्जि सौगात तै तालोयलाई पुन्याउन पठायौं भन्या स्मेत इत्यादि च्याछिं ७ वर्ष १० मैन्हा १९ दिन जादा १८५९ सालमा इन्तारीन युतारीन् अम्वाले चार काजीलाई लेषेको.....................

(Chinese *Ambans* to Four *Kazis* of Nepal mentioning about the sending of the draft of the *arji* and the presents being sent by the Nepalese King and Queen to the Ch'ing Emperor.)

Source : MFA, *Poka* No. Pa 64.

Appendix H

सर्सौगाद चढाउने विसयेमा १ साल माफी गरि दियाको हो. आफु वालष हुनुहुन्छ. काजिहरु पठाउदा देसको केहि कां विग्रला आफु वाङको टहल पनि पुगैन. हाम्रो चितमा करुणा मानी लेषेको हो. भोट नेपालको दोसाध सम्म पुऱ्याउनु चिनिञा भारदारलाई लिन पठाउला. पछी वुधीमान भयेपछी दस्तुर माफिक पठाउनु होला भंन्या इन्तारीन फुतारीन अम्वाले श्री ५ सर्कारका हजुरमा १८५९ साल वैसाष वदि १० रोज ३ मा लेषेको ....

(Chinese *Ambans* to King (Girwan Yuddha) referring to the allowing the Nepalese government to send the scheduled mission a year later.)

Source : MFA, *Poka* No. Pa 64.

Appendix I

५९ साल

चीन वादसाहके सौगात गयाको मार्फत र हस्ते काजी सर्वजीत पाडे ....

भाद्र सुदि १५ रोज

सौगात ....६२२१।८।१

श्री वादसाहके .... ५३३०॥८।१

मुगा माला १ के तो २६ के १३०	सुलतानी वनात थाँ ८ के	१०८०
किंषापथान २० के १०३५	वनात वस्ता ६ के	८१०
रुपौला तास थान २ के १९९ ॥८।	गलेता थान ४ के	१००

२ नाल्या वन्दुक १ के अं २००		हाति दात ४ के अं	१६०
लवाग धार्नि ६ के १२६		जायफल गोटा ११०० के	१३७॥.
गैंडा षाग २ के अं ५०		दालचिनी धा ३ के	१८ ॥।
सुनौला कवुजा तरोवार ३ के २८०		कन्दकारि कवुजा तरोवार १ के ११०	
सुनौला कटार २ के ६५		दक्षिरिा सुपारि धां ६ के	३०
सुपारि धार्नि १० के १०		षुडा २ के अं	१०
षुकुरि ४ के अं ३८			
तोडेवाल वन्दुक २ के अं.	१००		

थप

श्री ५ महाराजावाट पत्र चिन्ह किषाप जोडा १ के २९०
श्री महारानी वाट सुनौला तास थान १ के तो २८॥ के ९९॥।.
किषाप जोडा .... १ के २६१

ल्हासाका अम्वा .... २ के ८९०॥।.

सुलतानी वनात वस्ता २ के २७०	तरोवार २ के अं	२०
तोडेवाल वन्दुक २ के अं ९०	हाति दात २ के अं	८०
षुकुरि २ के अं १४	किषा जोडा १ के	१०४
सुपारि धार्नि ४ के ४	दालचिनी धार्नि १ के	६।
वदाम धार्नि २ के ५	गरिगोटा ३० के	३॥.
छोहरा धार्नि	४ के	३॥.
श्री महारानीवाट किषाप थान	२ के	२९०

अैजन सौगात लि जान्याहरु के पोसाक २१५३

काजी सर्वजीत पाडेके ५९५	सर्दार चामु भडारि के ४१४
मछिन्द्रके .... १२५॥	पध्मनाम काफल्या के १२२॥
भाजुमनि जैसि के ... ११७	इन्द्र सिं षडका के ११७
जवर थापा के ११२	अली वक्त के १२२
नारान दोभास्या के ११२	सर्वजीत कार्कि के ११२
जसिवंत षतृ के १०७	वंस राज के ९७

अैजन सौगात को माल वाधना के रषोल गैद्ध के ज्मां १९२

आश्विं वदि[४] रो

सौगात के गैडा षाग. ....१ के अं ५०
डोल्या भरिया के षर्च. .... ९९॥।.
दर्वारि षर्च के .... ४६॥.

कासीवाल थान ४ के ३२	मीर्जापुरि छिट् था २ के ९॥.

चौविसा थान .... २ के ५

चीन जान्या मानीसहरु के षर्च वाडना के .... २९९॥.

डिगर्चामा सौगात गयाको मार्फत. सर्वजीत पाडे चैत्र सुदी ९ रो
किंषाप थान .... १ के ५५ कासिवाल थान १ के १०
सहन थान .... १ के ५

(The detailed expenses and the list of presents sent along with the 1802 Nepalese Quinquennial mission to China under the leadership of *Kazi* Sarvajit Pande.)

Source : Royal Nepal Army Head-quarters (RNAH), Part 3, Serial No. 63 (53).

Appendix J

वादसाहवाट आफु वाङलाई र महारानी सुवर्ण प्रभालाई वकसी पठायाको सुनको पर्माना इनाम आइपुग्या पछी अर्जि चढाई पठाई दिनु होला भन्या च्याछींन ८ वर्ष ७ मैन्हा १२ दिन जादा संवत १८६० सालमा इन्तारीन युतारीन अंवाले श्री ५ सर्कारमा लेषेको ....

(Chinese *Ambans* to King (Girwan Yuddha) informing to send *arji* after receiving the *Parwana* and presents being sent by the Ch'ing Emperor to King Girwan and Queen Subarna Prabha.)

Source : MFA, *Poka* No. Pa 64.

Appendix K

श्री ५ वादसाहवाट पठाइ वकस्याको प्रमाना सौगात ल्हासा आइ पुग्यो. कुति संम पुऱ्याउन अंवावाट षटायाका हुनाले टींगरीमा आइ पुगे चाडो काजिहरुलाई लिन पठाउनु होला भंन्या च्याछीं ८ साल ८ मैन्हा २ दिन जादा १८६० सालमा गोर्षाका राजा भारा चार काजिलाई लेषेको १

(Chinese *Amban* to King of Gorkha and his *Bhardars* and Four *Kazis* informing to send *Kazis* to receive Chinese Emperor's *Parwana* and presents at Tingri Maidan.)

Source : MFA, *Poka* No. Pa 64.

Appendix L

सर्वजित पांडे काजिले संवन १८६० साल्मा ल्यायाको च्याछीन् ८ वर्ष १ मैन्हा २४ दिन जादाको प्रमाना १

ऐ. प्रमानाका भोटे अक्षरको उल्था.

तिम्रा वावा रण वहादुर शाह देषी असल चित्तले मेरा सर्कारका जस्तो काम चलाई साले पिच्छे माल चढाई जेसुकै काम्मा पनि टाढा मानिस तिमीहरुले सानु काम काज पनि नविरायेको देषदा वहुत षुसी भयौ. तिमी आमा छोराले वहुत

मानेको साचो रहेछ चीज वस्तुहरु पठाई दियाको छ वकस पाई षुसि मान्नु. दुनिञालाई मनपर्दो गर्न नलाउनु काम नविराउनु भन्या ईत्यादी हुकुम वक्सौ भन्या श्री ५ सर्कार गीर्वाण युद्ध विक्रम साहका हजुरमा आयाको च्याछीन ८ साल आश्वीन २१ गतेको प्रमानाको नक्कल ....

(Chinese Emperor's *Parwana* to King Girwan Yuddha Bikram Shah.)

Source : MFA, *Poka* No. Pa 64.

Appendix M

६१ साल

चीन वादसाह का परमाना सौगात लि आउन्या. ताल्वे के सिमानामा जाइ भेट् गर्दा. दिन्या सराजाम. मार्फत काजि वषतवार सिं थापा टौढि टक्सारि भाद्र सुदि १० रो ....

चिङ्गली को छाता १ के ५	मिठाइ धार्नि ..... १२ के ९
अलैचि दाना धार्नि ३ के ३॥.	प्याज धार्नि ...... ५ के १।.
लसुन धार्नि .... ५ के ।।।.	हिंग तोला ...... १५ के १
जिरा पाथि .... १ के ॥.	छोहारा धार्नि ... २ के ३॥.
वदाम धार्नि .... १ के २	लवाग तोला ...... २० के २
दालचिनी सेर .... १ के २	सुपारि धार्नि ..... २ के १॥२
दक्षिरिाा सुपारि धार्नि ... १ के ३।।।	जायफल गोटा .....५० के ३२
गरिगोटा .... १५ के १।।।२	सुषमेल तोला २० के २॥.
अमोंट् सेर .... ३ के अं ४	अदुवा धार्नि ५ के ॥२
हास गोटा .... ३० के १५	हासका फुल १०० के १॥
कुषुराको फुल .... ५२० के ५	जायपत्रि तोला ५ के २॥
चिनी धार्नि .... २ के १।।।	चलासेर .... १ के ।।।.
मिश्रि धार्नि .... १ के ३	प्याग गोटा १५ के २।।।२
भरिया जना .... ४७ के ६७	तरोवार .... १ के १०
वन्दुक .... १ के अं २५	ढाल .... १ के ७
किंषाप थान .... १ के ३५	षुकुरि ....१ के अं ७
सफा थान .... ५ के १७॥	कासिवाल थान ४ के ३०
पिटा थान .... ४ के ३	अधर्सा थान ६ के ११॥.
भिंवजी पाथी .... ५ के अं १	मैनकपडा थान ३ के ३॥.
मेही चावल मुरि ...... १ के अं ५	चिहुरा पाथि १५ के अं ३
केरा घरि .... ६ के अं ३	मोटा चावल मुरि २ के अं ८
भैकटहर गोटा .... १५ के अं १	रुष कटहर .... ४ के अं १
काक्रो गोटा .... ७ के अं ॥	षर्वुजा ...... २ के अं ॥
निवुवा .... २५ के अं ।।	दारिम ...... ५० के ।।।.॥

अम्वां भारि .... ५ के अं २॥ फर्सि .... ५ के अं ।२
चिचिंदा भारि .... १ के अं ।. तोरिया भारि ..... १ के अं ।
तामा र तुसा भारि .... १ के अं ॥
केरुं सम्म आउन्या ताल्वे के किंषाप थान .... १ के २५
अधर्सा थान .... १ के १।।।.
केरुं का केटा २ के सफा थान .... २ के ७
साथ आउन्या सतारा मिञा के ८५
साल जोडा .... १ के ५० किंषाप थान १ के ३५

षडानन्द पाध्या मेजर के साल फर्द .... १ के २५

(The detailed expenses and the list of presents given to the Chinese officials who handed over the presents sent by the Chinese Emperor to *Kazi* Sarvajit Pande in 1804.)

Source : RNAH, Part 3, Serial No. 63 (53).

Appendix N

श्री ५ चिन वादसाहवाट श्री ५ गिर्वाण युद्ध विक्रम साहका नाउमा लेषी आयाको च्याछीन ८ वर्ष १ मैन्हा २२ दिन जादाको ताहावाट पठायाको मामुली सौगाद आइ पुग्यो. आफुलाई र मुमालाई पठाई दियाको छ ....

(Chinese *Amban's* letter referring to the sending of the Chinese Emperor's presents to King Girwan and Queen Mother Subarna Prabha.)

Source : MFA, *Poka* No. Pa 64.

Appendix O

आफ्ना महाराजवाट सुनको प्रमानाको उत्तरा अर्जी पठायाको आइ पुग्यो श्री वादसाहका हजुरमा चढाई पठाञ्युं . आफुले पठायाको किनषाप २ थान लियौ आफुलाई केहि पठायाको छैन. पछि पठाउला भंने च्याछि ८ साल १२ मैन्हा २ दिन जादा १८६० साल्मा अंवाले काजी दामोदर पांडेलाई लेषेको...

(Chinese *Amban* to *Kazi* Damodar Pande referring to the sending of Nepalese King's reply *arji* to Chinese Emperor's *Parwana* and receiving of presents from *Kazi* Damodar Pande.)

Source : MFA, *Poka* No. Pa 64.

* * *

4

Kazi Bhaktabir Thapa's Mission of 1807

According to the arrangement of the mission system, Nepal was to send the next five-yearly mission to China in 1807. But like the mission of 1802, the fourth mission of 1807 also did not go to Peking, and just handed over the usual five-yearly presents to the Chinese officials at the border area of Kuti. By that time there had been much improvement in the political situation in Nepal, along with the assassination of Ran Bahadur Shah and the emergence of an influential political personality like Bhimsen Thapa. Even then Nepal, once again pleaded that she would send a mission to the border area, explaining that the King of Nepal was still a minor[1]. The Chinese seemed to have been convinced by the reason given by Nepal, which is why China once again allowed Nepal to send the mission only up to the border instead of to Peking to hand over the presents to the Chinese officials. Here it should be noted that the 1807 Nepalese quinquennial mission has not been mentioned in the Chinese Imperial records[2]. But the Nepalese archival documents clearly state of Nepal's dispatching of five-yearly mission to China in 1807. The Nepalese documents mention that the fourth Nepalese mission, led by *Kazi* Bhaktabir Thapa, left the country in 1807. The other members of this mission were *Subedar* Dambar Thapa, the deputy leader of the mission, Aiman Thapa, Krishna Singh Thapa, Singh Bir Thapa, interpreter Narayan Tewari, as well as twenty one soldiers[3]. On this occasion, the Nepalese presents to the Ch'ing Emperor Chia Ch'ing were estimated at approximately Rs. 4,656 ।.।[4]. The 1807 Nepalese mission had carried twenty three items as presents to the Ch'ing Emperor. Nepal also sent thirteen items as presents, which were valued at Rs. 608।। to the Chinese

1. Tri Ratna Manandhar and Tirtha Prasad Mishra, *Nepal's Quinquennial Missions to China* , Kathmandu: Purna Devi Manandhar and Puspa Mishra, 1986, p. 24.
2. J.K. Fairbank and S.Y. Teng, "On the Ch'ing Tributary System", *Harvard Journal of Asiatic Studies*, Vol. VI, 1941, pp. 195-198.
3. Royal Nepal Army Head-quarters (hereafter referred as RNAH), Part 3, Serial No. 63 (53). See Appendix B.
4. *Ibid.*

Ambans through the 1807 Nepalese mission[5]. Like the mission of 1802, this Nepalese mission of 1807 delivered the presents and *arji* to the Chinese officials at Kuti[6]. After nearly a year, in 1808, *Kazi* Bhaktabir Thapa, along with his party, went to Kuti to receive presents and *Parwana* from the Ch'ing Emperor Chia Ch'ing.[7] The Chinese officials, who handed over the Chinese Emperor's presents to *Kazi* Bhaktabir Thapa, were also given presents by the Nepalese government.[8]

The importance of the mission of 1807 lies in the fact that it was the second Nepalese mission that did not go to Peking itself, but only went up to the Nepal - Tibet border to hand over the usual five-yearly presents meant for the Chinese Emperor to the Chinese officials, on the grounds that the King of Nepal was very young. In this way, we see that the events of the fourth five-yearly mission to China were similar to those of the third Nepalese five-yearly mission, of 1802, in many respects.

Appendix A

सरसौगाद ली चिन जाने काजिहरु भाद्र १ गते कुति पुग्ने छ भनी लेषेकोमा ञाहावाट वाङ सोपिलाई लिन पठायाको छ भन्या च्याछीं १२ वर्ष ७ मैन्हा १५ दिन जादा १८६४ साल्मा श्री ५ सर्कारमा गीवार्णलाई ....

(Chinese *Amban* to King Girwan referring to the sending of Wang Sopi to receive the Nepalese mission at Kuti.)

Source : Ministry of Foreign Affairs, Kathmandu (MFA), *Poka* No. Pa 64.

5. *Ibid.*
6. Chinese *Amban* to King Girwan Yuddha, Chyachhin 12th year 7th month 15th day (1807), Ministry of Foreign Affairs, Kathmandu (hereafter mentioned as MFA), *Poka* No. Pa 64. See Appendix A; Wang Chuye (of Tingri) to King Girwan, 1864 B.S. Bhadra Sudi 2 Roj 6 (1807), MFA, *Poka* No. Pa 64. See Appendix C. But another source indicates that the Nepalese mission of 1807 went up to Lhasa to deliver the presents. See RNAH, Part 3, Serial No. 63 (53). See Appendix B.
7. Chinese *Amban* to Nepalese King, 1865 B.S. (Chyachhin 13th Year) Bhadra Sudi 8 Roj 2 (29 August 1808), MFA, *Poka* No. Pa. 64. See Appendix D.
8. See Appendix E.

Appendix B

<u>६४ साल</u>

चीन वादसाह छेउ सौगात गयाको. मार्फत काजि भक्तवीर थापा सुवेदार डम्बर थापा. मिति भाद्रवदी ६ रोज......

सौगात .... १३४७॥[२]/

श्री वादसाहके ... अंदाज .... ४६५६।.।

अर्जी १	मुगा माला १ के तो १७॥ के २१०
अै. वेन्हनाके तास तो ८। २ के १२।/	तास थान .... २ के ५९[२]
विहारि का रुमाल. २ के अं॥	वनात थान .... १३ के १७९७[२]
पहेलो माहा पगरि १ के अं १॥	किंषाप थान .... २० के १३२५।॥[२]
रुपौला गोटा हा १० के अं ।॥.	गलेता थान .... ४ के १७५
पहेलो रुवा सेर १॥ के अं १॥	दोनाल्या वन्दुक ..... १ के १३२
तोडेवाल वंदुक २ के अं ९०	तर्वार .... ३ के ३०
कटार .... २ के अं ३५	षुंडा .... १ के १०
षुकुरि .... ४ के अ २८	गैडाको षाग .... २ के ४०
हाती दात .... ४ के अ १६०	घोडा .... २ के ४००
सुपारि धार्नि ... १० के अं १०	लवाग धार्नी .... ६ के १२६
जायफल गोटा १००० के अं ६२॥	दक्षिरिा सुपारि धा ६ के ३०

दाल चिनी धार्नि .... ३ के १८ ।॥.

ल्हासा का अम्वा २ के अंदाज .... ६०८॥

तरोवार .... १ के	षुकुरि .... १ के
वनात थान ..... २ के २२२	किंषाप थान ....२ के ८०
तोडेवाल वन्दुक २ के ९०	तरवार .... २ के २०
षुकुरि .... २ के १४	हाति दात .... २ के १६०
वदाम धार्नि .... २ के ५	दालचिनि धार्नि ... १ के ६
सुपारि धार्नि ..... ४ के ४	छोहारा धार्नि ..... ४ के ३।॥

गरिगोटा ....३० के ३।॥.

कुतिसंम सौगात लिन आउन्या चिनिञा के .... ८२।॥[२]

किंषाप थान १ के ४०	मेहि चावल पाथी २१ के २०।
मसिना चिहुरा पाथी २० के ४	लवांग सेर .... १ के ७
दालचिनि सेरं ...... १ के २	सिपाहि .... २१ के ४२
छोहारा धार्नि .... १ के ।॥	भरिया .... २३ के ३४॥
मिश्रि धार्नि .... १ के ३	जायफल गोटा ..... १५ के ।॥[२]
केसर तोला .... ५ के ३।॥.	सुपारि धार्नि .... १ के १

फलफुल गैह् ....

सौगाति मालका षोल र वेठन के. अंदाज ६८

वनात हात .... १५ के ३०	अधर्सा थान १० के	२०
पिटा थान .... १५ के १५	कोरा थान ..... ४ के	॥.
षारुवा थान .... १ के ३		

दर्वारि षर्च के. अंदाजका मोल .... ९४।।।ˀ

कासिवाल थान ४ के ४०	मेहि अधर्सा थान ४ के	१०
अधर्सा थान .... ४ के ८	सफा थान ...... ४ के	१४
षारुवा थान .... २ के ६	पिटा थान .... ४ के	४
सुपारि धार्नि .... १ के १	लवाग सेर .... १ के	७
दालचि पाव .... २ के १	छोहारा सेर .... १ के	।ˊ
जायफल गोटा ..... २० के १।	चिनी धार्नि .... २ के	१।।।
गरि गोटा .... ५ के		॥ˀ

अैजन सौगात ल्हासा सम्म पुऱ्याउन जान्या मानीसहरु के षर्च		४१६॥
काजि भक्तवीर थापाके १५०	डम्वर थापा के	५०
अैमान थापाके ४०	कृष्न सिं थापा के	५०
सिंहवीर थापा के ४०	नारान के	१०
भरिया जना २३ के .... ३४॥.	सिपाहि जना २१ के	४२

(The detailed expenses and the list of presents sent along with the 1807 Nepalese mission to China under the leadership of *Kazi* Bhakta Bir Thapa.)

Source : Royal Nepal Army Head-quarters (RNAH), Part 3, Serial No. 63 (53).

Appendix C

ताहांवाट पठायाको अर्जि सौगाद श्री ५ वादसाहका हजुर्मा चढाउन्या अर्जि सौगाद लि काजी भारदार कुतीमा आइपुग्या. हामीलाई वकसी पठायाका चीजहरु पनि लियौं भंन्या १८६४ साल भाद्र सुदी २ रोज ६ मा श्री ५ सर्कार गीवार्ण युद्ध विक्रम साहका हर्जुमा टिगरीका वाङ चुयेको चीठी ....

(Wang Chuye of Tingri to King Girwan informing about the arrival of the Nepalese mission at Kuti for delivering the presents and *arji* to the Ch'ing Emperor.)

Source : MFA, *Poka* No. Pa 64.

Appendix D

श्री ५ वादसाहवाट वकसेको सुनको प्रमाना लिन काजिहरु ल्हासामा चाडो पठाई दिनु भंन्या च्याछीं १३ सम्वत १८६५ साल भाद्र सुदि ८ रोज २ मा श्री ५ सर्कारका हजुरमा युतारिन उतारिन अम्वाले लेषेको ....

(Chinese *Ambans* to Nepalese King informing to send the Nepalese *Kazi* to receive the presents and *Parwana* being sent by the Ch'ing Emperor.)

Source : MFA, *Poka* No. Pa 64.

Appendix E

६५ साल

चिन वादसाह लाइ ६४ सालमा गयाको सौगातको प्रति उत्तर परमाना र सौगात वादसाहवाट आउदा कुति सम्म लिन जादा वादसाहवाट आउन्या भारदारलाइ दिन्या सराजाम. मार्फत ताल्वे चुइ. हस्ते काजि भक्तवीर थापा. आश्विन वदि ६ रो. .... १३५८॥/

सौगात .... २१३॥²।

नगद छाता मिठाइ अदुवा लसुन गैह्र के. .... १५॥.

जिन्सी .... ११८²।

वाफदा थान ....१ के ३७॥	अधर्सा थान .... ५ के १०
फुसाम थान .... २ के १६	पिटा थान .... ९ के ६॥।
तरोवार ....१ के १०	लवाग सेर .... १ के ५
मिश्रि धार्नि .... के ३	केसर तोला .... ५ के अं ५
जायपत्रि तोला ....५ के ५	सुषमेल सेर .... ॥ के ३॥
जायफल गोटा ....२५ के २।/॥	छोहारा धार्नि ...... १ के १॥।²
दक्षिरिा सुपारि सेर .... १ के २	अगोट धार्नि .... १ के अं ३
दालचिनि सेर .... १ के २	चिनी धार्नी .... २ के २
सुपारि धार्नि .... १॥ के १।/	हिंग तोला .... १० के ॥²
गरिगोटा .... ५ के ॥।/॥।	मेहि चिऊरा पाथी ३० के अं ६
मसिना चावल पाथी ३० के अं ७॥	षुकुरि. .... २ के अं १०
षाल के रुक हात ६ के ॥।²	येस पालामा फर्मा तोडेवाल
पिटा थान .... ९ के ।²	वन्दुक .... १ के अं ४५
सरजाम गैह्रवाधना के धुवा कुतिका ढेवा २ के	मेहि सफा
थान .... ३ के ४॥	थान .... २ के ६

अैजन सौगात कुति सम्म पुर्‍याउन जान्याहरु के षर्च.......... ११४४॥।²

काजि भक्तवीर थापा के .... ६१८॥।²

पुर्वि पगरि थान १ के १७६ किंषाप थान १॥ के १७५

साल जोडा १ के २५०	कोचिन षगाम १ के ७
जरिवाल पटुका १ के ३।	माल्दहि हात १३ के ६॥

चौविसा का रुमाल .... १ के ३

नगद रु १५०

काजिका साथ जान्या मानीस के नगद रु ५३६

सुवेदार डमवर थापाके ६६	सुवेदार कृष्न सिं थापा के ६६
दोभास्या हरि कृष्न के २५	नारान दोभास्या के १०
मछिन्द्र के २५	सिंहवीर के २०
अैमान थापा के २०	सुवेदार फौद सि अधिकारि ...६०
चामु षडका के १५	ज्मादार स्मेत सिपाहि २१ के ७०
भाजुमनि जैसि के १०	दोल्या भरिया ६ के २४

अली वकत के १२५

(The detailed expenses and the list of presents given to the Chinese officials who handed over the presents sent by the Chinese Emperor to *Kazi* Bhakta Bir Thapa in 1808.)

Source : RNAH, Part 3, Serial No. 63 (53).

* * *

5

Kazi Bhaktabir Thapa's Mission of 1812

In accordance with the peace agreement between Nepal and China in September 1792, Nepal sent her the first two five-yearly missions to China in 1792 and 1795 respectively. Afterwards the third and fourth Nepalese missions of 1802 and 1807 to China did not go to Peking themselves, but only went up to the Nepal-Tibet border to hand over the usual five-yearly presents meant for the Chinese Emperor to the Chinese officials, on the grounds that the King of Nepal was very young. In 1812, once again Nepal showed her willingness to send a mission only up to the border area, like the earlier missions of 1802 and 1807, and not to Peking itself, repeating the same plea that the Nepalese King was still a minor. Unlike the two earlier occasions in 1802 and 1807, this time the Chinese *Ambans* did not comply with the Nepalese request. Perhaps the Chinese *Ambans* thought that Nepal would abandon the system of sending quinquennial mission to Peking itself in the near future if she was allowed to deliver presents and *arji* at the Tibetan border again and again. That is why the Chinese *Ambans* insisted that the Nepalese government send the Nepalese mission to Peking, with usual presents and *arji*, in time, "as the Nepalese King has now become able to control the state affairs".[1] As such, Nepal decided to send the five-yearly mission to Peking itself.

Nepal sent her fifth five-yearly mission to China in June 1812, under the leadership of *Kazi* Bhaktabir Thapa, who had led the Nepalese mission of 1807. Here it should be noted that the Chinese Imperial records have not mentioned about Nepal's sending of five-yearly mission to China in 1812.[2] But the Nepalese archival documents clearly state of Nepal's dispatching of quinquennial

1. Chinese *Ambans* to Nepalese *Kazis*, Chyachhin 17th year 2nd month 29th day (March 1812), Ministry of Foreign Affairs, Kathmandu (hereafter mentioned as MFA), *Poka* No. Pa 64. See Appendix C. For the correspondence between the Nepalese and Chinese government regarding the sending of the 1812 Nepalese mission, see Appendices A and B.
2. J.K. Fairbank and S.Y. Teng, "On the Ch'ing Tributary System", *Harvard Journal of Asiatic Studies*, Vol. VI., 1941, pp. 195-198.

mission to China in 1812. On this occasion, Nepal proposed to send a ninety one member mission to China. It was reported that the *Ambans* objected to it, but permitted a mission of not more than sixty persons.[3] Besides *Kazi* Bhaktabir Thapa, the mission of 1812 included *Sardar* Dambar Thapa, deputy leader of the mission, Khadananda Padhya, Machhindra, *Subedar* Maha Singh Thapa, Ram Chandra Thapa, grandson of *Subedar* Dambar Thapa, Padma Narayan Kafle, *Dhakre* Arjun Thapa and *Bhariya Nayak* (Chief porter) Padau. The total cost of the mission of 1812 was Rs. 19,690III/III and the presents to the Ch'ing Emperor were estimated Rs. 4,323I/.[4] On this occasion Nepal sent eighteen items as presents to the Ch'ing Emperor. Besides that the 1812 Nepalese mission had carried presents to *Dhewas* of *Kuti*, *Chuii* of Tingari, *Talloye* of *Digarcha*, Lama of *Digarcha,* the Chinese *Ambans,* the *Potala* Lama, Lama of Takayali, the four *Kajis* of Lhasa, *Chundu* of Chindafu and the *Chundu* of Sindafu[5]. The mission of 1812 was well received by the Chinese officials on the way[6] and it was reported to have returned home after a lapse of about fifteen months. Unfortunately, Ram Chandra Thapa, a member of the 1812 Nepalese mission died on the way[7]. The 1812 Nepalese mission seemed to have reached Kerung by Bhadra, 1870 (1813). The Chinese official carrying the Chinese Emperor's *Parwana* to Nepalese King[8] as well as escorting the Nepalese delegation returned from Kerung, and they were given some presents by the Nepalese mission.[9]

The importance of the mission of 1812 lies in the fact that

3. Chinese *Amban* to Nepalese King, Chyachhin 17th year 4th month 17th day (1869 B.S., June 1812), MFA, *Poka* No. Pa 64. See Appendix D.
4. Royal Nepal Army Head-quarters (hereafter referred as RNAH), Part 3, Serial No. 63 (53). See Appendix E.
5. *Ibid.*
6. Bhaktabir Thapa and Dambar Thapa's letter to Bhimsen Thapa and Randhoj Thapa, 1869 B.S. Asadh Sudi 3 Roj 7 (1812), MFA, *Poka* No. Pa 64, See Appendix F.
7. Chinese *Amban* to Nepalese King, Chyachhin 18th year 2nd month 16th day (1869 B.S.), MFA, *Poka* No. Pa 64. See Appendix G.
8. Draft letter of the Nepalese King to Chinese Emperor, 1870 B.S. Bhadra Sudi 7 Roj 5 (1813), MFA, *Poka* No. Pa 64. See Appendix H.
9. RNAH, Part 3, Serial No. 63 (53). See Appendix I.

after the second Nepalese five-yearly mission of 1795, it was the first mission to go to Peking itself after a span of seventeen years. Besides that, *Kazi* Bhaktabir Thapa had led the Nepalese mission to China continuously for the second time.

Appendix A

अव आउदो साल श्री ५ वादसाहका हजुर्मा चढाई पठाउनालाई अर्जि सौगाद तयार गरी राषनु भन्या च्याछिन १६ साल संवत १८६८ साल ज्येष्ठ सुदि १२ रोज २ मा श्री ५ गिर्वाणलाई पठाएको–यांतारिन छेन्तारिन अम्वाले................

(Chinese *Ambans* to King Girwan reminding the sending of the Nepalese mission to the Ch'ing court for the forthcoming year.)

Source : Ministry of Foreign Affairs, Kathmandu (MFA), *Poka* No. Pa 64.

Appendix B

चीन जान्या भारदारहरु कुन दिन कुन वाटोवाट कइले आइपुग्छ सो लेषी पठाउनु भन्या च्याछिन १७ वर्ष २ मैन्हा २९ दिन जादा १८६९ साल्मा श्री ५ गिर्वाणलाई यान्तारीन छिन्तारीन अम्वाले लेषेको ....

(Chinese *Ambans* to King Girwan asking to provide about the details of the departure of the Nepalese mission.)

Source : MFA, *Poka* No. Pa 64.

Appendix C

अधिका रीत वमोजिम ५।५ वर्षमा येक पल्ट अर्जि सौगाद दि काजिहरु पेचिन पठाउनु पर्नेमा राजा बालष हुनाले सौगाद साध सम्म पुऱ्याय हुन्छ भनी अघि लेषी पठायाको हो. राजा उमेरदार भै मुलुकको काम काज सवै गर्न जांन्या भयाःका हुनाले अधिका रीत वमोजिम अर्जि सौगाद दि पैचिन जान काजी भारदारहरु चाडै पठाई दिनु भन्यां च्याछीन १७ वर्ष २ मैन्हा २९ दिन जादा १८६९ साल्मा याङतारिन छिंतारीन अम्वाले काजीहरुलाई लेषेको..................

(Chinese *Ambans* to Nepalese *Kazis* instructing to send the Nepalese mission to Peking soon as the Nepalese King has become able to control the state affairs.)

Source : MFA, *Poka* No. Pa 64.

Appendix D

अघि पैचिन पठायेका काजी स्मेत ६१ जवानमा ४५ जवान गयेका हुन. हाल ९१ पठाउने कुरालाई धेरै पठाउनु हुदैन अघिका रित वमोजिम ५०।६० लाई पठाउनु होला. हिडेको मिती आउने वाटो लेषी पठाउने चीनीञा भारदार पठाई कुति सम्म लिन पठाउछौ भन्या च्याछिन १७ वर्ष ४ मैन्हा १७ दिन जादा १८६९ सालमा श्री ५ सर्कारका–हुतारिन छिंतारीन अम्वाले पठाएको ....

(Chinese *Ambans* to Nepalese King mentioning the permission of dispatching the Nepalese mission of not more than sixty persons instead of ninety-one persons.)

Source : MFA, *Poka* No. Pa 64.

Appendix E

<u>६९ साल</u>

चीन श्री वादसाहके सौगात गयाको. मार्फत र हस्ते काजी भक्तवीर थापा. सर्दार डम्वर थापा. मिति जेष्ठसुदि १३ रो. .... १९६९०।।।/।।।

श्री वादसाह के. .... ४३२३।/

मुगामाला १ के तो २१।८। के २३५^{२}सु.	तास थान २ के तो ४५ के ८४।^{२}
किंषाप थान २० के १३२५।।।^{२}	वनात ताषा १३ के १७९७।^{२}
गलेता थान ४ के ७५	दोनाल्या संदुकी वदुक १ के अं १३२
हाति दात ४ के अं १६०	लवाग धार्नि ६ के १३२
जायफल गोटा १००० के ६२।।	गैडा षाग २ के अं ४०
दालचिनी धार्नि ५ के ३०	तरोवार ४ के अं ४०
सुनौला रुपौला कटार २ के अं ३५	दक्षिरिाा सुपारि धा ६ के ३६
सुपारि धार्नि १० के १०	षुडा २ के अं १०
षुकुरि ४ के अं २८	सुनौला तोडेवाल वंदुक २ के अं ९०

कुति का ढेवा २ के कासिवाल अतलस थान .... २ के १६

टिगरि का चुइ के ११

कासिवाल अतलस थान १ के १० सुपारि धार्नि १ के १

डिगर्चाको ताल्वे के तपसील सदर ११

डिगर्चाको लामा के १९६

वनात ताषा .... १ के १४० किंषाप थान १ के २५

चौविसा थान .... २ के ७ हाती दातका कटौरा २ के अं १६

अलैची दाना धार्नि .... ४ के अं ८

ल्हासा का अम्वा २ के .... ६०७॥

वनात ताषा .... २ के २८०　　तरोवार .... २ के अं २०

तोडेवाल वन्दुक .... २ के अं ९०　　ठुलो हाती दात २ के अं　८०

षुकुरि .... २ के अं १४　　किंषाप थान २ के　८३ ।।।.

सुपारि धार्नि .... ४ के ४　　दक्षिरी सुपारि धार्नि २ के　१२

दालचिनी धार्नि ..... १ के ६　　वदाम धार्नि .... २ के　६

गरिगोटा .... ३० के ३।।।.　　छोहारा धार्नि ...... ४ के　८

पोताला लामा के .... १५१।

वनात ताषा १ के ८०।।।　　किंषाप थान १ के ३७॥

हाति दातका कटौरा २ के अं १६　　चौविसा थान २ के ७

अलैचि दाना धार्नि ४ के अं ८　　सुपारि धार्नि २ के २

तक्यालि का लामाजु के .... १४७।

वनात ताषा १ के ८०।।।　　किंषाप थान १ के ४३।।।

चौविसा थान २ के ७　　हाति दातका कटौरा २ के अं १६

ल्हासाका ४ काजि के .... ११६।।.

किंषाप थान ४ के ११२।।.　　सुपारि धार्नि ४ के.......... ४

छिन्दफु का चन्दु के .... १२०।।।

वनात ताषा .... १ के ८०।।।　　किंषाप थान १ के ४०

सिंधाफु का चन्दु के ४२

किंषाप थान .... १ के ४०　　सुपारि धार्नि २ के २

दर्वारि षर्च के .... २११३।।

जमुर्दि वनात ताषा १ के ११२।।।　　सवुज वनात वस्ता २ के　१७५।।।

किंषाप थान ९ के २५४।।　　फलाम अतलस था २० के　१००

चौविसा थान ३० के १०५　　वरैलि छीट् थान १६ के　७६

सुपारि धार्नि ५ के ५　　लवांग सेर ३।। के　२५।।।

दालचिनी धार्नि २ के १२　　सुषमेल सेर २ के　१६।।

दक्षिरिाा सुपारि धार्नि १ के ६　　वला धार्नि ५ के　१७।।.

...... धार्नि ५ के १०　　षुकुरि १० के अं　३०

...... धार्नि २।।। के ११।　　क्षारुवा थान २० के　५०

...... २ के ६०　　धुवां थान ३० के　४५

नगद मोहर रु १००

अैजन सौगात के काम काम के षर्च .... ३०७॥.
नगद रु. .... १७०।२
षुडा षुकुरि तरोवार का विडामा लाउना के सुन तोसा
२ के मो रु. ३४
अलैंचि दाना मोल १२
तरोवार ५ के मोल ३२
रुपौला कवुजा १ के ३
अतलस थान २ मा वुट्टा भर्ना के दतु मोल १८।२
षुडा षुकुरि का वीड रगाउना के रंग मोल ॥.
भरिया ४७ के षर्च ४७

जिन्सी .... १३७।२

सुनौला कवुजा .... ४ के अं	२०	म्यान के मषमलष २ के	१५
षोल के वनात गज १ के	६।।।.	वेठन्के षारुवा था ४ के	१०
अर्जि लेषन्या कागज के		मलमल हात ३ के	१।/
लेषन्या सुन तोला १।.।५ के	२१।	मैन कपडा थान १० के	२०
हतियार का षोल्के वनात ग ३॥ के	१४२।	अर्जि के तास तो ४।८। के	१६।।।.॥
रेस्मि डोरि .... १२ के अं	।।।.	भित्री के मष मलष १ के	८
पहेलो रुवा सेर ...... १ के	॥/	पहेलो पगरि थान ॥ के	।।।.
वेठन के अधर्सा थान ... १ के	३	रुपौला गोटा तोला ४ के	१२
अै. के धुवा थान .... ४ के	६	वेठन के चौविसा हा १६ के	२

अैजन सौगात लि चीन श्री वादसाहका हजुरमा जान्या भारदार पगरि गैह्रके
षर्च र पोसाक .... ११५२६।।।२॥
काजि भक्तवीर थापा के .... ३८९९।।

नगद रु.	३०००	साल जोडा .... १ के	३२२
सालका रुमाल ... १ के	२००	किंषाप थान ..... २ के	२८६
गुदर थान .... १ के	१६।/	कलंधरा माल्दहि थां १ के	६।/।।
सुरुष पुर्वि पगरि थां १ के	४०	लैस तोला ७ के	२८
विहारि का रुमाल १ के....	।२॥		

सर्दार डम्वर थापा के .... १४४२।।।.॥

नगद रु.	१०००	किंषाप थान १॥ के	१९२॥२
साल जोडा १ के	१७८	सालका रुमाल १ के	३५
३५ गजि पगरि १ के	१४	माल्दहि थान २ के	१८

चिङ्गली हात ४ के ३ रुवा धार्नी१ के १॥।
विहारी का रुमाल .... १ को२॥

षडानन्द पाध्या के .... ४६०।९

नगद रु. .... ३४९॥।२ साल फर्द १ के ५०
ला २२ गजि पगरि १ के ६ वाफदा थान १ के ३१।
कासिवाल थान ॥ के ९।२ मल्दहि थान १ के १०
चौविसा थान ॥ के १।२ चिङ्गली हात ३ के २।.
षासाका रुमाल .... १ के३१

मछीन्द्र के .... ६४६।३१

नगद .... ५०० किंषाप थान १ के ५९।२
साल फर्द .... १ के ५७ ला २२ गजी पगरि १ के ६
कासिवाल थान ॥ के ८॥।९ माल्दहि थान १ के १०
सालका रुमाल १ के ४५ षासाका रुमाल १ के ३१

सुवेदार महासिं थापा के .... ५०८।९।

नगद .... ४०० ला २२ गजी पगरि १ के ६
सालफर्द .... १ के ५० वाफदा थान १ के ३२॥
कासिवाल थान ॥ के ९।२ मल्दहि थान १ के १०
षासा का रुमाल .... १ के ३१

सुवेदार डंवर थापा को नाति रामचन्द्र थापा के ६१३१

पुर्वि पगरि थान १ के १४॥ वाफदा थान १ के ३५
कासिवाल थान ॥ के ६ फलाम थान १ के ५॥.
षासाका रुमाल .... १ के३१

पध्मनारान काफल्या के .... ३१०॥.।

नगद .... २०० पटनावाल पगरि १ के २३
सालफर्द .... १ के ५७ वाफदा थान १ के ३३२
माल्दहि थान .... १ के ८ चौविसा थान ॥ के १।२
चिङ्गली हात २॥. के १॥।२ षासाका रुमाल १ के ३१

ढाक्रया अर्जुन थापा के .... ३६०९॥।

नगद रु .... ३०८॥।९। २२ गजी पगरि १ के ६
वाफदा थान १ के ३२॥।९ फलाम थान १ के ५॥.
षासाका रुमाल .... १ के ३१

भरि नाएक पाडौ के .... १९८।४

नगद .... १७५ पटनावाल पगरि १ के २२

वुट्टेदार चिङ्गली थां ॥ के ५॥ फलाम थान ॥ के २॥।

तास हात २१ के १० चौविसा थान १ के २॥।

षासाका रुमाल .... १ के २१

काजिका साथमा जान्या मानीसहरु के षर्च नगद ३६००

(The detailed expenses and the list of presents sent along with the 1812 Nepalese Quinquennial mission to China under the leadership of *Kazi* Bhaktabir Thapa.)

Source: Royal Nepal Army Head-quarters (RNAH), Part 3, Serial No. 63(53).

Appendix F

सुन गुम्वा देखी माथी पुग्दा चुई र धैवुङको सर्दार संग भेट भयो श्रेष्टाचार वहुतै गऱ्या भन्या भंने १८६९ साल आषाढ सुदी ३ रोज ७ मा भिम्सेन थापा रणध्वज थापालाई भक्तवीर थापा डंवर थापाले पठायाको चिठी...............................

(Bhaktabir Thapa and Dambar Thapa's letter to Bhimsen Thapa and Randhoj Thapa mentioning their cordial meeting with *Chuii* and *Sardar* of Dhaibung across Sun Gumba.)

Source : MFA, *Poka* No. Pa 64.

Appendix G

चीन गयेका मानिस मध्ये भारदार रामचन्द्र वाटामा मरेको षवर च्याछीं १८ वर्ष २ मैन्हा १६ दिन जादा १८६९ सालमा श्री ५ सर्कारमा हर्जुमा हु अम्वा स्याङ अम्वाले लेषेको ....

(Chinese *Ambans* to Nepalese King informing about the death of Ram Chandra, a member of the Nepalese mission to Peking on the way.)

Source : MFA, *Poka* No. Pa 64.

Appendix H

हाम्रा काजि भक्तवीर जिम्मा श्री ५ वादसाहवाट पठाई वक्साको प्रमाना वुझि लिञ्यू भंन्या उत्तरा लेषेको १८७० साल भाद्र सुदी ७ रोज ५ च्याछीं १८ साल ७

मैन्हा २८ दिन जादा श्री ५ चीन वादसाहका हजुरमा लेषियाको षलिताको नक्कल ....

(Draft letter from Nepalese King to Chinese Emperor informing the receiving of the Chinese Emperor's *Parwana* sent through *Kazi* Bhaktabir.)

Source : MFA, *Poka* No. Pa 64.

Appendix I

७० साल

काजि भक्तवीर थापा चीनवाट फर्कदा वादसाह को परमाना केरुं सम्म पुऱ्याउन आउन्या चिंनिञा के मेजमानी गयाको भाद्रवदी १३ रोज अं ६२॥२

सुपारि धार्नि	१s१॥ के १॥	वदाम धार्नि	s१॥ के १॥
मरीच धार्नी	s॥२के ।२॥२	लवाग धार्नि	s। के १।॥
दालचिनी धार्नी ...	s॥. के १	गरिगोटा	५ के ॥२
वला धार्नि	s॥ के ॥/	छोहरा धार्नि	१ के २
चिनि धार्नि	५ के ४।२	सुषमेल धार्नि	s॥ के ३॥
जायफल गोटा ...	१५ के ॥।२	अलैचि धार्नि	s।१ के ।२
मिश्रि धार्नि	s१ के १	रुपौला कवुजा तरोवार	१ के अं ५
अधर्साका रुमाल	४ के ॥	भरिया	२४ के ३०
चिरुवादार	२ के ४	हल्कारा	१ के १
प्याग गोटा			८ के २

(The detailed expenses and list of presents given to the Chinese officials who escorted the 1812 Nepalese delegation under *Kazi* Bhaktabir Thapa up to Kerung, in 1813.)

Source: RNAH, Part 3, Serial No. 63(53).

* * *

Kazi Ranajoor Thapa's Mission of 1817

Inspite of her war with the British in 1814-1816, as per the Chinese government's instruction, Nepal sent her sixth quinquennial mission to China on time in 1817.[1] Here it should be pointed out that the Chinese Imperial records have not mentioned about the 1817 Nepalese quinquennial mission to China.[2] But the Nepalese documents clearly state of Nepal's sending of five-yearly mission to China in 1817. The mission of 1817 was led by *Kazi* Ranajoor Thapa[3]. The mission had carried an *arji* and presents to the Ch'ing Emperor. The total cost of this sixth Nepalese mission was Rs. 20,024॥.[4] The 1817 Nepalese mission seemed to have left Kathmandu for Peking in Ashad Sudi 13, 1874 B.S. (June 1817)[5] and returned home around September 1818.[6] It was reported that Nepalese *Mukhtiyar* (Prime Minister) Bhimsen Thapa had instructed this Nepalese mission of 1817 to make a personal appeal to the Ch'ing Emperor Chia Ch'ing for assistance, but the Ch'ing Emperor refused to assist Nepal.[7] Through this Nepalese mission of 1817, Ch'ing Emperor Chia Ch'ing was reported to have sent

---

1. Chinese Amban to Girwan Yuddha, Chyachin 21st year 8th month 22nd day (1816), Ministry of Foreign Affairs, Kathmandu (hereafter referred as MFA), *Poka* No. Pa 64. See Appendix A. Sharma has mistakenly referred the 1817 mission as the eighth Nepalese quinquennial mission to China. See Kunjar M. Sharma, *The Economic Theme in Nepali Foreign Policy: An Historical Analysis up to the end of the Anglo-Nepal War*, Unpublished Ph.D. dissertation, University of Denver, 1973, p. 189.
2. J.K. Fairbank and S.Y. Teng, "On the Ch'ing Tributary System", *Harvard Journal of Asiatic Studies*, Vol. VI., 1941, pp. 195-198.
3. Royal Nepal Army Head-quarters (hereafter mentioned RNAH), Part 3, Serial No. 63 (53). See Appendix C.
4. A document relating the total cost of the Nepalese mission led by *Kazi* Ranajoor Thapa, dated 1874 B.S. Ashad Sudi 13 Roj 6 (June 1817), MFA, *Poka* No. Pa 64. See Appendix B.
5. RNAH, Part 3, Serial No. 63 (53).
6. Margaret W. Fisher and Leo E. Rose, *England, India, Nepal, Tibet, China, 1765-1958*, Berkeley: University of California Press, 1959, pp. 2-12.
7. Leo E. Rose, Nepal: *Strategy For Survival*, Berkeley: University of California Press, 1971, p. 95.

various presents and a *Parwana* to the Nepalese King Rajendra Bikram Shah. Except for this, and, like the earlier Nepalese missions, no more is known about this Nepalese mission of 1817.

The importance of the 1817 Nepalese mission lies in the fact that despite Nepal fought the major war against the British in 1814-1816 and realized that the support she could obtain from China was marginal at best, Sino-Nepalese relations returned to their normal footing in 1817 with the dispatch of the sixth five-yearly mission to Peking. It was the first Nepalese five-yearly mission which was sent to China just immediately after the post 1814-1816 Anglo-Nepal war period.

Appendix A

फिरिंगी संग धेरै वर्ष सम्म लडाई भै हालमात्र मिलाप भयाको वषत हुनाले सररौगाद चाडो तयार गर्नु पर्दैन आउदो साल वोढो (?) चिन जान्या रीत वमोजीम् च्याछीं २१ वर्ष ८ मैन्हा २२ दिन जादा १८७३ सालमा श्री ५ सर्कार गीर्वाण युद्धलाई सितारिन अम्वाले लेषेको ....

(Chinese *Amban* to King Girwan asking not to collect the presents soon and reminding to send the Nepalese mission to Peking as scheduled in the forthcoming year.)

Source : Ministry of Foreign Affairs, Kathmandu (MFA), *Poka* No. Pa 64.

Appendix B

सम्वत १८७४ साल्मा काजी रणजोर थापा जादाको

काजी रणजोर थापा अर्जि सौगाद ली. श्री ५ चीन वादसाहका हजुर्मा दर्शन गर्न जादा रु. २००२४।।े खर्च भयाको फाटवारी सम्वत १८७४ साल आषाढ सुदी १३ रोज ६ को कागत् ....

(A document relating to the total cost of the 1817 Nepalese Quinquennial mission led by *Kazi* Ranajoor Thapa.)

Source: MFA, *Poka* No. Pa 64.

Appendix C

चीन श्री बादसाह छेउ पाच वर्षको मामुली सौगात गयाकोमा मार्फत काजी रराजोर थापा मिती आषाढ सुदि १३ रो. तपसिल ६९ साल बमोजीम तप्सील सदर.

(Presents sent along with the 1817 Nepalese Quinquennial mission to China under the leadership of *Kazi* Ranajoor Thapa.)

Source : Royal Nepal Army Head-quarters (RNAH), Part 3, Serial No. 63(53).

* * *

7

Kazi Dalbhanjan Pande's Mission of 1822

Due to the death of the Ch'ing Emperor Chia Ch'ing in 1820, Nepal had to send a special mission to Peking to congratulate the new Ch'ing Emperor, Tao Kwang. Following the precedent of the mission of 1795, on this occasion also Nepal requested the Chinese *Ambans* at Lhasa for permission to send a single mission a year later, with usual five-yearly presents and special presents for the new Ch'ing Emperor, Tao Kwang.[1] The Nepalese request was accepted by the Chinese authorities.[2] On this occasion, Nepal proposed to send a fifty-five member mission to China.[3] The Chinese *Ambans* objected to it but permitted a mission of not more than forty-five persons.[4] As such, the seventh Nepalese quinquennial mission, led by *Kazi* Dalbhanjan Pande left for Peking on Ashar 7, 1879 B.S. (June 1822).[5] Here it should be pointed out that the Chinese Imperial records have mentioned about Nepal's sending mission to China in 1823.[6] But the Nepalese archival documents clearly state of Nepal's dispatching of five-yearly mission to China in 1822. *Sardar* Devi Bhagat Khatri was the deputy leader of the mission, and *Subedar* Dambar Khatri, *Subedar* Krishna Dev Padhya,

---

1. Draft letter from Nepalese King to Chinese *Ambans*, 1877 B.S. (1820), Ministry of Foreign Affairs, Kathmandu (hereafter mentioned as MFA), *Poka* No. Pa 64. See Appendix B. For the correspondence between the Chinese and Nepalese government regarding the sending of a single Nepalese mission a year later with usual five-yearly presents and special presents to the new Ch'ing Emperor Tao Kwang, see Appendices A and C.
2. Chinese *Ambans* to Nepalese King, Tao Kwang, 1st year 4th month 21st day (1820), MFA, *Poka* No. Pa 64. See Appendix D.
3. Nepalese King to Chinese *Ambans*, 1879 B.S. Jestha Badi 1 Roj 3 (1822), MFA, *Poka* No. Pa 64. See Appendix I. For the correspondence between the Chinese and Nepalese government regarding the Nepalese proposal of sending a fifty-five member mission to China, see Appendices E, F, G, J and K.
4. Chinese *Ambans* to *Kazi* Dalbhanjan Pande, Tao Kwang, 2nd year 5th month 12th day(1822), MFA, *Poka* No. Pa 64. See Appendix J.
5. B.H. Hodgson, "Route of two Nepalese Embassies to Pekin with remarks on the water-shed and plateau of Tibet", *Journal of the Asiatic Society*, No. VI, 1856, p. 497.
6. J.K. Fairbank and S.Y. Teng, "On the Ch'ing Tributary System", *Harvard Journal of Asiatic Studies*, Vol. VI., 1941, pp. 195-198.

Ranbir, Interpreter Bhimsen, Interpreter Hemanta, *Bhariya Nayak* Pandau, *Jamadar* Chandra Bir and *Jamadar* Nain Singh Adhikari were other members of the mission. In addition to them, *Subba* Anup Singh Adhikari, Bakhtananda Vaidya, *Subedar* Dildhar Majhi, *Jamadar* Biru Khatri, *Jamadar* Ran Bhanjan Pande, *Jamadar* Bhotu Basnyat, *Chiruwadar* Bhawani Singh were also included in this mission of 1822.[7] On this occasion, Nepal asked the Chinese *Ambans* at Lhasa about the question of sending of elephants and horses. The Chinese *Ambans* reminded the Nepalese government of the earlier Chinese instructions of 1796 and 1800 stopping the presentation of those animals in the future. Then Nepal asked the Chinese *Ambans* about sending different types of palanquins, such as *Khadkhadiya, Myana* and *Palaki* as presents to the new Ch'ing Emperor.[8] The Chinese *Ambans* instructed them not to send those items,[9] and in case those items were dispatched from Nepal, the Nepalese were asked to drop those items on the way and not to carry them to Peking. But by that time, the Nepalese mission had already left the Nepalese capital.[10] Anyway, as per the Chinese *Amban's* instruction, the Nepalese mission did not carry those items to Peking.[11] This time, the usual five-yearly presents and special presents were estimated to be Rs. 3,917 ॥.॥।^{2} and Rs. 7,526 respectively, whereas the total cost of this seventh Nepalese mission was Rs. 27,109.[12] On this occasion Nepal sent eighteen items as ordinary presents and twenty nine items as special presents to the new Ch'ing Emperor. Besides that the 1822

---

7. Royal Nepal Army Head-quarters (hereafter referred as RNAH), Part 3, Serial No. 63(53).
8. Jnanmani Nepal, *Nepal-Bhot Chin Sambandha Ka Kehi Sanskritik Paksha* (Some Cultural Aspect of Nepal-Tibet China Relations), Kathmandu: Royal Nepal Academy, 2045 B.S., p.69.
9. Chinese *Ambans* to Nepalese King, Tao Kwang, 2nd Year (1822), MFA, *Poka* No. Pa 64. See Appendix H.
10. Nepal, f.n. no. 8, p.69.
11. Nepalese King to Chinese *Ambans*, 1879 B.S. Shrawan Badi 13 Roj 3 (1822), MFA, *Poka* No. Pa 64. See Appendix M.
12. RNAH, Part 3, Serial No. 63 (53). See also Appendix L. Regarding the estimation of the usual five-yearly presents to the Ch'ing Emperor in 1822, Manandhar and Mishra have mistakenly given it as Rs. 3937॥.॥^{2} instead of the correct figure of Rs. 3917॥.॥^{2}. See Tri Ratna Manandhar and Tirtha Prasad Mishra, *Nepal's Quinquennial Missions to China*, Kathmandu: Purna Devi Manandhar and Puspa Mishra, 1986, p.76.

Nepalese mission had carried presents to *Dhewas* of Kuti, *Chuii* of Tingri, *Talloye* of Digarcha, Lama of Digarcha, the Chinese *Ambans* , the *Potala* Lama, Raja Lama of Takayali, the four *Kajis* of Lhasa, the *Chundu* of Chindafu and the *Chundu* of Sindafu.[13] Between the course of their journey (from their arrival in Lhasa[14] and their departure from Lhasa to Peking), there were correspondence between the Nepalese mission and the Nepalese government.[15] This Nepalese mission arrived at Peking on Magh 12, 1879 B.S. (January 1823) and remained there for forty seven days.[16] The 1822 Nepalese mission returned home after a lapse of about fifteen months. Unfortunately, Mana Singh, a member of the 1822 Nepalese mission died on the way.[17] After their arrival in Lhasa from Peking, the Nepalese mission met the Chinese *Ambans*, the Dalai Lama and the Tibetan *Kajis*.[18] The Nepalese mission was given a warm send-off at Lhasa.[19] It seemed to have reached Kerung by Bhadra, 1880 (1823). The Chinese official carrying the Chinese Emperor's *Parwana* to Nepalese King as well as escorting the Nepalese delegation returned from Kerung, and they were given some presents by the Nepalese mission.[20]

The importance of the mission of 1822 lies in the fact that it was the second such mission to carry the usual five-yearly presents and special presents on the occasion of the new Ch'ing Emperor Tao Kwang's ascent to the throne. Another noteworthy feature of the 1822 mission was that it had recorded a systematic summary of the routes from Kathmandu to Peking as traversed by the Nepalese envoy to China and set down by his secretary at the close of each day's

---

13. RNAH, Part 3, Serial No. 63 (53).
14. Chinese *Amban* to Nepalese King, Tao Kwang 2nd Year (1822), MFA, *Poka* No. Pa 64. See Appendix N.
15. Nepalese King to *Kazi* Dalbhanjan Pande, 1879 B.S. Sukla Ashwin Sudi 12 Roj (1822), MFA, *Poka* No. Pa 64. See Appendix P.
16. Hodgson, f.n. no. 5, p.497.
17. Chinese *Ambans* to Nepalese King, Tao Kwang, 2nd year 8th month 24th day (1822), MFA, *Poka* No. Pa 64. See Appendix O.
18. Nepalese King to *Kazi* Dalbhanjan and others, 1880 B.S. Bhadra Sudi 6 Roj 4 (1823), MFA, *Poka* No. Pa 64. See Appendix W.
19. Chinese *Amban* to the *Kazis* of Nepal, Tao Kwang 3rd year 7th month 16th day (1823), MFA, *Poka* No. Pa 64. See Appendix Q.
20. RNAH, Part3, Serial No. 63 (53). For the receiving of the Chinese Emperor's *Parwana*, see Appendices R, S, T, and V.

journey.[21] Besides that, it was through the 1822 Nepalese mission *Mukhtiyar* Bhimsen Thapa received a Chinese title.[22]

Appendix A

गादि मुमारष र मामुली सौगात संग पठाउनु हुन्छ कि भनी लेषी पठायाको छ जो जवाफ आउला लेखी पठाउला अन्यां तौककाड. १ वर्ष १ मैन्हा ११ दिन जादा १८७७ सालमा श्री राजेन्द्रलाई युतारीन लिन्तारीन अम्वाले पठायाको चिठी............................

(Chinese *Ambans* to King Rajendra informing to wait the Ch'ing court's reply to the Nepalese government's request for permission to send a single mission with usual five-yearly presents and special presents for the new Ch'ing Emperor.)

Source : Ministry of Foreign Affairs, Kathmandu (MFA), *Poka* No. Pa 64.

Appendix B

गादि ममारष र ५ वर्षको सौगाद आउदो साल येकै पटक पठाउला भन्या १८७७ सालमा श्री ५ सर्कारवाट ल्हासाका २ अम्वालाई लेषियाको मसौदा.................

(Draft letter from Nepalese King to Chinese *Ambans* requesting for permission to send a single mission with usual five-yearly presents and special presents for the new Ch'ing Emperor.)

Source : MFA, *Poka* No. Pa 64.

Appendix C

चीनवाट पठायाको प्रमाना आइ पुग्यो लिन मानिस पठाउनु भन्ने श्री ५ लाई यूतारिन लिउतारीन् अम्वाले तौकाङ्ग १ वर्ष चैत्र सुदी १२ मा लेखेको...........

(Chinese *Ambans* to Nepalese King asking to send men to receive the Chinese Emperor's *Parwana*.)

Source : MFA, *Poka* No. Pa 64.

Appendix D

गादी ममारषको अर्जि सौगाद र मामुली सौगाद एक पटक पठाएमा दोहोरो हिडनु नपर्न्या हुन्छ. तोक्काङ २ साल्मा पठाउनु भन्या तौक्काङ १ वर्ष ४ मैन्हा २१ दिन जादा १८७८ सालमा श्री ५ लाई उतारिन लिनतारीन अम्वाले लेषेको.................................

---

21. Hodgson, f.n.no.5, pp. 491-497.
22. Nepalese *Kazis* to Chinese *Amban*, 1880 B.S. Ashwin 12 Roj 5 (1823), MFA, *Poka* No. Pa 64. See Appendix U.

(Chinese *Ambans* to Nepalese King instructing to send a single mission with usual five-yearly presents and special presents for the new Ch'ing Emperor.)

Source : MFA, *Poka* No. Pa 64.

Appendix E

मामुली र गादि ममारषको सगुन सौगाद र अर्जि स्मेत लि काजी दलभंजन पाडेहरु ६ मैन्हा भरीमा आइ पुग्छन् भनी अम्वा छेउ विन्ती गर्नु अधिका रीत वमोजिम ४५ जना हुन भंन्या इत्यादी १८७८ साल चैत्र वदि ७ रोज ६ जनरलवाट नायेक पानिजुलाई लेखेको...................

(Nepalese General to Nepalese *Nayak Paniju* of Lhasa instructing to inform the Chinese *Ambans* regarding the dispatching of forty-five member Nepalese mission to China under the leadership of *Kazi* Dalbhanjan Pande.)

Source : MFA, *Poka* No. Pa 64.

Appendix F

मामुली सौगाद र गादी मुमारष पठाउदा धेरै मानिस नपठाउनु. पहिले अनुसार पठाउनु. काजी र चाकरहरुको नाम लेखी पनी पठाउनु तौकाङ्ग २ मैन्हा १ दिन जादा १८७८ सालमा श्री ५ राजेन्द्रलाई उतारिन लिंतारीन अम्वाले लेखेको..........................

(Chinese *Ambans* to King Rajendra instructing not to send many persons and to send the name of the leader and the members of the forthcoming Nepalese mission to Peking.)

Source : MFA, *Poka* No. Pa 64.

Appendix G

दल भंजन ६ महिना भित्रमा आइपुग्ने. मानिस अधिका रीत वमोजीम ४५ हुनन्. सराजां सौगाद स्मेत हुदा दोवर होला भन्या १८७८ चैत्र वदी ७ रोज ६ मा लिन्तारिन अम्वालाई लेखेको ....

(Nepalese Government to Chinese *Amban* informing about the dispatching of forty-five member Nepalese mission to Peking under the leadership of *Kazi* Dalbhanjan Pande within six months.)

Source : MFA, *Poka* No. Pa 64.

Appendix H

चीनिञा वादसाहको लागी गादी मुमारष पहिले जस्तै पठाउनु पालकी म्याना पठाउनु पर्दैन भन्या तौकां २ साल अघिका मैन्हामा १८७९ मा श्री ५ मा

उतारीन पाउतारीन अम्वाले लेषेको ....

(Chinese *Ambans* to Nepalese King instructing to send the special presents for the new Ch'ing Emperor as usual and not to send *Palaki* and *Myana* as presents.)

Source : MFA, *Poka* No. Pa 64.

Appendix I

मामुली सौगाद र गादी मुमारष तयार गरी चीन वादसाह समक्ष काजी दलभंजन पांडे देवी भक्त षत्री स्मेत जना ५५ लाई असारका २ दिन जादा विदा गरी पठाउछौ भन्या १८७९ साल ज्येष्ठ वदी १ रोज ३ मा श्री ५ वाट ल्हासाका २ अम्वालाई लेखेको ....

(Nepalese King to Chinese *Ambans* informing about the proposal of sending fifty-five member Nepalese mission to Peking under the leadership of *Kazi* Dalbhanjan Pande.)

Source : MFA, *Poka* No. Pa 64.

Appendix J

चीन पठाउदा पहिले अनुसार पठाउनु १० जना वढी नपठाउनु भन्ने तौक्काड. २ साल ५ मैन्हा १२ दिन जादा १८७९ साल्मा काजी दलभंजनलाई उत्तारीन पाउतारीन अम्वाले लेखेको ....

(Chinese *Ambans* to *Kazi* Dalbhanjan Pande instructing to send only forty-five member Nepalese mission to Peking.)

Source : MFA, *Poka* No. Pa 64.

Appendix K

४५ जना मात्र पठाएको छ पढने २ जना पठाएको छ २ जनालाई ल्हासामा थामी ४५ जनालाई मात्र चीन पठाउने १८७९ साल आषाढ वदी ७ रोज ३ मा श्री वाट अम्वालाई.................................

(Nepalese King to Chinese *Amban* informing about the dispatching of only forty-five member Nepalese mission to Peking.)

Source : MFA, *Poka* No. Pa 64.

Appendix L

<u>७९ साल</u>

चीन श्री वादसाहके पाच वर्षको र गादि ममारष को स्मेत सौगात गयाको मार्फत काजि दलभंजन् पाडे आषाढ वदि १० रो.

पाच वर्षको मामुली

श्री वादसाहके.. ३९१७आ.॥।[२]

मुगा माला १ के तो १७५।५ के १३१॥[२]	किंषाप थान २० के १४६० ॥।/
गलेताथान ४ के १००	वनात वस्ता १३ के १४१९।[३]॥।२
दुइ नाल्या सदुकी वंदुक १ के १३२	सुनौला कवुजा कोथि स्मेतको
षुकुरि............४के अं ४८	तरोवार ४ के ५६

षुडा............ २ के अ २०	कटार २ के अं ३५
गैडा षाग........२ के ६२	तोडेवाल वदुक २ के अं ९०
सु.तास थान २ के तो ४०।२।५ के ५५।	हाति दात ४ के अं १६०
जायफल गोटा १००० के ३१।.	द. सुपारि धार्नि ६ के २४
सुपारि धार्नि १० के ८॥।.	लवाग धार्नि ६ के ८४
दालचिनी धार्नि.......................................३ऽ२॥[२] के १९।[२]	

कुतिका ढेवा २ के कासिवाल थान....................	२के ११।[३]।२
टिगरि का चुइके..	६॥ ॥[३]
कासिवाल थान १ के ५॥[३]॥३	सुपारि धार्नि ...१ के ॥।[२]

डिगर्चाका तालोय के सदर	६॥ ॥३
डिगर्चाका लामाज्यू के	१४०॥। ॥
वनात थान .... १ के ६८।॥	किंषाप थान १ के ४५ ॥।.
को. चौविसाथान २ के ७	अलैचि दाना धा ४ के ४
हाति दातका कटौरा......................	२ के अं १६

ल्हासाका अम्वा २ के	५७५[३]॥
किंषाप थान २ के १३१	वनात वस्ता २ के २०७ ॥।॥
तरोवार २ के ३०	तोडेवाल वंदुक २ के अ ९०
हाति दात ४ के अं ८०	षुकुरि २ के अं १४
सुपारि धार्नि ४ के ३॥.	द.सुपारि धार्नि २ के ८
दालचिनी धार्नि १ के ५	वदाम धार्नि २ के २॥[२]
गरिगोटा ३० के ४ ॥.	छोहारा धार्नि ४ के ३

पोतला लामाजु के	१५०।/
वनात वस्ता १ के ६०॥/	किंषाप थान १ के ६१
कोपा चौविसा थान २ के ७	सुपारि धार्नि २ के १॥।
अलैचि दाना धार्नि ४ के ४	हाति दातका कटौरा २ के अं १६

तक्यालि का राजा लामा के	१८१ऽ॥२
वनात वस्ता...........१ के १०३॥।.॥२	किंषाप थान १ के ५०।
कोपा चौविसा थान २ के ७	अलैचि दाना धार्नि ४ के ४
हाति दातका कटौरा.................................	२ के अं १६

ल्हासाका ४ काजि के............................	१६५।[२]
किंषाप थान ४ के १६१॥।[२]	सुपारि धार्नि.................... ४ के ३॥

छिंदफु का चुंदु के	१४४॥।[२]।
किंषाप थान १ के ४१।	वनात वस्ता ....१ के १०३॥[२]।

सिंधाफु का चुंदु के.. ४५।
किंषाप थान १ के ४३।। सुपारि धार्नि ....२ के १।।।

दर्वारि षर्च के मो रु १०००
अै. सौगात लि जान्या पगरिहरु के षर्च.............. ८६०२।।।ऽ२
काजि दलभंजन पाडे के .... ४२०५।२।।।२
नगद रु ....३००० जिन्सी रु............ १२०५।२।।।२

सर्दार देवी भगत षत्रि के .... १३९९।।।.।।१
नगद रु ....१००० जिन्सी रु ....३९९।।।.।।१

सुवेदार डम्वर षत्रि के .... ८३६।२।२
नगद रु ....६७५ जिन्सी रु .... १६१।२।२

सुवेदार कृष्नदेव पाध्याके .... ४३७।२।२
नगद रु ....३५० जिन्सी रु .... ८७।२।२

ररावीर के .... ५८६।२।३
नगद .... ५०० जिन्सी रु .... ८६।२।३

दोभास्या चिनीत्रा भीमसेन के .... ३२२।।।२।२
नगद रु .... २५० जिनसि .... ७२।।।२।२

भोधा दोभास्या हेमंत के .... २६८।।।३।२
नगद रु .... २०० जिन्सी रु .... ६८।।।३।२

भरिया नाएक पाडौ के .... २०८२।।
नगद .... १७५ जिन्सी .... ३३२।।

ज्मादार चन्द्रवीर के .... १७१२।२
नगद रु .... १२० जिन्सी .... ५१२।२

ज्मादार नैनसिं अधिकारि के .... १६५।।।२।।।२
नगद रु .... १२० जिन्सी .... ४५।।।२।।।२

१४९४५।.।।।३

गादि ममारष जादा वढता

श्री वादसाह के ७५२६
धुक धुकी स्मेत मोतिका मुगा माला १ के तो २२।३ के २६३।
माला ....१ के ४५० रुपौला तास थां १ के २२।३। के २५२
सु.तास थान २ के तो ५७५।५ के १८६।।।२ किंषाप थान २० के १४३६ ।।/
वनात ताषा ....८ के ९२१/।। वुट्टेदार चिङ्गली थां ४ के ५२
लषनौ छीट् थान ....६ के ६० नाल्या संदुकी वंदुक १ के १००
२ नाल्या वन्दुक ....१ के ३०० दुर्वेन ....२ के ७८।।
तरोवार .... ९ के २०६ कपर्दारि कोठाको तरोवार १ के अं १०
कटार .... २ के ४० तोडेवाल वन्दुक .... २ के अं ९०

पेस्कवुज .... २ के अं ६५	गैडा षाग .... २ के अं ७०
केसर तोला .... १०० के १८७॥	गुलाव का अतर तो ७२।.। के २८८
जायफल गोटा .... ५०० के १५॥[२]	लवाग धार्नि ....१२ के १६८
दालचिनी धार्नि ....३५२॥ के १९[२]॥२	गरि गो १०० के धार्नि ५ के १५
वदाम धार्नि ....६ के ७॥[२]	मैसराजाम सुर्य्य मुषि १ के ३७७[३]
मैसराजाम पाल्कि १ के १३६४ ॥.॥	म्याना.................१ के ३१४ ॥
षुकुरि ....२ के अं १४	हाति दात .... १० के अं ४००

षोटं थ्वाङ् के .... ३५१॥[२]।३

मुगा माला १ के तो १०।६के ७४५३	किंषाप थान २ के ९८ ॥
लवाग धार्नि .... १ के १४	वनात ताषा १ के १०३॥[२]।
तरोवार .... २ के ४५	हाति दात .... २ के अं १६

टुथ्वाङ् के .... ३४४॥[३]॥१

मुगामाला १ के तो १०।३ के ७२।॥१	किंषाप थान २ के १०९
लवाग धार्नि १ के १४	वनात ताषा १ के १०३॥[२]।
तरोवार .... २ के ३०	हाति दात .... २ के अं १६

केरुं का ढेवा २ के कासिवाल थान ....२ के ११।[३]।२

दर्वारि षर्च के जिन्सी मालको ज्मा रु ....११०७॥.॥१

अै.सौगात लि॰ जान्या मानीसहरु के षर्च ....२३०३[३]।२

काजि दल भंजन पाँडे के थप जिन्सी रु ....८२२।[२]

सुवा अनुप सिं अधिकारि के ....८३९।[३]॥

नगद रु ....८०८ जिन्सी रु ......३३१।[३]॥

वषतानन्द वैद के .... २८७[२]।२

नगद रु ....२०० जिन्सी रु ....८७[२]।२

सुवेदार दिल धर माझि के जिन्सी रु .... १६८॥[३]।२

ज्मादार विरु षत्रि के जिन्सी रु .... ३८॥[३]२

ज्मादार रराभंजन पाडे के जिन्सी रु .... ४७[२]।

ज्मादार भोटु वस्न्यात के जिन्सी रु ....४४[२]।

चिरुवादार भवानि सिं के ....५४॥.॥

नगद रु ....४० जिन्सी रु ...१४॥.॥

अैजन २ सौगातका काममा षर्च भयाको ....५१९।[२]

पाल्की वोकन्या पुतवार लुभु सैराका भरिया हल्कारा स्मेत के षर्च नगद रु.१९०

हात हतियार गैह्रका कोथि कंठीका जलप मार्ना के सुन तोला ६।७२।के. अं.१३५

अर्जि वेह्रना के र सौगात मालका षोल वेठन गैह्र के जिनसि रु ...१९४।[२]

१२१६४९॥३

(The detailed expenses and the list of presents sent along with the 1822 Nepalese Quinquennial mission to China under the leadership of *Kazi*

Dalbhanjan Pande.)

Source : Royal Nepal Army Head-quarters (RNAH), Part 3, Serial No. 63(53).

Appendix M

म्याना पालकी पठाएकोमा केरु टिगरी दिगर्चामा जाहा हुन्छ राषनु भन्या चीठी लेषी काजी दललाई चीट्ठी पठाएको छ भन्ने श्री ५ वाट १८७९ साल श्रावण वदी १३ रोज ३ मा अम्वा २ लाई लेषेको ....

(Nepalese King to Chinese *Ambans* referring to his instruction to the Nepalese mission of dropping the presents *Myana* and *Palaki* on the way and not to carry them to Peking.)

Source : MFA, *Poka* No. Pa 64.

Appendix N

दलभंजन पाण्डे ल्हासा आइ पुगेको श्री ५ लाई उतारीन पाउतारीन अम्वाले तौकाङ २ वर्ष मैन्हा १६ दिन जादा १८७९ श्री ५ लाई पठाएको...........

(Chinese *Ambans* to Nepalese King reporting the arrival of *Kazi* Dalbhanjan Pande at Lhasa.)

Source : MFA, *Poka* No. Pa 64.

Appendix O

पेचिन जाने काजी दलभंजन पाण्डेसंग गएको चाकर मनासिं लालि मुलुक पुग्दा वेथा लागी मऱ्यो भन्ने तौकाङ्ग. २ साल ८ मैन्हा २४ दिन जादा १८७९ सालमा श्री ५ लाई उतारिन पाउतारीन अम्वाले लेखेको ....

(Chinese *Ambans* to Nepalese King reporting the death of Mana Singh, a member of the Nepalese mission on the way.)

Source : MFA, *Poka* No. Pa 64.

Appendix P

हाल खवर यस्तै गरी पठाउदै गर्नु भनी काजी दलभंजन पाण्डे सर्दार देवीभक्त सुब्बा अनुपसीं अधिकारीहरुलाई १८७९ साल शुक्ल आश्वीन सुदी १२ रोजमा श्री ५ ले पठाएको ....

(Nepalese King to *Kazi* Dalbhanjan Pande and others instructing to communicate through letters.)

Source : MFA, *Poka* No. Pa 64.

Appendix Q

चीन जान्या काजिहरुलाई ञाहा दस्तुरसाथ भोज षुवाई इनाम वकसी पठाएको छ भन्या तौक्काङ ३ वर्ष ७ मैन्हा १६ दिन जादा १८८० सालमा अम्वाले काजीहरुलाई लेषेको ....

(Chinese *Amban* to the *Kazis* of Nepal informing about the cordial send-off of the Nepalese mission at Lhasa.)

Source : MFA, *Poka* No. Pa 64.

Appendix R

काजी दलभंजन पांडे जिम्मा मामुलीको अर्जि सौगाद र हामी गादीमा वस्दाको सगुण सौगात पठाइ दिएको आइपुग्यो भन्ने तौक्काड. ३ वर्ष १ मैन्हा ८ दिन जादाको प्रमाना ....

(Chinese Emperor's *Parwana* of the receiving of the usual five-yearly presents and special presents sent through *Kazi* Dalbhanjan Pande.)

Source : MFA, *Poka* No. Pa 64.

Appendix S

चीन वादसाहवाट पठाएको पर्माना लिन दोसाध सम्म सर्दार निर्भय सिंह थापालाई खटायूँ १८८० साल भाद्र शुदी ... रोज ... मा श्री ५ वाट पाउतारिन अम्वालाई लेषेको नक्कल ....

(Draft letter from Nepalese King to Chinese *Amban* informing about the dispatching of *Sardar* Nirvaya Singh Thapa at the Nepal-Tibet border to receive the Chinese Emperor's *Parwana.*)

Source : MFA, *Poka* No. Pa 64.

Appendix T

८० साल

काजि दलभंजन पाडे चीनवाट फर्कदा परमाना केरुं सम्म पुऱ्याउन आउने चिनीञा के मेजमानी भाद्र सुदी ५ रोज .... नगद रु-२१९॥. जिन्सी अघिलो वमोजीम सदर – २१८।३॥

(The expenses of the Chinese officials escorting the Nepalese mission of 1822 up to Kerung.)

Source : MFA, *Poka* No. Pa 64.

Appendix U

काजी भिमसेन थापालाई गजुर चीन वादसाहवाट पठाएको अम्वाको सिफारीसमा रातो गजुर कल्की पाउने आसा राखेको आदि आसयको पत्र १८८० साल

आश्विन १२ रोज ५ मा काजिहरुवाट ल्हासाका अम्वा पाउतारीनलाई लेखेको......................

(Nepalese *Kazis* to Chinese *Amban* referring to the Chinese Emperor's awarding *Gajur* to *Kazi* Bhimsen Thapa.)

Source : MFA, *Poka* No. Pa 64.

Appendix V

दलभंजन पाण्डे मार्फत पठाएको पर्माना आइपुगेको र पर्मानाको जवाफ (अर्जि) पठाएको - हाम्रा फार्सि अक्षर लेख्ने मुन्सी मरेको हुनाले हाम्रै अक्षरले मात्र लेखी चढाएको छ - १८८० साल आश्वीन शुक्ल १२ रोज ५ मा श्री ५ वाट पाउतरीन अम्वालाई लेखेको ....

(Nepalese King to Chinese *Amban* informing about the receiving of the *Parwana* sent through *Kazi* Dalbhanjan Pande and the sending of *arji* written in his own handwriting.)

Source : MFA, *Poka* No. Pa 64.

Appendix W

ल्हासामा आई अंवा, दलाई लामा चार काजीसंग सीस्टाचार भै हिडन्या काम वेस गरयौ – १८८० साल भाद्र शुदी ६ रोज ४ मा श्री ५ वाट काजी दलभंजन पाण्डे सर्दार देवीभक्त षत्री सुव्वा अनुपसिं अधिकारीहरुलाई लेषेको ....

(Nepalese King to *Kazi* Dalbhanjan and others expressing his pleasure at the Nepalese mission's meeting with Chinese *Ambans*, the Dalai Lama and the Four Tibetan *Kajis* at Lhasa.)

Source : MFA, *Poka* No. Pa 64.

* * *

8

Kazi Bir Keshar Pande's Mission of 1827

According to the arrangement of the mission system, Nepal sent her eighth quinquennial mission to China in June 1827 under the leadership of *Kazi* Bir Keshar Pande. Here it should be noted that the Chinese Imperial records have not mentioned about Nepal's dispatching of five-yearly mission to China in 1827.[1] But the Nepalese archival documents clearly state of Nepal's sending of mission to China in 1827. The other members of the 1827 Nepalese mission were *Sardar* Ranajung Karki, the deputy leader of the mission, *Khardar* Rudra Narayan Padhya, *Subedar* Chamu Basnyat, Interpreter Bhimsen, Interpreter Vansaraj Thapa, Lakshmi Narsingh, *Bhariya Nayak* Bir Bhadra and *Jamadar* Abdil Bista. In addition to them, Lhasa *Naikya* Shiva, *Subedar* Randhoj Pande, *Jamadar* Kalu Khatri, *Jamadar* Chandra Bir Thapa, *Jamadar* Surbir Majhi, *Jamadar* Gambhir Singh Adhikari, *Jamadar* Dambar Singh Adhikari and Ram Narayan Vaidya were also included in the mission.[2] There is the reference of the early departure of the mission from Kathmandu due to the auspicious day fixed by the astrologers.[3] This time, the presents to the Ch'ing Emperor Tao Kwang were estimated to be Rs. 6,117l[3]. The mission had carried eighteen items as presents to the Ch'ing Emperor.[4] It was given a very warm welcome in Peking. The mission members were entertained through the Chinese plays and dances.[5] At the time of sending mission to China, Nepal also sent presents to the Chinese and Tibetan authorities, such as *Dhewas* of Kuti, *Chuii* of Tingri, Lama of Digarcha, *Talloye* of Digarcha, the Chinese *Ambans*, the *Potala* Lama, Raja Lama of Takayali, the four *Kajis* of Lhasa, *Chundu* of Chindafu

1. J.K. Fairbank and S.Y. Teng, "On the Ch'ing Tributary System", *Harvard Journal of Asiatic Studies*, Vol. VI., 1941, pp. 195-198.
2. Royal Nepal Army Head-quarters (hereafter referred as RNAH), Part 3, Serial No. 63 (53). See Appendix C.
3. Chinese *Ambans* to King Rajendra, Tao Kwang 7th year 5th month 11th day (1827), Ministry of Foreign Affairs, Kathmandu (hereafter mentioned as MFA), *Poka* No. Pa 64. See Appendix A: Nepalese King to Chinese *Ambans*, 1884 B.S. Ashad Badi 8 Roj (1827), MFA, *Poka* No. Pa 64. See Appendix B.
4. RNAH, Part 3, Serial No. 63 (53). See Appendix C.
5. Chinese *Ambans* to Nepalese King, Tao Kwang, 8th year 5th month 19th day (1828), MFA, *Poka* No. Pa 64. See Appendix D.

and the *Chundu* of Sindafu.[6] While returning from Peking, the 1827 mission reached Thindafu by Jestha 1885 B.S. (1828)[7] and seemed to have reached Kerung by Bhadra 1885 B.S. (1828)[8].

The importance of the mission of 1827 lies in the fact that the leaders as well as the *Sardars* of the mission got an audience with the Ch'ing Emperor Tao Kwang seventeen times. Besides that, being happy with the Nepalese mission, the Ch'ing Emperor awarded Coral *Gajur* to *Kazi* Bir Keshar Pande and blue *Gajur Kalaki* to *Sardar* Ranajung Karki. Similarly the Ch'ing Emperor also awarded some other members of the mission with *Fatik Gajur* and White *Gajur*.[9]

Appendix A

काजीहरु हिडेको चाडो भयो. हडवड नगरी सुविस्ता साथ पठाउनु भन्या तौक्काङ ७ साल ५ मैन्हा ११ दिन जादा १८८४ मा श्री ५ राजेन्द्रलाई सुन्तारीन् कांतारीन अम्वाले लेषेको ....

(Chinese *Ambans* to King Rajendra making remarks at the early departure of the Nepalese mission from Kathmandu.)

Source : Ministry of Foreign Affairs, Kathmandu (MFA), *Poka* No. Pa 64.

Appendix B

साइत अगाडी नै आएकोले पठाएको हो विस्तारै सुस्त सुस्त जानु भंन्या इत्यादि १८८४ साल आषाढ वदि ८ रोज १ मा श्री ५ वाट ल्हासाका २ अंवालाई पठाएको ....

(Nepalese King to Chinese *Ambans* informing the early sending of the Nepalese mission due to the auspicious day fixed by the astrologers.)

Source : MFA, *Poka* No. Pa 64.

Appendix C

८४ साल

चीन श्री वादसाह छेउ ५ वर्ष का मामुली सौगात गयाको मार्फत काजि वीर केसर पाडे मिति आषाढ वदि १ रोज.............

श्री वादसाह के .... ६११७[३]

6. RNAH, Part3, Serial No. 63 (53). See Appendix C.
7. *Arji* of Bir Keshar Pande and Rana Jung Karki to the Nepalese King, dated 1885 B.S. Jestha 8 Roj 5 (1828), MFA, *Poka* No. Pa 64. See Appendix E.
8. *Arji* of Bir Keshar Pande to the Nepalese King, dated 1885 B.S. Bhadra Badi 4 Roj 5 (1828), MFA, *Poka* No. Pa 64. See Appendix F.
9. Chinese *Ambans* to the Nepalese King, Tao Kwang 8th year 5th month 19th day (1828), MFA, *Poka* No. Pa 64. See Appendix D.

मुगा माला १ के तो १६।५।८ के ११६ | सु.तास थान २ के तो ५३ के २१२
किंषाप थान ....२० के १८३३ | वनात ताषा ......१३ के २४३७ ॥।
तरोवार ....४ के १२० | षुकुरि .... ४ के ३२
षुडा .... २ के ४० | दोनाल्या वन्दुक ...१ के ४००
कटार .... २ के ७० | तोडेवाल वन्दुक ...२ के १००
गलेता थान ....४ के १०० | गैडा षाग .... २ के १०५
हाति दात गोटा ....४ के ४०० | जायफल गोटा ......1000के १८ऽ॥२
दक्षिराा सुपारि धार्नि ....६ के ३०॥।[३]। | सुपारि धार्नि ....१० के १०ऽ ॥
लवाग धार्नि ....६ के ६१॥।[२]॥। | दालचिनी धार्नि ......५ के २३॥[२]॥।

कुतिका ढेवा २ के कासिवाल थान .... २ के ११॥
टिगरिका चुइ के .... ६॥।[३]।
कासिवाल थान १ के ६। | सुपारि धार्नी ....१ के ॥[३]।

डिगर्चा का लामाजु के १७८
वनात वस्ता ....१ के ११२॥ | किंषाप थान ....१ के ३९
अधर थान ....२ के ६॥ | अलैचि दाना धार्नि ...४ के अं ४
हाति दातका कटौरा ....२ के १६

डिगर्चा का तालोये के .... ८॥।[३]।
कासिवाल थान .... १ के ८। | सुपारि धार्नि ....१ के ॥[३]।

ल्हासाका अम्वा २ के .... ७७२॥[३]
वनात वस्ता ....२ के ३०६ | किंषाप थान ....२ के १२८
तरोवार ....२ के ५२ | तोडेवाल वन्दुक .....२ के ९०
षुकुरि ....२ के ८ | हाती दात .... २ के १६०
सुपारि धार्नि ....४ के २॥।/ | दक्षिराा सुपारि धा २ के १०।.॥।
दालचिनी धार्नि ....१ के ४॥[३]/॥। | गरिगोटा .... ३० के ३॥.॥।
वदाम धार्नि ....२ के २॥।/॥।२ | छोहारा धार्नि .... ४ के ४।[३]।

पोतला लामाजु के .... २०१ ॥[३]॥
वनात वस्ता .... १ के ११८॥। | किंषाप थान .... १ के ५३
अधर थान .... २ के ६॥/ | सुपारि धार्नि .... २ के १।[२]॥
अलैचि दाना धार्नि ....४ के अं ४ | हाति दातका कटौरा २ के १८

तक्यालि का राजा लामा के .... १९६॥/
वनात वस्ता ....१ के १२५ | किंषाप थान ....१ कें ५५
अधर थान .... २ के ६॥/ | अलैचि दाना धार्नि ४ के अं ४
हाति दातका कटौरा ....२ के १६

ल्हासाका ४ काजि के .... १८६॥।/

किंषाप थान ....४ के १८४ सुपारि धार्नि ....४ के २॥।

छिन्दफु का चन्दु के .... १६४॥
किंषाप थान .... १ के ४६ वनात वस्ता .... १ के ११८॥।

सिंघाफु का चन्दु के .... ५०।[२]॥
किंषाप थान .... १ के ४९ सुपारि धार्नि .... २ के १।[२]॥

दर्वारि षर्च के गयाको .... २५१९[३]२
नगद रु ....१००० जिन्सी रु १५१९[३]२

अैजन सौगात पुऱ्याउन जान्या पगरिहरु के षर्च .... १११३३॥।[३]।२
काजि वीर केसर पाडे के .... २५८३।[२]।
नगद रु ....१००० जिन्सी रु .... १५८३।[२]।

सर्दार ररागंज कार्कि के .... १३६७॥।
नगद रु .... १००० जिन्सी रु ३६७॥।

षर्दार रुद्र नारान पाध्याके .... ५०१॥।[२]
नगद रु .... ३५० जिन्सी रु १५१॥।[२]

सुवेदार चामु वस्न्यात के .... ५३५[३]
नगद रु .... ४०० जिन्सी रु १३५[३]

दोभास्या चिनिञा भीमसेन के .... ४१८॥[३]
नगद रु .... २५० जिन्सी रु .... १६८॥[३]

दोभास्या वंसराज थापा के .... ३६४।[३]
नगद रु .... २०० जिन्सी रु १६४।[३]

लक्ष्मि नरसिं के .... ६१० ॥[२]
नगद रु .... ५०० जिन्सी रु .... ११०॥[३]

भरिया नाएक वीरभद्र के .... २०६।॥।[२]
नगद रु .... १७५ जिन्सी रु .... ३१।॥।२

ज्मादार अवदील विष्ट के .... २८७ ॥[३]
नगद रु .... २४० जिन्सी रु .... ४७॥[३]

काजि का साथमा जान्या मानीसहरु के षर्च ३६००
येस पटक मामुली भंदा वढता गयाका मानीस के वकस .... ६५९।[३]
ल्हासाका नाइक्या शिव के १००
नगद रु .... १०० जिन्सी रु ०

भोघा दोभास्या वंसराज थापा के पैरु ५०
सुवेदार रंधोज पाडे के जिन्सी .... ११७॥[३]
ज्मादार कालु षत्री के जिन्सी .... ४७॥[३]

ज्मादार चन्द्रवीर थापा के जिन्सी	४९³
ऐं. सुरविर माझी के जिन्सी रु	५२।³
ऐं. गंभीर सिं अधिकारि के जिन्सी रु	५१॥/
ऐं. डम्वर सिं अधिकारि के जिन्सी रु	५४॥/
राम नारान वैद के	१३६।/
अैजन सौगात के काम काममा लाग्या को षर्च	३९८॥³/२
भरिया के षर्च तरोवार षुकुरिका कवुजा कोथि के मोल्मा के सुना मोल स्मेत के	२५१।²
अर्जि वेह्रना र हात हतियार गैह्रका षोल के	१४७।/२

(The detailed expenses and the list of presents sent along with the 1827 Nepalese Quinquennial mission to China under the leadership of *Kazi* Bir Keshar Pande.)

Source :Royal Nepal Army Head-quarters (RNAH), Part 3, Serial No. 63 (53).

Appendix D

संवत १८८४ सालमा काजि वीर केशर जाँदा को

पेचीन जाने काजीहरुले श्री ५ वादसाहको १७ फेरा दर्सन पाया. नाच तमासा पनि देषाया. वहुतै संभार दया गरी राष्या भंन्या स्मेत इत्यादी वेहोरा र काजीले मुगाको र सर्दारले निलो गजुर कलकी पाए. अरु भला मानिसलाई फटीकको गजुर. सेतो गजुर पनी पाये भन्ने इत्यादी. तोक्काङ ८ साल ५ मैन्हा १९ दिन जादा १८८५ साल्मा श्री ५ सर्कारका हजुरमा दुवै तारीन् ककातारीन अम्वाले लेखेको......................

(Chinese *Ambans*' letter to the Nepalese King regarding the well receiving of the 1827 Nepalese mission by the Ch'ing court.)

Source : MFA, *Poka* No. Pa 64.

Appendix E

पेचीन सहर पुगी सौगाद चढाई विदा भै थिन्दफु आई पुग्यौं भन्या १८८५ साल ज्येष्ठ ८ रोज ५ मा वीर केशर पांडे रणजंग कार्कीहरुले चढायाको अर्जि.........

(Bir Keshar Pande and Ranjang Karki's *arji* referring to their arrival at Thindafu from Peking.)

Source : MFA, *Poka* No. Pa 64.

Appendix F

प्रायश्चीत गरी दर्शन गर्न आउछु भन्ने अर्जि वीर केशरहरुले १८८५ साल भाद्र वदी ४ रोज ५ ....

(Bir Keshar's *arji* referring to have an audience with the Nepalese King after performing the ceremony of purification.)

Source : MFA, *Poka* No. Pa 64.

* * *

9

Kazi Bir Keshar Pande's Mission of 1832

Here it should be pointed out that the 1832 Nepalese quinquennial mission has not been mentioned in the Chinese Imperial records[1]. But the Nepalese and Indian archival documents have stated that in accordance with the arrangement of the mission system, Nepal sent her ninth quinquennial mission to China in 1832. Going through the dispatch from Aing Ko, the Chinese *Amban* in Tibet, published in the 139th Gazette for the 11th year of Taon Kwang 1831, it seems that the Nepalese King Rajendra Bikram Shah had informed the Chinese *Amban* of his intention to dispatch a mission to Peking in 1832[2]. The 1832 mission was led by *Kazi* Bir Keshar Pande, the leader of the previous mission of 1827. Besides the *Kazi*, the mission of 1832 included *Sardar* Lakshabir Sahi, the deputy leader of the mission, *Khardar* Siv Narsingh, *Subedar* Dadal Singh Rawal, *Subedar* Surbir Adhikari, Chinese language interpreter *Jamadar* Hasta Bir Pande, Interpreter Vansaraj Thapa, Lakshmi Narsingh, *Jamadar* Abdil Bista, *Bhariya Nayak* Ramu, *Jamadar* Kalu Khatri, *Jamadar* Kasi Ram Khatri, Ram Narayan, Bhadra Singh, Surbir Majhi and Kanak Singh Khatri[3]. The delegates carried an *arji*[4] and presents from the Nepalese King Rajendra Bikram Shah to the Ch'ing Emperor Tao Kwang. The total cost of the mission of 1832 was Rs. 21,873॥^{2} ॥ whereas, the presents to the Ch'ing Emperor Tao Kwang were estimated to be Rs. 3,613।ॉ॥. The 1832 Nepalese mission had carried eighteen items as presents to the Ch'ing Emperor. Besides that the mission had also carried presents to the *Dhewas* of Kuti,

---

1. J. K. Fairbank and S.Y. Teng, "On the Ch'ing Tributary System", *Harvard Journal of Asiatic Studies*, Vol. VI, 1941, pp. 195-198.
2. Acting Secretary, Canton Macao to H.H. Prinsep Esq., Secretary to Govt. Fort William, Foreign Dept. Ext., 4 June 1832, No. 33, National Archives of India, New Delhi (hereafter referred as NAI). See also Appendix F.
3. Royal Nepal Army Head-quarters (hereafter mentioned as RNAH), Part 3, Serial No. 63 (53). See Appendix B.
4. Nepal Residency to Political Secretary to Government, Fort William, 1 December 1833, Foreign Dept. Polt., 19 December 1833, No. 12, NAI. See Appendix I.

Chuii of Tingri, *Talloye* of Digarcha, Lama of Digarcha, the four *Kajis* of Lhasa, Raja Lama of Takayali, the *Potala* Lama, the Chinese *Ambans,* the *Chundu* of Chindafu, and the *Chundu* of Sindafu[5]. On the auspicious day fixed by the astrologers,[6] *Kazi* Bir Keshar Pande's mission left Kathmandu on 18 June 1832[7]. The Nepalese government had requested the Chinese *Amban,* the *Potala* Lama and the Raja Lama to teach the required customs to the Nepalese mission.[8] Here it should be mentioned that Maddock, the British Resident in Kathmandu was not duly informed about the departure of *Kazi* Bir Keshar Pande's mission of 1832 to China[9]. This mission returned on 22 October, 1833[10], after a lapse of sixteen months. While in Peking, *Kazi* Bir Keshar Pande was entertained with fireworks. Besides sightseeing in Peking, he was also taken to the Royal Elephant stalls to see the elephants sent as tribute to the Ch'ing Emperor by various countries.[11] The Nepalese *Kazi* and some members of the Nepalese mission were duly awarded by the Ch'ing Emperor. Thus it seems that the Nepalese mission was well received by the Ch'ing court and it had reported to the Nepalese King about the audience with the Emperor and the handing over the Nepalese presents to the Emperor.[12] The 1832

5. RNAH, Part 3, Serial No. 63 (53). See Appendix B.
6. Nepalese King to Chinese *Ambans*, 1889 B.S. Jestha Sudi 9 Roj 5 (1832), Ministry of Foreign Affairs, Kathmandu (hereafter referred as MFA), *Poka* No. Pa 64. See Appendix A.
7. Maddock, Resident in Nepal, to Secretary, Govt. of India, 20 June 1832, Foreign Dept. Polt. C., 27 August 1832, No. 18, NAI. See Appendix G.
8. Draft letter of the Nepalese Government to the Chinese *Amban,* the *Potala* Lama and the Raja Lama, 1889 B.S. (1832), MFA, *Poka* No. Pa 64. See Appendix C.
9. Maddock, Resident in Nepal, to Secretary, Govt. of India, 20 June 1832, Foreign Dept. Polt. C., 27 August 1832, No. 18, NAI.
10. Maddock, Resident in Nepal, to Secretary, Govt. of India, 9 November 1833, Foreign Dept. Polt., 21 November 1833, No. 36, NAI. See Appendix H.
    See also William Wilson Hunter, *Life of Brian Houghton Hodgson*, New Delhi: Asian Educational Services, Reprint, 1991, p. 78.
11. Maddock, Resident in Nepal, to Secretary, Govt. of India, 1 December 1833, Foreign Dept. Polt., 19 December 1833, No. 12, NAI. See also Appendix I.
12. *Kazi* Bir Keshar Pande and *Sardar* Lakshabir Sahi's *arji* to the Nepalese King, 1890 B.S. Jestha Sudi (1833), MFA, *Poka* No. Pa 64. See Appendix D.

mission seemed to have reached Kerung by Bhadra Sudi 15, 1890 B.S.(1833). The Chinese officials carrying the Chinese Emperor's *Parwana* and escorting the Nepalese delegation up to Kerung were warmly sent off[13].

The noteworthy feature of this ninth Nepalese complimentary quinquennial mission was that its leader had led the quinquennial mission to Peking for the second time consecutively. Interestingly enough, most probably from this very mission of 1832, the British Residency succeeded in obtaining the Nepalese court's correspondences with the Ch'ing court[14].

Appendix A

असारको २ दिन जादा वढिया साइत ठहर्छ काजीहरुलाई वीदा गरी पठाएको छ– १८८९ ज्येष्ठ सुदी ९ रोज ५ श्री वाट ल्हासाका २ अंवालाई पठाएको.............
(Nepalese King to Chinese *Ambans* informing about the departure of the Nepalese mission to Peking from Kathmandu.)

Source: Ministry of Foreign Affairs, Kathmandu (MFA), *Poka* No. Pa 64.

Appendix B

८९ साल

चीन श्री वादसाह छेउ ५ वर्षको मामुली सौगात गयाको मार्फत काजी वीर केसर पाडे मिति आषाढ वदी ५ रोज .... २१८७३। ।[२]॥
श्री वादसाह के .... ३६१३।⁄॥
मुगामाला १ के तोला १८।७ के ११२[३] सु. तास थान २ के तो ४४।४। के ६१ऽ।

किंषाप थान ....२० के १३६०	वनात वस्ता .... १३ के १०३२।
गलेता थान ....४ के १०५.	तरोवार .... ४ के ५८
षुडा ....२ के १०	२ नांल्या वन्दुक ... १ के १७५
तोडेवाल वन्दुक ....२ के १३०	कटारि ....२ के ७०
षुकुरि ....४ के २०	गैडा षाग .... २ के ९५
हाती दात .... ४ के २८०	जायफल गोटा ......१००० के४६।।।[२]
दक्षिराग़ी सुपारि धार्नी ..६ के ३०	सुपारि धार्नि .... १० के ८।।।.
लवाग धार्नि ....६ के ३३	दालचिनी धार्नि .... ५ के १६।

कुतिका ढेवा २ के कासिवाल थान .... २ के १४ ।२

13. RNAH, Part 3, Serial No. 63 (53). See Appendix E.
14. Nepal Residency to Political Secretary to Government, Fort William, 2nd December, 1833, Foreign Dept. Polt., 19 December 1833, No. 11, NAI. See also Appendix J.

टिगरिका चुइके .... ७॥२

कासिवाल थान १ के ७ ऽ॥१ — सुपारि धार्नि .... १ के ॥[२]

डिगर्चाका लामा के .... १२२॥

वनात वस्ता ....१ के ५२॥ — अधर थान .... २ के ११

किंषाप थान ....१ के ३७ — अलैचि दाना धा ....४ के ६

हस्ति हाड कंटौरा .... २ के अं १६

डिगर्चाका तालोय के .... ७॥[२]॥

कासिवाल थान १ के ७ ऽ॥१ — सुपारि धार्नि .... १ के ॥[२]

ल्हासाका अम्वा २ के .... ५३०॥।

तरोवार ....२ के २८ — तोडेवाल वन्दुक ....२ के ६०

षुकुरि .... २ के १० — वनात ताषा ....२के १७०॥[३] ।

किंषाप थान ....२ के ९४ — हाती दात ....२ के १४०

सुपारि धार्नि ....४ के ३॥ — दक्षिराा सुपारि धा .....२ के १०

दालचिनी धार्नि ....१ के ३।. — गरि गोटा ....३० के ३॥[२]

वदाम धार्नि ....२ के ३॥. — छोहारा धार्नि ....४ के ४

पोतला लामा के .... १६५॥[२]

वनात वस्ता .... १ के ८३[२] — हाती दातका कटौरा २ के अं १६

किंषाप थान ......१ के ४८ — अलैचि दाना धार्नि ४ के ६

अधर थान ....२ के ११ — सुपारि धार्नि ...... २ के १॥.

तक्यालिका राजा लामा के १४७

वनात वस्ता ....१ के ७८ — अधर थान .... २ के ११

किंषाप थान ....१ के ३६ — हाति दातका कटौरा २ के अं १६

अलैचि दाना धार्नि ....४ के ६

ल्हासाका चार काजि के .... १८५॥.

किंषाप थान ....४ के १८२ — सुपारि धार्नी ...... ४ के ३॥.

छिन्दफु का चन्दु के .... १३९॥[२]

वनात वस्ता ....१ के १००॥[२] — किंषाप थान १ के.... ३९

सिंहाफु का चन्दु के .... ४४॥.

किंषाप थान ....१ के ४३ — सुपारि धार्नि ....२ के १॥.

दर्वारि षर्चके .... २०३१॥[२]॥

नगद मोरु .... १००० — जिन्सी रु....... १०३१॥[२]॥

अै. सौगात के काम काममा षर्च भयाको .... ४१६॥[२]॥

नगद भरिया षर्च र तर्वार षुकुरि कटारका कोथि

का जोमा मोल्मा के सुना मोल स्मेत के .... २२७॥.

षोल वेठन गैह्र के जिन्सी रु. .... १८९।[२]॥

अै. सौगात लि जान्या पगरिहरुके षर्च .... १४४४५॥[३]॥२

काजि वीर केसर पाडे के .... ५०८९।.॥

नगद रु............. ४००० जिन्सी रु. १०८९।.।।

सर्दार लक्षविर साहि के .... ३२७३।.

नगद रु.......... २८८० जिन्सी रु............. ३९३।

सर्दार सिव नरसिं के .... ४४१।।।.।१

नगद रु .... ३१५ जिन्सी रु............... १२६।।।.।१

ददल्सिं रावल सुवेदार के .... ३२८।।।.।१

नगद रु .... २०० जिन्सी रु.............. १२८।।।.।१

सुरविर अधिकारि सुवेदार के तपसिल सदर .... ३२८।।।.।१

चिनिञा दोभास्या ज्मादार हस्तवीर पाडे के .... ३४४।।।.।१

नगद रु .... २२५ जिन्सी रु .... १०१।।।.।१

लक्ष्मि नरसिं के .... ५४५।।।.।१

नगद रु .... ४५० जिन्सी रु............... ९५।।।.।१

ज्मादार अवदील विष्ट के .... २६१।।।.।१

नगद रु .... २१६ जिन्सी रु.............. ४५।।।.।१

भरि नाएके रामु के .... १८९।[३]।१

नगद रु .... १५७।। जिन्सी रु .... ३१।।।[३]।१

ज्मादार कालु षत्री के. जिन्सी रु .... ४५।।।.।१

ऐ. कासीराम षत्री के. अै. रु.. ४४।।।.।१

राम नारान के. अै. रु.. ८२।।।.।१

भाद्र सिं के अै. रु .... ५६।।।.।१

सुरविर माभ्फि के अै. रु .... ४६।।।.।१

कनक सिं षत्रि के अै. रु .... ४८।।।.।१

काजिका साथमा जान्या मानीस जना २० के मोरु....... ३०००

(The detailed expenses and the list of presents sent along with the 1832 Nepalese Quinquennial mission to China under the leadership of *Kazi* Bir Keshar Pande.)

Source : Royal Nepal Army Head-quarters (RNAH), Part 3, Serial No. 63 (53).

Appendix C

चीन वादसाहका हजुरमा सौगाद ली जान्या काजी विर केसर पांडेहरुलाई दस्तुर सिकाउनु भंन्या ल्हासाका अम्वा पोताला लामा राज लामाहरुलाई लेषियाको सम्वत १८८९ सालको चिट्ठीको नक्कल ....

(Draft of the Nepalese Government's letter to Chinese *Amban,* Potala Lama and Raja Lama to teach the manners (customs) to *Kazi* Bir Kishore Pande and the other members of the Nepalese mission to Peking.)

Source: MFA, *Poka* No. Pa 64.

Appendix D

पैचीन पुगी श्री ५ वादसाहको दर्सन गरी अधिका रीत वमोजीम् सौगाद चढाई फर्कि आयौं भंन्या काजी वीर केसर पाडे सर्दार लक्षवीर साहीहरुले १८९० साल ज्येष्ठ सुदी रोजमा चढाई पठायाको अर्जी ....

(*Kazi* Bir Keshar Pande and *Sardar* Lakshabir Sahi's *arji* to Nepalese King informing about the returning from Peking following the Chinese Emperor's audience to the Nepalese mission.)

Source: MFA, *Poka* No. Pa 64.

Appendix E

९० साल

काजि वीर केसर पाडे चीनवाट फर्कदा परमाना लिन केरुं सम्म जान्या सर्दार ररागंज कार्कि के षर्च र चिनिञा के मेजमानी. प्रथम भाद्र सुदि १५ रो.......

मेजमानी के. .... ४१॥[३]॥२

नगद मिठाइ प्याग डोरि गैह्र के १६

जिन्सी अंदाज .... २५॥[३]॥२

सुपारि धार्नि.	१॥ के १।	सुषमेल पाव ....२ के	४॥
जायफल गोटा	१५ के ॥।.॥	चिनी धार्नि ...... १ के	१
अलैचि सेर	१ के ।/	मिश्रि सेर ....१ के	१
लवाग पाव	१ के ॥[२]॥	मरीच धार्नि ....॥ के	१
छोहारा धार्नि	१ के १	वदाम सेर .... ॥ के	॥।[२]
दाल चिनी पाव	१ के ।.।२	अधर्सा हात ....१६ के	१।.
वदाम धार्नी	१ के १॥।	चिऊरा पाथी ....१० के	५
चावल मुरि	१ के ५	फलफुल गैह्र	

मेजमानि पुऱ्याउन जान्या सर्दार के डोल्या भरिया षर्च .... १५१।.

(The detailed expenses relating to the Chinese Officials who escorted *Kazi* Bir Keshar Pande up to Kerung in 1833.)

Source : RNAH, Part 3, Serial No. 63 (53).

Appendix F

From - Acting Secretary, Canton Macao

To - H.H. Prinsep Esq. Secretary to Government Fort William

The 139th Gazette for the 11th year of TaonKwang (Diet ?) 1831 contains a despatch from Aing Ko, the Chinese Resident in Thibet saying that he had received a very respectful petition from the King of the Gorkas, mentioning that since the last envoy went from him to Peking five years ago, they have had very prosperous seasons in Gorkha: that the 5th year the time (appropriate ?) for another Embassy, having arrived, he had prepared with great care and (uneration ?) all the articles of tribute, and had sent forward to Thibet thr Harc man Hokr as Envoy to proceed to his Imperial Majesty's Court.

Hingko and his colleagues say that they had made all necessary arrangements from the liberal reception of the envoy in Thibet, as the language of the King's Petition is extremely respectful and obedient.

The reply in His Majesty's own hand as the vermillion Pencil indicates was

"I know it. Respect this".

Source : Foreign Dept. Ext., 4 June 1832, No. 33, National Archives of India, New Delhi (NAI).

Appendix G

From - Nepal Residency

To - Secretary with G.G. Simla

20th June 1832

.... I take this opportunity of informing his lordship that the periodical Embassy from the Nipaul Government to the court of Pekin left Catmandhoo the day before yesterday. No official or formal intimation had been previously made to me that the mission was in preparation, though the court Moonshee had casually remarked in one of his visits to the residency sometime ago that it was intended to send an Embassy to China this season and I should not probably have been informal of its actual departure if I had not happened to meet the minister riding out yesterday evening, when he mentioned the circumstances.

Source : Foreign Dept. Polt. C, 27 August 1832, No. 18, NAI.

Appendix H

From - Nepal Residency

To - Political Secretary to Government Fort William

Nepal Residency November 9th 1833.

Sir,

I have the honor to acquaint you that Kajee Beer Kishwar Paundy, the Envoy to of this Court to Pekin, having on the 22nd ult reached the confines of the valley on his return, the MahaRaja attended by his Eldest son, by all his Chiefs, and by 3000 regular troops, proceeded on the 23rd to the Envoy's encampment.

The Envoy had the Imperial Epistle suspended round his neck in a large cylinder covered with brocade. When the MahaRaja reached the spot where he stood, His Highness descended from his Elephant and made three profound salams to the Emperor's letter. The Envoy was then seated on a spare Elephant and placed at the head of the cortege which returned with all military pomp to the capital, a royal salute having been first fired.

Since the establishment of the British Residency at Kathmandu, 4 missions have proceeded, at regular periods to Pekin, occupying about 16 months in going and returning. Heretofore in our time the office of fetching the Imperial Epistle from the Envoy's last encampment had devolved upon the Minister and was discharged, of course, with less pomp than on the recent occasion when the Raja himself performed the duty. But the change is accounted for here by the Raja's heretofore on .... and present majority for, it is added, the Prince himself had always been formerly, used to escort the Emperor's letter in the manner just practised. The Embassy is quad-rennial to bear tribute and acknowledgement inferiority to the feet of the Chinese Empeorr : and was fixed upon Nepal in 1792 in consequence of the utterly unprovoked irruption of the Nipalese into Tibet and their plundering the sacred city of Digarchee. No importance is attached by the Chinese to their relations with Nepal, and they are maintained by Nepal Chiefly or solely to be placed of against us, if need be.

I have the honor to be

Sir,

Your most obd. humble servant

BH Hodgson Res

Source : Foreign Dept. Polt., 21 November 1833, No. 36, NAI.

Appendix I

From : - Nepal Residency

To : - Political Secretary to Government Fort William

Dated 1st December 1833

Translation of the Darbar's addefs to the Emperor of China conveyed by the Nepalese Envoy *Beer Kishwar Pandey to Pekin.*

After Compliments

After the expiry of 5 months and 21 days of the present year I am despatching the Kajee Beer Kishwar Pandey to pay my respects to Your Majesty and to present on my part the following articles of tribute which are the best my poor country can furnish a little worthy of the might and greetings of Your Majesty but Your Majesty will be graciously pleased to accept them.

They are 11 elephant tusks 10 (Bhimawas ?) horns, 10 Pieces of Kun Khab, 10 of broad cloth 10 of fine muslin 10 of (Chintg ?), 10 of Bofta 10 of Swords 10 of Owling pieces, 10 (Bohehs ?) 10 ...., 10 (Kutri ?) 10 Knives and a quantity of cloves of (utmegs ?), Cinamom, Betelnut Dukhuni Betelnuts, all spice Besar Almonds .... and ottar of Roses.

From Pekin my country is far off; but should any foeeignee (wartonly ?) attack and invade me, I will hasten to (inplace ?) Your Majesty's protection and shall in such event aly upon obtaining it.

From the time when I became a dependant of Your Majesty up to this hour, I have uniformly shaped my thoughts and actions to obedience, looking to no one else. It is many years now since I became Your Majesty's dependant. I have now no quarrels about boundaries with any one. I execute justice in (nicery ?) and (equity ?) towards all my subjects who, by Your Majesty's auspices, are in the present enjoyment of security and happenings. Should in future any (occurrence ?) small, are (feeot ?) (eeqwe ?) it, I will hasten to communicate it, and will abide by Your Majesty's (mymtious ?) (threats ?). China is far from this. Your Majesty must in all aspects be kind and consider me.

Despatched from Nepal in the 15th Year of the month of the Emperor Lan quan's (eeyn ?).

(A.B. ?) (Mendieed ?) from the Parbatteah translation prepared for the use of the court, so also the reply. Both have Chinese counterparts.

True translation

The Emperor's reply through the same Channel

By Command, the Emperor's Mandate to the Ghoorkha Raja you have continued faithful and obedient since the commencement of your connexion with the Emperor. On the present occasion the Kajee Beer Kishore has delivered a letter and tribute, the contents of the letter have afforded satisfaction. The Kajee has been honoured with an audience, and has been feasted, Beer Kishwar has received a deefs and a knot for the cap. The other respectable companions of the Kajee have been presented with the same, according to established usage the Kajee's retinue and carriers, have had their expenses paid. The Kajee has been treated with an exhlution of fire works and under the conduct of Chinese Chiefs, he has been conducted (eound ?) the (geeot ?) Bajar to see the sights. He has been taken to the Royal Elephant stalls, and shown the Elephants sent as tribute to the Emperor by the 5 Kingdoms, Donlou & Myansyan & Leoo Cheoo & Syantoo and Choosooyan. The Kajee has acquitted himself with discretion & (peopeity ?) & has been honoured with the usual (malls ?) of (conegmity ?). All things have been done, as customary gone country must continue obedient as heretofore and in regard to boundary disputes you must attend to the Emperor's instructions (sigmfred ?) through the two Ambas at Lasa and abide by their (aceongements ?) Your merchants are permitted to trade (at Lahsa) as usual. You must keep your (mfuous ?) in due subjection and not suffer them to cause disputes. By so doing you will (expeener ?) the (feeotest ?) favor from the Emperor, Your country is far from hence. It is not (neofaey ?) for you to send any one here to acknowledge the favor done you by the letter and presents which Beer Kishwar conveys to you.

You will send that acknowledgement to the two ambas at Lahsa, who will forward it to the peesenel. Do all things with awe regard to the Emperor's Kindness and protection, and look to no other quarter.

On a separate paper is written

"His Majesty (obeids ?) me to enquire, in his name, after the health and welfare of your Raja and of your Chouteriah and of your other Chiefs and people and to add that by doing all things in obedience to His Majesty's Commands you will ensure a continuance of his favour".

The above is said to be His Majesty's personal (Shaer ?) in the interview with the Kajee, the enquaries being put through the Chinese (mutees ?) and interpreters of the Embassy.

True translation

Source : Foreign Dept. Polt. 19 December 1833, No. 12, NAI.

Appendix J

From - Nepal Residency
To - Political Secretary to Government Fort William
Dated 2nd December 1833.

Secret
Sir,

With the .... received by this Durbar for the last 18 months, I have deemed it addressable to procure copies of their correspondence with the Pekin on the occasion of the late Embassy to the court of the Emperor.

The enclosed papers are (Aeeurations ?) of the Durbar adeefs, through the Envoy, to the Emperor, and of His Majesty's reply by the same manner. They have on appearance of being genuine nor I have any reason to doubt that they are so in fact, though the 4 (teeml ?) contron 2 have thought it .... to observe in my measures for possessing them, has somewhat hampered my means of attaining full certainty on that head.

I have engaged the person who supplied these documents (an interpreter) to furnish me occasionally, ... notices of what is done and attempted by the Durbar at Lhasa.

I have the honour to be
Sir
Hodgson
Resident

Source : Foreign Dept. Polt., 19 December 1833, No. 11, NAI.

* * *

10

Chautariya Kazi Pushkar Shah's Mission of 1837

Here it should be pointed out that the 1837 Nepalese quinquennial mission has not been mentioned in the Chinese Imperial records[1]. But the Nepalese and Indian archival documents have stated that in accordance with the arrangement of the mission system, Nepal sent her tenth quinquennial mission to China in 1837 under the leadership of *Chautariya* (a collateral member of the royal family) Pushkar Shah, an important member of a collateral branch of the royal family. The *Chautariya* was accompanied by a retinue of *Sardar* Captain Kirti Dhoj Pande, the deputy leader of the mission, Ran Bikram Shah, *Khardar* Purna Nanda, Interpreter Vansaraj Thapa, Mahiman Karki, Chigadhi Vaidya, Ran Keshar Mahat, Shree Krishna Karki, Amrit Mahat, Dal Bir Khatri, Gajadhar Padhya, Bhau Singh, Yaktabar (Shaktabar) Jaisi, Mannu Miya, *Bhariya Nayak* Padma Narayan, Gotha Rana and Dambar Thapa[2]. The total cost of the mission was Rs. 34,663॥ and the presents to the Ch'ing Emperor Tao Kwang were estimated to be Rs. 7,133S॥2. The 1837 Nepalese mission had carried eighteen items as presents to the Ch'ing Emperor. Besides that the mission had carried presents to *Dhewas* of Kuti, *Chuii* of Tingri, *Talloye* of Digarcha, Lama of Digarcha, the four *Kajis* of Lhasa, Raja Lama of Takayali, the *Potala* Lama, the Chinese *Ambans*, the *Chundu* of Chindafu, the *Chundu* of Sindafu and Tu Thwang[3]. *Chautariya Kazi* Pushkar Shah's mission left Kathmandu on 14 July 1837[4]. It

1. J. K. Fairbank and S.Y. Teng, "On the Ch'ing Tributary System", *Harvard Journal of Asiatic Studies*, Vol. VI, 1941, pp. 195-198.
2. Royal Nepal Army Head-quarters (hereafter referred as RNAH), Part 3, Serial No. 63 (53). See Appendix C.
3. *Ibid.*
4. Leo E. Rose, *Nepal: Strategy For Survival*, Berkeley: University of California Press, 1971, p. 98. For the correspondence between the Nepalese and the Chinese government regarding the sending of the 1837 mission and dispatching of letter to *Kazi* Pushkar Shah, see Chinese *Amban* to Nepalese King, Tao Kwang 17th year 6th month 11th day (1837), Ministry of Foreign Affairs, Kathmandu (hereafter mentioned as MFA), *Poka* No. Pa 64. See Appendix B: Nepalese King to Chinese *Ambans*, 1894 B.S. Ashwin Badi 5 Roj 3 (1837), MFA, *Poka* No. Pa 64. See Appendix D.

seems that, being a religious person as well as a strict follower of the Hindu religion, *Chautariya* Pushkar Shah observed its rules and regulations strictly throughout his journey and did not even accept tea offered by others. He was reported to have taken food only cooked by his own personal cook.[5] The *Chautariya* was given a warm welcome in China.

Here it should be mentioned that in December 1835 Ranajung Pande, the political rival of *Mukhtiyar* Bhimsen Thapa, had written to the Chinese *Amban* in Lhasa stressing his family's traditional ties with Tibet and asking for the *Amban's* intercession with the Nepalese court.[6] In response the Chinese *Amban* wrote to the Nepalese King Rajendra asking that the King himself, and not *Mukhtiyar* Bhimsen Thapa, nominate the leader of the next five-yearly mission to Peking, and suggesting strongly that Ranajung Pande be chosen for this. King Rajendra did indeed undertake this task himself, but he nominated his favourite *Chautariya* Pushkar Shah, instead of the Chinese *Amban's* choice, Ranajung Pande.[7] But one source states that the Chinese *Amban* had suggested to King Rajendra not to send wicked Ranajung but to nominate another good (virtuous) person to lead the quinquennial mission to the Ch'ing Emperor's court[8]. It was reported that before the nomination of *Chautariya* Pushkar Shah, Jagat Bam Pande was nominated to lead the 1837 Nepalese five-yearly mission to Peking[9]. By the time *Chautariya* Pushkar Shah was on his way to Peking leading the quinquennial mission of 1837, there had been a great political upheaval in Nepal with the dismissal and

---

5. Jnanmani Nepal, *Nepal-Bhot Chin Sambandha Ka Kehi Sanskritik Paksha* (Some Cultural Aspect of Nepal-Tibet China Relations), Kathmandu: Royal Nepal Academy, 2045 B.S., pp. 111-112.
6. Chitta Ranjan Nepali, *General Bhimsen Thapa Ra Tatkalin Nepal* (General Bhimsen Thapa and Contemporary Nepal), Kathmandu: Ratna Pustak Bhandar, Third Edition, 2035 B.S., pp. 206-207.
7. Ludwig F. Stiller, *The Silent Cry*, Kathmandu: Sahayogi Prakashan, 1976, p. 273.
8. Chinese *Amban* to King Rajendra, Tao Kwang 16th Year (1893 B.S., Magh 21), MFA, *Poka* No. Pa. 64. See Appendix A.
9. Bhim Bahadur Pande Chhetri, *Rastra Bhakti Ko Jhalak: Pande Bamsa Ko Bhumika, 1596-1904 B.S.*, (A Glimpse of Loyalty to the Nation: Role of the Pande Dynasty, 1596-1904 B.S.), Kathmandu: Ratna Pustak Bhandar, 2034 B.S., p. 156.

imprisonment of *Mukhtiyar* Bhimsen Thapa, who had held the post of *Mukhtiyar* continiously for thirty one years. The Nepalese court not only duly informed the *Chautariya* about the political developments in Nepal, but also dispatched him a letter to hand over to the Ch'ing Emperor in which King Rajendra described Bhimsen Thapa as "pro-*Feringhi Bhardar* (Pro-British Courtier)".[10] Perhaps due to the great political upheaval in Nepal, the *Chautariya* tried to complete his journey as early as possible. That is why he completed the round-trip journey to Peking in less than fourteen months. Like the earlier mission of 1822, the mission of 1837 had also recorded a detailed and systematic summary of the routes from Kathmandu to Peking as travelled by the Nepalese envoy to Peking.[11] This mission of 1837 also did the same for the return trip. From the travel account, it seems that it took nearly six months to complete the journey from Peking to Kathmandu proper.[12] It was reported that two members of the Nepalese mission, i.e. one *Subedar* and one *Siphahi* (soldier) died on the way[13]. The Chinese *Amban* had duly informed King Rajendra about *Kazi* Pushkar's departure to Kathmandu from Lhasa.[14] The delegates returned home on 25 September 1838[15] along with the Chinese Emperor's *Parwana.*[16] B.H. Hodgson, the then British Resident in Nepal had also reported to his government regarding the

---

10. Nepali, f.n.no. 6, pp. 209-210.
11. B.H. Hodgson, "Route of two Nepalese Embassies to Pekin with remarks on the water-shed and plateau of Tibet", *Journl of the Asiatic Society*, No. VI, 1856, pp. 486-490.
12. Nepal, f.n.no. 5, pp. 401-411.
13. MFA, *Poka* No. Pa 64.
14. Chinese *Amban* to King Rajendra, 1895 B.S. (1838), MFA, *Poka* No. Pa 64. See Appendix E.
15. Hodgson to Secretary, Govt. of India, 3 October 1838, Foreign Dept. Sec., 26 December 1839, No. 139, National Archives of India, New Delhi (hereafter referred as NAI). But both Fisher and Rose as well as Sever have given the wrong date for the arrival of the Nepalese mission to Nepal, as October 1838. See Margaret W. Fisher and Leo E. Rose, *England, India, Nepal, Tibet, China, 1765-1958,* Berkeley: University of California Press, 1959, pp. 2-12, Adrian Sever, *Nepal Under the Ranas,* New Delhi: Oxford and IBH Publishing Co.Pvt.Ltd. 1993, p. 472.
16. Nepalese King to Chinese *Ambans*, 1895 B.S. Ashwin Badi 5 Roj 7 (1838), MFA, *Poka* No. Pa 64. See Appendix F.

return of the 1837 Nepalese mission[17]. Through this mission of 1837, the Nepalese government had requested for the Ch'ing court to either send troops or a subsidy of twenty million rupees to oppose the British[18], but the Nepalese delegation was said to have met with a stern refusal of its petition for monetary aid, and opposition to the furtherance of hostility by Nepal against the British.[19] Thus, the Ch'ing court did not respond to Nepal's call for anti-British activities.

One of the chief characteristics of the mission of 1837 was that it was the first Nepalese quinquennial mission ever led by the highest Nepalese official and a prominent political personality like *Chautariya* Pushkar Shah. That is why this very mission was quite distinct from other Nepalese quinquennial missions in many respects. Firstly, the deputy leader of the 1837 Nepalese mission happened to be Captain Kirti Dhoj Pande, the first time ever that the highest Nepalese military official to held the post of deputy leader of the quinquennial mission. Secondly, the mission carried many expensive presents to the Ch'ing Emperor. That is why the Nepalese presents were estimated to be Rs. 7,133S॥2, so far the highest estimated price for usual five-yearly presents. Thirdly, and most notably, soon after his return from Peking as the leader of the Nepalese quinquennial mission to China, *Chautariya* Pushkar Shah was appointed to the post of *Mukhtiyar* in 1838.[20] In this way *Chautariya* Pushkar Shah's mission of 1837 has its own importance in the long history of Sino-Nepalese relations.

Appendix A

श्री ५ वादसाहका हजुरमा यो षरावी रणजङलाई नपठाउनु अरु वढिया मानिस विचार गरी पठाउनु भन्या तौक्काङ १६ साल माघ २१ दिन जादा १८९३ सालमा श्री ५ राजेन्द्रलाई डौतारीन अम्वाले लेखेको ....

(Chinese *Amban* to King Rajendra instructing not to send wicked

---

17. See Appendix H.
18. Rose, f.n.no. 4, p. 98.
19. Hodgson to Govt. of India, 26 May 1838, Foreign Dept Sec., 13 June 1838, No. 10, NAI. See Appendix G.
20. H. Ambrose Oldfield, *Sketches from Nepal*, Vol. I, Delhi: Cosmo Publications, Reprint, 1981, p. 313.

Ranajung Pande but to nominate another good person to lead the Nepalese mission to Peking.)

Source : Ministry of Foreign Affairs, Kathmandu (MFA), *Poka* No. Pa 64.

Appendix B

चीनमा ससौगात ली जाने काजीहरुलाई ५ मैन्हाको १८ दिन जाँदा नेपालवाट पठाउछौं भनी लेषेकोमा पछी ६ मैन्हाको दीनमा मात्र पठाउछौ भंन्याको दस्तुर विगारेको हो. अव वढी ढीला नगर्नु चाडो गरी पठाउनु भन्ने तोक्काङ १७ वर्ष ६ मैन्हा ११ दिन जादा १८९४ सालमा श्री ५ सर्कारका हर्जुरमा ककाङतारिन डौतारिन अम्वाले लेखेको ....

(Chinese *Ambans* to Nepalese King informing to send the Nepalese mission to Peking soon.)

Source : MFA, *Poka* No. Pa 64.

Appendix C

<u>९४ साल</u>

चीन श्री वादसाह छेउ ५ वर्षका मामुली सौगात गयाको मार्फत चौतरीया पुष्कर साह कप्तान कीर्तिधोज पाडे मिति आषाढ सुदी ८ रो........... ३४६६३॥.

श्री वादसाहके .... ७१३३ऽ॥२

मुगा माला १ के तो ४७७॥ के ३८२	सु. तास थान २ के तो १५८ के ७३१।.
किंषाप थान .... २० के २७७९॥.॥	वनात वस्ता १३ के १८१४॥.२
गलेता थान :...... ४ के १००	तोडेवाल वंदुक २ के १००
तरोवार ....४ के ५४	षुकुरि .... ४ के ३२
षुडा ....२ के ४०	कटार .... २ के ५०
दुइ नाल्या वन्दुक ...१ के ४००	गैडा षाग ......२ के ७०
हाति दात .... ४ के ४००	जायफल गोटा १००० के ६२॥
दक्षिरिाा सुपारि धार्नि ६ के ३३	सुपारि धार्नि १० के १२॥.
लवाग धार्नि ....६ के ४८	दालचिनि धार्नि ५ के २३॥.

कुतिका ढेवा २ के कासिवाल थान ....२ के २४

टिगरि का चुइ के .... १३।.

कासिवाल थान १ के १२ सुपारि धार्नि ....१ के १।.

डिगर्चा का तालोय के तप्सील सदर ....१३।.

डिगर्चा का लामा के ....१४४[३]॥

वनात वस्ता ....१ के ६२^{३}॥ किंषाप थान ...... १ के ५०
मेहि अधर थान .....२ के १० अलैची दाना धार्नि ४ के अं ६
हाति दातका कटौरा ....२ के १६

ल्हासा का चार काजि के १५७
किंषाप थान .... ४ के १५२ सुपारि धार्नि ... ४ के ५

ल्हासाका तक्यालिका राजा लामा के १५३
वनात वस्ता ..... १ के ७१। किंषाप थान ......१ के ५०
मेहि अधर थान .... २ के १० अलैचि दाना धा ४ के अं ६
हाति दातका कटौरा .... २ के १६

ल्हासा का पोतला लामा के १५६
वनात वस्ता .... १ के ६७^{२}॥३ किंषाप थान १ के ५५
मेहिअधर थान .... २ के १० अलैचि दाना धार्नि ४ के अं ६
सुपारि धार्नि .... २ के २॥ हाति दातका कटौरा २ के १६

ल्हासा का अम्वा २ के ६०८
वनात वस्ता २ के १०८ किंषाप थान .... २ के १९२
तरोवार .... २ के १५ तोडेवाल वन्दुक ....२ के ९०
षुकुरि .... २ के ८ हाति दात .... २ के १६०
सुपारि धार्नि ४ के ५ दक्षिरिा सुपारि धार्नि २ के ११
दालचिनी धार्नि १ के ४॥। गरिगोटा ३० के धार्नि १ के ४।
वदाम धार्नि ....२ के ४॥। छोहारा धार्नि ...... ४ के ४।

छिन्दफु का चन्दु के २०७
वनात थान .... १ के १६८ किंषाप थान .... १ के ३९

सिंघाफु चन्दुके .... ४१॥
किंषाप थान .... १ के ३९ सुपारि धार्नी .... २ के २॥

येस सालमा थप टुंथ्वाङ् के .... की .... ८७९॥^{३}
किंषाप थान ..... २ के ५९९॥।/। ८ वन वनात थान १ के २१८॥।^{२}
गैडा षाग .... १ के १६ तोडेवाल वंदुक ..... १ के ४५

दर्वारि षर्च के .... २२४७॥।^{३}
नगद मोरु .... १००० जिन्सी रु .... १२४७॥।^{३}

अै. सौगात पुऱ्याउन जान्या मानीसहरु के षर्च कपडा के रु .... ३१५४ऽ।

चौ. पुष्कर साह के....११६९।.।।। स. किर्तिधोज पाडे के ७६३॥.।२

रराा विक्रम साह के ..२०३॥. ॥१ अमृत महत के ९९ ३ ३

षर्दार पुर्ाा नन्द के ....१२४।।।.॥१ दलवीर षत्री के ...... १०६।.॥१

दोभास्या वंसराज थापा के.. ११४।.॥१ गजाधर पाध्या के ..... ५७।.॥१

महिमन कार्कि के .....५७।.॥१ भाउ सिं के .... ५६॥.॥१

चिगधी वैद के ......४६ २ १ यक्रवार जैसि के .. ५५।.॥१

रराकेसर महत के .....५५।.॥१ मनु मिज्ञा के ...... ५३।.॥१

श्री कृष्न कार्कि के .....५२।.॥१ भरिया नाएक पद्मनांरा ५८ २ ॥१

येस साल थप

गोठ राना के .... ४०।।।.॥१ डम्वर थापा के ...... ४०।।।.॥१

अैजन मानीस के नगद मोरु. ११९८१

चौतरिया पुष्कर साह के. जेष्ठ सुदि १ रो. १२०००

सर्दार कीर्तिधोज पाडे के १२५०

अरु मानीस गैह्र के ५९३१

अैजन सौगात को काम काममा षर्च लाग्या को .... ५४९।।। २ ॥

नगद रु. .... २६४॥ जिन्सी रु. .... २८५।।॥

(The detailed expenses and the list of presents sent along with the 1837 Nepalese Quinquennial mission to China under the leadership of *Chautariya Kazi* Pushkar Shah)

Source : Royal Nepal Army Head-quarters (RNAH), Part 3, Serial No. 63 (53).

Appendix D

हाम्रा दुष दर्दको विस्तार चौतरीया काजी पुस्कर साहवाट आफु छेउ विन्ती विस्तार गऱ्या हुन काजीहरुलाई पठायाको चिट्ठी दया गरी पठाई दिउ – श्री ५ वाट १८९४ साल आश्वीन वदी ५ रोज ३ मा ल्हासाका २ अंवालाई लेखेको............................

(Nepalese King to Chinese *Ambans* requesting to dispatch letter to *Kazi* Pushkar Shah.)

Source : MFA, *Poka* No. Pa 64.

Appendix E

चौतरीया काजी पुस्कर साह ल्हासावाट हिडे नेपालमा आइ पुग्ला भंन्या तौक्वाङ १८ वर्ष श्रावण मैन्हाको २७ दिन जादा १८९५ साल्मा श्री ५ राजेन्द्रलाई ककान्तारीन ल्यैंतारीन अंवाले लेखेको ....

(Chinese *Ambans* to King Rajendra informing about *Chautariya Kazi* Pushkar Shah's departure from Lhasa to Kathmandu.)

Source : MFA, *Poka* No. Pa 64.

Appendix F

श्री ५ चीन वादसाहवाट पठायको पर्माना आइ पुग्यो- १८९५ साल आश्वीन वदी ५ रोज ७ श्री ५ वाट २ अंवालाई पठाएको ....

(Nepalese King to Chinese *Ambans* reporting the receipt of the Chinese Emperor's *Parwana.)*

Source : MFA, *Poka* No. Pa 64.

Appendix G

From - Nepal Residency
To - Secretary with G.G.
May 26th 1838

4. I beg leave further to report that Puskar Sah, the Nepalese Envoy to Pekin, is said to have met with a stern refusal to his petition for monied aid, and countenance in furtherance of hostility by Nepal against our (fort ?), and that other are summoned to have evaded or declined all cooperation with the Goorkhas.

Source : Foreign Dept. Sec., 13 June, 1838, No. 10, National Archives of India, New Delhi (NAI).

Appendix H

From - Nepal Residency
To - Secretary to Government of India
Nepal Residency, October 3rd 1838.

Sir,

I have the honor to acquaint you that the Nipalese Envoy to Pekin made his public entry, on his return from the quinquennial mission upon the 25th ultimo, and that official intimation thereof was made to me yesterday.

2. The return of the Envoy and reception of the Celestial Emperor's mifsives were marked with less than the usual ceremony, whilst the official intimation to me is an unwanted courtesy and one accompanied by the presentation of several Chinese curiosities for myself and for my assistant.

3. Whether these circumstances are to be attributed to some chagrin conceived by the Durbar against the Emperor for non concurrence with its restless views, or whether, just now, the Durbar seek to propitiate or to delude me, I cannot at present satisfy myself. But real solution may be a compound of all these motives.

4. The Trifles presented to myself and Doctor Campbell have been appropriated by us, according to custom, the value of them nearly having been given to the bearers thereof to the Residency.

I have the honor to be
Sir,
Your most obedt. Servt.
B H Hodgson
Resident

Source: Foreign Dept. Sec., 26 December 1839, No. 139, NAI.

* * *

11

Kazi Jagat Bam Pande's Mission of 1842

In accordance with the arrangement of the mission system, Nepal sent her eleventh quinquennial mission to China in 1842 which was led by *Kazi* Jagat Bam Pande, the grandson of *Kazi* Damodar Pande. There is the reference of the Nepalese King informing the Chinese *Amban* in 1841 regarding the procuring of present items from India in order to send the Nepalese mission to Peking in 1842.[1] The Chinese Imperial records have also mentioned about the 1842 Nepalese quinquennial mission.[2] It was reported that over the opposition of the Fateh Jang Shah ministry, King Rajendra Bikram Shah approved the appointment of Jagat Bam Pande.[3] Here it should be mentioned that, by that time, Ranjung Pande had already been dismissed from the post of *Mukhtiyar*, and *Chautariya* Fateh Jang Shah had been appointed *Mukhtiyar*. Also there were Chinese reverses in the opium war of 1839-1842. Perhaps due to the new political developments in China also, King Rajendra appointed Jagat Bam Pande,a prominent member of the anti-British faction, as the leader of 1842 Nepalese quinquennial mission. The Nepalese mission left Kathmandu on 3 July, 1842.[4] In addition to Jagat Bam Pande, the forty-five member mission of 1842 included *Sardar* Bir Bhadra Karki, the deputy leader of the

---

1. Nepalese King to Chinese *Amban*, 1898 B.S., Jestha Sudi 5 Roj 4 (1841), Ministry of Foreign Affairs, Kathmandu (hereafter mentioned as MFA), *Poka* No. Pa 64. See Appendix A.
2. J.K. Fairbank and S.Y. Teng, "On the Ch'ing Tributary System", *Harvard Journal of Asiatic Studies*, Vol. VI, 1941, pp 195-198.
3. Leo E. Rose, *Nepal: Strategy For Survival*, Berkeley: University of California Press, 1971, p. 100.
4. Hodgson to Secretary, Govt. of India, 2 July 1842, Foreign Dept. Sec., 10 August 1842, No. 126, National Archives of India, New Delhi (hereafter referred as NAI) and Bikram Jit Hasrat, *The History of Nepal as Told by Her own and Contemporary Chronicles*, Hoshiarpur: V.V. Research Institute, 1970, p. 314. See also Appendix L. But Sever has given the wrong date of the departure of the Nepalese mission from Kathmandu as 13 July, 1842. See Adrian Sever, *Aspects of Modern Nepalese History*, New Delhi: Vikas Publishing House Pvt. Ltd., 1996, p. 170.

mission[5], *Subedar* Bir Mardan Bhandari, *Khardar* Siddhi Narsingh, Chinese language interpreter Hari Krishna, *Ajitan* Kanak Singh Khatri,Indra Singh, *Jamadar* Nain Singh Adhikari, Bhotu Bakheti, *Bhariya Nayak* Padma, Indra Bir Khatri and Devi Prasad Pande. The total cost of the mission was Rs.29,012||′ whereas the presents to the Ch'ing Emperor Tao Kwang were estimated to be approximately Rs. 6,613|||^{3}2.[6] The 1842 mission had carried seventeen items as presents to the Ch'ing Emperor. Besides that the 1842 Nepalese mission had carried presents to *Dhewas* of Kuti, Talloye of Digarcha, Lama of Digarcha,the four *Kajis* of Lhasa, Raja Lama of *Takayali*, the Chinese *Ambans*, *Chundu* of Chindafu and the *Chundu* of Sindafu. Through this mission, Crown Prince Surendra had also sent an *arji* as well as a present to the Ch'ing Emperor Tao Kwang.[7] The delegation was reported to have remained in Peking for thirty three days.[8] While in Peking, the members of the Nepalese mission were entertained with Chinese plays and dances, swimming, wrestling and fireworks.[9] Besides that they were also given presents by the Ch'ing court. Thus it seems that the Nepalese mission was well received by the Ch'ing court.

Here it should be mentioned that the Chinese reverses in the opium war encouraged the Nepalese court, then dominated by the bitterly anti-British Pandes, to seek Chinese support against the British through the mission of 1842. That is why *Kazi* Jagat Bam Pande was instructed to beg for monetary aid with which to make

---

5. Nepalese King to Chinese *Ambans*, 1899 B.S. Baisakh Badi 1 Roj 2 (1842), MFA, *Poka* No. Pa 64. See Appendix B.
6. Royal Nepal Army Head-quarters (hereafter mentioned as RNAH), Part 3, Serial No. 63 (53). See Appendix C.
7. RNAH, Part 3, Serial No. 63 (53) and Nepal Government's Letter to the Chinese Government,dated 1899 B.S. Ashad Badi 8 Roj 6 (23 June 1842), National Archives of Nepal, Kathmandu (hereafter referred as NAN), *Poka* No. 5, Letter No. 44. But the Chinese *Amban* seemed to have detained the *arji* and the present of the heir apparent Surendra designed for the Ch'ing Emperor stating that they were contrary to usage. See Hodgson to Secretary, Govt. of India, 27 September 1842, Foreign Dept. Sec., 19 October 1842, No. 70, NAI. See Appendix M.
8. Tri Ratna Manandhar and Tirtha Prasad Mishra, "Cavenagh and Rose on Nepal's Mission to China", *Rolamba*, Vol 3, No. 1 (January-March 1983), p. 46.
9. Description of the activities of the 1842 Nepalese mission at Peking, MFA, Undated, Unnumbered *Poka*. See Appendix F.

an attack on British territory with twenty to forty thousand men, according to the amount of the subsidy solicited.[10] According to the British Resident's records, the Nepalese envoy Jagat Bam Pande spoke to Chinese *Amban* at Lhasa the concerning of the large amount of monetary aid (three or four *crores* i.e. Rs. 3,000,0000 - Rs. 4,000,0000) sought by Nepal. The Chinese *Amban* was reported to have told the Nepalese envoy he had better write to Kathmandu to ascertain the true recokoning.[11] In a letter sent to the Ch'ing Emperor through Jagat Bam Pande, King Rajendra stated;" .... we request you to help us by sending your army to fight the British. The Chinese army can reach Calcutta within twenty or twenty five days if it moved through the eastern way i.e.Sikkim and it takes about thirty five or forty days to reach Delhi if the Imperial army marched through the western side i.e. Taklakhar. Be it not possible to send army so far, give us some seventy or eighty million rupees so that we can expel the British Resident from our country and make an attack on India. If the Chinese Emperor did not help us in either way, it becomes very difficult for us to protect our country......... Secondly, we request you to propose an exchange of the Tibetan district of Taklakot for the vassal principality of Mustang in Nepal."[12] Furthermore, another proposal was made by *Kazi* Jagat Bam Pande, who suggested to Meng-pao, the Chinese *Amban* in Lhasa, a dual Tibetan-Nepalese administration of Kerung and Kuti, under which Lhasa would administer these districts for ten years and Kathmandu for three years. Meng-pao's reply clearly indicated amazement that Nepal would even presume to make such a very unusual suggestion. By the time Jagat Bam Pande reached Peking the opium war had been settled, and China was filled with dismay at the thought of disturbances in the Himalayan area, that is, the Dogra-Tibetan war of 1841-1842. Peking instructed *Amban* Meng-pao to reject Nepal's request for

10. Hodgson to Secretary, Govt. of India, 2 July 1842, Foreign Dept. Sec., 10 August 1842, No. 126, NAI. See Appendix L.
11. Hodgson to Secretary, Govt. of India, 27 September 1842, Foreign Dept. Sec., 19 October 1842, No. 70, NAI. See Appendix M.
12. *Arji* to the Chinese Emperor dated 1899 B.S. Ashad Badi 8 Roj 6 (23 June 1842), NAN, *Poka* No. 5, Letter No. 44. See Appendix D; Chinese *Amban* to Nepalese King, 1899 B.S. Poush Badi 2 (1842), MFA, *Poka* No. Pa 64, See Appendix E.

assistance on the grounds that it was not China's policy "to send troops to protect the countries of the foreign barbarians", such as Nepal.[13] Thus one sees that Nepal attempted to exploit the Anglo-Chinese (Opium) war of 1839-1842 in order to seek Chinese support against the British, but the Chinese refused to be drawn in. In this way Nepal tried to make use of the 1842 mission against the British but China stood by its policy of 'impartial benevolence'. It also clearly indicated that the Chinese would not encourage Nepalese militarism in any way.

The special feature of this eleventh Nepalese quinquennial mission was that fate did not side with the leader of the mission, for following the appointment of Mathabar Singh Thapa as *Mukhtiyar* in December 1843, the prominent Pandes were executed in Nepal while the Nepalese mission of 1842 was on its way back to its home country. The Nepalese government assured *Kazi* Jagat Bam Pande that it would not take any action against him,[14] but in spite of that, *Kazi* Jagat Bam Pande and *Sardar* Bir Bhadra Karki too did not think it proper to return to Nepal, and managed to escape to India from Tibet[15] in disguise. Later on, while in India, Jagat Bam Pande became involved in ousting Prime Minister Jang Bahadur from power. One language interpreter and one *Siphai* of the 1842 Nepalese mission were reported to have died on the way.[16] The other members of the 1842 Nepalese mission returned to Nepal by Kartik 1900 B.S. (1843). The Chinese officials carrying the Chinese Emperor's *Parwana*[17] and escorting the Nepalese delegation were given a warm send-off from Kerung.[18]

---

13. Rose, f.n.no. 3, pp. 100-101.
14. Nepal Government's Letter to *Kazi* Jagat Bam Pande, 1900 B.S. Marga 2 Roj 5 (1843), MFA, *Poka* No. Pa 64. See Appendix G.
15. Nepalese King to Chinese *Ambans*, 1900 B.S. Falgun Sudi 1 Roj 5 (1844), MFA, *Poka* No. Pa 64. See Appendix H.
16. MFA, *Poka* No. Pa 64.
17. Chinese Emperor's *Parwana* dated 1900 B.S. Falgun 17 (1844), MFA, *Poka* No. Pa 64, See Appendix J; *Arji* to the Chinese Emperor, 1900 B.S. Magh Badi 9 Roj 1 (1844), MFA, *Poka* No. Pa 64. See Appendix K.
18. RNAH, Part 3, Serial No. 63(53). See Appendix I.

Appendix A

हाम्रो देसमा नहुन्या टाढा मधेसवाट झिकायाको चीज आई पुग्या पछी आउदो साल आफुहरु मार्फत श्री ५ चीन वादसाहको दर्सन गर्न पठाउन्या काम गरुला– १८९८ साल ज्येष्ठ सुदी ५ रोज ४ मा श्री ५ वाट ल्हासाका अम्वालाई लेखेको.......................

(Nepalese King to Chinese *Amban* informing to send the Nepalese mission to Peking in the forthcoming year after procuring the present items from India.)

Source : Ministry of Foreign Affairs, Kathmandu, (MFA), *Poka* No. Pa 64.

Appendix B

काजी दामोदर पाण्डेको नाती काजी जगतवम पाण्डे सर्दार वीर भद्र कार्की स्मेत ४५ जनालाई ल्हासा पुगी सवै दुःखदर्द विन्ती गर्नु आफुहरुका अर्ति सिक्षा ली पेचीन जानु भंन्या इत्यादी १८९९ साल वैशाष वदी १ रोज २ मा श्री ५ वाट ल्हासाका २ अंवालाई लेखेको ....

(Nepalese King to Chinese *Ambans* mentioning the dispatching of the forty-five member Nepalese mission under the leadership of *Kazi* Jagat Bam Pande, the grandson of *Kazi* Damodar Pande and instructing the Nepalese mission to learn lessons from the Chinese *Ambans* before their departure to Peking.)

Source: MFA, *Poka* No. Pa 64.

Appendix C

<u>९९ साल</u>

चीन श्री वादसाहलाइ ५ वर्षको मामुली सौगात गयाको मार्फत काजि जगतवम पाडे सर्दार वीर भद्र कार्कि आषाढ वदि ९ रोज....................... २९०१२।।´

श्री वादसाह के अंदाजका मोल.. ६६१३।।।[३]२

मुगा माला १ के तोला ४३।५।के ३४८ तास थान २ के तो १३०।३।के ५२१[३]

किंषाप थान २० के २७७९।।	वनात वस्ता १३ के	१८१४।।२
गलेता थान ४ के १००	तोडेवाल वन्दुक २ के	१००
तरोवार ४ के ५४	षुकुरि ४ के	३२
षुडा २ के ५५	२ नाल्या वन्दुक १ के	४००
गैडा षाग २ के ७०	हाति दात ४ के	१६०
जायफल गोटा १०० के ६२।।	द. सुपारि धार्नि ६ के	३३

सुपारि धार्नि १० के १२॥	लवाग धार्नि ६ के	४८
दालचिनी धार्नि ५ के २३॥।		
कुतिका ढेवा २ के अंदाज		२१।
कासिवाल थान २ के २०	सुपारि धार्नि १ के	१
डिगर्चाका तालोय के अंदाज..		११।
कासिवाल थान १ के १०	सुपारि धार्नि १ के	१।
डिगर्चा का लामा के अंदाज..		१४०^{३}॥
किंषाप थान १ के ५०	वनात वस्ता १ के	६२^{३}॥
अधर थान २ के १०	अलैचि दाना धार्नि ४ के	६
हाति दात का फुरु २ के	....	१२
ल्हासाका ४ काजि के अंदाज.......................................		१५७
किंषाप थान ४ के १५२	सुपारि धार्नि ४ के	५
ल्हासाका तकयालि राजा लामा के अंदाज..................		१५१॥।
किंषाप थान १ के ५०	वनात वस्ता १ के	७१
मेहि अधर थान २ के १०	अलैचि दाना धार्नि ४ के	६
सुपारि धार्नि २ के २॥	हाति दात का फुरु २ के	१२
ल्हासाका अम्वा २ के अंदाज.......................................		६०
किंषाप थान २ के १९२	वनात वस्ता २ के	१०८
तरोवार २ के १५	तोडेवाल वन्दुक २ के	९०
षुकुरि २ के ८	हाति दात २ के	१६०
सुपारि धार्नि २ के २॥	द. सुपारि धार्नि २ के	११
दालचिनी धार्नि १ के ४॥।	गरिगोटा ३० के धा १ के	४।
वदाम धार्नि २ के ४॥।	छोहारा धार्नि ४ के	५।
छिन्दफु का चन्दु के अंदाज..................................		२०८
किंषाप थान १ के ४०	वनात वस्ता १ के	१६८
सिंघाफु का चन्दुके अंदाज..		४२॥
किंषाप थान १ के ४०	सुपारि धार्नि २ के	२॥
दर्वारि खर्च...		२३२३। ।
नगद मोरु		१०००
जिन्सी अंदाज...		१३२३। ।
किंषाप थान ७ के ३५०	वनात वस्ता ३ के	३१२
वाफदा थान २ के ७०	कासीवाल थान २० के	२००
१४ ह. फर्कावादि थां १६ के ९६	षारुवा थान २० के	६०
चौविसा थान ३० के ९०	धुवा थान १५ के	१८॥।
पिटा थान ३० के ३०	लवाग सेर ३॥ के	९।।
द. सुपारि धार्नि १ के ५॥	वदाम धार्नि १ के	२।^{२}
सुपारि धार्नि ५ के ६।	गरि गो ४० के सेर ४ के	५॥^{२}॥

दालचिनी धार्नी २ के ९॥ सुषमेल सेर २ के १८
वला धार्नि ५ के १० षुकुरि १० के ३०
श्री वादसाहलाइ श्री युवराजाधिराजवाट अर्जि जादा थप सुनौला तास थान १ के तोला ४३।९।के ....

काम पऱ्यो भन्या षर्च गर्नु काम परेन भन्या फिराइ ल्याउनु भन्या काजिका जिम्मा गयाको अंदाज..१७४०
किंषाप थान ७ के ७०० वनात वस्ता १० के १०४०

अैजन सौगात पुऱ्याउन जान्या मानीसहरु के षर्च................. १६३६२।॥३॥

काजि जगतवम् पाडे के .... ६६३२।॥.॥
नगद कल्दार मोरु .... ५५६२॥
जिन्सी रु. .... १०७०।.॥
.... पगरि १ अं. १५ साल जोडा १ के ६००
.... का रुमाल १ के ८० किंषाप थान २ के अं ३००
माल्दहि थान १ के अं. १५ साल्का पटुका १ के ६०
.... का हात.. २॥ के अं ।.॥

सर्दार वीरभद्र कार्कि के १९९५३
नगद मोरु १६००
जिन्सी रु. ३९५३
...... गजि पगरि १ के अं. ५ सालजोडा १ के १७०
साल्का रुमाल १ के अं ५० किंषाप थान १॥ के अं. १५०
माल्दहि २ के अं. २० षामा हात २ के अं ३॥

आठ पगरि का जना ८ के

सुवेदार वीरमर्दन भडारि के .... ६४५।॥३॥
नगद मोरु .... ४५४॥
जिन्सी.. १९१।३॥
........गजि पगरि १ के अं. ४ सालफर्द १ के ६७॥
किंषाप थान १ के अं १०० वेस कासीवाल थान ॥के अं. ६।
माल्दहि थान १ के अं. १२॥ चिङ्गली हात २॥ के अं. १
..........हात .... २ के अं. ३॥

.... पाडे के .... ६४१।३॥
नगद मोरु ४५०
जिन्सी सदर.. १९१।३॥

षर्दार सिद्धिनर सिं के .... ५०६।३॥
नगद मोरु ....२२५ जिन्सी तप्सील सदर १९१। ३॥

चि. दोभास्या हरि कृष्ण के .... ४१६।३॥
नगद मोरु................. ३१५ जिन्सी सदर १९१।३॥

आजिटन कनक सिं षत्री के .... ३७१।^{३}॥
नगद मोरु ....१८०जिनसी तप्सील सदर .... १९१।^{३}॥

इन्द्रसिं के नगद ३६०० मध्ये जिन्सी सदर......................... १९१।^{३}॥
ज्मादार नैनसिं अधिकारि के .... २६५॥।^{३}॥
नगद मोरु .... १८४॥
जिन्सी रु. .... ८१।^{३}॥
२७ गजि पगरि १ के अं. ४ किंषाप थान १ के अं. ६०
वेस कासिवाल थां ॥ के अं. ६। औरंजेवी माल्दहि थां १ के अं. १०
चीङ्गली हात २॥ के अं. १ षासा हात २ के अं. ^{३}॥

भोटु वषेति के .... २६५॥।^{३}॥
नगद मोरु १८४॥ जिन्सी सदर ८१।^{३}॥

<u>६ पगरि जना ६ के</u>

भरिया नाएक पदम के .... १८७।^{३}॥
नगद मोरु .... १५७॥
जिनसि अंदाज.. २९॥।^{३}॥
प. पगरि थान १ के ३ को चौविसा थान १ के ३॥
सिलिंतोस फर्द १ के ७ वे. कासिवाल थान ॥ के ६।
वुट्टेदार चिङ्गली हा ९ के ९ चिङ्गली हात २॥ के १
षासाका रुमाल.. १ के ^{३}॥

इन्द्रविर षत्रि के नगद ३६०० मध्ये जिन्सी अंदाज............ ५५।^{३}॥
प. पगरि थान १ के ३ ३५अं. किंषाप थान १ के ३५
औरंजेवी माल्दहि थां १ के १० वेस कासिवाल थान ॥ के ६।
चिङ्गली हात २॥ के १ षासा हात २ के ^{३}॥

.........मित्रा के नगद ३६०० मध्ये जिन्सी सदर ....
.........वीर षत्रि के सदर.. ५५।^{३}॥
.... मान के सदर.. ५५।^{३}॥
...... देवि प्रसाद पाडेके नगद ३६०० म. जिन्सी .... ९५।^{३}॥
.... गजि पगरि १ के अं. ३ वाफदा थान १ के ३०
साल फर्द १ के ४५ औरंजेवी माल्दहि थां १ के अं १०
कासिवाल थान ॥ के अं. ६। चिङ्गली हात २॥ के अं. १
षासाका रुमाल.. १ के अं ^{३}॥

.... पगरि मध्ये जना १ ६पगरि मध्ये जना ५ तिलंगा गै
.... २९ काजिका साथ जान्या ज्मा जना ३५ के षर्च नगद मोरु... ३६००
यस साल ४५ जना वाहेक थप जान्या जना २ के षर्च .... ३२४॥।^{३}
...... नन्द कारिगर के अंदाज का मोल................................ १५४॥।^{३}॥
.... रु .... १०० प. पगरि थान १ के ३

.... कोचिन ष गो ८॥के ३६	को. चौविसा थान १ के	३॥
.... विसा थान १ के ३॥	प. विहारि थान १ के	३॥
.... थान ॥ के ५ षासा हात २ के ^{३}॥		

.... जोसि के अंदाज का मोल..		१७०^{३}॥
नगद रु. १२०	प. पगरि थान १ के	३
चौविसा थान १ के ३॥	चौविसा थान १ के	३
..... हारि थान १ के ३॥	कासिवाल थान ॥ के	५
कोचिन षगा के ३२षासा हात २ के ^{३}॥		

अैजन सौगातको काम काम काम के षर्च		४१५।⁄॥
.... मजुरि गैह्र के नगद रु................................१०७		
.... नाल पातामा मोल्मा के कल्दार असर्फि ५ के अं.१२५		
.... षोल थैला गैह्र के जिन्सी रु. अंदाज के मोल १८३।⁄॥		
.... तोला २० के ८०	वनात गज ३।^{२} के	१०^{२}
.... हात १२ के ६	गोटा तोला १ के	३
रुवा पाव १ के ^{२}॥	सुति मषमल्षगा ९ के	१८
अतर मासा २ के १	सु. कलावतु तो ।५।के	२
रेसम तोला ३।के ^{३}	गुछ्ली लैस तो ।६।के	६
विहारि हात ४ के ।^{३}	पिटा थान १४॥ के	१४॥
षारुवा थान ३ के ९	चौविसा थान ४ के	१२
धागो तोला ४ के ⁄	गजि पगरी १ के	१॥
ले. सुन तो ।७।३ के १९	ले. चादि तो ।१।४।के	।^{२}

(The detailed expenses and the list of presents sent along with the 1842 Nepalese Quinquennial mission to China under the leadership of *Kazi* Jagat Bam Pande.)

Source : Royal Nepal Army Head-quarters (RNAH), Part 3, Serial No. 63 (53).

Appendix D

श्री:

उप्रांत अकास्म मानका .... का हजुरमा अर्जि सौगात् चह्राइ दर्सन् दंडवत् गर्न काजी भारादार पठाउन्या वर्ष यहि हो . हाम्रो देस पहाड्मा हुन्या चिज याहा षोजी यहा नहुन्या टाढा देस मध्येसवाट झीकाई मन्को भावसीत अधिकारीत वमोजीम सव्थोक् तयार गरि ल्हासा बध्न्या (वस्न्या?) अंवाहरुका अर्ति सिक्ष्या माफिक् पेचिन.......... का हजुरमा पुगि हाम्रा दुषदर्दको जाहेर गरि आउनु भनि हाम्रा वहुत प्रतीत् विश्वास भयाको काजी दामोदर पांडेको नाति काजी जगत्वंम पांडे र सर्दार विर भद्र कार्कि षरिदार सुवेदार दोभास्या अरु चाहिया माफिक् भला मानिसहरुलाइ याहावाट विदा गरि पठाञ्यौं अघि .... वाट तिमिले

निमक्को सोभ्को चिताउनु हाम्रा दक्षीण ढोका नेपाल्का तिमि छौ . प्रजा प्राणिको पालना गर्नु ५ वर्षको मामुलीत् सौगात् ली हाम्रा हजुरमा दर्सण गर्न आउनु . तिमि साना मुलुकका राजा छौ . तिमिमाथि कौनै कुराको भये आइलाग्यो भन्या सहाय गर्न्या हामि छौ . दक्षीण तर्फ अनेत्र मुलुकवाट नेपाल लिनाको मानसुवा गरि कोही आयो ताहांका प्रजाप्राणीलाई दुष दिन लाग्यो . तिमीलाइ मिचि चिनलाई नमानि हामिलाइ मान् भनी भंन आयो भंन्या यो गोर्षाका मुलुकको गादी .... वाट हामिलाई वक्साको छ .... वादसाहलाई मात्र हामि जांदछौ अरु कसैलाइ जांदैनौ भंन्या कुराको जवाफ दिनु. जवाफ दिदा मानेन भन्या साचो कुरो ठहऱ्याई अर्जि लेषि आफ्ना दर्वारका पत्यायाका काजिलाई हाम्रा हजुरमा पठाइदिनु. हाम्रा तजवीजसंग पठायाका फौजलाइ थामनसकिन्याछ भन्या फौज पठाई बक्सौंला थाम्न सकिन्या छैन भन्या दौलथ वक्सी पनि तिमी माथि आइलाग्न्या वैरिलाइ धपाइ दिउला इ २ कुराको थिति वाधि गोर्षाको नेपालराज हाम्रो हो यति षातिर जामा तिमिलाई वक्स्याको छ . अघि देषि पनि तम्म्रो पीछया हामिले लीयाको हो. कैल्हे केहि परि आयो भन्या विंती गरी पठाउन भनी .... वाट हामिलाई षातीर जामाको धर्मपत्र पर्वाण र पंजा हाम्रा .... जिज्यु वाज्य रणबहादुर साहलाई वक्स्याको ली साल ४९ का आश्वीन महीन्हामा काजी देवदत्त थापा आयोथ्यो भन्या याहाका अघिका बुढा जान्याहरु भंन्छन् . उसै हुकुमको आधार राषी.............. का प्रतापले यो हाम्रो मुलुक रह्याको थियो उसै आधारमा हाम्रा श्री वुवाज्यू गिर्वाणजुद्ध वीक्रम साह रहनु भयाको हो तिन पुस्तासम्म हजुरका पंजाका दरले पछीम तर्फ सिष र दक्षिण तर्फ फिरंगीले गोर्षा माथि ....को बहुतै मेहर करुणा छ. गोर्षासँग चल्नु छैन भनी दव्याकै थियो हाम्रा श्री वुवाज्यु गिर्वाणजुद्ध विक्रम साह र हाम्रा श्री वाज्यज्यू २७।२८ दिं को फरक भै सितलाकाका बेरामले १८ वर्षका उमेरमा परलोक हुनु भयो उस वषत्मा ३ वर्षका उमेरका श्री वुवाज्यू हुनु हुदो रहय छ अघि ...... बाट हाम्रा पुर्षालाई धर्मपत्र गरि वक्स्याको यस्ता वेहोराको धर्मपत्र पर्वाण छ भन्या कुरा कसैले जाहेर गरेनछन्. श्री वुवाज्यु वालष हुनाले केहि थाहा पाउनु भयेन अघि हाम्म्रा पुर्षालाई नेपालको राज्य भोग गराइ दिन्या र .... का पिछामा हामिलाई राषिदिन्या हाम्रा पुर्षाले पत्याइ कजाइको पगरि दि राष्याको काजि दामोदर पाडेलाइ हो. हाम्रो दरवारको पुरानु बुंन्यादी .... का हजुरमा पनि जाहेर भयाको. अघि वकस्याको धर्मपत्रको वेहोरा जान्या पनि उही हो काजि दामोदर पांडे मऱ्यापछि हाम्रा दर्वारमा पत्यारन भयाको वाहिरीया सानु मानिस भिमसेन थापा मुक्तीयारि हुनु गयेछ. अघि .... वाट वकस्याको धर्मपत्रको पर्वाण दवाइ दी फिरंगीसग मिलि ७१ सालमा गारन् रवाल भन्याका इ दुइ फिरिंगीलाई नेपालला डाकी इ २ संग मिलाप गरि हाम्रा दर्वार देषी ॥ (आधा?) कोस उत्तर्रानिवारिमा कोठि लाउन दिये छ केहि पुर्व केहि पछीम केहि दक्षिणको मुलुक पनि सोपेछ. अघि हाम्रा सोभ्को गर्न्या भैयाद भारदार पर सारि फिरंगीको ढाक देषाइ श्री वुवाज्युलाई पनि भारदारलाई पनि हप्काई ३४ वर्ष सम्म आफै मालिक भयाको रहेछ. फिरंगी नेपालमा ल्याई राख्याको २८ वर्ष

भयेछ पछि श्री वुवाज्यूको १७।१८ वर्षको उमेर भया पछि थाहा हुन जादा यो मुलुक .... का दया करुणाले हामिलाई बक्सनु भयाको हो .... को हुकुम नभै कस्का हुकुमले फिरंगीलाई ल्याइस् भनि भिमसेनथापालाई सासना गर्नाको मनसुवा गर्दा फिरंगीले लीयाको मुलुक पनि ल्याइदिन्छु . याहा वस्याका फीरंगीलाइ पनि धपाइदिंछु भनि साल ९२ मा आफ्नु भतिजो माथवरसिंथापालाई कलकत्ता लाठसंग पठायो फिरंगीले लीयाको मुलुक पनि ल्याउन सकेन नेपालमा रह्याका फिरंगीलाई पनि धपाउन सकेन .... को हुकुम नपाइ मलाइ दवाइ फिरंगीलाइ ल्याउन्या निमकहरामी गरि फिरंगिसँग मिल्न्या त को होस भनि ९४ सालका श्रावण महिन्हामा भिमसेन थापालाइ कयद गरि राष्याको थियो. उस्का षान्कीमा डामोदर पाडेका छोरा रणजङपांडेलाई मुषतीयारी दियाको थियो । भिमसेन थापाले आफनु मुनासिवले फिरंगीसंग मील्याका कुरा सवै .... का हजुरमा षुलस्त जाला र मेरो झन सासना होला भनि आफनु गलो आफैले काटि मऱ्यो श्री वुवाज्यूले थाहा नपाई भिमसेन थापाले अघि अघि मामुलित सौगात र अर्जि ली जौन काजिहरुलाई ताहा पठाउथ्यो. फिरंगीले यहा वेजाइ गऱ्याको कुरा केहि पनि विंति गरिपठाउदो रहेन छ फिरंगी नेपालमा आइरहेछ भन्या कुरा .... का हजुरमा विंती नगर्नु हाम्रा महाराजा षुसि हुनु हुंछ. प्रजा प्राणिहरु पनि षुसि छन् भनि अर्जिमा लेषि चह्राइ पठाइदो रहेछ उसले गऱ्याको काम कुरा आजकाल मलाई थाहा हुन जादा कसका हुकुमले याहा वसी रहिछस् भनि फिरंगीसंग छेडषानिका कुरा गर्दा फिरंगीले हामिलाई जवाफ दियाका कुरा चिनको .... का भरोसाले हामिलाई, चिह्राउछौ भन्या क्य होला वढीयै छ चिन....... का मुलुक क्कांताङ भन्याको सहर हामिले अंवल गरि सक्यौ चिन्का भरोसाले तिमिलाई पुग्न्या छैन पछीम्तर्फवाट सिषले लदाक्ग तोंफ तात्का षार लोचेरा (लेचिरा?) नुन् षानी सुन षानी सिषको राजा सेर सिंले लियो उसलाई तिम्रा .... ले क्या गऱ्या. चिनको ढाक तिमिले हामिलाई देषाउनु पर्दैन ढेरै वर्ष सम्म लडाइ नगऱ्याका हुनाले चिनीया फौज लडाइ गर्न जादैनन् क्कांताङतिरका लडाइमा २/३ टापु हामिले लिञ्यू कम्पनिसँग दोस्ती राषी क्काताङतर्फवाट हामि र ल्हासा तर्फवाट तिमिहरुले मनसुवा राष्यौं भन्या ल्हासा ली सहजै चिन् सम्म अंवल हुन्या छ भंन्या यस्ता कुरा गर्दा यो कुरा हामिलाई नसुनाउ हामिले अघि देषी मानी आयाका चिनका .... लाइ यो कुरा मनले पनि चितावन सक्तैन भंन्या जवाफ दिञ्यू ताहा......... संग पनि अज्यौलि गरि क्कांताङमा पनि लडाइ गर्न लागी रहेछ याहा हामि संग पनि यस्ता कुरा गर्न लागि रहेछ यो मुलुक .... को हो फिरंगीले यहा सम्म वेजाजि गऱ्यामा पनि हाम्रा हजुरमा गोर्षाले केहि कुरा विंति गरि पठायेन भंने षवकी होला भंन्या डरले अर्जि लेषि विंति गरि पठायाको छ १४।१५ पुस्ता देषि हाम्रा पुर्षाले पत्याइ आयाका हाम्रा दर्वारका प्रतितवाला पुराना वुंन्यादी मुलकाजी ताहा.......... का हजुरमा पनि जाहेर भयाको काजी दामोदर पाडेका नाति हामिले पनि पत्याइ राष्याको काजि जगत वं. पांडेलाई हाम्रा दुष दर्दको अर्जि र ञाहा फिरंगीले वेजाइ वोहुत गऱ्याको विती गर्नाको निमित दर्शण गर्न पठायाको छ . यस वेलामा तिमिहरुले पनि फिरंगीसँग

मुहडा जोर भनि .... वाट हुकुम आउछ फौजको पनि वक्सीस भै आउछ भन्या पुर्व सुषीम्‌वाट फिरंगीको कलकता २०।२५ दिनको वाटो छ पश्चिम तर्फवाट फौज वक्सींछ भन्या ताकलाषारदेषि डिल्ली ३५।४० दिनको वाटो छ ७।८ कडोर डौलथ् वक्सीस भै आउछ भन्या याहा वस्याको फिरंगीलाई उठाउछौ लडाइ पनि गर्दछौ र इ कुरामा यक कुराको पनि .... वाट मंजुर गर्नु भयेन भन्या दुइ मुलुकका विचमा पऱ्याका छौं दुइतिर मांनालाई हाम्रा वर्गतले पुगी आउदैन हुकुम भया माफिक सवैथोक गर्न सकन्यै छौ. दौलथ पनि वक्सीस भयेन मद्दत पनि वक्सीस भयेन भन्या मुलुक थामन जस्ता तरहलें हुछ सो कुरा आफुहरुकै दयाले हुन्या छ विति गरि पठायाका कुराको मेहर करुणा भै आयेन भन्या यो .... को दक्षिण ढोका थाम्न सकीन्या छैन मैले र मेरा पुत्र जवराजधिराजले मनका भावसित चह्राइ पठायाका अर्जि र (२) .... का हजुरमा पुग्न्या काम गरिदिनु भया वढिया होला. येस पटक लेषिया वमोजिमका र अरु अरु कुराको सवै विस्तार विंति गर्न हाम्रो वहुत विश्वास प्रतीत भयाको काजी जगतवंपाडेलाइ पठायाको छ यस्ले विंती गऱ्याको कुरा प्रमाण प्रतित जांनु होला ५ वर्षको मामुलीयेत सौगातका संगमा मात्र अर्जि चह्राइ पठाउदा टाढाको पध्न्हा पर्न जानाले आफ्ना दुष दर्दका अर्जिहरु ....का हजुरमा पुगी सक्दैन भंना निमित जरुरि पऱ्यामा अघिपछि पनि अर्जि चह्राइ पठाउन्या कुराको अर्जिमा पनि विति गरि पठायाको छ यो कुरा पनि .... का हजुरमा जाहेर गरि अघि पछि पनि आफ्ना दुषदर्दका अर्जि आफहरु मार्फत .... का हजुरमा पुग्न्या र केहि हाम्रा दुषदर्द पऱ्यामा याहावाट भारादार गै आफुहरु संग विंती ची गर्न पाउन्या वन्दोवस्त वाधि दिन्या काम भया. दुषद पऱ्यामा भारादारहरुलाइ आफहरु छेउ पठाउनालाइ वढीया होला वाकि हिजो नेपाली राजा प्रतापमल्लका पालामा भिमलकाजिले केरुं र ठुगा मारि टे गरि छिचोलि उतावाट मुहडा फिराइ कुतिसम्म आइ फेरि साके र डिगर्चाको मन्सुवा गरि जादा ताहाका लामाज्यु सुलतनात्‌का वातचित्त सध्न्याह गरि वन्देजवाध्याको केरुं र कुति आधा नेपालको अंवल गरि भोट चह्रन्या महाजन वेपारि गैह्रसित क्तीर दै दस्तुर लै लगायेत् आम्दानि गैह्र भोट्‌को लाग् नास्ती नेपालैको लगीत् गरि ३२ कोठि ल्हासामा वसाइ ३२ कोठीको मिर्दा नाइक्य १ राषि नेपालका टक भोटमा चलाइ १ रुपैयाको १३ मासा चादि १२ रुपैयाको १ तोला वुकी सुन ३ माथि (पाथि) नुनको भाव नेपाल दाषिल गर्नु भोटको चिज मध्येस मध्येसको चिज भोट पुर्व तर्फको रस्ता नषुलाउनु नेपालैको रस्ता चलाउनु भन्यां. यति कुराको वन्देज वाधि लामाज्यूहरुले दियाको नजरआना प्रसस्त दोलथलि भिम्‌लकाजि फिऱ्याका हुन यो वन्देजको रस्त चल्याको थियो गोर्षावाट नेपालमार्दा २०।२५ वर्षसम्म घेरा पर्दा नेपालैको रस्ता कचवचिन गयो र पुर्व सुषिमको रस्ता षुलन गयाको थीयो श्री ज्यूज्यू वाज्याज्यु सिंह प्रताप साहका पालको चलन सच्याउन निमित्त टक्सारि प्रतापसिंहलाइ हुकुम वमोजिम भोटमा गै लामाज्यूहरुसँग सध्न्याह गर्दा कुति र केरुं छाडी अघिको पुरानु वन्देज सवै सच्याइ पुर्व तर्फको रस्ता वंध गरि नेपालैको रस्ता चलाई आया र पुरानै दरभरमा सुनचादि नुन इत्यादि सवै चिज

आइपुग्याको थियो श्री वाज्याज्यु रणवहादुरसाहका पालामा १०।१२ वर्षका विचमा यो चलन हराउँदै जांदा टक्सार वंद भै आम्दानी घटन जांदा क्या निमित्त यो चलन हराउदै गयाको रहेछ जाचि वनाइ आउनु भनि तहा देषित क्राजिको वेहोरा भै ठुलो घामघुम उठन गयाको हो. हिजोको वन्देज सवै यसै तक्राजिमा भेटीयाको भया ३२ कोठी र नाइक्या पनि ताहा रहन पाउन्या होइन विचमा तक्राजी भै कचवचिन गयाको भया पनि नेपालको षोट हो भोटको नेपाल हो अघि देषिको दोस्ति पनि छंदैछ .... वाट पनि पुरानु वन्देज मेटीवक्स्याको छैन ३२ कोठिको वन्देज पनि छंदैछ केरुं र कुति पनि छोडीदियाको छंदैछ मेटीया सवै कुरा मेटीन्या हो. रह्या सवै कुरा रहन्या हो सुन चादि औ जिन्सी र रस्ता कचवचियाको क्या वेहोराले हो. वन्देज छुटन जांदा याहा टक्सार साह्रै वन्द भै आम्दानि घटी रहेछ तस निमित्त नेपालको र भोटको सरत दोस्ति रहन्या हिजोको वन्देजमा चलन जस्ताको तस्तो व्येहोरा ताहा ला (ई) भया सवै कुरालाई वढिया होला. औ अघि राजालामावाट यो पातलालामाज्यू न(गा) दिमा कथीन भयो आफना वल षजानाले नपुग्या पछि वलले मिचिकन पनि तेस तर्फ लडाइलाई वाटो षुला गर्न्या छ अघि देषि हाम्रा पुर्षाले मानि आयाको .... लाइ हो हामिले पनि मन सा (मा) वाचा कर्मणले भन्यैको छ हाम्रा ता हजुर हुनु हुंछ पीछया परेकाको धर्म रहन्या र प्रजा प्रणीको पालना हुन्या जस्ता तरहले हुंछ गरिवक्स्याजावस यो राज्ये हजुर कै हो. दोश्रो कुरा ताकलाषार भन्याका जगा अघि जुमलि राजाका पालामा जुमलाको अम्वल हो. पछि भोट तर्फवाट मोस्तांङ सहादि ताकलाषार भोट तर्फ गयाको रहेछ. त्यो ताकलाषार भन्याको भोटको जगा. हाम्रा मुलुक जुमलाका सिवानासँग मिल्दो जगा पर्न जांछ. तस निमित तेस ताकलाषारका वदलामा हाम्रा मुलुकको मोस्तांङ सहालि त्यो ताकलाषार भंन्या जगा हामिलाइ वक्सीस् भया. भोटका उपर सिष चढि आयाका वेलामा भोटसंग सामेल भै सिषलाइ हटाउन्या काम गरियेला. यस पटक लदाकदेषि यसो भोट तर्फलाइ सिषको सर्दार जोरावर भन्यांले ढेरै लस्कर ली चह्राइ गर्दा येस वषतमा सिषलाई भोट तर्फ चह्रन दिन्या होइन. भोटलाई मद्दत दिनु पर्छ भनि हाम्रा जुमलाका र भोटका सीवाना संम्म हामिले फौज पठायाको हो. हाम्रो लस्कर फर्की आयो. तेश्रो कुरा लदाकको मुलुक सिषले अंवल गऱ्याको ७।८ वर्ष भयो आज पनि भोटसंग लडाञि गर्नाको सिषवाट तयारि हुन लागिरहेछ. तस निमित भोटसंग सामेल भै लदाक हान्नालाई रस्ता वक्सीस भया. सिषसँग लडाइ गरि लदाकको मुलुक अम्वल गरि तेसतर्फ वाट भोट् तर्फ सीष आउन वन्द गरि रहन्या काम गरियेला. लदाकले अघि .... लाइ जो चह्रायाको हो सो कुरा सौगात्का तवरसँग.......... लाइ हामीले चह्राउन्या काम गरौला. चौथो कुरा ५।७ वर्ष देखि फिरंगीले सुषिमको नगीज भोट् ल्हासा तर्फ वाटाको गम् उन्या गरि दोर्ज्यलिं भंन्या जगा सम्म वाटो सडक सम्म षनि छाउनी वनाइ वसि रहेछ तस निमित्त सुषिम देखि माथि ल्हासादिगर्चाका मुलुकवाट पाहाडको रस्ता धर्माका मुलुकसम्म १ कोस भरको चौडा वाटो वक्सीस भया धर्माका सीवानासम्मलाई कोश भर चौडाका हीसावले ल्हासा दिगर्चाको मुलुक जति

ज्मीन पर्दछ तेस ज्मीनको वदला मील्दो जगाडेढो दोवर सम्म वढता हुन्या गरि हाम्रा मुलुकको जमिन् सट्टा दिन्या काम गरौला. यस्कुराको सुषीमको अडा पनि वलीयो होला तेस्तरफका साना ठुला षवर पनि विंति गरि पठाउदै रहुला. इ लेषिया वमोजिम का र अरु कुराको पनि विस्तार विंती गर्नु भनि काजी जगत्वम पाडेलाई अह्राइ पठायाको छ यस्ले विंती गऱ्याका प्रमाण जानि सेवक हुनु भनि ... वाट हाम्रा उपर दया करुणाको मेहरवानी भै आयो भन्या यो ... को दक्षीण ढोका थामिरहन्या काम गरौला मेहेर करुणा भै आयेन भन्या हामि साना मुलुकका राजाले यो दुष दर्दका कुराको अर्जिहरु ५ वर्षका सौगातका संगमा मात्र चह्राइ पठाउदा टाढाको पधना (पध्रा) पर्नजांछ कदाचित केही जरुरी कुरा विचमा चह्राइ पठाउनु पऱ्यो भन्यो नेपालवाट लेषि पठायाको अर्जि हाम्रा हजुर्मा चह्राइ पठाउनु भन्य ल्हासाका अंवाहरुलाई हुकुम भै आया देषि केहि जरुरि पऱ्यामा अर्जि लेखि विंति गरि पठाउला भंन्या विस्तार स्मेत हाम्रा सवै दुष दर्दका कुराको .... का हजुरमा मेरा तर्फवाट र मेरा पुत्र जवराजधिराजका तर्फवाट अर्जि लेषि विंति गरि पठायाको छ अघि देषि हाम्रा दुषदर्द .... का हजुरमा जाहेर गरि दिन्या ल्हासाका अंवाहरु हुन आज पनि आफुहरु हुनु हुंछ हामिता श्रीफ् आफहरुलाई मात्रै जांदछौं सवै कुरा आफुहरुकै भरोसा छ. हाम्रा उपर दया करुणा राषि विंती गरि पठायाका अर्जिको ..का हजुरमा जाहेरगरि हामि पिछ्रा पऱ्याकाको धर्म रहन्या र प्रजा प्राणीको पालना हुन्या वध्न्या कुरा लेषि आउदा अधिकारित वमोजिम संगुण चिजहरु काजि हस्ते पठायाको छ दाषिल होला इति सम्वत् १८९९ साल मिति आषाढ वदि रोज ६ मुकाम् कांतीपुर श्रम्म्.................

(Nepal Government's Letter to Chinese Government seeking China's help sent through *Kazi* Jagat Bam Pande on 1899 B.S.Ashad Badi 8 Roj 6.)

Source : National Archives of Nepal, Kathmandu (NAN), *Poka* No. 5, Letter No. 44.

Appendix E

पेचीन जान अर्जि सौगाद लि काजी जगत वं पाडे आइ पुगे अर्जिमा अंग्रेजसंग लडनलाई दौलथको मद्दत देउ कि सिमान कुर्न सिपाही षटाई दिनु भन्ने र देश साटने कुरा स्मेत लेषियाको रहेछ. रीत दस्तुर नमिलेको चर्चा. तौकाङ २२ सम्वत् १८९९ साल पौष वदी २ रोजको दाषिला अम्वाको चिठी श्री ५ सर्कारका हजुरमा पठायाको ....

(Chinese *Amban* to Nepalese King mentioning the arrival of *Kazi* Jagat Bam Pande at Lhasa along with the presents and the *arji* to the Ch'ing Emperor seeking the Chinese support against the British and proposing the exchange of districts.)

Source : Ministry of Foreign Affairs, Kathmandu (MFA), *Poka* No. Pa 64.

Appendix F

९९ साल सौगात पुऱ्याउन जाने काजि जगत वम पाडे आषाडको २ दिन जादा त्राहावाट गयाका माघका दिन १२ जादा पछाडी दी वाकी ६ भंदा पेचिन पेचिन सहरमा दाषिला भयाका रहयाका छन् – माघ १८ दिन जादा सौगात वुझाया छन फाल्गुनवदि ५ रोज १ मा श्री ५ चिन वादसाहको दर्सन गऱ्याका रहयाछन तलाउमा षेल्याका तमासा देषि माघको दिं २३ जादा दर्वार भित्र पहलमानको कुस्ती हेऱ्याछन् फागु १ वदी १३ रोज ७ मा सिपाहि केटाहरुके भरी टाक १० र कुचिन थान १ कपडा समेत मिलेछ दर्वार भित्र लामाहरुको नाच हेऱ्याछन्- फालगुन सुदि ३ रोज ६ मा दर्वारवाट कुचिन वक्स भयेछ फाल्गुन सुदी १३ रोज १ मा थामी गयाका आतास वाजीको तमासा देख्याछन् फाल्गुनका दिन १५ जादा मंगलवार कलकी पनी मिले साझ विहान २ वषत दर्शन गऱ्या छन्..............................

(Description of the activities of *Kazi* Jagat Bam Pande's mission at Peking.)

Source: MFA, Undated, Unnumbered . *Poka* No. Pa 64.

Appendix G

कम्माडर इन चिफ भिमसेन थापालाई विगार्नेहरुले सजाये पाए . तेरो कसुर वेराम केही छैन . हाम्रा हजुरमा हाजीर हुन आइज . तलाई भये छैन भन्या काजी जगत्वम पांडेलाई १९०० साल मार्ग २ रोज ५..............

(Nepal Government's Letter instructing *Kazi* Jagat Bam Pande to return to Nepal assuring his safety.)

Source : MFA, *Poka* No. Pa 64.

Appendix H

अघिको भन्दा १ महिना ढिला भयो पेचिन जाने काजीहरुको खोज तलास गर्दा ढिला हुन गयाको हो. काजी सर्दार आफुको मुलुक टिगरी पहाडको वाटो गरी मधेस भागी गया भन्या सुनिदा अव त्राहा नआयेता पनि अर्जि लेखी रवाना गरी पठाएको छ भन्या १९०० साल फागुन शुदी १ रोज ५ मा श्री ५ सर्कारवाट २ अंवालाई ....,...........

(Nepalese King to Chines *Ambans* informing *Kazi* (Jagat Bam

Pande) and *Sardar*'s (Bir Bhadra Karki) escape to India from Tibet.)

Source : MFA, *Poka* No. Pa 64.

Appendix I

१९०० साल

काजि जगत वं पांडे चीन जादा साथका मानीसहरु चीनवाट फर्कदा श्री वादसाहका परमाना लिन केरुं सम्म लिन जान्या सर्दार....... चन्द्र साहि हस्ते चिनवाट आउन्या भारादारहरुके मेजमानी गया कार्तिक सुदि १४ रो............

मेजमानी के ४०

मिठाई र प्याङ के नगद रु. .... १५।

जिन्सी रु. अंदाज... २४॥।´॥।

सुपारि धार्नि १॥ के १॥।[२] — जायफल गोटा १५ के ॥।[३]

दालचिनि पाव १ के ।[२]। — सुषमेल पाव २ के ४॥

मरीच धार्नि ॥ के १ — छोहारा धार्नि १ के १।´

वलासेर ॥ के ।´ — मिश्रि सेर १ के १

.... पाव १ के ॥[२]॥ — वदाम धार्नि १ के २।[२]

..........पाव ५ के १॥।.। — चिनी धार्नि १ के १।

अलैचि सेर १ के ।´ — अधर्सा हात १६ के १[२]।

चिउरा पाथी १० मसिना चावल मुरि १ फलफु गैह्र नुवा ...... अडैका नाउमा पुर्जि ६

मेजमानी पुऱ्याउन जान्याहरु के डोल्या भरिया षर्च पैसा रु....... ५७॥

(The detailed expenses of the Chinese officials who escorted the 1842 Nepalese mission up to Kerung in 1843.)

Source : RNAH, Part 3, Serial No. 63(53).

Appendix J

हाम्रो मुलुकमा फिरङ्गीले थिचो मिचो गरेको हुनाले ताहावाट ठूलो फौज र दौलथको मद्दत वक्सी हाम्रो गोहार गरिवक्सीयोस भनि र देस र देस सारी वक्सीयोस भनी साविक भन्दा वढता कुरा षुसामत गरि अर्जिका थपी पठायाकालाई आफ्ना प्रजालाई माया गरी आफ्ना मुलुक वहाल गरी वलियो गराई अरु केही कुरामा अर्काका मुलुकको मन्सुवा नगर्या केही फसाद परी आउदैन आफसे आफ प्रजालाई पनि सुख हुन्छ औ अघि आरम्भै देखी फौज दौलथको मद्दत दिने रं देस साटने काम चीनवाट केही भयाको छैन भनी यो कुराको जवाफ तोक्काङ १८ सालको पर्वानामा प्रष्ट लेषी पठायाको हो. वाङ भन्नाको क्या हो भने मुलुकको सव काम समाहली राख्ने भनेको हो. वाङले हलौ झुठ्ठा

कुरा सुनन्नु हुदैन. तसर्थ साध सिमानाका राजाहरु संग यथा योग्य काम गर्नु फेरी भ्कुठा कुरा पत्याई षुसामत गर्ने काम नगर भन्या इत्यादी वेहोराको तोक्काङ २३ फागुन १७ दिन जादा सम्वत १९०० सालमा पेचीन जाने काजी जगत वम पाँडेले ल्याको प्रमाना ....

(Chinese Emperor's *Parwana* dated 1900 B.S Falgun 17 (1844) brought by *Kazi* Jagat Bam Pande.)

Source: MFA, *Poka* No. Pa 64.

Appendix K

काजी जगतवम पाडे जीम्मा वक्सी आयाको प्रमाना र सौगादको मालहरु सवै बुझी लियौं भन्या सम्वत १९०० साल माघ वदी ९ रोज १ मा श्री ५ वादसाहका हजुरमा लेखीयाको अर्जीको नक्कल ....

(*Arji* to the Chinese Emperor referring to the receiving of *Parwana* and presents sent through *Kazi* Jagat Bam Pande.)

Source: MFA, *Poka* No. Pa 64.

Appendix L

From - The Resident Nepal
To - T.H. Maddock Esq. Secretary to Government of India,
July 2, 1842
Secret.
Sir,

I have the honour to report to you that Jagat Bum Panday, the periodical envoy of this court to that of Pekin takes his departure tomorrow. It is credibly reported that he has secret instructions emanating from the Palace faction to solicit pecuniary aid from China, and to offer to attack the British territories with 20, 30 or 40,000 men according to the amount of the subsidy solicited. By the route taken by the Embassy about three months are consumed on the way to Pekin, and as many on that back again but including halts on the way and at Pekin the time of absence of the mission from Cathmandoo is commonly about 15 months. There is however a house Imperial (seppefs?) available whereby communication can be held with Cathmandoo from Pekin in 50 days.

It is supported by Jagatbum's party that if the Emperor be worsted by our troops at Pekin he will retire easterly in the direction of Kham and will then give orders for stirring up to attack on our Indian Empire his various nominal and actual allies dependents in this direction among whom Nepal has been reckoned twice (go?) where a very large Tartar army crossed the snows, and having beaten the Nepalese in a severe battle at Dhaiboong about 25 miles, northwest from Catmandoo, made the Nepalese pafs(?) under the yoke and agree to the present quinquennial mission as a permanent token of subjection. The opposite or peace party in this Durbar rely on our good fortune in arms, and considering it certain that the Emperor will have been reduced to terms by us before Jagat Bum Panday's arrival, believe that he will only support himself and party to redicule here by the failure of their............... would the Envoy carry any written instructions of a hostile tenour (detour) to us I have no doubt. I shall be able ere long to profess myself of a transcript of them.

In connection with trans-himalaya affairs I have the honour to submit herewith (app No. 1) copy of a letter just received by me from the Commissioner of Kumaon and Garhwal 19 June.

I have the honour to be
Your most obedient servant
BH Hodgson
Resident

Source : Foreign Dept. Sec., 10 August 1842, No. 126, National Archives of India, New Delhi (NAI).

Appendix M

From - The Resident Nepal
To - T.H. Maddock Esq. Secretary to Government of India with the Governor General Simla.
September 27th 1842
Secret

Sir,

I have the honor to submit herewith (app. No. 1) translation of a paper of secret Intelligence conveying the substance of the proceedings had at Lassa on the arrival of the Nipalese Embassy there, enroute to Pekin

I have the honor to be
Sir,
Your most obedt. Servt.
BH Hodgson
Resident

Appendix No. 1 Resident Nepal's despatch of 27th September 1842

Paper of Secret Intelligence

Jagut bum Pandey's letters from Lassa have just arrived - one is a letter of the Envoy and one of the Viceroy, both addressed to the Maha Raja.

The Viceroy says that the Kharita & presents of the Heir Apparent designed for the Emperor are contrary to usage; also a great part of what the Raja had written : that he cannot suffer the going of any of these noverties to Pekin through the Envoy without orders; that he will write for such orders & act accordingly, on receipt of them; and that meanwhile Jagatbum the Envoy must proceed on his Embassy with the usual letter & presents only.

With regard to what the Maha Raja had written of affairs in China & Western Tibet, the Viceroy answers that His Highness had heard greatly exaggerated accounts of the contest with the English in which the Chinese had at first been severely handled no doubt, but had lately rallied & that there was no cause of anxiety on that score whilst on the score of Tibet there was still less for that the Imperial troops had been completely successful there against the Invaders as Zo-raver Sing's head exposed over the city gate might satisfy the Maha Raja's Envoy & his party from Cathmandoo. Jagatbum the Durbar's Envoy writes that he had had a very flattering reception at Lassa and had exhibited the documents & presents entrusted to his care : but that neither words nor things in excess of customs could be allowed to go on to Pekin without orders; that the Viceroy would write instantly for such orders, and, if the answer was in the assent, would send on the letters and presents now detained so that they should reach the Envoy ere he got to Pekin. The Envoy goes on to say that when he broached to the Viceroy the matters of the large monied aid (3 or 4 Crores) sought by Nepal, the Viceroy asked him what he called a Crore ? & when the Envoy had informed him, told the Envoy he had better write to Cathmandoo to ascertain the true reckoning. About the Taklakhar gold mine, the Viceroy seemed rather more seriously inclined adds the Envoy who concludes that he had done his best at Lassa which he should quit on the 10th September & proceed to Pekin where also whatever was possible should be attempted & effected.

(True translation)
BH Hodgson
Resident

Source : Foreign Dept Sec., 19 October, 1842, No. 70, NAI.

* * *

Part Two

Rana Period 1847-1906

12

Kazi Surath Singh Pantha's Mission of 1847

Here it should be pointed out that the decline of Imperial China in the 1840's (following the Anglo-Chinese (Opium) War of 1839-1842) also coincided with major political changes inside Nepalese court in 1846. Jang Bahadur emerged as the most powerful Nepalese Prime Minister following the Kot and Bhandarkhal massacres of 14 September 1846 and 30 October 1846 respectively. Queen Laxmi Devi was exiled to Banaras, India and King Rajendra also followed the Queen, appointing Crown Prince Surendra as his representative in Nepal. As soon as the opportunity arose, Jang Bahadur managed to instal Surendra Bikram Shah as the new King of Nepal on 12 May 1847. The major political developments of 1846 and 1847 did not affect Nepal's relations with China. Leo E. Rose has stated that "One of the side effects of Jang Bahadur's rise to power in 1846 was the decision to cancel the quinquennial mission to Peking scheduled to depart in 1847".[1] Twitchett and Fairbank too have accepted the statement of Rose.[2] But the view of Leo E. Rose is not true at all. The Nepalese documents prove that Jang Bahadur sent the quinquennial mission to China in 1847 at the usual time. Jang Bahadur seemed to be very eager to get Chinese recognition for King Surendra, the new ruler of Nepal. He was quite well aware of the fact that the recognition of the new Nepalese King by both British India and China would certainly help to institutionalize his government. So he himself took the initiative to send a five-yearly mission to China.[3] Here it should be pointed out that the 1847 Nepalese quinquennial mission has not been mentioned in the

---

1. Leo E. Rose, *Nepal: Strategy For Survival*, Berkeley: University of California Press, 1971, p. 107.
2. Denis Twitchett and J.K. Fairbank (eds.), *The Cambridge History of China*, Vol 10, Late Ch'ing, 1800-1911, Part I, Cambridge: Cambridge University Press, 1978, p. 405.
3. Jnanmani Nepal, "Jang Bahadur Ko Bidesh Niti Ra Sambat 1904 Ko Pechin Jane Pratinidhi Mandal" (Jang Bahadur's Foreign Policy and Mission to Peking of 1904 B.S.), *Contributions to Nepalese Studies*, Vol. VIII, No. 2 (June 1981), p. 187.

Chinese Imperial records.[4] Fisher and Rose have also presented an incomplete record of Nepalese quinquennial missions to China without referring the 1847 Nepalese five-yearly mission.[5] But the Nepalese archival documents have stated that in accordance with the arrangement of the mission system, in June 1847, Jang Bahadur sent the Nepalese complimentary five-yearly mission to China under the leadership of *Kazi* Surath Singh Pantha.[6] Going through the Nepalese documents, it seems that in February 1847, the Chinese *Ambans* reminded the Nepalese King Rajendra to send the quinquennial mission to China in proper time.[7] Likewise there is also the reference of the correspondence between the Chinese *Ambans* and the new Nepalese King Surendra regarding the sending of the Nepalese mission to China.[8] The Nepalese King was also instructed to send the name of the *Kazi*, leading the mission beforehand.[9] On receiving the *Ambans*' letter, Jang Bahadur took quick actions to dispatch mission to the Ch'ing court. In July, the Nepalese King informed the Chinese *Ambans* that the Nepalese mission under the leadership of *Kazi* Surath Singh Pantha had left Kathmandu on 14 Ashad 1904 B.S. (June 1847).[10] This mission

---

4. J.K. Fairbank and S.Y. Teng, "On the Ch'ing Tributary System", *Harvard Journal of Asiatic Studies*, Vol VI, 1941, pp 195-198.
5. Margaret W. Fisher and Leo E. Rose, *England, India, Nepal, Tibet, China, 1765-1958*, Berkeley: University of California Press, 1959, pp. 2-12.
6. For the detailed account of this mission, see Ministry of Foreign Affairs, Kathmandu (hereafter referred as MFA), *Poka* No. Pa 64; Royal Nepal Army Head-quarters (hereafter mentioned as RNAH), Part 3, Serial No. 63 (53). See Appendix E; Nepalese King to Chinese *Ambans*, 1904 B.S. Jestha Sudi 13 Roj 7 (July 1847), National Archives of Nepal, Kathmandu (hereafter referred as NAN), *Poka* No. 2, Letter No. 158; Tri Ratna Manandhar and Tirtha Prasad Mishra "Cavenagh and Rose on Nepal's Mission to China", *Rolamba*, Vol 3, No. 1(January-March 1983), pp. 46-47 and Nepal, f.n. no. 3, pp. 175-206.
7. Chinese *Ambans* to King Rajendra, Tao Kwang Year 27 and 18 day of Falgun 1903 B.S. (February 1847), MFA, *Poka* No. Pa 64. See Appendix A.
8. Chinese *Ambans* to King Surendra, Tao Kwang Year 27 and 25th day of Jestha 1904 (June 1847), MFA, *Poka* No. Pa 64. See Appendix B.
9. Manandhar and Mishra, f.n.no. 6, p. 47.
10. Nepalese King to Chinese *Ambans*, 1904 B.S. Dutiya Jestha Sudi 14 Roj 1 (July 1847), MFA, *Poka* No. Pa 64. See Appendix D.

consisted of forty-five persons.[11] *Sardar* Ahibarna Basnyat was the deputy leader of the mission[12] and some other important members of the mission were *Sardar* Bhakta Singh Adhikari,[13] Harkha Bahadur Pantha, Ujir Singh Basnyat, Ambar Dhoj Pantha, Santa Bir Basnyat, Chhatra Singh Khadka and Khardar Ranga Nath Padhya.[14] With them, *Bhariya Nayak* Tikhulia, Gambhir Pantha, Jorawar Singh, Tikhul Singh, Ram Narsingh, Interpreter Ram Narayan and Indra Singh Khawas were also included in this 1847 Nepalese mission.[15] The leader and the deputy leader had included their sons Ambar Dhoj Pantha and Santa Bir Basnyat respectively as members of the mission.[16] The delegates carried an *arji* and presents from the Nepalese King Surendra to the Ch'ing Emperor Tao Kwang. The total cost of the mission of 1847 was Rs. 22,673|||^{3} whereas, the presents to the Ch'ing Emperor Tao Kwang were estimated to be Rs. 4,789. The 1847 Nepalese mission had carried eighteen items as presents to the Ch'ing Emperor. Besides that the mission had also carried presents to the *Dhewas* of Kuti, *Talloye* of Digarcha, Lama of Digarcha, Raja Lama of Takayali, the four *Kajis* of Lhasa, the *Potala* Lama, the Chinese *Ambans* and the *Chundu* of Chindafu.[17]

The Nepalese mission reached Lhasa on Bhadra 16, 1904 B.S. (August 1847).[18] While in Lhasa the Nepalese delegation discussed with the Chinese *Ambans* concerning the overtaxation of the goods of the Nepalese merchants in Kuti-Kerung area, of which the *Ambans* assured the Nepalese mission of redressing Nepalese grievances. The Chinese *Ambans* had also informed the Nepalese King about the date of the departure of the Nepalese mission from

---

11. Nepalese King to Chinese *Ambans*, 1904 B.S. Pratham Jestha Sudi 1 Roj 7 (July 1847), NAN, *Poka* No. 2, Letter No. 158. See Appendix C.
12. In February 1843, he had been sent by the Nepalese Court to India to bring up General Mathabar Singh Thapa to Nepal.
13. Jnanmani has referred to Bhakta Singh Adhikari as Bhakta Bir Adhikari, see Nepal, f.n.no.3, p. 182.
14. Jnanmani has referred to Ranga Nath Padhya as Ranga Lal Upadhaya, see Nepal, f.n. no. 3, p. 182.
15. RNAH, Part 3, Serial No. 63 (53). See Appendix E.
16. *Ibid.* and Nepal, f.n. no.3, p. 182.
17. RNAH, Part 3, Serial No. 63(53). See Appendix E.
18. Chinese *Amban* to Nepalese King, Tao Kwang Year 27 and 16 day of Bhadra 1904 B.S. (August 1847), MFA, *Poka* No. Pa 64. See Appendix F.

Lhasa to Peking.[19] Afterwards the Nepalese delegation reached Peking on Falgun 16, 1904 B.S. (1848).[20] The Chinese Emperor Tao Kwang gave an audience to the members of the Nepalese mission, and, as usual presented a *Gajur* of *Manik* and a *Parwana* to the Nepalese King, and minor presents to the members of the Nepalese delegation.[21] A great feast was also arranged in honour of the mission.[22] The mission members were reported to have been entertained through Chinese plays, dance programmes, swimming, wrestling and fire works. The Nepalese mission left Peking on Chaitra Sudi 6, 1904 B.S. (1848)[23] and arrived at Lhasa in November 1848.[24] But the return journey of the Nepalese mission of 1847 was not happy one. Firstly, a porter ran away with the loads of goods.[25] Next, twenty six year old Ram Narayan, Chinese language interpreter and a member of the 1847 Nepalese mission, died of malaria fever in Szechuwan province.[26] Similarly, *Sardar* Ahibarna Basnyat, the deputy leader of the mission, died in Lhasa due to illness.[27] Above all, *Kazi* Surath Singh Pantha, the leader of the mission, also met with the same fate,[28] for he passed away at Lhasa just a day before he proposed to leave Lhasa for Kathmandu. Both *Kazi* Surath Singh Pantha and *Sardar* Ahibarna Basnyat were cremated at Lhasa according to Nepalees rites by their sons.[29] The remaining members of the mission, led by a son of late *Kazi* Surath Singh Pantha, arrived at Kathmandu in Falgun, 1905 B.S. (March 1849)[30] after a lapse of nearly twenty months.[31] The mission

19. Chinese *Ambans* to Nepalese King, Tao Kwang 27th year 8th month (1904 B.S.), MFA, *Poka* No.Pa 64. See Appendix G.
20. Nepal, f.n. no. 3, p. 183.
21. Tikhul Singh to Jang Bahadur, 1905 B.S. Jestha Badi 5 Roj 3 (May 1848), MFA, *Poka* No. Pa 64. See Appendix H.
22. Manandhar and Mishra, f.n.no. 6, p. 47.
23. Nepal, f.n.no. 3, p. 183.
24. Manandhar and Mishra, f.n.no. 6, p. 47.
25. Nepal, f.n. no. 3, p. 183.
26. *Ibid.*, p. 184.
27. Chinese *Ambans* to Nepalese King, Tao Kwang, 28th year 11th month 4th day (December 1848), MFA, *Poka* No. Pa 64. See Appedix I.
28. Draft Letter from Nepalese King to Chinese *Ambans*, 1905 B.S. Poush Badi 11, Roj 7 (December 1848), MFA, *Poka* No. Pa 64. See Appendix J.
29. Nepal, f.n.no. 3, p. 184.
30. *Ibid.*

members were warmly welcomed in Kathmandu. They were escorted by the musical bands and dancing groups to the royal palace, Hanuman Dhoka, where the *Parwana* sent by the Ch'ing Emperor Tao Kwang was duly presented to King Surendra.[32]

This twelfth five-yearly mission of 1847 was important due to the following reasons : Firstly, it was the first Nepalese quinquennial mission to China sent by Jang Bahadur, the founder of Rana regime in Nepal. Secondly, it was due to this mission that Chinese recognition of Nepalese King Surendra came in September 1847 earlier than British recognition. It was reported that as soon as the Ch'ing Emperor Tao Kwang knew of the arrival of the 1847 Nepalese five-yearly mission at Lhasa, he instructed the *Ambans* to recognize the new ruler of Nepal. Jang Bahadur in turn had also proudly informed the Ch'ing Emperor Tao Kwang about the Alau incident (in which ex-King Rajendra was easily defeated by Jang Bahadur's army) through the Nepalese envoy to China, *Kazi* Surath Singh Pantha, who was at that time on his way to Peking.[33] Thirdly, it was the first Nepalese complimentary five-yearly mission to China in which both the leader and the deputy leader of the mission passed away while they were on their way back to Nepal. Above all, it was perhaps through the 1847 Nepalese mission, Jang Bahadur seemed to have received information regarding the wide spread prevalence of opium smoking in China as well as the demand for opium in the Chinese market following the opium war of 1839-1842. That is why he initiated the technique of making a large profit by involving the 1852 Nepalese quinquennial mission to China in the opium trade. Thus the 1852 Nepalese mission inaugurated the system of carrying opium to sell in China, and the system continued till the last Nepalese mission to China in 1906.[34]

---

31. But Manandhar and Mishra have stated that the 1847 Nepalese quinquennial mission returned home after twenty two months. See Tri Ratna Manandhar and Tirtha Prasad Mishra, *Nepal's Quinquennial Missions to China*, Kathmandu: Purna Devi Manandhar and Puspa Mishra, 1986, p. 27.
32. Nepalese King to Chinese *Ambans*, 1906 B.S. Baisakh Sudi 10 Roj 4 (May 1849), MFA. *Poka* No. Pa 64. See Appendix K.
33. Manandhar and Mishra, f.n.no. 6, pp 47-48.
34. Vijay Kumar Manandhar, *Cultural and Political Aspects of Nepal-China Relations*, Delhi: Adroit Publishers, 1999, pp. 69-70.

Appendix A

सौगाद चाडै पठाउने – तौककाङ २७ वर्ष फागुन १८ जादा १९०३ सालमा श्री ५ राजेन्द्रलाई छिन्तारिन युतारिन अम्वाले लेखेको ....

(Chinese *Ambans* to King Rajendra instructing to send the Nepalese mission to Peking soon.)

Source : Ministry of Foreign Affairs, Kathmandu (MFA), *Poka* No. Pa 64.

Appendix B

मामुली सौगात पठाउन र आफु वाङ गादिमा राज गरेको अर्जि रित मिलेको रहेछ भन्ने चढाई पठाउला भन्या तौककाङ २७ ज्येष्ठ मैन्हा २५ जादा १९०४ सालमा श्री सुरेन्द्र छिन्तारीन युतारीन अम्वाले लेषेको ....

(Chinese *Ambans* to King Surendra referring to the sending of the Nepalese mission with presents and the forwarding of the newly ascended Nepalese King's *arji* to the Ch'ing court.)

Source : MFA, *Poka* No. Pa 64.

Appendix C

सं. १९०४ साल प्रथम जेष्ट सुदि १ रोज ७ श्री ५ वाट ल्हासाका अंवा २ के...............

उप्रांत अधिकारीत वमोजिम सौगात काजिहरुको नाम नभेसि अगावै लेषि पठाउनु भंन्या अर्ति शिक्षालेषी आउंदा टाढा देस मधेसवाट मगाउन्या चीज मगाई हाम्रा मुलुकमा भयाको चीज तयार गरि राष्याको छ असार महिनामा यहावाट हिडाई अधिकारीत वमोजिम ताहा पुगन्या गरि विदा गरौंला .... का दर्शन दंडवत गर्न जान्या अधिकारीत बमोजिम् काजी सर्दार षर्दार भला मानिसको नाम तमिसि समेत सुसायतमा ञाहावाट हिडदछन् भनि अगावै आफुहरु छेउ पठाउला भनि सं. १९०३ साल चैत्र सुदि १३ रोज २ का दिन हामिवाट आफुहरुलाई लेषि गयाको हो. पुगी विस्तार बुझ्नु भयो हो. आफुहरुका अर्ति माफीक ञाहा नहुन्या चीज टाढा देस मधेसवाट झिकाई अधिकारीत वमोजीम ५ वर्षको मामुली सौगात अर्जि समेत् .... को दर्शन दंडवत गर्न पैचिन जान षटायाका काजी सुरत सिं पंथ सर्दार अहि वर्ण वस्न्यात षरिदार सुवेदार ज्मादार दोभास्या अरु वाहीया माफिक भला मानीस गरि अधिकारीत वमोजीम् जना ४५ लाई कुतिको वाटो गरि ल्हासा पुगी आफुहरुको दर्शन गरि हाम्रा दुष दर्द सवै विंति गरि आफुहरुको अर्ति शिक्षा लि पैचिन जानु भनि अह्राई आषाड महिनाका १४ दिन जांदा ञाहावाट विदा गरि पठाउंछौं. वाटमा ढिल नगरि सरासर जानन् ....

(Nepalese King informing the Chinese *Ambans* regarding the

dispatching of forty-five member Nepalese mission under the leadership of *Kazi* Surath Singh Pantha.)

Source : National Archives of Nepal, Kathmandu (NAN), *Poka* No. 2, Letter No. 158.

Appendix D

अघि वुवाज्यूका पाला देखी आफुहरुका अर्ति शिक्षा माफिक श्री ५ वादसाहका शरण पिछ्या परी मानी आएको हो . असारका १४ जादा काजी सर्दारहरुलाई अर्जि सौगाद दिई विदा गरी पठाएको छ - १९०४ द्वितीया ज्येष्ठ सुदी १४ रोज १ मा श्री ५ वाट ल्हासा २ अंवालाई ....

(Nepalese King informing the Chines *Ambans* about the departure of the Nepalese mission from Kathmandu.)

Source : MFA, *Poka* No. Pa 64.

Appendix E

<u>१९०४ साल</u>

चीन श्री वादसाहलाई ५ वर्षको मामुलि सौगात गयाको मार्फत काजि सुरथ पंथ सर्दार अैवर्ण वस्न्यात दुतिय जेष्ठ वदि १३ रोज..............................

श्री वादसाह के ४७८९

मुगाको माला १ के दाना १०९ के तोला ....४३।७५।के........ ३३८[२]॥

सुनौला तास थान १ के तोला .... १३५।४।के .... २४५।.॥

किंषाप थान .... २० के .... १९५०॥/॥

रंगरंगका वनात वस्ता .... २३ के .... १०००।[३]२

गलेता थान .... ४ के अं. १००

कोठि र मोहरिमा सुनौला तार कसिका।को तोडेवाल्वदुक २ के .. १३०

सुनौला मोल्माकोथिकंठी सुनौला कवुजा तरोवार ४ के अं. ५४

तावामा सुनौला मोल्मा हस्तीहाड का वी डर्क २।२ स्मेत

मेगजीनको षुकुरी ४ के अं. ३२

तावामा सुनौला मोल्मा विराकोथी मेगजीन का षुडा २ के अं. ५५

सुनौला तार कसिपाना सेरषान कटार ....२ के ७४

केपवाला मैसराजाम स्मेत संदुकी वन्दुक १ के अं. ४००

गैडा षाग .... २ के अं. ७०

ठुला हाति दात .... ४ के अं. १६०

जायफल गोटा ....१०००के. अं. .... ६२॥

जाहाजी सुपारि धार्नि ....१० के. अं. .... १२॥

दक्षिणि सुपारि धार्नि ....६ के अं. ३३

लवाग धार्नि .... ६ के अं. ४८
दालचिनि धार्नि .... ५ के अं. .... २३॥

कुति का ढेवा २ के अंकवाल कासिवाल थान .....२ के अं. २५
टिगरिका चुइ के अंदाज .... १३॥
अं. कासिवाल थान १ के १२॥ सुपारि धार्नि ....१ के १।

डिगर्चा का तालोय के .... १३॥
अं. कासिवाल थान १ के १२॥ सुपारि धार्नि १ के १।

डिगर्चा का लामा के १७६
किंषाप थान १ के ४८ सुलतानी वनात थान १ के अं.१०४
मेहि अधर थान १ के अं.४ अलैचि दाना धार्नि ४ के ... ८
हस्ति हाड का फुरु .... २ के अं..... १२

ल्हासा तक्यालिका राजालामा के १७३
किंषाप थान १ के ४५ सुलतानी वनात थान १ के अं.१०४
मेहि अधर थान १ के अं. ४ अलैचि दाना धार्नि ४ के ... ८
हस्ति हाड का फुरु २ के अं. १२

ल्हासाका ४ काजि के १६१
किंषाप थान ४ के १५६ सुपारि धार्नि ४ के अं. ... ५

ल्हासाका पोतला लामा के .... १८४॥
किंषाप थान १ के ५० सुलतानी वनात थान १ के अं.१०४
मेहिअधर थान २ के अं. ८ सुपारि धार्नि २ के अं. .... २॥
अलैचि दाना धा ४ के ८ हस्तिहाड का फुरु २ के अं. १२

ल्हासाका अम्वा २ के .... ५६६॥३॥
किंषाप थान ....२ के २१६
सुलतानि वनात वस्ता ....२ के ९९
तावाको मोल्मा कवुजा कोथि भयाको तरोवार ....२ के अं. १२
मोहरिर कोथिमा सुनौला तार्कसिकाम भयाको तोडेवाल बन्दुक २ के अं. १००
तावामा सुनौला मोल्मा काजो कोथी कर्द २।२ स्मेत अं. २०
षुकुरि ....२ के अं. ६
गरिगोटा ३० के धार्नि ....१६२॥२के अं. ३॥३॥
छोहारा धार्नि ....४ के अं. ५।
ठुलो हाति दात ....२ के अं. ८०
दक्षिणि सुपारि धार्नि ....२ के अं. ११
वदाम धार्नि ....२ के अं. २॥।
सुपारि धार्नि ....४ के अं. ५।
दालचिनि धार्नि ....१ के अं. ५॥।

छिन्दफु का चन्दु के १४४
किंषाप थान १ के ४० सुलतानी वनात वस्ता १ के अं. १०४

दर्वारि षर्च		१९३८॥
नगद मोहर रु		१०००
जिन्सि		९३८॥
किंषाप थान ७ के २२६	वाफदा थान २ के	२१॥।
सुलतानी वनात वस्ता २ के ८१॥/१२ह.	फर्कावादि छी १६ के अं.	८०
लाल वनात वस्ता १ के अं. ६६	षारुवा थान २० के अं.	६०
कासिवाल थान २० के अं. २००	चौविसा थान ३० के अं.	९०
गरि धार्नि २९१॥ के अं. १०॥	लवांग धार्नि १५॥ के अं.	९॥
दालचिनी धार्नि २ के अं. ११॥	दक्षिणि सुपारि धा १ के अं.	५॥
सुषमेल धार्नि ९२ के अं. १८	वदाम धार्नि १ के अं.	१।
वलाचिनी धार्नि ५ के अं. १०	सुपारि धार्नी ५ के अं.	६॥/
छालाको म्यान षुकुरि	१० के अं.	३०

येस साल श्री वादसाह लाइ श्री ५ महाराजाधिराजवाट गादि मा राज गर्नु हुदा षवरको अर्जिजादा पत्र चिन्ह के सुनौला तास थान १ के तोला ४१ के . २०५

अैजन सौगात पुऱ्याउन जान्या मानीसहरुके षर्च र कपडा		१४८४६
काजि सुरथ पंथ के		३९०३॥
नगद मोरु		३०००
जिन्सी		९०३॥
.... पगरि थान	१ के अं.	१५
सालजोडा	१ के	४००
सालका रुमाल	१ के	७०
.... का कमर वन्द	१ के	१००
किंषाप थान	२ के अं.	३००
दलंधरामाल्दही थान	१ के अं.	१५
विहारि थान	२ के अं.	३
षासा हात	२ के अं.	॥

सर्दार अैवर्ण वस्न्यात के		३९९१॥॥
नगद वालि मोरु		३६००
जिन्सी अंदाज		३९१॥॥
३४ गजी पगरी १ के ५	साल जोडा १ के	१७०
साल्का रुमाल १ के ५०	किंषाप थां १॥ के	१५०
माल्दहि थान २ के १५	चिङ्गली हा ४ के	१॥।
षासा हात	२ के	॥

<u>आठ पगरि ८ के</u>

सुवेदार भक्तसिं अधिकारी के	६०६।
नगद मोरु	४५४॥
जिन्सी	१५१॥।

२७ गजी पगरि १ के अं.३॥	साल फर्द १ के	५०
किंषा थान १ के अं. ८०	वेस्माल्दहि थां १ के अं.	१२॥
कासिवाल थां ।१ के अं. ५	चिङ्गलि हा २ के	॥।

हर्ष वहादुर पंतके .... ४३२।[३]॥
नगद मोरु .... २५६॥
जिन्सी........ १७५॥।[३]॥

२७ गजी पगरि १ के अं. ३॥	साल फर्द १ के	८०
कासिवाल थां ॥के अं५	किंषाप थां १ के अं.	८०
वेसमाल्दहि थां १के अं. ६।	चिङ्गलि हा २॥ के अं.	१
षासा हा	२ के अं.	[३]॥

उजीर सिं वस्न्यात के .... ३५३॥[३]॥
नगद मोरु .... २५६॥
जिन्सी अंदाज........ ९७[३]॥

२७ गजि पगरि १ के ३॥	सालफर्द १ के	२५
वेस्माल्दहि थां १ के १२॥	किंषाप थां १ के	५०
चिङ्गली हा २॥ के १	कासीवाल्थां ॥ के	५
षासा हात........	२ के	[३]॥

अम्वरधोज पंथ के .... ३५३॥[३]॥
नगद मोरु .... २५६॥

२७ गजि पग्री १ के ३॥	साल्फर्द १ के	२५
कासिवाल थां ॥ के ५	किंषाप थां १ के	५०
वेस्माल्दहि थां १ के १२॥	चिङ्गली हा २॥ के	१
षासा हात........		२ के [३]॥

संतवीर वस्न्यातके .... ३४५ ॥।[३]॥
नगद मोरु .... २५६॥
जिन्सी अंदाज........ ८९।[३]॥

२७ गजि पग्री १ के ३॥	साल्फर्द १ के	२५॥।
कासिवाल्थां ॥ के ५	चिङ्गली हा २॥ के	१
वेस्माल्दहि थां १ के १२	किंषाप थां १ के	४२
षासा हात २ के		[३]॥

छत्रसिं षडका के .... ३४५।[३]॥
नगद मोरु .... २५६॥
जिन्सी अंदाज........ ८८॥।[३]॥

२७ गजि पग्री १ के ३॥	सालफर्द १ के	२५॥।
कासिवाल थान ॥ के ५	चिङ्गली हा २॥ के	१
वेस्माल्दहि थान १ के १२॥	किंषाप थान १ के	४१
षासा हात........	२ के	[३]॥

.... दार रंगनाथ पाध्या के .... ३५०³॥
नगद मोरु .... २५६॥
जिन्सी.. ९३ ॥³॥
२७ गजी पग्री १ के अं. ३॥ वेस्माल्दहि था १॥ के अं. १८
कासिवाल था ॥ के अं. ५ किंषाप थान १ के ४१।
सालफर्द १ के २४ चिङ्गली हात २॥ के अं. १
षासा हात...२ के अं. ³॥

दोभास्या के .... ७९॥³॥
नगद छतीस सय मध्ये x
जिनसि .... ७९॥³॥
२७ गजी पग्री १ के अं. ३॥ कासिवाल्थां ॥ के अं. ५
किंषाप थान १ के ३८॥ माल्दहि थान १ के अं. ७॥
सालफर्द १ के २४ चिङ्गली हा २॥ के अं. १
षासा हात .... २ के अं. ³॥

<u>६ पगरि का जना ६ के</u>

भरिया नाएक टिषुल्या के .... २०९।³॥
नगद मोरु .... १५७॥
जिन्सी.. ५१॥।³॥
२२ गजि पग्री १ के अं ३ कोपाचौविसा थां के अं. ३॥
किंषाप थान १ के २९। कासिवाल थां ॥ के अं. ५
..........स फर्द १ के अं. १० चिङ्गली हात २॥ के अं. १
षासा हात..२ के अं. ³॥

.... पंथ के .... ५५³॥
नगद छतीस सय मध्ये ....
जिन्सी.. ५५³॥
२२ गजि पग्री १ के अं. ३ वेस्माल्दहि थान १ के अं. १०
किंषाप थान १ के ३६ चिङ्गली हात २॥ के अं. १
कासिवाल थां ॥ के अं. ५ षासा हात २ के अं. ³॥

.... वस्न्यात के .... ५७॥³॥
नगद छतीस सय मध्ये ....
जिन्सी अंदाज... ५७॥³॥
२२ गजि पग्री १ के अं. ३ कासिवाल्थान ॥ के अं. ५
किंषाप थान १ के ३६ चिङ्गली हात २॥ के अं. १
वेस्माल्दहि थान १ के अं. १२॥ षासा हात २ के अं. ³॥

जोरावर सिं के .... ६०³॥
नगद छतिस सय मध्ये ....

जिन्सी अंदाज... ६०^{३}॥

२२ गजी पग्री १ के अं. ३		वेस्माल्दहि थां १ के अं.	१२॥
किंषाप थान १ के ३८॥		चिङ्गली हात २॥ के अं.	१
कासिवाल थान ॥ के अं. ५		षासा हात २ के अं.	^{३}॥

रामनर सिं के ... ५४ ॥^{३}॥

नगद छतिस सय मध्ये ...

जिन्सी अंदाज... ५४॥^{३}॥

२२ गजि पग्री १ के अं. ३		कासिवाल थान ॥ के अं.	५
किंषाप थान १ के ३३		चिङ्गली हात २॥ के अं.	१
वेस्माल्दहि थां १ के अं. १२॥		षासा हात २ के अं.	^{३}॥

इन्द्रसिं षवास के ... ४६॥^{३}॥

नगद छतीस. सय मध्ये ...

जिन्सी अंदाज...

४६॥^{३}॥

२२ गजि पग्री १ के अं. ३		कासिवाल्थां ॥ के अं.	५
किंषाप थान १ के २५		चिङ्गली हात २॥ के अं.	१
वेस्माल्दहि थां १ के अं. १२॥		षासा हात २ के अं.	^{३}॥

आठ पगरि मध्ये १ छ पगरि मध्ये ५ तिलंगा जना २९ को मा काजिका साथ जान्या जना ३५ के षर्च मोरु ३६००

फर्मायसी माल षरीद के जिम्मा काजि सर्दार मोरु ... १x

जिम्मा षर्दार रंगनाथ धिमिन्या सलांषर १ के चाति तो ३८।१ के

अैजन सौगात जादा षोल वेठन गैह्न काम काम के ... ४३७

अर्जिका संदुस के अंदाज... ७४^{२}॥

सुनौला तास तोला १६।२।५ के ६५		रुपौला गोटा तो ।६। के	१॥
रुवा पाव १ के ^{२}॥		जर्द विहारि हा ६के	॥।
... हा ... ८ के ४		जर्द वनात गज ॥ के	२
... अत्तर तोला ... ।२। के			॥।

श्री ५ महाराजाधिराजवाट गादिमा राज गर्नु भयाका ... र का अर्जिका संदुस के अंदाज ... ७१॥1।

... तोला १६।३। के ६५^{३}		स. गोटा तोला ।६। के	१॥
रुवा पाव ... १ के ^{२}॥		विहारि हात ६ के	॥।
... हात ४ के २		जर्द वनात गज ॥ के	२

... षोल गैह्न के अंदाज... ६४^{२}

वनात गज ८।^{२} के ३३॥		रेसम तोला १।२। के	॥।^{२}
... वतु तो २।५। के १०		मषमलष गां १। के	२॥
... थान १५ के १५		चौविसा हात १५ के	२।

सौगात का भारि कुति सम्म पुऱ्याउन जान्या लुभु सेरा का भरिया जना ६० के

षर्च पै रु .... ९०॥
अर्जि राषन्या संदुसमा चित्रकार लेषन्या भाजु मोचा चित्रकारि के पै रु.२
संदुस वनाउन्या कर्मिहरु के पै रु. ५
सौगातका काज काम गर्न्या ल्छे साना कौसिका वैठकया ३ टहलुवा २ जम्मा जना ५ के अंदाज.. १२९॥[२]॥
.... ४ गजी पग्री ३ के १५ अं. कासिवाल थां १॥ के २७
.... अधर थान ३ के १८ कोचिंष गां ६ वावत् मोरु ४२
पटनावाल विहारी थां ३ के १०॥ षासा हात ६ के ॥[२]॥
.... चौविसा थान ३ के १०॥ टहलुवा २ के चौवि थां २ के ६

(The detailed expenses and the list of presents sent along with the 1847 Nepalese Quinquennial mission to China under the leadership of *Kazi* Surath Singh Pantha.)

Source : Royal Nepal Army Head-Quarters (RNAH), Part 3, Serial No. 63 (53).

Appendix F

मामुली अर्जी सौगात र आफु वाङ गादीमा राज गर्‍याको अर्जि सौगात लिई सुरथ सिं पन्त ञाहा आइपुगे तोक्काङ २७ भाद्र मैन्हाका १६ दिन जादा १९०४ मा श्री ५ मा वड्ा यिन्तारीन अम्वाले लेखेको ....

(Chinese *Amban* informing the Nepalese King about the arrival of the Nepalese mission in Lhasa.)

Source : MFA, *Poka* No. Pa 64.

Appendix G

८ मैन्हाका २४ दिन जादा ल्हासावाट हिडछन् - तोक्काङ २७ साल ८ मैन्हा .... दिन १९०४ श्री ५ मा यिन्तारीन युतारीन अम्वाले लेषेको ....

(Chinese *Ambans* informing the Nepalese King about the date of the departure of the Nepalese mission from Lhasa to Peking.)

Source : MFA, *Poka* No. Pa 64.

Appendix H

पेचीन पुगी श्री ५ वादसाहको दर्सन गरी श्री ५ सर्कारलाई माणिकको गजुर ४५ जवानलाई साविक मामुली वमोजिम वक्स भयो . विदा भै फर्की सिंगाफु आइपुग्यौ भन्ने प्राइममिनिष्टरलाई १९०५ साल ज्येष्ठ वदी ५ रोज ३ मा तिखुल सिं ले पठाएको ....

(Tikhul Singh informing Prime Minister Jang Bahadur about the Chinese Emperor granting an audience to the members of the Nepalese mission and presenting a *Gajur* of *Manik* to the Nepalese

King.)

Source : MFA, *Poka* No. Pa 64.

Appendix I

काजी सुरथ सिं पन्त ल्हासावाट हिडन्या वषत्मा आकास चलिका वेथाले मुक्त भयो. निजका छोरा र प्रमाना त्राहावाट ११ मैन्हाका १३ दिन जादा पुऱ्याउन पठाऱ्यू. लिन पठाउनु तौकाङ्ग २८ साल ११ मैन्हा ४ दिन जादा १९०५ साल्मा श्री ५ मा युतारीन छुतारीन अम्वाले लेषेको ....

(Chinese *Ambans* to Nepalese King reporting the death of *Kazi* Surath Singh Pantha at Lhasa.)

Source : MFA, *Poka* No. Pa 64.

Appendix J

काजी सर्दार दुवै जना ल्हासामा मुक्त भयाको षवर आफुहरुवाट लेखी आउदा वहुतै फिकी भयो. आफुहरुवाट पनी भरिसक्ये उपाये गर्दा पनि केही नलागी दैवको इच्छा गरी टर्दो रहेनछ भन्दा इत्यादि १९०५ साल पौष वदी ११ रोज ७ श्री ५ वाट ल्हासा २ अंवालाई लेखेको नक्कल ....

(Draft letter from Nepalese King to Chinese *Ambans* expressing grief at the deaths of both the leader and the deputy-leader of the Nepalese mission at Lhasa.)

Source : MFA, *Poka* No. Pa 64

Appendix K

सम्वत १९०५ साल फागुन सुदी १३ रोज ४ श्री ५ चीन वादशाहका हजुर्मा श्री ५ सर्कारवाट गयाको अर्जीको मसौदा. वादसाहवाट वकसी पठाउनु भयाको पर्माना आउछ भन्ने षवर आई पुगनी वित्तीकै सवै भला मानीस ली नाच तमासा उत्सव गरी टाढा सम्म लिन गै कांतिपुर दर्वारमा ल्याई गद्दि सिंहासनमा राषी दर्सन दण्डवत गयौ. हुकुं चित्त लगाई सुन्यौ. आफ्ना वुवाज्यूको रजाई मुखपेट येकत्व भै सरण पिछामा रही अंवाका अर्ति शिक्षा वमोजिम काम गऱ्या देषी म षुसी हुंला भंन्या इत्यादी वेहोराको यो अर्जि फिर्ता भै १९०६ साल बैशाष सुदी १० रोज४ का दिन. अर्को लेषी गयो भन्या लेषियाको अर्जिको मसौदा............१

(Nepalese King to Chinese *Ambans* informing about the grand reception of the Nepalese mission in Kathmandu.)

Source : MFA, *Poka* No. Pa. 64.

* * *

13

Kazi Gambhir Singh Adhikari's Mission of 1852

In accordance with the arrangement of the mission system, Nepal sent her thirteenth quinquennial mission to China in 1852. The 1852 Nepalese quinquennial mission has not been mentioned in the Chinese Imperial records.[1] But the Nepalese and Indian archival documents clearly state of Nepal's sending of five-yearly mission to China in 1852. Going through the Nepalese documents, it seems that in 1850, the Chinese *Amban* informed the Nepalese government about the death of Emperor Tao Kwang and the accession of the new Ch'ing Emperor Hsien Feng. He also instructed the Nepalese government to send special presents and the usual five-yearly presents to the new Ch'ing Emperor along with the forthcoming 1852 Nepalese quinquennial mission to Peking.[2] Accordingly Nepal sent her five-yearly mission to China under the leadership of *Kazi* Gambhir Singh Adhikari at the scheduled time in 1852.[3] But the ill fate of the 1852 Nepalese mission started at the beginning, when both the leader and the deputy leader designate *Kazi* Ran Mehar Singh Adhikari and *Sardar* Bir Man Thapa were to be dropped on account of their illnesses. *Kazi* Gambhir Singh Adhikari and *Sardar* Samsher Jang Thapa were appointed in their

---

1. J.K. Fairbank and S.Y. Teng, "On the Ch'ing Tributary System", *Harvard Journal of Asiatic Studies*, Vol. VI, 1941, pp. 195-198.
2. Chinese *Amban* to King Surendra, Hon Fong 1st year 10th month 12th day (1851) and Hon Fong 2nd year 3rd month 7th day (1852), Ministry of Foreign Affairs, Kathmandu (hereafter mentioned as MFA), *Poka* No. Pa 64. See Appendices C and F. See also, Jnanmani Nepal, *Nepal-Bhot Chin Sambandha Ka Kehi Sanskritik Paksha* (Some Cultural Aspect of Nepal-Tibet China Relations), Kathmandu: Royal Nepal Academy, 2045 B.S., pp 437-438.
3. It is interesting to note that one writer has mentioned that Prime Minister Jang Bahadur himself led the Nepalese quinquennial mission to China in 1853 and on that occasion he received the Chinese title *Thong-Lin-Pimma-Kokang-Wang-Shang* from the Chinese Emperor, which is not true at all. See Ramji Upadhyaya, *Nepal Ko Itihas Arthat Digdarshan* (History of Nepal or Survey), Banaras: *Subba* Homnath Kedarnath, 2007 B.S., p. 275.

place.[4] The 1852 Nepalese mission included *Sardar* Bhimsen Rana, Badal Singh Adhikari, Bharat Karki, Dal Bhanjan Adhikari, Pitambar Sahi; Kalu Khatri, *Khardar* Bhim Nar Singh, *Bhariya Nayak* Dhan Bir, *Jamadar* Karbir Adhikari, Gambhir Bista, Bhairab Singh, Keshar Basnyat and Ridhi Man. This Nepalese mission had carried the usual five-yearly presents and special presents to the new Ch'ing Emperor, Hsien Feng.[5] Regarding the usual five-yearly presents as well as special presents to the Ch'ing Emperor, it was estimated to be Rs. 8666।।। and Rs. 10399′ respectively. The total cost of the 1852 mission was estimated to be Rs. 44,955।।।^{2}।।।. It had carried eighteen items as five-yearly general presents to the Ch'ing Emperor. Besides that the mission had also carried presents to the *Dhewas* of Kuti, the four *Kajis* of Lhasa, Raja Lama of Takayali, the *Potala* Lama, the Chinese *Ambans*, the *Chundu* of Chindafu and the *Chundu* of Sindafu.[6] The 1852 Nepalese mission had carried twenty six various items as special presents to the new Ch'ing Emperor Hsien Feng. Some of the important items of the special presents carried by the 1852 mission to the Ch'ing Emperor included necklaces of pearls and corals, weapons, clothes, spices, binoculars, rhinoceros horns, ivory, etc. The Nepalese mission had also carried special presents to *Talloye* of Digarcha, Khotu Thuwang and Tuthuwang.[7]

The Nepalese mission left Kathmandu in August 1852[8],

---

4. Nepalese King to Chinese *Amban,* 1908 B.S. Poush Sudi 6 Roj 1 (1851) and 1909 B.S. Jestha Sudi 12 Roj 1 (30 May 1852), MFA, *Poka* No. Pa 64. See Appendices D and E. See also Tri Ratna Manandhar and Tirtha Prasad Mishra, *Nepal's Quinquennial Missions to China*, Kathmandu: Purna Devi Manandhar and Puspa Mishra, 1986, pp. 27-28.
5. Royal Nepal Army Head-quarters (hereafter referred as RNAH), Part 3, Serial No. 63 (53). See Appendix G.
6. *Ibid.*
7. *Ibid.*, See also Tirtha Prasad Mishra, "Shree Panch Surendra Ko Chinia Badshah Lai Upahar" (King Surendra's presents to Chinese Emperor), *Garima*, Year 8 No. 1, Vol. No. 93, Bhadra 2047 B.S., pp. 35-37.
8. While reporting to the government of India in May 1854, British Resident Ramsay has stated that the 1852 Nepalese mission left Kathmandu in August 1852. See Ramsay to Secretary, Govt. of India, 6 May 1854, Foreign Dept. Sec., 26 May 1854, No. 50, National Archives of India, New Delhi (hereafter mentioned as NAI). See Appendix A. But in another report to the government of India in June 1866, the same British Resident Ramsay had mistakenly mentioned that the 1852 Nepalese mission left Nepal in

and despite the deaths of the Nepalese mission's horses and yaks in Lojhome area[9] reached Peking on schedule, and was received with the usual formalities and friendliness. But the journey of the 1852 Nepalese mission was not happy one. Firstly, *Kazi* Gambhir Singh Adhikari, the leader of the Nepalese mission, died on the way in around Magh, 1909 B.S. (1853).[10] Next, *Sardar* Samsher Jang Thapa, the deputy leader of the mission, also met with the same fate, for he passed away at Siling Jhayang town due to illness in 1910 B.S. (1853).[11] Moreover, the 1852 mission had met with great hardships while returning from Peking, and in addition to the leader and deputy leader, several other members of the mission passed away while returning from Peking.[12] The 1852 Nepalese delegates also seemed to have lost some of their goods during their journey to China.[13] Due to the deaths of the leader and deputy leader, the leadership of the 1852 mission passed to Bhimsen Rana. At the time of the return journey of the Nepalese mission from Peking, the T'aiping rebellion in China had reached alarming proportions. That is why Bhimsen Rana was compelled to follow an indirect route to Tibet. According to Nepalese accounts,[14] the delegates suffered all sorts of humiliations and maltreatment on the return journey, especially in the Kham areas of eastern Tibet. The British sources,[15] however, state that Jang Bahadur exaggerated the issue of the maltreatment of the 1852 Nepalese mission as a pretext to

---

July 1852. See Ramsay to Secretary, Govt. of India, 9 June 1866, Foreign Dept. Polt A, June 1866, No. 163, NAI.

9. Chinese *Amban* to Nepalese King, Hon Fong 2nd year 9th month 7th day (1909 B.S.), MFA, *Poka* No. Pa 64. See Appendix H.
10. Samsher Jang Bahadur Thapa's letter dated 1909 B.S. Magh Sudi 15 (1853), MFA, *Poka* No. Pa 64. See Appendix I.
11. Bhimsen Rana's *arji* to Gen. Krishna Bahadur Rana dated 1910 B.S. (1853), MFA, *Poka* No. Pa 64. See Appendix J.
12. Bhimsen Rana's *arji* to *Shree Tin* Jang dated 1910 B.S. (1853), MFA, *Poka* No. Pa 64. See Appendix K.
13. Chinese *Amban* to Nepalese King, Hon Fong 4th year 9th month 17th day (1854), MFA, *Poka* No. Pa 64. See Appendix L.
14. Pudma Jung Bahadur Rana, *Life of Maharaja Sir Jung Bahadur*, Kathmandu: Ratna Pustak Bhandar, Reprint, 1980, p. 173, and Prem R. Uprety, *Nepal-Tibet Relations 1850-1930*, Kathmandu: Puga Nara, 1980, pp. 62-63.
15. Ramsay to Secretary, Govt. of India, 6 May 1854, Foreign Dept. Sec., 26 May 1854, No. 50, NAI. See Appendix A.

declare war against Tibet in 1855. The mission seemed to have reached Kerung by Baisakh Badi 7, 1911 B.S. (1854).[16] It had also recorded a detailed and systematic summary of the routes from Nepal's Tatopani area to Peking as travelled by *Sardar* Samsher Jang Thapa, the deputy leader of the 1852 Nepalese mission.[17] Finally the Nepalese mission arrived at Kathmandu in 1911 B.S. Jestha Badi 11 Roj 2[18] (22 May, 1854)[19] after a lapse of about twenty one months. Interestingly the old tradition of granting a warm welcome to the Nepalese quinquennial mission was not observed this time due to the ill-treatment of the Nepalese mission by the Chinese government and Tibetan authorities.[20] Meanwhile the *Parwana* sent by the Ch'ing Emperor Hsien Feng was duly presented to King Surendra amidst the usual function.[21]

This thirteenth five-yearly mission of 1852 was important due to the following reasons : Firstly, this mission happened to be the third such Nepalese mission which had carried the usual five-yearly presents as well as special presents to the new Ch'ing Emperor. Secondly, the mission indeed proved to be most crucial, for the alleged abuse of this 1852 mission by the Khampas of Tibet prompted Nepal to declare war against Tibet in 1855. Thirdly, due to the unfavourable reception accorded to this 1852 Nepalese mission, relations between China and Nepal were interrupted and no Nepalese quinquennial mission was dispatched until 1866. Fourthly, it was the second such Nepalese quinquennial mission to China in which both the leader and the deputy leader of the mission passed away during their journey to China. Above all, the 1852 Nepalese mission had carried a lot of commodities, including nearly

16. RNAH, Part 3, Serial No. 63 (53). See Appendix M.
17. Kamal Dixit, *Mahachin* (Greater China), Lalitpur: Jagdamba Prakashan, 2055 B.S., pp. 7-9.
18. "Nepal Desh Ko Itihas" (History of Nepal), A Manuscript in the National Archives of Nepal, Kathmandu, Published in *Ancient Nepal*, No. 27, April 1974, p. 6.
19. Ramsay to Secretary, Govt. of India, 25 May 1854, Foreign Dept. Sec., 30 June 1854, No. 42, NAI. See Appendix B. See also H. Ambrose Oldfield, *Sketches From Nepal*, Vol. I, Delhi: Cosmo Publications, Reprint, 1981, pp. 411-412.
20. Purushottam Sham Shere J.B. Rana, *Jung Bahadur Rana: The Story of His Rise and Glory*, Delhi: Book Faith India, 1998, p. 80.
21. *Ibid.*, p. 81 and Oldfield, f.n.no. 19, p. 412.

three *Lakh* rupees (Rs. 3,00,000) worth of opium duty free, with the diplomatic privilege to sell them in China in spite of its legal ban in that country. It was also reported that the immense quantity of opium being smuggled into China was sold at high prices. Thus the 1852 Nepalese mission started the commercial activities by inaugurating the system of carrying opium to sell in China, and the system continued till the last Nepalese mission to China in 1906.[22]

Appendix A

From : Major G. Ramsay
Resident at Nepal

To : T.P. Grant Esqr.
Sec. to the Govt. of India
Foreign Dept.
Fort William

Dated Nepal Resd.
6th of May 1854

Sir,

I have the honour to report for the information of the noble the Governor Genl. in Council some occurrences at this Court.

Some days ago General Jung Bahadoor informed me that he has lately received a letter from Lahsa from a Lieutenant, a Nepalese officer who accompanied the quinquennial mission to China (that left Khatmandoo in the month of August 1852 and has not yet returned).... that he had lately had an interview with the Chief Umbah of Lahsa on the subject of the civil war now raging in China; and that, in replies to a question of the Umbah's, he had told him that he reports his Minister would send a body of troops to the Emperor of China's assistance if a requisition were made to him to do so.

General Jung Bahadoor......... for an opinion upon this subject, and begged my advice either in an official or in a private form, but I told him that, as my own government had remained strictly neutral with reference to the present state of affairs in China, I could not consistently with my duty give him any advice, or attempt to

---

22. For the details of the 1852 Nepalese mission's opium trade in China, see Vijay Kumar Manandhar, *Cultural and Political Aspects of Nepal-China Relations*, Delhi: Adroit Publishers, 1999, pp. 69-72.

influence him in the matter; moreover, that I could not at present trouble His Lordship the Governor General by a reference in so highly improbable a case.

His Excellency expressed himself disappointed and said that he felt himself placed in a dilemma; - that he had an equal regard for the two great Asiatic powers "the British Government in Hindostan" and "China", although his country was tributary only to the latter, and that he is anxious, if called upon to do so, and the British Government does not take umbrage at it, to send an army of 12 to 14000 men either into Thibet, or wherever else their presence may be useful in supporting the present Chinese dynasty; and he assured me that it is his intention to make a formal representation to the British Government on the subject, the moment he has any real grounds for believing that the Court of Pekin intend seeking the Goorkha aid.

I cannot but think that........ circumstances have occurred in Thibet that have placed this Durbar in an embarassing position and that the desire to send troops across the snows arises from some indignity that has been offered to the Nepalese embassy; regarding which, all kinds of rumours are afloat; - amongst others, that the Chief Sardars who were in charge of its have been murdered, and that the Emperor of China indignantly refused the presents that were taken to him, saying that, as Jung Bahadoor chose to go to England with presents for Queen Victoria, he should either come to Pekin, or there should be war between the two countries - I totally discredit these reports, for I have seen an interesting letter descriptive of Pekin, and of the kind reception the mission....... with from the Emperor, which was addressed to the Minister here, by the Lieutenant who is now in charge of it. That officer reported the deaths of the principal Sirdars his superiors in the mission and of several other persons, and stated that it had met with great hardships and privations, and had been obliged to halt in several places, or to make considerable detours to avoid falling in with parties of troops hostile to the existing Government of China.

On several occasions the Minister has represented to me that he and his brothers are in a state of great anxiety about this mission for that they had........... into China by its means, fully three lacs of rupees worth of opium, Pearls.......... Just after the mission left Khatmandoo his Excellency professed to have sent........ only a very few thousand rupees worth of opium (he now says at least 2 lacs worth) and that he prevented his brothers and the Sirdars from adding to it a much larger quantity; for fear of detection and disgrace - but I am disposed to credit his present admission as being more in accordance with the Nepalese character.

The large sum of money the proceeds of the sale of all this smuggled property should now be in the charge of the Lieutenant, who may perhaps have been playing false, and have proved unable to resist the temptation of enriching himself, and who could easily find partisans amongst the notoriously corrupt and venal Chinese officials in Thibet. It is not at all improbable that he may have appropriated to himself this large sum of money and that the despatch of troops towards Lassa is in order to recover it - but, this is mere surmise on my part, or the Chinese authorities knowing as they necessarily must do how large a treasure is in his custody may have exacted heavy payments from him, and perhaps detained him (the mission is now several months overdue) on his refusing to comply with their demands.

The....... that the Emperor of China will now (he might have done to.......) call upon the Nepalese Government for assistance appeared to me to be so unlikely that I determined not to trouble His Lordship the Governor General by reporting which General Jung Bahadoor had communicated to me on the subject; at all events until I heard something more about it. ....

Source : Foreign Department Secret, 26 May 1854, No. 50, National Archives of India, New Delhi (NAI).

Appendix B

From : Ramsay, Resident at Nepal

To : Secretary to the Government of India , Foreign Department Fort William

Dated May 25th 1854

.... The Mission also somewhat unexpectedly made its appearance, bearing a letter for the Maharajah from the Emperor of China.

.... His Excellency states that Lt. Bheem Sen Rana who succeeded to the charge of the Chinese mission on the death of its principal leader, had interviews both with the Chinese umbah or

Governor of Lhasa, with the four Tibetan Kajees or umbahs who were formerly for a short period tributary to Nepal.

Source : Foreign Department Secret, 30 June 1854, Nos.42-43, NAI.

Appendix C

मामुली सौगात र गादीमा राज भयाको सगुन सौगात आउदो साल पठाउनु भन्ने हानफोन १ साल १० मैन्हा १२ दिन जादा १९०८ सालमा श्री ५ सुरेन्द्रलाई युतारीन अंवाले लेखेको ....

(Chinese *Amban* to King Surendra instructing to send the Nepalese mission to China next year.)

Source : Ministry of Foreign Affairs, Kathmandu (MFA), *Poka* No. Pa 64.

Appendix D

ञाहा भएको र मधेसवाट झीकाउन्या चीज जति सवै तयार गरी काजि रणमेहर सिं अधिकारी सर्दार वीरमान थापाहरुलाई षटन गरी राखेको छ भन्या १९०८ साल पौष सुदी ६ रोज १ मा श्री ५ वाट ल्हासाका युतारीन अम्वालाई लेषेको...............................

(Nepalese King to Chinese *Amban* informing about the collecting of the presents to be sent along with the Nepalese mission under the leadership of *Kazi* Ran Mehar Singh Adhikari and *Sardar* Bir Man Thapa.)

Source : MFA, *Poka* No. Pa 64.

Appendix E

अघि षटन भयाका काजी सर्दारहरु असक वेरामी हुदा फेरी क़ाजी गंभीर सिं अधिकारी सर्दार सम्सेर थापाहरु ४५ जना असारको २१ दिन जादा आउछन्– १९०९ साल ज्येष्ठ सुदि १२ रोज १ मा श्री ५ वाट युतारीन् अम्वालाई लेषेको.............................

(Nepalese King to Chinese *Amban* informing about the new appointment of *Kazi* Gambhir Singh Adhikari and *Sardar* Samsher Jang Thapa in place of the leader and deputy leader designate of the Nepalese mission.)

Source : MFA, *Poka* No. Pa 64.

Appendix F

मामुली सौगातको र नञा गादिमा राज गऱ्याको सगुन को मालको फाट षोली पठाउनु भन्या र नञां डोअम्वा स्वर्गे हुनु भयो भन्या हान फोङ २ साल ३ मैन्हा

७ दिन जादा १९०९ सालमा श्री ५ मा युतारीन अम्वाले लेखेका.................
(Chinese *Amban* to Nepalese King instructing to send the detailed list of the general and special presents to be sent along with the Nepalese mission to the Ch'ing court.)

Source : MFA, *Poka* No. Pa 64.

Appendix G

१९०९ साल

चीन श्री वादसाहलाइ सौगात गयाको मार्फत काजि गंभीर सिं अधिकारी सर्दार सम्सेर जङ् थापा मिति श्रावराा वदि १ रोज .... ४४९५५।।।[२]।।।

५ वर्ष को मामुली

श्री वादसाह के .... ८६६६।।।
मुगामाला १ दाना १०९ के तोला ३८।५। के मोरु........ २६९।।
सुनौला तास थान २ के तोला ८२ ।.। के लाठ्साही..... १५३।।।
किंषाप थान २० के पैसा रु .... ५७१६।।।
...का वनात वस्ता ....१३ के मोरु.... १४५२।[२]
गलेता थान .... २ के पै रु .... ३६१′
कोठि र मोहरिमा सुनौला तार कसी काम
तोडेवाल वन्दुक .... २ के मोरु १००
सुनौला कोथि र कंठी कवुजा मषमलको म्यान भयाको
तरोवार .... ४ के मोरु ४०
...मा सुनौला मोल्मा का जो काथि हस्ति हाडका वीड
का म्यान कर्द २।२ स्मेतको षुकुरि ... ४ के मोरु २०
...मा सुनौला मोल्मा कोथी मषमलका म्यान भयाको
सेरषान कटार .... २ के मोरु २०
...मा सुनौला मोल्मा विरा कोथी मषमलका म्यान
भ... को पुडा .... २ के मोरु ... १०
मेगजीन को मैसराजाम स्मेतका दुइ नाल्या संदुकी
बन्दुक .... १ के मोरु... १००
गैडा षाग .... २ के मो रु ... २५
हाति दात .... ४ के मोरु ... २५०
जायफल गोटा .... १०१ के पै रु ... ४७।।[३]
दक्षिरिाा सुपारि धार्नि .... ६ के पैरु २१
सुपारि धार्नि .... १० के पैरु..... १२।।
लवाग धार्नि .... ६ के पैरु..... २७
दालचिनी धार्नि .... ५ के पैरु..... ४०

कुतिका ढेवा २ के कासिवाल थान ....२ के ५७।।
टिगरिका चुइ के कासिवाल थान ....१ के २७।।

डिगर्चाका लामा के.................................. २७६।[३]॥
किंषाप थान १ के १५९।[३]॥ ...... वनात वस्ता १ के मो १०२
चौविसा थान २ के ६ ...... हस्तीहाडका फुरु २ के मो ३
अलैचि दाना धार्नि ...... ४ के मोरु ६

ल्हासा का ४ काजि के ....४८२[२]।१
किंषाप थान ४ के ४७७[२]।१ ...... सुपारि धार्नि ४ के पै ५

ल्हासा तक्यालिका राजा लामा के ६४१
किंषाप थान १ के ५२५ .... वनात वस्ता १ के मो १०१
चौविसा थान २ के ६ .... हाति दात को फुरु २ के मो ३
अलैचि दाना ....धार्नि ४ के मो ६

ल्हासाका पोतला लामा के .... २९३॥
किंषाप थान १ के १६९ .... चौविसा थान ... २ के पैरु ६
हस्तिहाडका फुरु २ के मो ३ ..... सुपारि धार्नि ... २ के पै २॥
अलैचि दाना .... धार्नि ...... ४ के पैरु ६

ल्हासाका अम्वा २ के .... ७४६॥
किंषाप थान २ के २५०
तावामा सुनौला मोल्मा कोथि कठी कवुजा वेलाइति मषमल्का
म्यान भयाको तरोवार .... २ के मोरु ... २०
मोहरिर कोठिमा सुनौला तार कसी काम भयाको तोडेवाल
वन्दुक .... २ के मोरु... १००
सुनौला मोल्मा काजो कोथी हस्तिहाडका वीड
मषमल्का म्यान भयाको षुकुरि ... २ के मोरु... १०
वनात वस्ता .... २ के मोरु... २०९
हातिदात .... २ के मोरु.... १२५
दालचिनि धार्नि .... १ के पैरु ८
सुपारिधार्नि .... ४ के पैरु.... ५
दक्षिरिाा सुपारि धार्नि ...... २ के पैरु... ७
वदाम धार्नि .... २ के पैरु... ३।।।
गरिगोटा ३० के धार्नि ...... १ के पैरु ... ३।
छोहारा धार्नि ...... ४ के पैरु... ५।।।
अघि पाला पालमा याहावाट गयाको एस साल श्री मिनिष्टर साहेवका पालामा बुझ्दा नजान्या ठहर्दा फिर्ता भै आयो

छिन्दफु का चन्दु के.. १६०
किंषाप थान १ के ६० वनात वस्ता १ के मोरु १००

सिंहाफु का चन्दु के .... ६२॥
किंषाप थान १ के ६० सुपारि धार्नि १ के पै २॥
अघि पाला पालामा याहा वाट गयाको एस साल श्री मिनीष्टर साहेवका पालामा

वुझदा नजान ठहर्दा फिर्ता भै आयो

गादिम मारष को

श्री वादसाह के १०३९९

हिरा पन्ना जडाउ धुकधुकी लट्कन स्मेत मानीक दाना

सानु पन्ना दाना १६ मोतिदाना ६४ स्मेत माला १ के मोरु .. ७००

मुगामाला १ के दाना ११७ के तोला ... ३२।८। के मोरु .. २३३

तास थान .... ३ के लाठ् ... १९९॥[२]॥

सुनौला थान २ के तोला ७९।२।के ... १४८ ॥

रुपौला थान १ के तोला ३४।३।के ५१।[२]॥

किंषाप थान .... २० के पैरु .... ६९६४ऽ।

रंगरंगका वनात वस्ता.... ८ के मोरु..... ८२०॥[२]

बुट्टेदार चिङ्गली थान...... ४ के मोरु.... ३२

लषनौ छीट् थान .... ६ के मोरु ४८

कोथी र मोहरिमा सुनौला तार कसिको तोडेवाल

वन्दुक .... २ के मोरु... १००

मैसराजा स्मेत चापवाला २ नाल्या वन्दुक ... १ के मो २००

कोथिकंठी कवुजा मषमल्का म्यान तरोवार ... ४ के मो ४०

तावामा सुनौला मोल्मा कोथी वेलाइति मषमलका

म्यान सुनौला पाता सेरषान कटार २ के मोरु... २०

अै. वेहोराको पेस्क वुज .... २ के मोरु... २०

तावामा सुनौला मोल्मा काजो कोथी हस्ती हाडका

वीड मषमल्का म्यान कर्द २।२ स्मेतको षुकुरी..... २ के मो १०

मैसराजाम स्मेतको सुयूर्य मुषि.... १ के मोरु... ७५

दुर्वेन .... २ के मोरु ... २००

गैडा षाग........... २ के मोरु... २५

केसर तोला............. १०० के पैरु... ६२॥

गुलावका अतर तोला .... ७२।.। के मोरु ... १४४

जायफल गोटा............ ५१० के पैरु... २३॥

लवाग धार्नि............ १२ के पैरु... ५४

दालचिनी धार्नि............. ३ऽ२।[३] के पैरु... ३०॥

गरिगोटा १०० के धार्नि..... ४ऽ के पैरु... १३

वदाम धार्नि................ ६ऽ के पैरु... ११।

मझौला हाती दात ....१० के मोरु... २७२॥

लाठ्साही .... १९९॥[२]॥

मोरु .... ३०४०[२]

पैसा रु .... ७१५९ऽ।

डिगर्चा का तालोय के पैरु .... २७॥

किंषाप थान ....१ के २६। सुपारि धार्नि... १ के १।

षोटु थ्वाङ्‌ के .... १०४८॥[३]
मुगा माला ... १ के दा १०९ के तोला १२।३।के मोरु... ४९।
किंषाप थान... २ के पैरु............ ७५०[३]
जर्द वस्ता.... १ के मोरु............ १०५
मेगजीनको तावामा सुनौला मोल्मा कवुजा कोथी
कसी वेलाइति मषमलका म्यान तरोवार... २ के मो ... २०
मझौला हाति दात ...... २ के मोरु.......... १२०
लवाग धार्नि ...... १ के पैरु .... ४॥
अघि पालामा ञाहावाट गयाको एस साल श्री मिनिष्टर साहेवका पालामा वुझदा नजान्या ठहर्दा फिर्ता भै आयो

टुथ्वां के .... ९८२॥[३]
मुगादाना .... १०९ के तोला १२।.। के... ४८
किंषाप थान .... २ के पैरु .... ६८४[३]
जर्द वनात वस्ता .... १ के मोरु १०६
मेगजीनको तावामा सुनौला मोल्मा कबुजा कोथी कसी
वेलाइति मषमल्का म्यान तरोवार ...२ के मोरु... २०
मझौला हाति दात .... २ के मोरु... १२०
लवाग धार्नि .... १ के पै.... ४॥

तेरीज सौगात को

लाठ साही .... ३५३॥[२]॥ .... मोरु ६६९१।
५६॥ .... पैरु १६७६६ऽ॥१
षर्च .... २८१३।/॥३
नगद मोहर रु. १000
किंषाप थान .... ५ के पैरु..... ५९०
...थान .... ४ के पैरु..... ३६७
वनातवस्ता .... ३ के मोरु..... ३२४॥
कासिवाल थान ..... २० के पैरु..... २३४
वादि छीट्‌ थान ..... १६ के मोरु..... ४८
षारुवा थान ..... २० के मोरु.... ६०
...थान ..... ३० के मोरु ६०
थान ..... ३० के मोरु.... ३०
लवाग धार्नि ..... १ के पैरु ..... ४॥
दक्षिरिाा सुपारि धार्नि ... १ के पैरु ..... ३॥
वदाम धार्नि .... १ के पैरु ...... १॥[२]
गरिगोटा ४० के धार्नि ... १ऽ१ के पैरु.... ४। ।१
सुषमेल धार्नि .... ऽ२ के पैरु.... १२॥[२]॥२
वला धार्नि .... ५ के पैरु .... १२॥

कंद धार्नि .... २ के पैरु..... ८।

दालचिनि धार्नि .... २ के पैरु १६

मेगजीनको कर्द २।२ स्मेत छालाका म्यान भयाको षुकुरी .....१० के मोरु..३०

सुपारि धार्नि ५ के पैरु ६।

मोरु १०००

जिन्सी .... १८१३। । ॥३

मोरु .... ५२२॥

पैरु .... १२९०॥ ॥३

अैजन सौगात पुऱ्याउन जान्या मानीसहरु के षर्च १५८४

काजि गंभीर सिं अधिकारि के.................................... ४१११॥[3]१

नगद मोरु.. ३०००

जिन्सी .... ११११॥[3]१

पगरी १ के १२ .... सालजोडा १ के ३२५

सालका रुमा १ के ११३ साल्का पटुका १ के ९०

किंषाप थान १ के २४९॥ किषाप थान १ के .... ३०३॥ ॥१

कलंधरामाल्द थां १ के १५ षासा थान २ के ४

सर्दार सम्सेर जङ् थापाके .... ४४९०॥[3]

नगद १० सालको वाली षर्च ३६००

जिन्सी .... ८९०॥[3]

४ हा. पग्री १ के १० ..... साल जोडा १ के २७५

साल जामा थान १ के ८० किंषाप थां १॥के .... ४९५॥[3]

कलंधरा माल्दहि थान .... २ के ३०

<u>८ पगरि जना ८ के</u>

भिमसेन राना के .... ५४३॥

नगद मोरु .... २५६॥

जिन्सी .... २८६॥ ॥

पगरि १ के १० साल जोडा १ के ८०

...थान १॥ के १७८॥ अं. कासीवाल्थां १ के १८॥

वदल्सिं अधिकारि के .... ४६०॥[2]३

नगद मोरु .... २५६॥

जिन्सी .... २०४[2]३

पग्री १ के २...... किंषाप थान १ के १४३॥[2]३

साल फर्द १ के ४० अं. कासीवाल्थां १ के १८॥

भारत कार्कि के .... ३५१॥

नगद मोरु .... २५६॥

जिन्सी ९५

पग्री १ के २..... वाफदा थान १ के .. ३१

कासीवाल्थां १ के १८॥	सालफर्द १ के	४०
नौरंजेवी थान .... ॥ के	....	३॥
...भंजन अधिकारि के...		५५०॥।
नगद मोरु..		४५४॥
जिन्सी		९६
...पग्री १ के २	वाफदा थान १ के...	२४॥
कासीवाल्थां १ के २६।	सालफर्द १ के.......	४०
नौरंजेवी थान .... ॥ के	....	३॥
अधिकारि के		३३७॥
नगद मोरु		२५६॥
जिन्सी		८१
...पग्री १ के २....	अं. कासिवालथां १ के...	३२
वाफदा थान १ के ३२....	सालफर्द १ के	१५
पिताम्वर साहि के		३३१
नगद मोरु		२५६॥
जिन्सी		७४॥
२२ गजी पगरी १ के २....	वाफदा थान १ के ...	३९
अं. कासिवाल्थां १ के १८॥	सालफर्द १ के	१५
कालु षत्री के		८४॥
नगद ३६०० वाट		
जिन्सी		८४॥
२२ गजी परी (पगरी) १ के २	वाफदा थान १ के ...	४४
सालफर्द १ के १५	माल्दहि थान १ के ...	५
अं. कासिवाल थान .... १ के		१८॥
षर्दार भिमनरसिं के................................		४४६॥[3]॥
नगद मोरु		२५६॥
जिन्सी		१९०[3]॥
२२ गजी पगरि १ के २....	किषाप थान १ के ..	१२२॥[3]॥
अं. कासीवाल्थां १ के १८॥..	सालफर्द १ के	४०
नौरंजेवी थान .... १ के............		७

६ पगरि जना ६ के

भरिया नाएक धनवीर के		२२४।[2]
नगद मोरु		१५७॥
जिन्सी		६६॥।[2]
२२ गजी पगरि १ के २....	चौविसा थान १ के....	२
अं. कासिवाल्थां १॥ के ३१।[2]	वाफदा थान १ के ...	३१।
जमादार करवीर अधिकारि के		५३॥।

नगद ३६०० वाट ....
जिन्सी .... ५३॥।
२२ गजी पगरि १ के २ ... वाफदा थान १ के. २५॥
अं. कासिवाल थान .... १ के ...२६।

...विष्ट के .... ६१।
नगद ३६ (३६००) मध्ये..
जिन्सी .... ६१।
२२ गजी पगरि १ के २ ... वाफदा थान १ के.. ३३
अं. कासिवाल थान .... १ के ...... २६।

भैरव सिं के .... ८६।
नगद ३६०० मध्ये ....
जिन्सी .... ८६।
२२ गजी पगरि १ के २ ..... वाफदा थान १ के....... ५८
अं. कासिवाल थान .... १ के .... २६।

...सर वस्न्यात के .... ७५॥।
नगद ३६०० मध्ये ....
जिन्सी .... ७५॥।
२२ गजी पगरि १ के २ .... वाफदा थान १ के ..४४
कासिवाल्थान १ के २६। .... नौरंजेवी थान ॥के ...३॥

...मान के.. ४६॥[२]
नगद ३६०० मध्ये..
जिन्सी .... ४६॥[२]
२२ गजी पगरि १ के २ ...... वाफदा थान १ के.....२९॥
कासिवाल थान ॥ के १३[२] ..चौविसा थान १ के ..२

पगरि ६ पगरि मध्ये ५ तिलंगा २९ ज्मा काजिका
जान्या जना ३५ के षर्च नगद मोरु ३६००

माल षरिद के जिम्मा काजि सर्दार मोरु २०००
सौगात जादा षोल वेठन गैह्र काम काम के ...... ४१९[२]।१
...का संदुस के .... ५४॥[३]

वासाके तास तोला .... १४।७ के............... ४७
गोटा स्मेत २॥ह. अग्रेजी मल मल हात ३ के.......॥।
मुगा वेहृना के अै. हात ... ७ के ....३॥
रुवा धार्नि .... १[३] के ....।
जर्द वनात गज ...... ॥ के २
१८ गजी पगरि थान .... ॥ के ....॥[२]
गुलाफ का अतर तोला ... ।२।५ के ....॥

येस साल गादिम मारषको सौगात जादा अर्जिका

संदुस के .... ५६।।।
वासाको तास तोला ....११।७॥ के...... ४७
अंग्रेजी २॥ ह मलमल हात ३ के.......... १॥
रुपौला गोटा तोला ...... ।२।८ के .... ।।।´
अरु सदर .... ७।^{३}

षोल वेठन गैह्र के .... ३०७॥^{३}।१
जर्द वनात गज ....१३॥ के....... ५४
स थान ....९ के ९
अर्जि लिषना के .... ।।।
पटना वाल मसि तोला .... ३ के .... ॥
पिनसल कलम .... १ के .... ।

विहारि हात .... ५ के .... ।^{२}॥
अर्जि लेषन्या कागजमा लेषना के लेषन्या
सुन तोला .... ।९।३ के मो...........२५
अर्जि लेषन्या कागज वनाउना के ... १।।।
पैसा रु १
प्यु गोली तोला ... ६ के ....।।।

तेरीज

नगद रु .... ३९२१८ऽ।।।१
लाठ् साहि .... ३५३॥^{२}॥
मोरु .... २२०४२।
२० गजी .... ५६।/।।
१६ गजी रु .... १६७६६ऽ।।१

जिन्सी .... ५७३७॥ /।।३
मोरु १८८७
पैरु .... ३८५०॥ /।।३

.... ४४९५५॥^{२}।।

(The detailed expenses and the list of presents sent along with the 1852 Nepalese Quinquennial mission to China under the leadership of *Kazi* Gambhir Singh Adhikari.)

Source : Royal Nepal Army Head-quarters (RNAH), Part3, Serial No. 63(53).

Appendix H

आफु वाङका चीन जाने काजीहरुले लोभ्फोम भन्या जगामा पुग्दा घोडा चौरी

मर्दा घोडा चौरी नपाई वाटामा ढिल हुने भयो भनी ञाहा लेखी पठायाका हुनाले श्री वादसाहका हर्जुमा अर्जि लेखी पठायाको छ भन्या हानफोङ २ साल ९ मैन्हा ७ दिन जादा १९०९ साल्मा श्री ५ मा युतारीन अम्वाले लेखेको...................

(Chinese *Amban* to Nepalese King informing about the delaying of the Nepalese mission's journey to Peking due to the deaths of their horses and yaks in Lojhom area.)

Source : MFA, *Poka* No. Pa 64.

Appendix I

काजी गंभीर सिं परलोक भया भन्या र सिंधाफु सहरको वयान श्री जनरल ज.व.रा का नाउमा सम्वत १९०९ साल माघ सुदी १५ रोजमा सर्दार सम्सेर जं वहादुर थापाले लेखेको ....

(*Sardar* Samsher Jang Bahadur Thapa informing about the death of *Kazi* Gambhir Singh.)

Source : MFA, *Poka* No. Pa 64.

Appendix J

पेचीन पुगी वादसाहलाई सौगाद चढाञ्यूं .. हामीलाई दिनु पर्ने दस्तुरात दिये २ मैन्हाको मुकां गरी विदा भै पेचीनवाट फिऱ्यौ – सिलिङ भ्याङ भन्या सहरमा पुग्दा सन्नीपातका वेथाले सर्दार सम्सेर जं थापा परलोक भए. १९१० साल्मा जनरल कृष्न वहादुर कुवर राणालाई सुव्वा भीमसेन रानाले लेषेको अर्जि......

(*Subba* Bhimsen Rana's *arji* to General Krishna Bahadur Rana informing about the death of *Sardar* Samsher Jang Thapa.)

Source : MFA, *Poka* No. Pa 64.

Appendix K

पेचीन पुगी सौगाद चढाएको – साविक भन्दा वढी थप खितावहरुको भाग स्मेत वक्स भयो . पेचीनवाट हिडयौ भंन्या र काजी गंभीर सिं सर्दार सम्सेर जं थापा सुवेदारहरु अरु मरेको – अन्य पेचीन चीन सम्वन्धी खवर श्री ३ जंगलाई १९१० मा भीमसेन रानाले पठाएको अर्जि.......................................

(Bhim Sen Rana's *arji* to *Shree Tin* Jang informing about the deaths of *Kazi* Gambhir Singh, *Sardar* Samsher Jang Thapa, *Subedars* and others.)

Source : MFA, *Poka* No. Pa 64.

Appendix L

सौगाद पुऱ्याउन जान्या पगरीहरुको वाटोमा हराएको माल षोजी पठाई दिनु भनी तार्चिन्देउमा चिनिया भारदारलाई लेखी पठायाको छ भन्या हानफोङ ४ वर्ष ९ मैन्हा १७ दिन जादा १९११ सालमा श्री ५ मा युउतारीन अंवाले लेखेको.................................

(Chinese *Amban* to Nepalese King informing about the searching of the lost goods of the Nepalese mission in Tarchendeo area.)

Source : MFA, *Poka* No. Pa 64.

Appendix M

१९११ साल

सुवा भिमसिं राना चिन वाट फिर्दा केरुं सम्म लिन जादा चिनवाट
चिनिञा भारदारहरु के वैशाष वदि ७ रोज ....
लिन जान्या वकील विष्नु प्रसाद पंडीत के षर्च मोहर्रुपैया १००
मेजमानी के .... ३३॥।
चिनि धार्नि १ के ...... मोरु १ छोहरा धार्नि ऽ१॥।[२] के मो... ॥।ऽ२
टिगिंन् च्यूरा मुरि १ के.... ऐं ४[३]॥ मिठाइ धार्नि के ऐ. १३
मसिना चावल़ मुरि १ के.. ऐ. ५॥[३]।३ फलफुल गैह्र के पैरु ८
सराजाम राषन्या प्याङ वाधना के
प्याङ् ३ के पैरु ॥।[३]..................... डोरि मोल्

चिनवाट आयाका असवाफका भारिमा छाप मारि ल्याउना
के लाहा वत्ति मोल् पैसा रु .... २ भारि लिन जान्या
लुभु सेराका मोहि ३३ के षर्च पैसा रु .... ५४॥
नाइक्या .... १ के २ .... भरिया ...... ३५ के ....५२॥

(The detailed expenses of the Chinese officials who escorted *Subba* Bhim Sen Rana of the 1852 Nepalese Quinquennial mission up to Kerung in 1854.)

Source : RNAH, Part 3, Serial No. 63 (53).

* * *

14

Kazi Jagat Sher Sijapati's Mission of 1866

At the time of sending the five-yearly mission to China in 1857, the political situation in the Himalayan region was somewhat disturbing. The Nepal-Tibet war of 1855-56 was just over following the treaty of 1856, and China did not help Tibet against Nepal in this war. Moreover, China was greatly threatened by T'aiping rebellion. In view of this situation, the Ch'ing Emperor, through the *Amban*, instructed Nepal to send only *arji* instead of the usual five-yearly mission with huge presents.[1] Accordingly, the Nepalese government sent only *arji* and not presents to the Ch'ing Emperor Hsien Feng in 1857.[2]

In 1862, five years later, the political situation of both Tibet and China were not good. Tibet was on the verge of civil war, whereas China was also being troubled in some provinces due to the T'aiping rebellion. Under such circumstances, the Ch'ing government permitted Nepal to cancel the Nepalese mission of 1862[3]. But here it should be mentioned that in August 1861, the Ch'ing Emperor Hsien Feng died and he was succeeded by T'ung-Chih. In reply to the new Ch'ing Emperor T'ung-Chih's *Parwana* announcing the death of Emperor Hsien Feng, Nepal sent an *arji* to the new Ch'ing Emperor.[4]

In June 1866, Jang Bahadur decided to send a mission to Peking after the receipt of several overtures from the Chinese *Amban* at Lhasa inviting him to reestablish the relations that formerly existed between China and Nepal, and promising on the part of the Emperor that any future mission that may be sent to him

---

1. Chinese *Ambans* to King Surendra, Hon Fong 7th year 2nd month 8th day (March 1857), Ministry of Foreign Affairs, Kathmandu (hereafter mentioned as MFA), *Poka* No. Pa 64. See Appendix F.
2. *Arji* to the Chinese Emperor, dated 1914 B.S. Jestha Badi 8 Roj 1 (1857), Nepalese Government to Chinese *Amba*n 1914 B.S., Ashwin Badi 14 Roj 5 (1857),*Ibid.*, See Appendices G and H.
3. For the correspondence between Nepal and China till the cancellation of 1862 Nepalese mission, see Appendices I, J, K, L and M.
4. Chinese Emperor's *Parwana*, Throndi 1st year 7th month 1st day (Auguat 1862), *Ibid.*, See Appendix N.

by Nepal would be received with high honours and consideration.[5] One important factor which seemed to have prompted Jang Bahadur to dispatch a mission to Peking was to secure the very valuable presents that were sent in return by the Chinese government as well as the great profits coming from the mission's trading activities. Thus after a lapse of fourteen years, Nepal sent her mission to China in 1866. The Chinese Imperial records have mentioned of Nepal's dispatching five-yearly mission to China in 1865[6]. But the Nepalese and Indian archival documents clearly state of Nepal's sending of five-yearly mission to China in 1866[7]. The 1866 Nepalese mission was led by *Kazi* Jagat Sher Sijapati, the son of Colonel Lall Singh Sijapati. The mission consisted of altogether forty-five persons, including *Sardar* Mullay Jung Pande, the deputy leader of the mission, *Subba* Motay (Moti ?) Lal Khatri, *Subedar* Jangbir Khatri, and Tepul Singh. It was reported that due to the hardships experienced by the last Nepalese mission in 1852, no Nepalese officials consented to accompany the mission of 1866. That is why persons of lower ranks were promoted for the occasion. The Nepalese mission left Kathmandu on 2 August, 1866.[8]

From the Tibetan capital Lhasa[9], the 1866 Nepalese mission was only able to reach Ta Tsin Deo (Ta-Chien-lu), about half way to Peking, near the China-Tibet border. From there, the mission was not allowed to proceed to Peking due to a Muslim

---

5. Ramsay to Secretary, Govt. of India, 9 June 1866, Foreign Dept. Polt. A. June 1866, No. 163, National Archives of India, New Delhi (hereafter referred as NAI).
6. J.K. Fairbank and S.Y. 'Teng, "On the Ch'ing Tributary System", *Harvard Journal of Asiatic Studies*, Vol. VI, 1941, pp. 195-198.
7. For the details of the 1866 Nepalese mission, see MFA, *Poka* No. Pa 64: Ramsay to Secretary, Govt. of India, 7 August 1866, Foreign Dept. Polt. A. August 1866, No. 104, NAI. See Appendix A.
8. Ramsay to Secretary, Govt. of India, 7 August 1866, Foreign Dept. Polt. A. August 1866, No. 104, NAI. But Sever has wrongly stated that the Nepalese mission left Kathmandu on 15 August 1866. See Adrian Sever, *Aspects of Modern Nepalese History*, New Delhi: Vikas Publishing House Pvt. Ltd., 1996, p. 170.
9. For the details of Nepalese mission's departure and arrival at Lhasa, see Appendices O, P, Q and R.

rebellion in western China[10]. Several months later, the Chinese authorities asked the Nepalese envoy *Kazi* Jagat Sher to turn over the presents for the Emperor and promised to forward them to Peking.[11] The Nepalese envoy unwillingly agreed to this, but waited for nearly two years at Ta Chien-lu for permission to proceed to Peking.[12] According to Bishop Chauvean[13], head of the French Jesuit mission at Ta Chien-lu, *Kazi* Jagat Sher insisted on going to Peking, but the Chinese authorities persisted in their refusal. The Nepalese envoy made many endeavours to advance to Peking, but it was without success. Once he had even thought of commencing his journey towards Peking at his own expenses. However, having already handed over the Nepalese presents for the Ch'ing Emperor to the Chinese mandarins, and due to the inability to selling the huge amount of merchandise carried by the Nepalese mission, the Nepalese envoy gave up the idea of going to Peking at his own expenses. His failure to visit Peking caused the Nepalese envoy to become ill from which he suffered for several months. When all hopes of going to Peking had vanished and the merchandise had not been sold, *Kazi* Jagat Sher then thought of returning to Nepal. In the meantime, the Nepalese mission had also received the return presents from the Ch'ing court. Therefore, on 15 July 1868, *Kazi* Jagat Sher left Ta Tsin Deo with his party and all their luggage *en route* in their return journey to Kathmandu.[14] In this way, this Nepalese mission of 1866 was greatly humiliated when it was not allowed to visit Peking on the grounds of a Muslim rebellion in western China.

It is beyond doubt that the 1866 Nepalese mission suffered severe hardships. It was reported that several persons connected

---

10. Leo E. Rose, *Nepal: Strategy For Survival*, Berkeley: University of California Press, 1971, p. 135.
11. *Santarins* to Jagat Sher, Throndi 6th year 2nd month 4th day (1867), MFA, *Poka* No. P: 4. See Appendix T.
12. Ramsay to Secretary, Govt. of India, 29 July 1867 and 3 August 1867, Foreign Dept. Polt. A, August 1867, Nos. 53-54, NAI. See Appendices B and C: Ramsay to Secretary, Govt. of India, 16 January 1869, Foreign Dept. Polt A. March 1869, No. 208, NAI. See Appendix D.
13. Translation of a French document sent by Bishop Chauvean regarding the Nepalese mission to China, 17 July 1868, Foreign Dept. Polt. A. March 1869, No. 208, NAI. See Appendix D.
14. *Ibid.*

with the mission had also died[15]. All the more, upwards of a *lakh* of rupees (Rs. 1,00,000) worth of opium and valuable goods were destroyed by the inclement weather experienced in traversing the numerous snowy passes and mountains intervening between the Nepalese frontier and the Chinese border.[16] Here it should be mentioned that besides a lot of other merchandise, a huge quantity of opium, valued at four and a half *lakhs* of rupees (Rs. 4,50,000), was sent with the mission of 1866 for sale in China. That merchandise mostly belonged to Jang Bahadur and his brothers. *Sahu* Dharma Narayan Manandhar, a Newar merchant, monopolist and a close associate of Jang Bahadur[17], had also sent with this 1866 Nepalese mission one of his own nephews with a vast quantity of opium, cloth, spices and other goods.[18] But as no market was being found, it was laid down in the Nepalese godowns at Lhasa, and thus the Nepalese court was at a loss how to dispose of them. It was reported that as half the amount of opium carried by the 1866 Nepalese mission proved unsaleable, the remaining opium, consisting of four hundred coolie loads, was brought back to Lhasa by the Nepalese mission. As it became difficult to dispose of the opium, at least half the amount was brought back to Kathmandu.[19]

---

15. Ramsay to Secretary, Govt. of India, 29 July 1867, Foreign Dept. Polt. A, August 1867, No. 53, NAI. See Appendix B.
    Chinese *Amban* to King Surendra, Throndi 6th year 3rd month 16th day (1867), MFA, *Poka* No. Pa 64. See Appendix U.
16. Ramsay to Secretary, Govt. of India, 29 July 1867, Foreign Dept. Polt. A, August 1867, No. 53, NAI.
17. For the details of *Sahu* Dharma Narayan, see Vijay Kumar Manandhar, "*Sahu* Dharma Narayan Manandhar: A Financier And Member of the Bureaucratic Elite of the Nineteenth Century", *Voice of History*, Vol. XIV, No. 1 (June 1999), pp. 19-36.
18. Ramsay to Secretary, Govt. of India, 29 July 1867, Foreign Dept. Polt. A, August 1867, No. 53, NAI.
19. Daniel Wright, Officiating Resident to Secretary, Govt. of India, 27 February 1875, Foreign Polt. A, May 1875, No. 104, NAI. For the details of the 1866 Nepalese mission's opium trade in China, see Vijay Kumar Manandhar, *Cultural and Political Aspects of Nepal-China Relations*, Delhi: Adroit Publishers, 1999, pp. 72-76. See also Commander-in-Chief to *Kazi* Jagat Sher, 1923 B.S. Bhadra Badi 13 Roj 6 (1866), MFA, *Poka* No. Pa 64. See Appendix S. See also Jagat Sher's *arji* to the Nepalese Government dated 1925 B.S., MFA, *Poka* No. Pa 64. See Appendix X.

The Chinese government's motive in refusing the 1866 Nepalese mission's permission to proceed to Peking is not clearly known. However, Bishop Chauvean, the head of the French Jesuit mission at Ta Chien-lu and an acquaintance of Nepalese envoy Jagat Sher, guessed that the Chinese were trying to "bring down the storm" of Nepal's wrath on Tibet by sending the mission back to Kathmandu dissatisfied, with the hope that China would be able to take advantage of the Nepalese-Tibetan conflict to regain its former position in Tibet.[20] This view does not seem to be correct, for China wanted to have closer relations with Nepal[21]. It seems that the inhospitable attitude towards the 1866 Nepalese delegates was due purely to their smuggling activities[22]. Here it should be pointed out that the 1852 Nepalese mission, which had carried a huge amount of opium, valuing nearly three *lakh* rupees (Rs. 3,00,000) under the cover of diplomatic privileges, had aroused suspicion among the Chinese authorities, who did not like the entry of contraband objects, i.e., opium in their country in spite of its legal ban. Although the Chinese authorities did not react immediately in 1852, at the time of the Nepalese mission of 1866 however, they did not allow the mission, which had carried a large quantity of opium for sale in China to proceed to Peking from Ta Chien-lu on the grounds of a Muslim rebellion in western China[23]. Also Mr. T.T. Cooper, the English traveller in China who had met the Nepalese delegation of 1866 in Tibet, was also under the impression that the Nepalese mission's progress to Peking was arrested owing to its possession of opium.[24] According to T.T. Cooper, after much persuasion, *Kazi* Jagat Sher was allowed to proceed as far as Chen-tu in order to dispose of several chests of opium brought for sale in China, and then return home. He soon reached Chen-tu, and hoped to proceed

20. Translation of a French document sent by Bishop Chauvean regarding the Nepalese mission to China, 17 July 1868, Foreign Dept. Polt A, March 1869, No. 208, NAI.
21. Rose, f.n. no. 10, p. 138.
22. Tri Ratna Manandhar, *Nepal: The Years of Trouble (1877-85)*, Kathmandu: Purna Devi Manandhar, 1986, p. 141.
23. Tri Ratna Manandhar and Tirtha Prasad Mishra, *Nepal's Quinquennial Missions to China*, Kathmandu: Purna Devi Manandhar and Puspa Mishra, 1986, pp. 39-40 and p. 58.
24. R.C. Lawrence to C.U. Aitchison, 10 September 1870, Foreign Dept. Sec. I, 1870, No. 400, NAI.

further, but the Chinese authorities made this impossible, for he was allowed to have neither coolies nor boats, and, what was worse, no one would buy his opium; it was too strong, and the people preferred the native drug. He spent several months at Chen-tu, vainly pressing his request for leave to proceed to Peking. The Chinese officials treated the Nepalese envoy with great discourtesy, hoping by this means to force him to return, and had lodged him in a dirty hovel outside the city.[25] Moreover, it was also reported that the Ch'ing Emperor did not intend to receive the 1866 Nepalese mission, which, according to custom, should have been dispatched in 1857 and 1862.[26] However, the main reason why the Nepalese mission was turned back by the Chinese from Ta Chien-lu of the Chinese province of Szechuwan seemed to be because of the large quantity of opium the Nepalese authorities (Ranas) had sent with it and which, under ordinary circumstances, would have been sold free of duty and taxes as a privilege of the delegates. It was beyond doubt that the Nepalese mission's involvement in the opium trade in China was indeed a misuse of the diplomatic mission for the personal pecuniary benefit of Prime Minister Jang Bahadur Rana and his brothers. It is strong evidence of how the Ranas misused the diplomatic relations between the two countries. The Ranas' lust for wealth could not be satisfied by the cxploitation of national resources only, so the Ranas compelled the officials to smuggle the contraband goods like opium to China, sometimes even female to sell[27]. The Nepalese mission of 1866 had to return home humiliated by the Chinese authorities[28]. It seems that the mission returned to Kathmandu after a lapse of nearly three years[29].

This fourteenth five -yearly mission of 1866 was important due to the following reasons: Firstly, this mission happened to be

---

25. E.C. Baber, Consular officer at Chungking to Hugh Fraser, Her Majesty's Charge d'Affaires at Peking, 2 August 1878, Foreign Dept. Sec., December 1878, No. 27, NAI. See Appendix E.
26. Ramsay to Secretary, Govt. of India, 29 July 1867, Foreign Dept. Polt. A, August 1867, No. 53, NAI.
27. Manandhar, f.n. no. 19, p. 88.
28. For the Nepalese Government's correspondence with the Chinese Government regarding the returning of the Nepalese mission, see Appendices V,W and Y.
29. Draft letter from Nepalese King to Chinese Emperor, 1926 B.S. Jestha Sudi 15 Roj 5 (1869), MFA, *Poka* No. Pa 64. See Appendix Z.

the third[30] and the last quinquennial mission sent to China during the thirty-one-year Premiership of Jang Bahadur. Secondly, this mission was the fourth such Nepalese mission which had carried the usual five-yearly presents and special presents to the new Ch'ing Emperor (T'ung Chih). Thirdly, this mission happened to be the first Nepalese mission which was not allowed to visit Peking on the plea of a Muslim rebellion in western China and had to return home humiliated from Ta Chien-lu, about half way to Peking near the China-Tibet border. Fourthly, the extreme discourtesy meted out to the Nepalese mission by the Chinese officials in Chen-tu and the deaths of several members of the mission in eastern Tibet not only irritated[31] but also led Jang Bahadur to seriously consider sending Nepalese mission to China in future. As such, relations between China and Nepal were interrupted and no Nepalese mission was dispatched until 1877. Above all. another important feature regarding the 1866 mission was that, upon its return to Kathmandu, the leader of the mission, *Kazi* Jagat Sher met the then British Resident, Colonel R.C. Lawrence, furnished some information about the mission, and handed over the private travel diary that he kept, in which there were notes of the journey from Kathmandu to Lhasa, and from thence to Thin-da-foo in western China, with the distance in miles between the different stages, and a brief account of the habits and customs of the people, including the important subject of the cultivation of opium in China.[32]

Appendix A

From – Colonel G. Ramsay, Resident at Nepal
To – Secretary to the Govt. of India, in the Foreign Dept., with the Governor General, Simla

---

30. But Rose and Fisher, believing that Jang Bahadur did not send a quinquennial mission to China in 1847, concluded that during his thirty-one-year rule, Jang Bahadur sent only two quinquennial missions to China. See Leo E.Rose and Margaret W.Fisher, *The Politics of Nepal: Persistence and Change in an Asian Monarchy,* Ithaca and London: Cornell University Press, 1970, p. 147.
31. Nepalese King to Chinese *Amban*, 1925 B.S. Kartik Sudi 9 Roj 7 (1868), MFA, *Poka* No. Pa 64. See Appendix Y.
32. R.C. Lawrence to C.U. Aitchison, 10 September 1870, Foreign Dept. Sec. I, 1870, Nos. 400-401, NAI.

No. 27, dated the 7th August 1866

I have the honour to report that the Nipalese Mission referred to in my letter, No. 15, "Political" of the 9th of June last, left Khatmandoo for China on the 2nd instant.

1. Owing to the hardships experienced by the last Mission in 1852 no Sirdars would consent to accompany the present one, and persons of lower grades were promoted for the occasion; the leader being a young man, a son of Colonel Lall Sing of the Goorkha Artillery, who was made a Kajee.
2. The following are the names of the Officers of the Mission:-

Kajee Juggut Shere Khuttree.
Sirdar Mullay Jung Panday.
Soobah Motay Lall Khuttree.

with 42 attendants, writers, subadars, &c.

Source : Foreign: Dept. Polt. A, August 1866, No. 104, National Archives of India, New Delhi (NAI).

Appendix B

From – Colonel G. Ramsay, Resident at Nepal

To – Secretary, Govt. of India, in the Foreign Dept., with the Governor General, Simla

No. 21, dated the 29th July 1867

I have the honor to report that rumors have been afloat for sometime past at Khatmandoo that serious disasters have happened to the Nepalese Embassy that left for Pekin about 11½ months back, and that military preparations have been commenced here with the view to the despatch of a body of troops towards Thibet soon after the Dusserah festival, as was done in 1855-56 when a war occurred between the Goorkhas and Thibetans. One person, an artizan in the arsenal, lately mentioned in the Residency lines that orders have been issued for the preparation of 25 small guns, and that as many musket as can be put into serviceable order are at once to be got ready; and in the city the subject is freely spoken of.

2. Quarrels between Thibetans and the subjects of Nepal at Lhassa, the refusal of redress to the latter by the courts of

justice, the murder of a Newarree merchant, and oppressive exactions of duty upon all merchandize sent across the border, were the alleged reasons for the last war; but I reported at the time that I believed it to have been chiefly caused by outrages offered to the Nepalese Embassy then on its way back from China, which, after being detained for four or five months upon its journey, returned to Khatmandoo under the charge of the junior officer of all who had originally accompanied it, his seniors having all been reported to have died.

3. It was not possible to ascertain here what really did happen to that Embassy, as beyond vaguely stating that it had long been detained and its members insulted, Maharajah Jung Bahadoor avoided all references to the subject, and prohibited its being talked about by any one; but the Superintendent of Darjeeling, on the authority of Cheeboo Lama, the Sikkim Rajah's Vakeel (since dead, I believe), who was in frequent communication with Eastern Thibet, reported that the Sirdars of the mission had been grossly ill-treated and one of them mutilated.

4. Upon that occasion an immense quantity of opium was smuggled into China and sold at large prices, and when the last Embassy left in August 1866 a still larger quantity of that drug and much other merchandize, the property of Maharajah Jung Bahadoor and his brothers, was sent up with it; and Dhurrumnarain Sahoo, the Newarree merchant and, monopolist, also sent with it one of his own nephews with a vast quantity of opium, cloth, spices, &c., &c.

5. Four or five months ago the Maharajah told me that letters had been received from the Embassy, stating that it had suffered severe hardships; that several persons connected with it had died; and that the officer in charge of it had reported that upwards of a lakh of rupees worth of opium and of valuable goods had been destroyed by the inclement weather experienced in traversing the numerous snowy passes and mountains intervening between the Nepalese Frontier and the Chinese border.

6. It is now reported here that the Emperor of China will not receive this Embassy, which, according to custom, should have been despatched seven years ago, and again in 1865; and that it has been opposed in its progress, and that many casualties have

occurred in it.

7. Adverting to these reports, which the Maharajah presumed had reached my ears, His Excellency a few days ago sent me the following message:-

   He said that he had not himself heard from any person in Thibet regarding the China Embassy for about three months, but that a letter had just been received by one of his brothers from the Nepalese Vakeel at Lhassa to the effect that reports were in circulation at that place that the mission was then at Ta Tsin Deo, the first large Chinese post on the south-western border of that country, and that large bodies of rebels were close to the place, for which reason the Governor of the district had refused to allow it to march by the usual route to Pekin, and had suggested that it should make a long detour, to which the Nepalese Kajee in charge of it had objected. The Vakeel further reported that it is said a reference has been made to the Emperor of China upon the subject, and that, until his mandate has been received, the mission will halt where it now is, and he added the following curious and very improbable story, viz., that Umbahs of Lhassa had recently received back from Ta Tsin Deo a letter originally addressed by the chief Chinese Umbah of Lhassa to the Emperor, which had fallen by an accident into the hands of the Embassy. The rebels are said to have intercepted and attacked the party, the bearers of the letter, and killed four sowars; but instead of taking away the letter with them they left it upon a large stone upon the road side, where it was found by some Bhoteas, who took it, not to the authorities of the country, nor to the Chinese officers in attendance upon the Embassy, but to the Nepalese Kajee, at whose suggestion it was returned to Lhassa.

8. This, the Maharajah said, is all he knows of the matter. He believes that the Embassy, which ought to have reached Pekin in March last, is still at Ta Tsin Deo (about half way); and it has encountered severe hardships, but that whether it will proceed onwards or return to Nepal is still a matter of uncertainty.

9. I have reported these circumstances in some detail, as exaggerated reports of military preparations here may reach His Excellency's ears, which I desire thus to account for.

10. Prior to the last campaign in Thibet there was a positive panic at Darjeeling; troops were applied for the defence of that province, and the name of the General, who was reported to have actually left Khatmandoo to command the force destined for its invasion, was seriously mentioned to the Government, and much uneasiness prevailed along the Morung border and even in Tirhoot and Chumparun.
11. I have no hesitation in stating now, with as much confidence as I did in 1855, that if active military preparations be made here, they will be caused entirely by the receipt of further disastrous intelligence from Thibet connected with the position of the Embassy now on the border of China.

Source: Foreign Dept. Polt. A, August 1867, No. 53, NAI.

Appendix C

From – Colonel G. Ramsay, Resident at Nepal
To - Secretary Govt. of India, in the Foreign Department, with the Governor General, Simla.
No. 21, dated the 3rd August 1867

In continuation of my letter, No. 21, Political, of the 29th ultimo, I have the honor to report that Maharajah Jung Bahadoor has just sent to inform me that he has heard from the Nepalese Embassy that it is positively about to return to Khatmandoo by order of the Emperor of China, who has desired that the tribute letter, &c., &c., destined for himself, may be received from it, and return presents made to it at Ta Tsin Deo, the disordered state of the country rendering its onward journey to Pekin impossible.

2. The Maharajah says that he feels much aggrieved at this treatment, the Embassy having been despatched by invitation of the Emperor, to whom the state of the country must surely have been known, who promised that it would be treated with greater consideration and receive higher honors from his Government than had ever been paid to any former one.
3. His Excellency has sent me a most interesting letter from some Catholic Missionaries in Thibet who had visited the Kajee, the head of the Embassy, and who have at his instigation written me an account of their severe trials and sufferings.

4. I propose to transmit a copy of the letter in question for the information of the Government in the course of a few days.

Source: Foreign Dept. Polt. A, August 1867, No. 54, NAI.

Appendix D

Translation of a French document sent by Bishop Chauvean regarding the Nepalese Mission to China dated Ta Tsien Fou, the 17th of July 1868

As the public would, perhaps, wish to know how the mission of the last Nepalese Ambassador to China has terminated, of which some mention has been made in a preceding note, we devote the following lines to this subject:-

We left Sir Juggut Shere at Tchenton, the capital of Letchonan, in the middle of October 1867, living in a poor and very small house outside the walls of the town. It has been mentioned that, at that time, the men of the suite of the Nepalese Ambassador were almost all ill with fever, but he himself was enjoying good health. That state of affairs only lasted for a time; some of the fevers disappeared, but others resisted all remedies. A little later Sir Juggut Shere fell sick in his turn, and had not thoroughly recovered whilst at Ta Tsien Fou. He attributed the loss of strength that he felt to the bad quality of the water, and it would not be surprizing if that cause had something to do with his sickness, for, though the plain of Tchenton is one of the most beautiful districts of the empire, it must be allowed that the water leaves much to be desired. It is, however, much more probable that the opposition he met with has been the chief cause of a malady which rendered every moment restless.

Sir Juggut Shere insisted on going to Pekin, but the Chinese authorities persisted in their refusal. They pretended to have received two despatches from the Supreme Government, still more and more decided in opposing the onward journey of Nepalese Embassy. These despatches did not say "we forbid;" "we refuse to receive;" &c., &c. The Chinese expressions were milder, and may be correctly translated into English thus: "it is not proper; " "we cannot admit;" &c., &c.

The authorities of Tchenton adhered to the orders that had been transmitted to them; and, to a certain extent, they were right. They would have found themselves in a very difficult position if Sir Juggut Shere, alleging in his turn the orders that he had received from Sir Jung Bahadoor Rana, and the treaties long ago concluded, had commenced his journey at his own expense and proceeded towards Pekin.

At one time he thought of doing so, but several considerations prevented him, one of the chief of which was, that the presents of the Maharaja his master were already in the hands of the mandarins, and he could not present himself at Pekin with empty hands. In addition to this, his merchandise had not yet been sold, and he did not like to trust goods of considerable value, and which, besides, belonged in great part to the Nepalese Government, to the care of hands so little to be trusted as those of the Chinese.

He was thus obliged to give up the idea most pleasing to himself, viz., that of presenting in person to the young Emperor of China the respects of his Sovereign; but he could not relinquish this design without feeling great grief, and for my part I shall always believe that this bitter sacrifice was the cause of the illness from which he suffered for several months.

All hope of going to Pekin having vanished and the merchandise not being able to be sold, Sir Juggut Shere could only think of returning to Nepal. Moreover, the Chinese authorities took care to recall him, and pressed him frequently to set out in terms which did not err through excess of politeness (bienveillance). It is true I have not heard the Nepalese Envoy make complaints on this subject, but I have the fact from so certain a source, that I have no doubt of it myself, and do not hesitate to assert it.

The day of his departure was fixed on Wednesday, the 29th May, and a start was, indeed, made, but only by a portion of the men and their baggage. Sir Juggut Shere with the remainder did not set out till some days later. The first part of this journey, as far as Ta Tsien Fou, has been fortunate and undisturbed, except by the troubles which are almost inevitable in these countries, such as the difficulty of procuring porters, the overflowing of rivers, the bad state of the roads, and other things of this kind. One measure taken by the Chinese Government was especially unpleasant to the Nepalese Ambassador, and may cause him trouble of all kinds even as far as Lhassa. This circumstance was the following:-

In accordance with the Treaty formed between Nepal and China, the Nepalese Envoy ought to have all the expenses of his journey defrayed by the Chinese mandarins. They give him 25 ounces of silver daily, in addition to provisions, forage, and palanquins. From his entry into China, Sir Juggut Shere himself received the 25 ounces of silver, and disposed of it according to his own pleasure; but when he commenced his return, the Marshal Fesony, Officiating Governor of Letchonan, made a change in this state of affairs. The silver is now weighed out to an interperter, the very man of whom they have had to complain during two years, and it is this interpreter who has to supply the expenses of the travellers. But it appears that this good interpreter has an avaricious disposition. He takes all, and he disburses but little; so that Sir Juggut Shere has been obliged to pay out of his own purse. But he does more than this. In the conveyance of all the property of the Nepalese Embassy (I have Sir Juggut Shere's own assurance) only 680 beasts of burden are necessary; but the interpreter demands many more (say 12 or 1,400) and he applies to his own benefit the animals supplied by the poor people. He buys goods on his own account; he conveys those entrusted to him by the mandarins and merchants, and we may be sure he takes care that his services are repaid. He enriches himself no doubt; but the odium of all these practices falls upon the Nepalese Ambassador, who is quite aware of the ill use that is made of his name without being able to prevent it.

The halt at Ta Tsien Fou this time has not been so long as in last year. On the 15th July Sir Juggut Shere left this with his party and all their baggage: may God conduct them in peace to Katmandoo! While he remained among us we did everything for him that lay in our power, acting towards him as towards the representative of a power friendly to France and England. It pleased him frequently to express to us his gratitude, and, not to take literally the exaggeration there might be in his expression of it, we think he will retain a favourable recollection of the Europeans whom he has met in China; and that it is not without reason that he has given them the name of friends.

Sir Juggut Shere has remained in China for nearly two years: supposing that they gave him every day the sum of 25 ounces of silver, he would have received nearly 18,250 Taels, or 136,875 Francs, about 54,750 Rupees. In this account are not included the enormous expenses incurred for transport; it is the poor people who pay all this: "they sweat blood and water;" but in China, and especially in Thibet, it seems to be agreed that the blood of the people is only clear water.

The Nepalese Embassy then has caused considerable expense, and we may ask, with what object ? The Chinese all say that Nepal pays tribute to their empire. I doubt much whether such is the intention of the Nepalese Government. What is there to fear from the Chinese in the present day ? The only point of contact that there is between them is at Lhassa, but it is very certain that the Nepalese are much more powerful at Lhassa than the Chinese, and it would not be surprizing if they expelled them altogether some day. Already the Calcutta journals have published that Sir Jung Bahadoor has views on Thibet, the conquest of which does not appear very difficult for an army trained in the European way. The Chinese understand thoroughly the danger that threatens them from that side; but in accordance with that blindness on which I have remarked elsewhere, and which is noticeable on all sides, they have behaved towards the Nepalese Embassy in a way calculated to bring down the storm which seems to be gathering in the plains of Goorkha. Sir Juggut Shere withdraws discontented, and I pray that the failure in proper respect of which he complains may be borne patiently by his master the Maharaja, and not become an occasion for a dreadful contest between Pekin and Katmandoo.

An official letter which arrived this very morning (18 July) from Tchenton, from the Marshal, Officiating Governor of the Province, has disclosed to us a fact of which we had no knowledge, and which is an honor (*gloire*) in our opinion to the Nepalese Government. I would eagerly seize on the opportunity of publicly testifying our lively gratitude. Let us state the facts as briefly as possible. When Sir Juggut Shere arrived at Batang in the end of 1866, he found there three Missionaries driven from the country they had occupied for several years previously. They had been insulted, brutally beaten, and plundered. Their houses had been burned, several of their Christian converts murdered, and even one of their companions killed at the moment of his throwing himself on the rope of a flying (*coulant*) bridge. The letter containing all these details was addressed to Colonel Ramsay, Resident at Katmandoo, and may be read in the *Indian Catholic Chronicle* of Calcutta and the *Bombay Catholic Examiner*. This gallant Colonel, in accordance with the prayer of the Missionaries, had the kindness to present this letter to the Maharaja of Nepal. The latter, moved by the misfortunes which had befallen us, and recalling the kindness with which he had been received at Paris by His Majesty Napoleon III (who was then (in 1850 or 1851) only President of the Republic, addressed a despatch to the Thibetian Government, demanding an explanation of what had taken place with regard to the French Missionaries, and suggesting some ideas which had not as yet penetrated as far as Lhassa, the country of the gods ! This is the communication come from Tchenton, of which we spoke just now. It is long, and this is not the place to give a translation of it. The Maharaja said, in substance, that the French Missionaries had made known to him all the violence of which they had been victims; that these events were no secret to any one; and that the Press had made them public throughout India and Europe. That he was a friend of the Thibetan Government, and for that very reason he advised them to consider a little what they were doing. That formerly both their Governments had agreed in trying to exclude strangers from their respective territories; but that now circumstances were greatly changed. That the great Empire of China itself had been forced to come to terms with England and France, and that, if they paid no attention at Lhassa to the observations he addressed to them, he could not be answerable for what might occur, and in any case he declared he was unable to give any assistance to the Thibetian Government.

It is easy for us to judge from the letter of the Imperial Embassy at Lhassa that these candid (and illegible) remonstrances of the noble Maharaja have produced a decided impression (*grande sensation*). One of the Ministers, by name Kopoon Sin, has endeavoured to reply to it. One of the reasons he has given against our admission into the interior of Thibet is, that ever since the time we have only been on the borders, pestilential diseases succeed each other almost without interruption, and insects destroy the crops. Such assertions could hardly have been confirmed by Humbold or Cuvier ! At least there is an appearance of at last wishing to do justice to our complaints, which we have in vain demanded for two years. If justice is rendered to us, we ought first to thank God, and after God, a generous Government, which out of its bounty has given us assistance, which we have long been refused by men who had the power, and whose duty, perhaps, it was, to aid us more effectually.

Source: Foreign Dept. Polt. A, March 1869, No. 208, NAI.

Appendix E

Dated Chungking, 2nd August 1878

From - E.C. Baber, Esq., Consular Officer at Chungking,

To - Hugh Fraser, Esq., H.M.'s Charge d'Affaires at Peking.

The following passage from Mr. Cooper's 'Travels of a Pioneer of Commerce' will recall to your memory the result of the previous Nipalese Mission under Juggut Share :-

"On the following day" (29th February 1868)" His Excellency Juggut Share, the Nipalese Ambassador, arrived. He was a young man of very courteous bearing, but seemed ill, and his conversation soon showed me that he was not only ill in body, but greatly depressed in spirits. His position was anything but pleasant, and he confided to me the history of his Embassy on its way so far towards Peking. He had left Katmandu nearly two years before, and after a long journey through Tibet, had arrived without encountering any serious difficulties at Ta-tsien-lu, the border town of China. Here he met his first repulse; a messenger from Peking brought him an Imperial order to deliver the presents sent by Jung Bahadoor to the Emperor at that place, and return to Nipal, as the road to Peking was rendered unsafe by the Nien-fei rebels. This the young Ambassador refused to do, pleading his instructions from Jung Bahadoor, which compelled him to deliver the presents in person. The authorities were determined to enforce the Emperor's orders, and Juggut Share was equally determined to proceed to Peking. Another application accordingly had to be made to the Emperor, for a reply to which he waited several months. When it came, it was in the form of a permission to him to proceed as far as Chen-tu (Ch'eng-tu) in order to dispose of several chests of opium brought for sale in China, and then to return home. He soon reached Chen-tu, and hoped to proceed further, but the authorities made this impossible. He could hire neither coolies nor boats, and, what was worse, no one would buy his opium; it was too strong, and the people preferred the native drug. At the time of my arrival, he had spent several months at Chen-tu, vainly pressing his request for leave to proceed to Peking. The officials treated him with great discourtesy, hoping by this means to force him to return, and had lodged him in a dirty hovel outside the city, which, as he said, was so filthy, that he was ashamed to ask me to visit him in it". - (Page 158; and see page 398).

Juggut Share did not succeed in getting beyond Cheng-tu, and on his return to Nepal was, I understand, severely punished for his failure. The present Legate seems an officer of much determination, having reached Ta-Chien-lu in spite of the obstacles placed in his way by the Chinese officials. It is very probable that he will reach Cheng-tu, and unless he takes the high road through the famine district, which is unlikely, he must continue his journey, via Chungking, and so down the Yangtse. He is certain, in that case, to call upon me, to obtain whatever assistance he may expect I can afford him. This will put me in a very awkward position *vis-à-vis* the local authorities, and I am not sure that I care to be associated in the Chinese mind with tribute-bearers. Common civility, however, will bind me to offer him, if desired, those little services which are so useful to strangers in a far land; and I presume there will be no harm in giving him a letter of introduction to Mr. Hughes, which will entail no more trouble than the putting the Legate on board a steamer and sending him to Shanghai with perhaps a letter to the Consul-General. Considering our relations with Nipal, this much at least seems called for.

The reason why the Chinese Government keep the Nipalese at a distance is probably that it is by no means anxious to maintain close relations with a country so nearly connected with India. The Mission is examined both on its entry into Thibet, and again on its return through that country, to satisfy the officials that it includes no Englishmen among its members. Another reason is that, as the tribute Missions are little more than disguised trade ventures, the Chinese fear they will sooner or later develop into a commercial establishment in Western China. Nipalese encroachments are much dreaded by the Lhassa Government, and their anxiety seems, of late years, to have spread to the Chinese, who are apprehensive, not for the integrity of their frontier, but for the security of its bulwark, or rather buffet, Thibet.

Source : Foreign Dept. Sec., December 1878, No. 27, NAI.

Appendix F

५ वर्षको मामुली सौगात चढाउन्या वषत होला पनी भोट गोर्षाको झगडा हुदा दु:ख पायाको हुनाले लडाई थामिया पछि सौगाद चढाउन आउदा प्रजा प्राणीलाई दु:ख होला भन्ना निमित यस पल्टको मामुली सौगाद चढाउन आउनु पर्दैन भन्या हुकुं आयो भन्या हाङफोङ ७ साल २ मैन्हा ८ दिन जादा श्री सुरेन्द्र विक्रम साहका हजुरमा संवत १९१३ सालमा छेन्तारीन यानतारीन अंवाले लेखेका.........

(Chinese *Ambans* to King Surendra instructing not to send five-yearly mission to China due to the sufferings of the outbreak of Nepal-Tibet War.)

Source : Ministry of Foreign Affairs, Kathmandu (MFA), *Poka* No. Pa 64.

Appendix G

अघिका रित वमोजिम सौगादका चिज विजहरु तयार पारी काजी भारदारहरु स्मेत षटाई जान तयार भयेका बषत्मा भोट गोर्षाको झगडा भै दुःष पायाको हुनाले यस पल्टको मामुली सौगाद पठाउनु पर्दैन भन्या हुकुम आयो भनी अम्वाहरुले लेखी पठाउदा सौगादका मालहरु थामी अर्जि चढाई पठायाको छ भन्यां १९१४ साल जेष्ठ वदी ८ रोज १ मा श्री ५ वादसाहका हजुरमा लेषीयाको अर्जिको नक्कल ....

(Nepalese Government's *arji* to the Chinese Emperor mentioning about the sending of *arji* instead of the usual five-yearly mission with presents.)

Source : MFA, *Poka* No. Pa 64.

Appendix H

हामीले आफुहरु मार्फत चढाई पठायाको अर्जि श्री ५ वादसाहका हजुरमा पुगी नजर भै सोझो चित्त गरी मान भाव संग पिछा परी एकत्व भैरहेको देषदा म वहुतै हर्ष भत्रा भंने इत्यादी हाम्रा उपर दया करुणको हुकुं भै आयाको विस्तार १९१४ साल आश्वीन वदी १४ रोज ५ मा श्री ५ सर्कारवाट यान्तारीन अंवालाई लेषेको ....

(Nepalese Government to Chinese *Amban* expressing happiness at the Chinese Emperor's reply to the Nepalese government's *arji.*)

Source : MFA, *Poka* No. Pa 64.

Appendix I

मामुली अर्जी सौगाद अघिका रित वमोजिम तयार गरी राषनु भनेर सठान सहरमा जाने वाटामा कुल्याहरुले कुल गर्न लाग्याको अझसंम थामिएको छैन भंने कुरा साचो ठहरीया पछि लेखी पठाउला भंने हाङफोन १० साल ११ मैन्हा १७ दिन जादा १९१७ साल्मा श्री ५ सर्कार सुरेन्द्र विक्रम साहका हजुरमा यान्तारीन अंवाले लेखेका ....

(Chinese *Amban* to King Surendra informing about the continuation of rebellion in Sathan town.)

Source : MFA, *Poka* No. Pa 64.

Appendix J

चीन जाने भारदारहरुलाई कुनै खतरा नभए, सरासर जान (पेकिङ) पाउने भए आफुहरुका चित्तमा ठहर्छ भने हाम्रो देसमा नहुने मध्येसवाट झिकाई होफोन १२ सालमा आफुहरुका अर्ति वमोजीम भारदार पठाउला भन्या १९१७ साल माघ सुदी २ रोज २ मा श्री ५ वाट यान्तारीन इन्तारीन अंवालाई लेखेको.............

(Nepalese King to Chinese *Ambans* seeking assurance for the Nepalese mission's safety and permission to reach Peking.)

Source : MFA, *Poka* No. Pa 64.

Appendix K

सठान सहरको वाटो षुला छैन यस पाला सौगाद चढाउनलाई पर्खी रहनु हाङफुन १७ सालमा चढाउन पठाउनु पर्छ भन्या हानफोङ १७ सालमा ८ मैन्हा ३ दिन जादा १९१८ सालमा श्री ५ सुरेन्द्रका हजुरमा यान्तारीन छिन्तारीन अंवाले लेखेको ....

(Chinese *Ambans* to King Surendra informing about the blocking of roads to Sathan town.)

Source : MFA, Poka No. Pa 64.

Appendix L

श्री ५ वादसाहलाई मान्या कुरामा हामी वहुतै खुसी छौ. कुल्याहा साम्य भया नभयाको र मामुली सौगात जानु पर्न्या नपर्न्या आफुहरु वाट तजविज गरी जवाफ पठाई दिनु भया देस देसवाट झिकाउनु पर्ने चीजहरु झिकाउन पठाउन्या काम गरौला-१९१८ साल आषाढ वदि ८ रोज १ मा श्री ५ वाट अंवालाई...

(Nepalese King to Chinese *Amban* making inquiries about the suppression of rebels and the dispatching of Nepalese mission to China.)

Source : MFA, *Poka* No. Pa 64.

Appendix M

आफु वाङले मामुली सौगाद चढाउन पठाउनु पर्दैन भन्या हुकुम भै आयाको प्रमाना पठाई दियाको छ सिमाना सम्म लिन पठाउनु होला. भन्या थोङदि २ साल २ मैन्हा १६ दिन जादा १९२० सालमा श्री ५ लाई आन्तारीन अम्वाले लेखेको ....

(Chinese *Amban* to Nepalese King informing about the cancellation of the dispatching of five-yearly Nepalese mission to China.)

Source : MFA, *Poka* No. Pa 64.

Appendix N

वाटामा लडाई परेको हुनाले यस पाला मामुली सौगाद नपठाउनु भन्या थोन्द्री १ साल ७ मैन्हा १ दिन जादा श्री ५ चिन वादसाहवाट आएको प्रमाना................

(Chinese Emperor's *Parwana* about the cancelling of the Nepalese mission to China.)

Source : MFA, *Poka* No. Pa 64.

Appendix O

फेरी सौगाद पठाउनु पर्ने वेला भयो. टाढावाट आउनु पर्ने हुनाले थोङद्री ६ सालमा आउनु हाम्रो मेहरवानी संझी ल्हासा वस्न्या अम्वाहरुका अर्ति सिक्षा मानी काम गर्नु भन्या इत्यादी पमाना लेषीयाको रहेछ – १९२० साल श्रावण सुदी ८ रोज ६ मा श्री ५ वाट अंवा.............................

(Nepalese King to Chinese *Amban* informing about the Chinese Emperor's *Parwana.*)

Source : MFA, *Poka* No. Pa 64.

Appendix P

काजी जगत्सेर ५ वर्षको सौगाद र गादी मुमारष सगुन लिई ल्हासा आइपुगेको तर अर्को चीठ्ठी दस्तुर नमिलेको हुनाले हालै नपठाउने पछि वीचार गर्ने-थोन्द्री ५ साल १० मैन्हा १० दिन जादा १९२३ सालमा श्री ५ सर्कारका हर्जुमा चिन्तारीन अम्वाले लेखेको ....

(Chinese *Amban* to Nepalese Government informing about the arrival of *Kazi* Jagat Sher at Lhasa.)

Source : MFA, *Poka* No. Pa 64.

Appendix Q

अर्जिका साथमा चीट्ठी नजाने कुरालाई अर्जिका साथमा नजाने भएता पनी सो कुरा हामीले जाहेर गर्नु पर्ने हुनाले अर्को अर्जी आफुहरु मार्फत चढाई पठायाको छ १९२३ साल माघ सुदी १५ रोज २ मा श्री ५ वाट यीन्तारीन अम्वालाई लेखेको ....

(Nepalese King to Chinese *Amban* informing about the sending of *arji* to the Chinese Emperor.)

Source : MFA, *Poka* No. Pa 64.

Appendix R

५ वर्षको मामुली सौगाद लि जादा अघी वेरामी हुदा पनी हिडनु पर्थ्यो अव उप्रान्त वेरामी भयामा नहिडनु भंन्या इत्यादि १९२३ साल आषाढ सुदी १२ रोज ३ मा काजी जगत्सेर षत्री सर्दार मलय जङ पांडेहरुका नाउमा गयाको नक्कलको मोहर ....

(Draft letter from Nepalese Government to *Kazi* Jagat Sher Khatri and *Sardar* Malaya Jang Pande instructing not to continue the journey of the mission at the time of illness.)

Source : MFA, *Poka* No. Pa 64.

Appendix S

मलाई र श्री ३ माहाराज दाज्यैज्यूका हर्जुरमा लेष्याको अर्जि २ आइ पुग्यो विस्तार जाहेर भयो – सर्कार वाहेक अरुको अफिमका भारी लिलाम गरेनौ भंन्या तिमीहरुलाई जरिवाना होला भन्या १९२३ साल भाद्र वदी १३ रोज ६ मा श्री कम्मांडर इन चीफवाट काजी जगत्सेरलाई ....

(Commander-in-Chief's warning to *Kazi* Jagat Sher regarding the disposition of opium.)

Source : MFA, *Poka* No. Pa 64.

Appendix T

ठाउँ ठाउमा वाटो वन्द गरी कुल्याहाहरुले विगाई विहृत गरेको हुनाले गोर्षाका

अर्जि सौगात पुऱ्याउन आउने काजीहरु पेचिन सम्म नआउनु भन्या भयाको छ. तिमीहरु फर्की आफ्ना राज्यमा जाउ अर्जि सौगाद चढाई जो भयाको वक्सीसहरु पठाई दिउला भन्ने थोन्द्री ६ वर्ष २ मैन्हा ४ दिन जादा ताचिनदेउका तुटुफमान भयाका सनतारीनहरुले काजी जगत्सेर षत्रीलाई ....

(*Santarins* to Jagat Sher requesting to turn over the presents for the Chinese Emperor and promising to forward them to Peking.)

Source : MFA, *Poka* No. Pa 64.

Appendix U

सुवेदार जंगवीर षत्री र वौधका लामा टेपुलसीं दमका वेथाले मरे. आफु वाङवाट पठायाको सारी हेर्दा निति थीतीमा नमिल्या कुरा धेरै रहेछ. हामीले वनाई दिएको मसौदा वमोजिं चाडो लेखी पठाउनु र वादसाहका हर्जुमा चढाई पठाउला भन्या थोन्द्री ६ साल ३ मैन्हा १६ दिन जादा १९२४ सालमा श्री ५ सुरेन्द्रलाई चिन्तारीन अंवाले लेखेको ....

(Chinese *Amban* to King Surendra informing about the death of *Subedar* Jangbir Khatri and Bauddha's Lama Tepul Singh.)

Source : MFA, *Poka* No. Pa 64.

Appendix V

श्री ५ वादसाहका हर्जुमा अर्जि सौगात पठाउन जाने काजीहरुले पेचिन जान नपाई सोसी सहरमा लडाई भै ठींनपुरका चुन्दुले चढाउन लगेको श्री वादसाहवाट वक्सेको प्रमाना षिलत स्मेत ली आउदा चोर डाकुको वचाउ गरी पठाउन व्यवस्था मिलाउन अंवालाई अनुरोध – १९२४ साल पौष वदी १३ रोज २ मा ....

(Nepalese Government to Chinese *Amban* requesting for the safety of the Nepalese mission while returning from Thinpur.)

Source : MFA, *Poka* No. Pa 64.

Appendix W

चीन जाने काजीहरुले दु:ख पाएको . श्री चीन वादसाहवाट वक्सेको असवाफ वचाई ल्याउन सकन असंभव. आवश्यक व्यवस्था गर्न अनुरोध. वैशाख सुदी १० रोज २ मा श्री ५ वाट ल्हासाका अंवा ....

(Nepalese King to Chinese *Amban* informing about the sufferings of the Nepalese mission and requesting for providing protection to the Chinese Emperor's presents to the Nepalese mission.)

Source : MFA, *Poka* No. Pa 64.

Appendix X

सम्वत १९२५ साल्मा काजी जगत्सेर सिजापतीहरुले ल्हासावाट लेखेको– ञाहावाट लगेको अफिमको भारी मालसामान भीकी कपट मिलाए भन्या इत्यादि अर्जि ....

(*Kazi* Jagat Sher Sijapati's *arji* to the Nepalese Government regarding the opium carried by the Nepalese mission.)

Source : MFA, *Poka* No. Pa 64.

Appendix Y

अघि अंवाहरुले वाटो खुला छ भनी लेखेकोले काजीहरु पठाएको . वादसाहको दर्सन नपाई फिर्दा सरम पनि भयो दुःख पनी पाए – १९२५ साल कार्तिक सुदी ९ रोज ७ मा श्री ५ वाट चिन्तारीन अंवालाई ....

(Nepalese King to Chinese *Amban* mentioning about the humiliation and sufferings of the Nepalese mission.)

Source : MFA, *Poka* No. Pa 64.

Appendix Z

वाटामा लडाई हुँदा येतावाट गयाका काजीहरु ठिन्दुपुरमा पर्षि मामुली सौगाद र गादीको सगुन सौगादहरु श्री ५ वादसाहका हजुरमा पुगी वक्सीस प्रमाना लि ठिन्दुपुर वाटै विदा भै आयाका आइ पुगे भन्या श्री ५ वाट वादसाहको हजुरमा जाने अर्जीको मसौदा – १९२६ साल ज्येष्ठ सुदी १५ रोज ५ ....

(Draft letter of the Nepalese King to the Chinese Emperor stating the arrival of the Nepalese mission in Nepal.)

Source : MFA, *Poka* No. Pa 64.

* * *

Kazi Tej Bahadur Rana's Mission of 1877

The extreme discourtesy and humiliation meted out to the 1866 Nepalese mission by the Chinese officials by not allowing the Nepalese mission to visit Peking and compelling them to return home humiliated from Ta Chien-lu, about half way to Peking near the China-Tibet border and the deaths of several members of the mission in eastern Tibet led Nepalese Prime Minister Jang Bahadur to think seriously about not sending any further mission to China at all. But the lure of huge commercial profits, especially through the opium trade, was too strong to resist, for the Nepalese missions had long ceased to have any political significance and had assumed the character of lucrative trading ventures. This is because the Nepalese ruling elite were well aware of the fact that in spite of all odds and all sorts of harrassment by the Chinese officials, the five-yearly mission system indeed provided a golden opportunity for them to dispose of a considerable cargo of opium in the western provinces of China without paying the heavy maritime duty and "*lekin*" taxes[1]. As such Jang Bahadur decided to dispatch the next mission to Peking in 1871. For that purpose, Nepal sent a letter to the Chinese *Ambans* in 1871 saying that she would send her mission if it would be allowed to reach Peking without any trouble.[2] The Ch'ing Emperor T'ung Chih could not give this assurance but rather allowed the Nepalese government to send *arji* and presents only to the Nepal-Tibet border[3]. Nepal was not satisfied with this reply and wrote that she would send her mission to Peking when the Emperor would instruct her to do so.[4] Under such conditions, the

---

1. Proposed Mission from Nipal to China, Foreign Dept. Sec. E, September 1876, Nos. 129-133, National Archives of India, New Delhi (hereafter referred as NAI).
2. Nepalese King to Chinese *Amban*, 1928 B.S. Kartik Sudi 4 Roj 5 (16 November 1871), Ministry of Foreign Affairs, Kathmandu (hereafter mentioned as MFA), *Poka* No. Pa 64. See Appendices J and L.
3. Chinese *Amban* to Nepalese King and *Sri Tin* Jang Bahadur, Throndi 10th year 12th month 29th day (1871), MFA, *Poka* No. Pa 64. See Appendix K.
4. Nepalese Government to Chinese *Ambans*, 1929 B.S. Marga Sudi 12 Roj 5 (12 December 1872), *Ibid.*, See Appendix M.

Nepalese government, which had been irritated by the failure of its 1866 mission to reach Peking, did not favour to send another mission to China at the scheduled time in 1871. At last, the proposed mission was allowed to be cancelled[5].

Going through the memorial from Sung Kwei, Acting Chinese Resident in Tibet, published in the *Peking Gazette* on 11 May 1876, it seems that Jang Bahadur had informed the Chinese *Amban* of his intention to dispatch a mission to Peking in 1877[6]. But before the mission could be sent to China, Jang Bahadur died on 25 February, 1877, and was succeeded by his brother Ranauddip Singh. The new Prime Minister faced strong internal opposition from the sons of Jang Bahadur, who questioned the legality of his accession to the prerogatives and powers of the offices held by their father before his death. That is why with a view to get Chinese recognition to his rule, within five months of his assumption of power, Ranauddip Singh dispatched a mission to China in July 1877[7] after a lapse of eleven years. The Chinese Imperial records have mentioned of Nepal's dispatching five-yearly mission to China in 1878, 1879 and 1880[8]. But the Nepalese and Indian archival documents clearly state of Nepal's sending of five-yearly mission to China in 1877 only. The 1877 Nepalese mission consisted of forty-five persons. It was led by *Kazi* Colonel Tej Bahadur Rana, son of late Prime Minister Bam Bahadur Rana[9] and a nephew of Ranauddip Singh. The other two prominent members of the mission were Lieutenant Bal Bahadur Pande, the deputy leader of the mission and *Subba* Bir Dhoj Adhikari.[10] The Nepalese mission left Kathmandu on 1934 B.S.

---

5. For the cancellation of the Nepalese mission, see Appendices N and O.
6. Memorial from Sung Kwei, Acting Resident in Tibet, Published in the *Peking Gazette*, 11 May, 1876, Foreign Dept Sec. E, September 1876, No. 130, NAI. See Appendix A.
7. Leo E. Rose, *Nepal: Strategy For Survival*, Berkeley: University of California Press, 1971, p. 137.
8. J.K. Fairbank and S.Y. Teng, "On the Ch'ing Tributary System", *Harvard Journal of Asiatic Studies*, Vol . VI, 1941, pp. 195-198.
9. Purushottam Shamsher Jang Bahadur Rana, *Sri Tin Haruko Tathya Brittanta* (Factual Description of *Sri Tins*), Banaras: Parambir Shamsher J.B.R., 2047 B.S., p. 184.
10. F. Henvey, Officiating Resident in Nepal to T.H. Thornton, Secretary, Govt. of India, 15 July 1877, Foreign Dept. Sec., October 1877, No. 149,

Ashad Sudi 5[11] (July 1877), carrying five-yearly general presents, special presents[12] and an *arji*[13] from King Surendra to the new Ch'ing Emperor Kwang Hsu.

Once again, the 1877 Nepalese mission faced difficulties in its efforts to reach Peking, although the Chinese government had earlier given the Nepalese mission permission to proceed to the Chinese capital. In November 1877, the Chinese authorities at Peking sent instructions to the Chinese *Ambans* at Tibet stating that "owing to the interruption of communication along the post roads caused by the unusually severe famine in the provinces of Shansi and Shensi", the Nepalese mission should be asked to surrender the presents and the letter to them (*Ambans*) to be forwarded to Peking and to return from there to their country.[14] By the time these instructions reached Lhasa, the Nepalese delegation had already left Lhasa for Peking. The *Ambans*, however, informed Ranauddip Singh about this instruction. In response, Ranauddip Singh (in the name of the Nepalese King) sent letters to the Chinese *Ambans* requesting for them to allow the Nepalese mission to visit Peking. He even argued that it would be a great humilitation to Nepal if her mission would be compelled to return from mid-way.[15] When the

---

NAI. See Appendix B. For the details of the 1877 Nepalese mission, see Tri Ratna Manandhar, *Nepal: The Years of Trouble (1877-85)*, Kathmandu: Purna Devi Manandhar, 1986, pp. 140-143, See also Tri Ratna Manandhar and Tirtha Prasad Mishra, *Nepal's Quinquennial Missions to China*, Kathmandu: Purna Devi Manandhar and Puspa Mishra, 1986, p. 29, 40 and pp. 58-59.

11. "Nepal Desh Ko Itihas" (History of Nepal), A Manuscript in the National Archives of Nepal, Kathmandu, Published in *Ancient Nepal*, No. 27, April 1974, p. 18.
12. Nepalese King to Chinese *Amban*, 1934 B.S. Jestha Badi 30 Roj 2 (1878), MFA, *Poka* No. Pa 64. See Appendix P.
13. Translation of a letter from King Surendra to the Chinese Emperor, 20 July 1877, Foreign Dept. Sec. E, September 1895, No. 124, NAI. See Appendix F.
14. *Peking Gazette*, 24 March 1879, Foreign Dept. Sec., June 1879, No. 23, NAI. See Appendix D. See also Chinese *Amban* to Nepalese King, Kwang-hsu 4th year 4th month 2nd day (1935 B.S.), MFA, *Poka* No. Pa 64. See Appendix V.
15. Nepalese King to Chinese *Amban*, 1934 B.S. Chaitra Sudi 12 Roj 1 (14 April, 1878), MFA, *Poka* No. Pa 64. See Appendix Q. See also Manandhar, f.n. no. 10, pp. 141-142.

Nepalese mission reached Ta Chien-lu, a Chinese town on the frontier of Tibet, on 1 July, 1878, the Chinese authorities stopped the mission[16] and asked them to surrender the presents and return from there. However, the leader of the Nepalese mission, *Kazi* Tej Bahadur Rana, refused to obey the Chinese instructions and told the Chinese authorities that his mission would not return until "my government orders to do so".[17] Following the exchange of correspondence between the Peking authorities and Ta Chien-lu officials for several months, the Nepalese mission was allowed to proceed further, and it reached Szechuan on 2 February, 1879. The Szechuan authorities entertained the Nepalese mission in the usual fashion. The Nepalese delegation appealed to the Szechuan authorities to allow them to proceed to Peking and even offered them presents of silk and articles of food. Meanwhile, the Szechuan authorities received a formal letter from Peking allowing the Nepalese mission to proceed to Peking. The Peking authorities also asked the Szechuan officials to send instructions along the road that proper attention be shown to the Nepalese mission.[18]

Finally, the Nepalese mission reached Peking by December 1879. Although the Nepalese mission reached Peking, it felt much humiliated as its members were lodged in the dirty building assigned to the missions of tributary states, near the British Legation.[19] The leader and the higher officials of the mission were reported to have received an audience in the Ch'ing court as 'vassals'[20], and the Chinese officer in charge of the mission even

16. R. Hughes, Her Majesty's Consul at Hankow to Salisbury, Foreign Secretary, 17 August 1878, Foreign Dept. Sec., January 1879, No. 91, NAI. See Appendix C. See also Chinese *Amban* to King Surendra, Kwang-hsu 4th year 4th month 2nd day (1878), MFA, *Poka* No. Pa 64. See Appendix R.
17. Manandhar, f.n.no. 10, p. 142. For the correspondence between Chinese and Nepalese government regarding the Nepalese *Kazi's* refusal to return from mid-way, see Appendices S and T.
18. Peking Gazette, 24 March 1879, Foreign Dept. Sec., June 1879, No. 23, NAI. and *Peking Gazette*, 9 April 1879, Foreign Dept. Sec., July 1879, No. 8, NAI.
19. T.F. Wade, Her Majesty's Minister at Peking to Viceroy of India, 16 January 1880, Foreign Dept. Polt. A, April 1880, No. 98, NAI. See Appendix G.
20. Her Majesty's Minister at Peking to Ripon, Viceroy of India, 1 November 1880, Foreign Political A, January 1881, No. 84, NAI. See Appendix H.

attempted to prevent the mission meeting the British representative at Peking. It was only after much persuasion (by applying through *Li Fan Yuan* and *Tsungli Yamen*) that the British representative Sir T.F. Wade, Her Majesty's Minister at Peking succeeded in meeting the Nepalese mission. Accordingly, on 10 January, 1880, the Nepalese envoy *Kazi* Tej Bahadur Rana, along with one colleague, called on the British representative at his British Legation. The British Minister also returned their visit two or three days later.[21] Furthermore, one or two messages passed between the British Minister at Peking and the visiting Nepalese mission in Peking.[22] The British Minister Sir T.F. Wade had described Nepalese envoy *Kazi* Tej Bahadur Rana as "a bright, intelligent man".[23] The Nepalese mission remained at Peking until May 1880. The announced departure date of the mission was deferred on several occasions, but it finally left Peking on 30 May 1880[24] after having had at least one audience with the Ch'ing Emperor, Kwang Hsu. While on its homeward journey, the Nepalese mission arrived at Ta-Tsian-lu (Ta Chien-lu) around April 1881.[25] Finally the 1877 Nepalese mission reached the Nepalese capital of Kathmandu in 1939 B.S. Ashad Sudi 3 Roj 1[26] (18 June, 1882), and was accorded a warm welcome by an escort of two regiments with bands playing.[27] The return journey of the Nepalese mission was quite peaceful[28], except that their goods had been stolen on the way.[29]

---

21. T.F. Wade to Viceroy of India, 16 January 1880, Foreign Dept. Polt. A, April 1880, No. 98, NAI.
22. Her Majesty's Minister at Peking to Ripon, Viceroy of India, 1 November 1880, Foreign Polt. A, January 1881, No. 84, NAI.
23. T.F. Wade to Viceroy of India, 16 January 1880, Foreign Dept. Polt. A, April 1880, No. 98, NAI.
24. Her Majesty's Minister at Peking to Ripon, Viceroy of India, 1 November 1880, Foreign Polt. A, January 1881, No. 84, NAI.
25. Girdlestone to Secretary, Govt. of India, 28 June 1881, Foreign Dept. Polt. B, July 1881, No. 156, NAI. See Appendix E.
26. "Nepal Desh Ko Itihas" (History of Nepal), *Ancient Nepal*, No. 27, April 1974, p. 24.
27. Girdlestone to Secretary, Govt of India 19 June 1882, Foreign Dept. Sec. July 1882, No. 155, NAI. See Appendix I.
28. For the correspondence between the Nepalese and Chinese government regarding the return journey of the Nepalese mission, see Nepalese King to Chinese *Ambans* 1938 B.S. Asadh Badi 10 Roj 3 (1881), MFA, *Poka* No. Pa 64 and Chinese *Ambans* to Nepalese Government, Kwang-hsui 7th

Here it will not be out of context to mention as to what may have caused the Chinese government's harsh attitude towards the 1877 Nepalese mission firstly by attempting to prevent it from reaching Peking and thereafter by harrasing or humiliating the mission in Peking. It seems that the Chinese greatly suspected that the 1877 mission, too was carrying opium along with other merchandise, and that the Chinese did not at all like the Nepalese mission's involvement in the opium trade. That is why similar to the 1866 mission, this time too, the Chinese stopped the Nepalese mission once again at Ta Chien-lu with the intention of preventing the Nepalese mission's visit to Peking. Later on, although the Nepalese mission was allowed to visit Peking only at the insistence of the Nepalese government, the Chinese (who were truly dissatisfied with the arrival of Nepalese mission in Peking) left no stone unturned to humiliate them. It appears that the Chinese seemed to have taken all these measures in order to harass or humiliate the Nepalese mission, whom the Chinese believed to be engaging in opium-trading (smuggling) activities. Thus considering the Chinese response it can be assumed that the 1877 Nepalese mission too was carrying a large quantity of opium for sale in China; if not, the Chinese would not have humiliated the Nepalese mission[30]. Besides that, Sir T.F. Wade, the British Minister at Peking who met the leader of 1877 Nepalese mission, interestingly remarked that the leader of the Nepalese mission did not like to say that the object of the mission was commercial, but the British Minister took it to be in reality. The British Minister had further remarked that like most missions from other countries to China, the Nepalese mission had brought various articles, some of course to be

---

year 6th month 13th day (1881), MFA, *Poka* No. Pa 64. See Appendices X and Z.

29. For the sufferings and the theft goods of the Nepalese mission, see Nepalese King to Chinese *Amban*, 1935 B.S. Jestha Badi 2 Roj 7 (1878), MFA, *Poka* No. Pa 64. See Appendix U; Nepalese King to Chinese *Amban*, 1937 B.S. Sudi 1 Roj 1 (1880), MFA, *Poka* No. Pa 64. See Appendix W, and Draft Letter from Nepalese King to Chinese *Amban,* 1939 B.S. Kartik Sudi 6 Roj 5 (1882), MFA, *Poka* No. Pa. 64. See Appendix Y.
30. For the details of the 1877 Nepalese Mission's involvement in opium trading activities in China, see Vijay Kumar Manandhar, ***Cultural and Political Aspects of Nepal-China Relations***, Delhi: Adroit Publishers, 1999, pp. 77-78.

presented as gifts to the Ch'ing Emperor, but the rest for sale. Here it should be noted that since the time of the 1852 Nepalese mission, opium had emerged as the most profitable trading item of the mission. In this way it seems that the 1877 Nepalese mission was also involved in opium trading activities and, due to that factor, the journey of the mission became significantly longer; this mission returned home after nearly five-years. Normally, the Nepalese mission to China took around two years to complete the journey[31].

This fifteenth five-yearly mission of 1877 was important due to the following reasons: Firstly, it was due to this mission that the Ch'ing Emperor Kwang Hsu recognized the new Nepalese Prime Minister Ranauddip Singh by decorating him the Chinese title of *Thong Ling Pimma Kokang Vang Syan (Thong Ling Pimma KoKang Wang Shang)* in January 1878, even before the arrival of the 1877 Nepalese mission at Peking. Here it should be mentioned that through the 1877 Nepalese mission, King Surendra had sent a letter informing the Ch'ing Emperor of Ranauddip Singh's assumption of power and in the meantime also requesting for him the same Chinese title obtained earlier by Jang Bahadur in 1871. Secondly, this mission happened to be the fifth Nepalese mission which had carried the usual five-yearly presents and special presents on the occasion of the new Ch'ing Emperor Kwang Hsu's ascending the throne in 1875. Thirdly, out of the fifteen five-yearly missions sent by Nepal over a period of eighty five years, i.e. from 1792 to 1877, this 1877 mission returned home after the lapse of about five years, the longest time so far taken by the Nepalese mission to complete the journey. Above all, it was the first Nepalese quinquennial mission ever led by the son of a Nepalese Prime Minister.

Appendix A

(Translation)

Projected Embassy from Nipal to China (manuscript edition of the *Peking Gazette* dated 11th May 1876).

Sung Kwei, Acting Resident in Thibet, memorialises as follows:-

A petition having been received from Nipal requesting information with regard to the period for sending tribute, your slave has

---

31. *Ibid.*, p. 78.

informed himself that according to regulation the King of Nipal should send a person once every five years to Pekin to make offering of a respectful address and of tribute. A Mission was due in 1872, with reference to which a rescript was received from His Majesty granting exemption on that occasion. Another period of five years will expire in 1877, and as the rescript of His Majesty (issued after the death of the late Emperor) commanded that a period of 27 months should elapse before offerings are laid before the Throne, the proper period will be reached in the 5th moon of next year. On perusal of a translation of the letter received from the King aforesaid, your slave finds it couched in language reverentially submissive and expressive of the most devoted loyalty. He accordingly makes report thereof for the Imperial information, and looking upwards would ask of the Celestial Grace whether permission may be granted to send the tribute offerings at the regular date, or whether there shall be a postponement of the period. On these points, upon which your slave does not venture to take the responsibility of decision, he prostrate awaits instructions. He has to add that the King aforesaid makes mention of the birth of a grandson, his first, (or, the child of his eldest son), which he thinks it his duty to report. Your slave has expressed congratulations in reply, and has sent back an Imperial donation of two rolls of embroidered satin, to which he has added on his own account a roll of wide satin by way of congratulatory largesse, in furtherance of his sovereign's desire to cherish tenderly the foreigner with a liberality that knows no bounds.

Rescript issued to the Grand Council in reply to the foregoing. Let the tribute be forwarded at the proper period.

Memorial published in the manuscript edition of the *Pekin Gazette*, 11th May 1876. Chinese Character.

Source : Foreign Dept. Sec. E., September 1876, No. 130, National Archives of India, New Delhi (NAI).

Appendix B

No. 35 P., dated Nipal Residency, 15 July 1877

From - F. Henvey, Esq., Officiating, Resident in Nipal

To - T.H. Thornton, Esq., D.C.L., C.S.I, Offg. Secy. to Govt. of India, Foreign Dept.

I have the honor to report, for the information of the Governor-General in Council, that a party consisting of

Colonel Tej Bahadur Rana, cousin of late Sir Jung Bahadur,
Lieutenant Bal Bahadur Pande,
Subah Bir Dhoj Adhikari,
and 42 petty officers and soldiers,

will leave Kathmandu after three or four days on a mission to the Court of Peking.

2. It has been announced to me on the part of the Nipalese Government that there is nothing special in the deputation of the persons to China. It is merely a return to the old practice of sending a quin-quennial mission to Peking, which practice fell into abeyance for a considerable time owing to disputes with the Thibetans.
3. The journey to Peking is said to take seven or eight months, and the party will probably not return to Nipal in less than two years.

Source : Foreign Dept. Sec., October 1877, No. 149. NAI.

Appendix C

N. 13, dated Hankow, 17 August 1878

From - R. Hughes, Esq., Her Majesty's Consul at Hankow
To - Marquis of Salisbury, Secretary of State for Foreign Affairs

I learn from Mr. Baber, who has addressed Her Majesty's Charge d'Affaires on the subject, that an Envoy from Nipal with tribute for the Chinese Government arrived at Ta Chien - lu, a Chinese town on the frontier of Thibet, on the 1st of July. He is delayed there in consequence of the authorities objecting to his further progress.

Mr. Baber seems to think that permission will ultimately be given him to proceed to Peking. The Envoy will probably endeavour to obtain the advice and assistance of British officials if he meets with them, and in the event of his proceeding *via* Hankow, Mr. Baber proposes to give him a letter of introduction to me.

I think it is doubtful that the Envoy will take this route if allowed to proceed to Peking. In any case, his moments are likely to be slow.

The mission is probably more or less in the nature of a trading speculation. It has doubtless other objects, but what they are is not known here at present.

Source : Foreign Dept. Sec., January 1879, No. 91, NAI.

Appendix D

From the Manuscript Edition of the Peking Gazette, 24th March 1879.

Memorial from Heng-Hsun, Manchu Commander-in-Chief in Sze-chwen, and Ting Pao-Chen, Governor-General of Sze-chwen, reporting the arrival in Sze-chwen of tribute-bearing Envoys from Nipal.

Owing to the interruption of communication along the post roads caused by the unusually severe famine in the provinces of Shansi and Shensi, your Ministers submitted a memorial in November 1877, requesting that the letter and tribute from Nipal might be intercepted in Tibet, and thence forwarded by a (Chinese) official to Cheng-tu (the capital of Sze-chwen), whence it could be sent on to the capital; and, in reply thereto, they had the honor to receive an Imperial Decree assenting to the course proposed.

Subsequently, Sung-Kwei, the Imperial Resident in Tibet, having reported that the tribute-bearing Envoys had already arrived in Tibet, and had been sent on their way, another Decree was received in the following words:- "When the tribute-bearing Envoys reach Sze-chwen, let an officer be despatched with the letter and tribute to Peking.

This Decree was reverently communicated to the Commissioner, and at the same time an officer was sent to Chamdo to convoy the tribute.

The Nipalese Envoy, Ko-chi, and others arrived in Sze-chwen on the 2nd of February last, and were entertained in the usual fashion, in order to make manifest our Emperor's magnanimity and his kindness towards strangers. The Envoys, evincing great joy, and knocking their heads on the ground, delivered over the petition of the Ruler of their country, dated July 1878, in which reference was made to the desire of his wild subjects to become civilized, to the glory conferred upon him by the previous admission of his Envoys to the Imperial presence, and to the tranquility which has prevailed in his dominions since his reliance has been placed in the far-reaching influence of His Imperial Majesty's might and protection.

The Envoys appealed to your Ministers to memorialize on their behalf, praying that, as heretofore, they might be allowed to proceed to Peking, so that they might with up-lifted eyes gaze on His Majesty, and offer the tribute in person. Their appeal, so respectful in tone and so sincere in feeling, your Ministers cannot venture to withhold from the throne; and as all has been quiet in Shansi and Shensi since rain fell last autumn, and there is no danger of difficulties being encountered along the post roads, they would refer for His Majesty's decision whether the Envoys shall be graciously permitted, as heretofore, to proceed to Peking.

Your Ministers would further add that the Ruler of Nipal and the tribute-bearing Envoys have offered them presents of silk and articles of food, which they would not venture to accept without permission, and they accordingly await His Majesty's pleasure on the subject.

To the above memorial the Grand Council has received the following Decree:- "Let the Nipalese Envoys be permitted, as is customary, to come to Peking; and let the Manchu Commander-in-Chief and his colleagues send instructions along the road that proper attention be shewn them. As to the question of accepting the presents offered to the Manchu Commander-in-Chief and his colleague, let the existing regulations be followed. The proper department will take note."

Source : Foreign Dept. Sec. E., June 1879, No. 23, NAI.

Appendix E

No. 39 P. of 1881

From - C.E.R. Girdlestone Esqre, Cs. Resident in Nepal

To - The Secretary to the Government of India, in the Foreign Department Simla.

Nepal Residency, the 28th June 1881

Sir,

Adverting to my letter No. 15 P. dated April 1880 (to which no answer has been received in this office) I have the honour to say that this Durbar has heard of the safe arrival of its Envoy and suite at Tasunloo, on the western border of China, about two months ago.

I have the honour to be,
Sir,
Your most obedient servant
Girdlestone
Resident

Source : Foreign Dept. Polt. B, July 1881, No. 156, NAI.

Appendix F

Translation of a letter from the Maharaja Adhiraj Surendra Bikram Sah of Nepal to the Emperor of China, dated Friday, the 10th of Asar Sudi Samvat 1934 (=20th July 1877).

Heading

To His Imperial Majesty the Emperor of China, who has at his command all the enjoyments and pleasures of this vast universe in all their various and multitudinous forms and shapes.

Petition

The present is the year in which it is incumbent upon me to submit the tribute petition, pay my respects, and make my prostrations to His Imperial Majesty the Emperor.

My country being in hills, such articles as cannot be found here, though searched for, have to be sent for from distant countries, consequently having procured the articles from India, and having mindfully and according to ancient custom prepared all the complement, I, in accordance with the note of instructions from the Umbahs stationed at Lhassa, send hence Kazi Tij Bahadur Rana Sirdar Bul Bahadur Panre and Khudar, Subadar, Interpreters and other suitable gentlemen, with the view that they may, waiting upon His Imperial Majesty at Peking, lay in his august presence the tribute petition, obtain reverential sight of His Imperial Majesty and making prostration to him return hither.

As the Umbahs stationed at Lhassa have, even before this, constituted the channel for conveying representations of my troubles and pains this day to the troubles and pains of the child as I am who being ignorant of the due formalities by reason of his living in a small (insignificant) hilly kingdom so remote from Pekin, will be made known to the Emperor through the medium of the Umbahs of Lhassa.

My ancestors too have borne allegiance to and have remained under the shelter of His Imperial Majesty. I too with all my head and heart (mouth and stomach, i.e. sincerity and zeal), and with all singleness of heart, beg to remain loyal and under the shelter of His Imperial Majesty. The bestowal of the kind consideration by His Majesty upon the child, viz., myself, that Gurkha (myself), who living in His Majesty's big country is serving the Emperor, is his slave, will dissipate and remove all my troubles and cares. Hereafter decade after decade for perpetuity living under His Imperial Majesty's protection, I will continue to dance attendance upon the Emperor. Dated Friday, the 10th of Asar Sudi Samvat 1934 (=20th July 1877).

Source : Foreign Dept. Sec. E., Sept. 1895, No. 124, NAI.

Appendix G

No. 2, dated Peking, 16th January 1880

From - Sir T.F. Wade, Her Majesty's Minister at Peking

To - His Excellency the Viceroy and Governor- General of India

A Mission from Nipal, of the approach of which we have been hearing for months, arrived here some three or four weeks ago. Its members were lodged in the dirty building assigned to the missions of tributary nations, at no great distance from this Legation.

After waiting a few days I sent to enquire after the health of the envoys, and to ask whether I could be of any service to them.

As I expected the Chinese in charge of the mission made some slight attempt to prevent intercourse with it. At least it is thus that I interpreted his reference to the Li Fan Yuan, an office in general charge of the Mongolians and other dependent races, through which alone, he said, would communication be possible.

I applied to the Tsungli Yamen, and, after a little longer delay, succeeded in getting into communication with the Nipalese, if indeed the use of the term be not inappropriate, where such difficulties beset the simplest conversation. The envoy speaks the language of his country to, I presume, a Nipalese, who interprets it in Tibetan to a Chinese of Ssu-Chuan, who interprets this to us.

The envoy and a colleague, both, as far as I could learn, military men, called on me on the 10th instant, and I returned their visit two or three days later; but I learned little except that from the sickness of one of the mission, it is likely to be here another month.

It is possible that the Chief, a bright intelligent man, did not like to say that its object was commercial, as I take it in reality to be. Like most missions from these countries to China, this one has brought various articles of home manufacture, some of course to be presented as tribute, but the rest for sale.

The names of the two envoys, as written in Chinese, should be Pa na pa ha je and Ti tzu pa hap tu git. At my request the chief of the mission had them written for me in Deva Nagari. I enclose the slip containing their names.

Source : Foreign Dept. Polt. A., April, 1880, No. 98. NAI.

Appendix H

No. 13, dated Pekin, 1st November 1880

From - Her Brittanic Majesty's Minister, Pekin.

To - His Excellency the Marquis of Ripon, K.G. Viceroy and Governor-General of India.

I beg to acknowledge receipt of a letter from the Secretary to the Government of India referring me to an earlier letter of the 14th of last May in which I was requested to report the departure of the Nipalese Mission.

In my letter of the 16th January last I had the honor to report to Your Excellency's predecessor an exchange of visits between myself and the heads of this Mission. One or two messages passed between us subsequently and their departure was again and again announced, but for some reason, to me unknown, again and again deferred, and the Mission finally left Pekin without my knowledge.

It must, however, have started in the summer, for in the Pekin Gazette of 27th August the Mission is stated to have arrived on its return journey at An-Yang Hsien upon the Honan frontier on the 18th of June last. An-Yang Hsien is 1,170 li, or twenty stages, something less than 400 miles, from Pekin, so that the Mission probably left upon the 30th of May.

The Chiefs had audience as vassals, but beyond this I was unable to ascertain anything of their proceedings. The probability is indeed that, as in the case of all similar Missions, there was absolutely nothing of importance to ascertain.

Source : Foreign Polt. A., January, 1881, No. 84., NAI.

Appendix I

No. 63 P., dated Nipal Residency Katmandoo, 19th June 1882

From - C.E.R. Girdlestone, Esq., C.S., Resident in Nipal
To - C. Grant, Esq., C.S.I., Secretary to the Government of India, Foreign Dept.

With reference to correspondence ending with No. 1490 E.P., dated 13th July 1881, from the Foreign Office, I have the honor to report that the mission deputed hence to China in 1877 returned here yesterday. The mission has brought a letter and presents from the Emperor of China to the Maharaj Adhiraj of Nipal, and was consequently for the last two miles into Katmandoo honored with an escort of two regiments with bands playing. In honor of the occasion two salutes of twenty-one guns each were fired at short intervals in the forenoon of yesterday.

Source : Foreign Dept. Sec., July 1882, No. 155, NAI.

Appendix J

वाटोमा रोक टोक नभै अघिका रीत वमोजिम सरासर पेकिङ गै वादसाहको दर्सन पाउन सक्ने भए ५ वर्षको सौगात पठाउने र हाम्रा मुख्य वजिरलाई इलकाव पायेका वारेमा स्मेत उन्का तरफवाट अर्जी चढाउन पाउनका सल्लाह – १९२८ साल कार्तिक सुदी ४ रोज ५ मा श्री ५ वाट अंवा....................

(Nepalese King to Chinese *Amban* informing about the Nepalese government's intention to dispatch mission to China if it would be allowed to reach Peking without any trouble.)

Source : Ministry of Foreign Affairs Kathmandu (MFA), *Poka* No. Pa 64.

Appendix K

सांसीन्भन्या सहरगा लडाई भएको र नथामीएको हुनाले भारदार पठाउंदा दुःख हुन्छ मामुली अर्जी सौगात दोसाध सम्म पुऱ्याउन पठाउनु. हामी ताहा सम्म लिन पठाउला भंन्या थोन्द्री १० साल १२ मैन्हा २९ दिन जादा १९२८ साल्मा श्री ५ लाई र श्री ३ सर्कार जङ्ग वहादुर राणाजी हजुरमा इन्तारीन तोतारीन अंवाले लेखेको ....

(Chinese *Ambans* to Nepalese King and *Sri Tin* Jang Bahadur Rana instructing to send *arji* and presents to the Nepal-Tibet border instead of sending mission to Peking due to the rebellion in Shanshin town.)

Source : MFA, *Poka* No. Pa 64.

Appendix L

देस देसावर वाट साना ठूला अव गोर्खा दरवारलाई श्री ५ चीन वादसाहको दया

मेहरवानी छुटेछ दर्सन दंडवत गर्न पनी पायेनन्. मामुली सौगाद लि दर्सन गर्न जान पनि पाएन होच्याउने ठाउ पाउने – यसर्थ चीन वादसाह दर्सन गर्न आउनु भन्या लेषी आयाको पठाउने – श्री ५ वाट १९२८ साल चैत्र सुदी ३ रोज ५ मा तेतारीन अम्वालाई ....

(Nepalese King to Chinese *Amban* informing about Nepalese government's intention of sending mission to Peking.)

Source : MFA, *Poka* No. Pa 64.

Appendix M

अव उप्रान्त मामुली सौगाद जैले ल्याउनु भन्या ल्याउनु भन्या श्री वादसाहवाट भै आउला. उसै वेला चढाई पठाउन्या काम गरौला भंन्या १९२९ साल मार्ग सुदी १२ रोज ५ मा श्री ५ सर्कारवाट ल्हासाका २ अम्वालाई लेखेको............

(Nepalese Government to Chinese *Ambans* informing that Nepal would send her mission to Peking when the Emperor would instruct her to do so.)

Source : MFA, *Poka* No. Pa 64.

Appendix N

सान्सी भन्यां देसमा लुष्दै भन्याका कुल्याहा ले कल गर्न लागेको नथामिएको हुनाले यस पटक आफु वाङको अर्जि सौगात चढाई पठाउनु पर्दैन भन्या हुकुं भै आयो – थोन्द्री ११ साल ९ मैन्हा १४ दिन जादा १९२९ सालमा श्री ५ लाई उन्तारीन अंवाले लेखेको ....

(Chinese *Amban* to Nepalese King informing not to dispatch mission to Peking due to the rebellion in Shanshi.)

Source : MFA, *Poka* No. Pa 64.

Appendix O

श्री ५ वादसाहका हर्जुमा सौगात चढाउने गैह्रको सोक सुर्ताको वखत हुनाले ३ वर्ष थाम्नु भन्ने लेषि आयाको छ . सो मान्नु होला भन्ने ककांस्यु १ वर्ष ५ मैन्हा २६ दिन जादा १९३२ साल्मा श्री ५ सुरेन्द्रलाई सितारीन अंवाले लेखेको...........

(Chinese *Amban* to King Surendra informing to postpone sending mission to China for three years due to the mourning period.)

Source : MFA, *Poka* No. Pa 64.

Appendix P

५ वर्षको मामुली सौगाद र गादी मुमारष सगुन सौगाद. काजी तेज वहादुर राणा, सर्दार वल वहादुर पांडे आषाढ २ दिन जादा श्री ५ चीन वादसाहको दर्सन गर्न पठाउने – १९३४ साल ज्येष्ठ वदि ३० रोज २ मा श्री ५ सर्कारवाट

ल्हासाका सुन्तारीन अंवालाई लेखेको ....

(Nepalese Government to Chinese *Amban* informing about the dispatching of the mission to Peking carrying general and special presents under the leadership of *Kazi* Tej Bahadur Rana and *Sardar* Bal Bahadur Pande.)

Source : MFA, *Poka* No. Pa 64.

Appendix Q

अघि २३ सालमा जस्तै फर्केर आउनु नपरोस भनी लेखी पठाएकोमा अघि जस्तो हुदैन भन्ने जवाफ आउदा श्री ५ को दर्सन गर्न पठाएको हो. यो साल फर्की आएमा वेइज्जत हुने – १९३४ साल चैत्र सुदी १२ रोज १ अंवालाई लेखेको..................................

(Nepalese King informing the Chinese *Amban* that it would be a great humiliation to Nepal if her mission would be compelled to return from mid-way.)

Source : MFA, *Poka* No. Pa 64.

Appendix R

सांसी र संसी भन्या सहरमा अनिकाल परी प्रजा प्राणीलाई दुःख हुनाले अर्जि सौगात सिठन्मा राखी फर्की जानु पर्खि रहनु पर्दैन वकसीक प्रमाना चीज वीज यामुन वाट पठाउला भन्या सिन्दुका चुन्दुले लेषी पठायाका छ भन्ना इत्यादि काङ्का स्यूई ४ साल ४ मैन्हा २ दिन जादा १९३५ सालमा श्री ५ सुरेन्द्रका हर्जुरमा कुइतारीन अम्वाले लेषेको ....

(Chinese *Amban* informing King Surendra about the Chinese authorities' instructing the Nepalese mission for surrendering the presents and returning from Sithan.)

Source : MFA, *Poka* No. Pa 64.

Appendix S

चीनका मुलुकमा अनिकाल परेको (संसि) चीन जाने काजीलाई फर्क भनी लेखी पठायाको. हाम्रा सर्कारको हुकुं नआई फर्कदैनौं भनी लेखी पठाए – कंस्यूई ४ साल १ मैन्हा १७ दिन जादा १९३४ साल्मा श्री ५ लाई सुन्तारीन फूइतारीन अंवाले लेखेको ....

(Chinese *Ambans* to Nepalese King informing about Chinese government's instruction to Nepalese *Kazi* to return from mid-way due to famine in Shanshi and the Nepalese *Kazi's* refusal to return from there.)

Source : MFA, *Poka* No. Pa 64.

Appendix T

सिठानवाट सौगात लिउन फोपुन २ ले काजीहरुलाई अर्जि सौगाद वुझाई फर्क भन्दा वीचवाट हामीले फर्कनु हुदैन सौगाद फिराई लान्छौ भन्छन्. फर्काई लैजादा रिसानी होला, आफु वाङले मान्नु होला छ भंन्या क्काङस्यूई ४ साल ४ मैन्हा ६ दिन जादा १९३५ साल्मा श्री ५ सर्कारका हजुरमा कुइतारीन अंवाले लेखेको ....

(Chinese *Amban* to Nepalese Government informing about the Nepalese *Kazi's* refusal to return from mid-way.)

Source : MFA, *Poka* No. Pa 64.

Appendix U

यो साल दु:ख हुदैन भनी पठाएकोमा ठाउँ ठाउँ धेरै मुकाम भएको. सीधा दस्तुर नदी वेसाई खानु भनेको, किन्न पनी नपाई दु:ख पाएको हुनाले अर्जि सौगात चढाउन विश्वास जाने भएकाले खास व्यवस्था हुनु पर्ने. १९३५ साल ज्येष्ठ वदी २ रोज ७ मा श्री ५ वाट सुन्तारीन कुइतारीन अंवालाई लेखेको...................

(Nepalese King to Chinese *Ambans* informing about the sufferings of the Nepalese mission and requesting for special arrangements for the mission.)

Source : MFA, *Poka* No. Pa 64.

Appendix V

सांसी र संसी भन्या सहरमा अनिकाल भै प्रजाप्राणीलाई दु:ष हुने हुनाले साह्रै दु:ख होला अर्जि सौगात वुझी श्री वादसाहवाट वकसीस भयाको चीज वीज अंवा मार्फत दोसाध सम्म पुऱ्याउन पठाउनु भन्या हुकुं आया वमोजिम लेखेको भनी सिठुंका टुचाङ तुवुथाम अंवाले कांस्यूई ४ साल ४ मैन्हा २ दिन जादा १९३५ सालमा श्री ५ मा ....

(Chinese *Amban* to Nepalese King informing about the Chinese Emperor's instruction of Nepalese mission's surrendering of *arji* and presents to the *Ambans* to be forwarded to Peking and the returning of the Nepalese mission from the mid-way due to the severe famine in Shansi and Shensi.)

Source : MFA, *Poka* No. Pa 64.

Appendix W

हराएका मालमता पत्ता लगाई र पत्ता नलागे नगद भराई पठाई दिनु भया वढिया होला भन्ने १९३७ साल सुदी १ रोज १ मा श्री ५ वाट सैतारीन अंवालाई लेखेको ....

(Nepalese King to Chinese *Amban* requesting for searching the Nepalese mission's lost goods or its compensation.)

Source : MFA, *Poka* No. Pa 64.

Appendix X

अव ता यो पाला जस्तो ठाउँ ठाउँमा माल भारीहरु चौरिन्यां हराउन्या र धेरै दिन मुकाम गर्नु पर्न्या ढिला हुदैन. श्री ५ वादसाहका हुकुमले अर्का पाला देखी अर्जि सौगात चढाउना दर्सन दंडवत गर्न जान्या काजिहरुलाई सुष आनन्द होला भन्या १९३८ साल आषाढ वदि १० रोज़ ३ मा श्री ५ वाट ल्हासाका २ अंवालाई..................................

(Nepalese King to Chinese *Ambans* expressing hope for the safety and comfort for the future Nepalese mission to China.)

Source : MFA, *Poka* No. Pa 64.

Appendix Y

सौगात चढाउन जाने काजीहरुको हरायाको माल मध्ये दाहिना वाज़ां संष २ ठुला मुगा ८ साना मुगाके माला ४ के दाना ७९४ चादी ४ पोकाके टाक ७३ भिस्कन ५ हाम्रा वकिल मे.क. महावीर गठतौला जिम्मा वुझाई अरु षोज तलास भया वढीया होला भन्या १९३९ साल कार्तिक शुदी ६ रोज ५ मा श्री ५ वाट सैतारिन अंवालाई लेषियाको मसौदा ....

(Draft letter from Nepalese King to Chinese *Amban* requesting for searching of the Nepalese mission's goods being stolen on the way.)

Source : MFA, *Poka* No. Pa 64.

Appendix Z

काजी तेज वहादुर राणा, सर्दार वल वहादुर पाडेहरु श्री ५ वादसाहको दर्सन गरी फीरेको पर्नी वर्ष दिन भयो अझ आई पुगेन्न. अव आउदो साल फेरी अर्जि सौगात लिइ दर्सन दंडवत गर्न काजी सर्दार षटाउने वेला भयो. नीजहरुलाई छिटो नेपाल आइ पुग्न्या गरी झिकाई दिनु भया वढीया होला भन्यां ल्हासा यामुनवाट सिठान चुङ यामुनमा लेषी पठायौं भंन्या इत्यादि क्कास्यूई ७ वर्ष ६ मैन्हा १३ दिन जादा श्री ५ सर्कारका हर्जुमा सैतारिन वैतारिन अंवाले लेखेको....................

(Chinese *Ambans* to Nepalese Government informing about the calling soon of the mission to Nepal.)

Source : MFA, *Poka* No. Pa 64.

* * *

Kazi Ran Bikram Rana's Mission of 1886

According to the arrangement of the mission system, Nepal was to send the next five-yearly mission in 1882, but Nepal did not send a mission to China in 1882. For the 1882 mission was postponed by the death of the Emperor's Dowger, Tsu Au. In 1885, Prime Minister Ranauddip Singh was reported to have informed the Chinese *Amban* that he was willing to send another mission in time[1], but before he could send the mission to China, Ranauddip Singh was assassinated on 22 November, 1885, and his successor, Bir Shamsher sent the Nepalese mission to China in 1886. Before sending the mission in 1886, the Nepalese government formally informed the Ch'ing court through the Chinese *Ambans* at Lhasa, in order to get the imperial sanction for the dispatch of the Nepalese mission[2]. Here it should be pointed out that Bir Shamsher, who attained power by assassinating Ranauddip Singh, seemed anxious to obtain Peking's recognition of his position. That is why even towards the end of 1885, Bir Shamsher sent a dispatch in the name of the Nepalese King Prithvi Bir Bikram Shah to the Ch'ing Emperor Kwang Hsu justifying the assassination of Ranauddip Singh and requesting for the Emperor, "as in former cases, to bestow upon (Bir Shamsher) the title of 'Valiant Prince', together with an official uniform"[3]. The 1886 Nepalese quinquennial mission has not been mentioned in the Chinese Imperial records[4]. But the Nepalese and Indian archival documents clearly state of Nepal's dispatching of five-yearly mission to China in 1886. This sixteenth Nepalese mission was headed by *Kazi* Ran Bikram Rana,

1. Tri Ratna Manandhar and Tirtha Prasad Mishra, *Nepal's Quinquennial Missions to China*, Kathmandu: Purna Devi Manandhar and Puspa Mishra, 1986, p. 29.
2. *Peking Gazette*, 22 November 1893, Foreign Dept. Sec. E, February 1894, No. 463, National Archives of India, New Delhi (hereafter referred as NAI). See Appendix A.
3. Leo E. Rose, *Nepal: Strategy for Survival*, Berkeley: University of California Press, 1971, p. 143.
4. J.K. Fairbank and S.Y. Teng, "On the Ch'ing Tributary System", *Harvard Journal of Asiatic Studies*, Vol. VI, 1941, pp. 195-198.

the eldest son of Colonel Tej Bahadur Rana, who had led the previous Nepalese mission of 1877. *Sardar* Drighaman Singh Basniat happened to be the deputy leader of the mission[5]. The Nepalese mission departed for Peking in 1943 B.S. Ashwin Badi 1 Roj 3[6] (13 September, 1886).[7] carrying an *arji* from King Prithvi Bir Bikram to Ch'ing Emperor Kwang Hsu[8]. Like the previous mission of 1877, this mission of 1886 also took nearly five years to complete the journey. By 1948 B.S. (1891), the Nepalese mission seemed to have reached Lhasa[9], and it finally returned to Kathmandu in June 1891[10].

The 1886 Nepalese mission too seemed to have been involved in opium trading activities, because in spite of the full cooperation of the Chinese officials on this occasion, this Nepalese mission also took nearly five years to complete the journey, in contrast to eighteen months, which had been normal duration prior to 1852. The Nepalese sources clearly indicate that the 1886 Nepalese mission was indeed involved in opium trading in China, for according to the Nepalese government's instructions to the leader of the Nepalese mission to China dated 11 September 1886,

---

5. Girdlestone to H.M. Durand, Secreatry to the Govt. of India, 15 September 1886. Foreign Sec. E, October 1886, No. 1, NAI. See Appendix B.
6. 'Nepal Desh Ko Itihas' (History of Nepal), A Manuscript in the National Archives of Nepal, Kathmandu, Published in *Ancient Nepal*, No. 27, April 1974, p. 29.
7. Girdlestone to H.M. Durand, Secreatry to the Govt. of India, 15 September 1886, Foreign Sec. E, October 1886, No. 1, NAI. But Rose and Sever have given the date of the departure of the 1886 Nepalese mission as 14 September, 1886 and 17 September, 1886. See Rose, f.n.no. 3, p. 144 and Adrian Sever, *Aspects of Modern Nepalese History*, New Delhi: Vikas Publishing House Pvt. Ltd. , 1996, p. 170.
8. For the correspondence between the Nepalese and Chinese government regarding the Nepalese mission's allowances and the escorting of the Nepalese mission by the Chinese Military officers, see Appendices D, E, F and H.
9. Chinese *Amban* to Nepalese King, Kwang Hsu 17th year 3rd month 20th day (1891). Ministry of Foreign Affairs, Kathmandu (hereafter mentioned as MFA), *Poka* No. Pa 64. See Appendix I.
10. H. Wylie, Resident in Nepal to Secretary, Govt. of India, 9 July 1894, Foreign Dept. Sec. E, July 1894, No. 184, NAI. Sever has given the date of the arrival of the 1886 Nepalese mission in Kathmandu as 17 June, 1891. See Sever, f.n. no. 7, p. 170. For the details of the arrival of the Nepalese mission at Kerung and Kathmandu, see Appendices J, K and L.

it seemed that the mission's members were also allowed to take some opium for their own trading purposes, but that they were strictly warned to sell the opium belonging to the ruling family first. If any member of the mission tried to sell his own article (opium) while neglecting the goods (opium) belonging to the ruling family, he was to be fined by the leader of the mission on the spot. However, if the leader of the mission was involved in such activities, he was to be fined by the Nepalese government upon his return to Nepal.[11] Thus it seemed quite clear that not only the Rana rulers but also the members of the 1886 Nepalese mission themselves were engaged in opium trading in China. It was also reported that just like the 1866 Nepalese mission, the Nepalese mission of 1886 also could not dispose of the narcotics, because the opium carried by the 1886 mission to Peking proved to be of inferior quality. *Kazi* Ran Bikram Rana, the leader of the 1886 mission, reported to *Maharaja* Bir Shamsher that no Chinese were willing to buy the Nepalese opium, for it had lost its flavour and its stickiness[12].

Here it will be interesting to note that in December 1888, William Woodville Rockhill, an American diplomat at Peking, met the Nepalese mission of 1886 while it was on its return journey from Peking to Kathmandu in T'ung-Kuan, a point of much strategic importance, as the trunk roads between Eastern China and the west and the Northwest met there, and the main route to Tibet, Burma, India and Turkestan lay through it. Rockhill met the Nepalese mission at the inn where he had stopped for breakfast. According to him, the Nepalese mission had left Peking in November 1888, but had travelled the route through Ho-nan. About the Nepalese mission, Rockhill has made interesting remarks :

> *"The mission was in no hurry to get home, as the chiefs and even the servants were in receipt of a daily allowance from the Chinese government as long as*

---

11. Nepalese Government's instructions to the leader of the mission, 1943 B.S., Bhadra Sudi 13 Roj 7 (11 September 1886), MFA, Unnumbered *Poka*. See Appendix C. See also Vijay Kumar Manandhar, *Cultural and Political Aspects of Nepal-China Relations*, Delhi: Adroit Publishers, 1999, pp. 78-79.
12. Prem R. Uprety, *Nepal-Tibet Relations 1850-1930*, Kathmandu: Puga Nara, 1980, p. 165.

they were in the empire, and were transported, fed, and lodged free of all expense, nor did they have to pay any duties or octroi dues on their goods, either when going to Peking or when returning home. There were about forty persons in the mission, a number of them Chinese from the Tibetan border-land or from Lhasa, these latter acting as interpreters for the Goorkhas, with whom they conversed in Tibetan".[13]

Once again in Ya-Chou, Rockhill saw a line of coolies carrying the luggage of the returning Nepalese mission to Ta-Chien-lu. The Nepalese mission was expected in Ta-Chien-lu in about a month, when they would take another good rest before starting for Lhasa. There was no need to impress on them the Tibetan formula, *Kale peb*, "Go slowly", for they seemed to have mastered all the intricacies of the piano e sano mode of travelling.[14]

This sixteenth five-yearly mission of 1886 was important due to the following reasons : Firstly, this mission happened to be the first mission sent to China during the sixteen year Prime Ministership of Bir Shamsher (1885-1901). Secondly, following this mission of 1886, the Ch'ing Emperor Kwang Hsu recognized the new Nepalese Prime Minister Bir Shamsher by decorating him the Chinese title of *Thong Ling Pimma Kokang Vang Syan (Thong Ling Pimma Kokang Wang Shang)* in 1946 B.S. Bhadra Sudi 6 Roj 1[15] (28 August 1889). Thirdly, since 1852 this happened to be the first Nepalese mission to which the Chinese officials fully cooperated in several ways. As such, the Nepalese government offered thanks to the Chinese *Ambans*[16]

---

13. William Woodville Rockhill, *The Land of the Lamas,* New Delhi: Asian Publications Services, Reprint, 1975, p. 19.
14. *Ibid.*, p. 310.
15. 'Nepal Desh Ko Itihas' (History of Nepal), *Ancient Nepal*, No. 27, April 1974, p. 31.
16. Draft letter from Nepalese King to Chinese *Amban*, 1946 B.S. Baisakh Sudi 15 Roj 4 (15 May 1889), MFA, *Poka* No. Pa. 64. See Appendix G.

Appendix A

Translation of Memorial from K'uei Huan, Resident in Thibet, in *Peking Gazette* of 22nd November 1893.

It is the duty of the Prince of Nepal to send tribute to Peking once every five years by one of his Ministers of State.

The tribute for the 8th year of Kuang Hsu (1882) was sent in proper order. Another mission became due in the 13th year of Kuang Hsu (1887), I have now received a petition from the Prince of Nepal as follows:-

"The articles composing the prescribed tribute for the 13th year of Kuang Hsù are of great bulk. I do not dare to delay longer, nor do I dare to exhibit the slightest presumption. I, therefore, beg you will proceed to memorialise the Throne for instructions as to whether the tribute should be presented. Upon receipt of His Imperial Majesty's commands, I will in respectful obedience make the necessary arrangements.

Your slave would humbly observe that the prescribed tribute presented. by the Prince of the said State was originally offered as a mark of his respectful fealty and sincerity. It rests entirely with the Imperil Grace to permit the presentation; your slave would not dare to presume to take upon himself the decision. He humbly submits the circumstances for Your Majesty's Sacred glance and Imperial commands.

Rescript with the vermilion pencil.

"Let him be permitted to present the tribute".

An Imperial decree

Source : Foreign Sec. E, February 1894, No. 463, National Archives of India, New Delhi (NAI).

Appendix B

No. 47 P., dated Nepal Residency, the 15th September 1886.

From : C.E. R. Girdlestone Esq. C.S. I., Resident in Nepal,

To : H.M. Durand, Esq., C.S.I., Secretary to the Government of India, Foreign Department.

With reference to my No. 63 P, dated 19th June 1882, to your address, I have the honor to report that another mission for Pekin started from Katmandu two days ago. The head of the mission is Kazi Run Bikrum, son of a well-known Colonel in the Nepalese army, named Tez Bahadur. With him is associated Sardar Drigman Singh Basniat. The mission is of the usual complimentary character.

Source : Foreign Sec. E., October 1886, No. 1, NAI.

Appendix C

सं १९४३ काजी रण विक्रम पेकिङ जाँदाको :-

चीन जाने-सवाल वमोजिम काम गर्ने- कति घटी वढी नगर्ने- वढता इनाम पाउ भन्ने विन्ती नगर्नु

– साविक दस्तुर मालिक हुकुं मर्जी वमोजिम कति फरक नपारि अर्जि चिठी सौगात आफ्नो जिम्मा लिई जाहा जाहा वुझाउनु पर्न्या हो वही पुऱ्याई वुझाउनु

– श्री ५ को तरफबाट लैजानु पर्न्या मालको नाप तौल गंति जम्मा र सो माल पऱ्याका मोल यति यति हो . यस्मा भरिसक्य किफायत पारी जुंन जुन ठाउमा विक्री हुन्छ विक्री गर्नु भंन्या तर्फ तर्फका छाप लाग्याको ढडार सो ढडा वमोजिमको माल वुझी ली लंवर छुटयाई प्याकीज गरी भारी हाल्नु सो वुझियाको माल भर्पाई दिनु

– वाटोमा आगो पानीको वचाउ गरी नविगारी संभारसित कुती पुर्याई साविक दस्तुर माफिक जस जस्का जिम्मा लगाई दिने

– समय समयमा ठाउँमा भारी जाच्ने

– श्री ५ सर्कारको तिमीहरु जिम्मा लाग्याको अफिम लगायत माल असवाफ पैल्हे श्री ५ को सर्कारको विक्री नगरी तिमीहरुले उही जातको माल विक्री नगर्नु, कसैले विक्री गरेमा जरिमाना गर्नु

– कुती देखी उस तरफ जाहा जाहा जति माल खरिद गर्न्या मानिसहरु आउछन् उनीहरुसंग भरीसक्य कसकास गरी तिमीहरु काजी, सर्दार भरीया नायक सल्लाहले ठहराई विक्री गर्नु . फर्मायाका जती माल षरिद गरी ल्याउंनु

– जुन जुन चौपाया खरिद गर्दा कसकास गरी खरिद गर्नु, खरिद भएको विवरण लेखी पठाउनु

– चौपायालाई भएको खर्चको विवरण लेख्नु

– प्रत्येक ठाउँको विवरण र उल्लेखनीय वुंदाहरु लेखी पठाउनु किताप खडा गरी ल्याउने

– तहवीलको दाम कसैलाई सापट नदिनु

– दोभासे भर्ना गर्ने, अस्थायी भर्ना गर्ने

जम्मा पेश्की गएको कालामोहर थान २३६४४२ ॥।′॥

इति सम्वत १९४३ साल मिति भाद्र सुदी १३ रोज ७

(Nepal Government's instruction to the leader of the mission dated

1943 B.S. Bhadra Sudi 13 Roj 7 (11 September 1886).)

Source : Ministry of Foreign Affairs, Kathmandu (MFA), Unnumbered *Poka*.

Appendix D

चीन जान्या काजीहरुले यो साल ध्यांडोताया भंन्या जगामा अनिकाल परेको हुनाले सिधा दस्तुर नभयाको रहेछ पछिलाई दस्तुर विग्रने छैन पाउनेछन भन्या ककास्यूई १३ साल ८ मैन्हा १ दिन जादा १९४४ साल्मा श्री ५ सर्कारका हजुर्मा वन्तारिन अम्वाले लेषेको ....

(Chinese *Amban* to Nepalese Government informing about the Nepalese mission not getting allowances due to famine in Dhyantodaya area and assuring of providing allowances to the mission.)

Source : MFA, *Poka* No. Pa 64.

Appendix E

कारवाई गरेकोमा खुसी व्यक्त. १९४४ साल पौष वदी ५ रोज २ मा अम्वालाई लेषन जाहेर गरेको साधक ....

(Draft letter of Nepalese Government to Chinese *Amban* expressing happiness over taking action.)

Source : MFA, *Poka* No. Pa 64.

Appendix F

सौगात लि' जाने काजीहरुले साविक वमोजिम छांदोताये भन्यां जगामा सिधादस्तुर नपायाको रहेनछ . भोटका मुलुकमा मात्र नपायाको रहेछ फर्कि आउदा दिनु भनि लेषि पठायाको छ भंने काकास्यूई १३ साल ११ मैन्हा २१ दिन जादा श्री ५ सर्कारका हजुर्मा वन्तारिन अम्वाले लेखेको ....

(Chinese *Amban* to Nepalese Government informing Nepalese mission receiving allowances in Chhandotaya area and not receiving in Tibet area.)

Source : MFA, *Poka* No. Pa 64.

Appendix G

हाम्रा काजी भारदार पेचिनवाट फर्की आउदा वाटामा तकलिफ पर्ला भनी घोडा

षल्मा सिधा दस्तुर अघिका रित वमोजिम दिनु भन्यां श्री ५ वादसाहवाट मेहेर्को हुकुं वक्साकको विस्तार आउदा वहुत षुसी लाग्यो भन्या १९४६ वैशाष सुदी १५ रोज ४ श्री ५ वाट अम्वालाई लेषन जाहेर गरेको ....

(Draft letter from Nepalese King to Chinese *Amban* offering thanks for fully cooperating the Nepalese mission.)

Source : MFA, *Poka* No. Pa 64.

Appendix H

सौगाद पुऱ्याउन जाने काजीलाई अघिका रित वमोजिम पैचिनवाट रमाना भया पछी अडा अडावाट पल्टंका अफिसर सिपाही षटाई पुऱ्याउन जान्या फाफुन संग लगाई पठाउनु पर्छ भन्या उर्दि भै आयाको विस्तार वढिया लेषी आयेछ . खुषी लाग्यो भन्या श्री ५ वाट १९४६ साल आषाढ वदि २ रोज ७ मा अम्वालाई लेख्न जाहेर गरेको साधक ....

(Draft letter from Nepalese King to Chinese *Amban* expressing happiness over the Chinese government's notice of escorting the Nepalese mission by the military officers at the time of the mission's return journey.)

Source : MFA, *Poka* No. Pa 64.

Appendix I

चीन जाने काजीहरुलाई विदा गरी पठायौं सिवाना सम्म भारदार लिन पठाई तहा पुगे पछि सौगात आइ पुगेको र मुष्ये वजिर लाई को काङ वाङ स्यानको षिताव वक्सेको प्रर्माना स्मेत आइपुग्यो भन्या २ अर्जि चढाई पठाउनु भन्यां काङस्यूई १७ साल ३ मैन्हा २० दिन जादा १९४८ सालमा श्री ५ का हजुरगा सोन्तारीन अम्वाले लेषेको ....

(Chinese *Amban* to Nepalese King mentioning about the sending-off of the Nepalese mission from Lhasa and instructing to send two *arjis* to the Chinese Emperor mentioning about the receiving of Imperial gifts and the Emperor's *Parwana* of conferring the Chinese title upon the Nepalese Prime Minister.)

Source : MFA, *Poka* No. Pa 64.

Appendix J

आफुहरुको दया संभी वहुत षुसि भञ्यूं केरुं सिमानासम्म इनां प्रमाना लिन मेजर कप्तान हिक्मत सिं वस्न्यात छेत्री र अरु भला मानिस खटाई पठायाको छ.

काजीहरु इनां प्रमाना लि काङ वाङ स्यानको षिताव आई पुग्नया वित्तिकै अधिकारित वमोजिम २ अर्जि लेषी आफुहरु मार्फत श्री ५ वादसाहका हजुरमा चढाई पठाउला भन्या १९४८ साल आषाढ वदी १२ रोज ७ मा श्री ५ सर्कारवाट अम्वालाई लेषन जाहेर गरेको साधक ....

(Draft letter from Nepalese Government to Chinese *Amban* informing about deputing of Captain Hikmat Singh Basnyat Chhetri to welcome the Nepalese mission at Kerung border and sending of two *arjis* to the Chinese Emperor.)

Source : MFA, *Poka* No. Pa 64.

Appendix K

५ वर्षको मामुली सौगात चढाई काजि रण विक्रम राणाले प्रमाना लि आउदा श्री ५ वादसाहको ठूलो मेहरवानी भयो . मेरो र मुख्य वजिर सवैका मनमा हर्ष भयो भन्या इत्यादि १९४८ साल भाद्र शुदि १५ रोज ६ मा श्री ५ वादसाहका हजुर्मा श्री ५ सर्कारवाट मामुली अर्जि लेषी पठाउन जाहेर गरेको साधक.................

(Draft letter from Nepalese Government to Chinese Emperor expressing happiness at the arrival of *Kazi* Ran Bikram Rana at Kathmandu carrying *Parwana* from the Emperor.)

Source : MFA, *Poka* No. Pa 64.

Appendix L

श्री ५ वादसाहवाट काङ वाङ स्यानको प्रमाना लिन जाने काजी सर्दार संगै आयाका छन् . अघि नेपाल सम्म पुऱ्याउन आउदथ्ये . सर्कारको इनाम स्मेत पाउथ्यौं यो पाला हामी अभागी हुनाले हामीले दर्सन गर्न आउन पाएनौं भन्या लेषेकोलाई नेपाल आउदा मात्र वक्स दिने दस्तुर हो ता पनि दुष पायेको हुनाले मोरु १०४ वक्स दियाको छ भन्यां श्री ३ महाराज वाट केरुङ्गका मातोलोयलाई लेषी पठाउन ४८ साल आश्वीन सुदी ५ रोज ४ मा जाहेर गरेको.............

(Draft letter from *Sri Tin Maharaj* to Kerung's *Talloye* informing him of rewarding Rs. 104/- at the receiving of the *Parwana* conferring the Chinese title upon him (*Sri Tin*).)

Source : MFA, *Poka* No. Pa 64.

* * *

Kazi Indra Bikram Rana's Mission of 1894

The next Nepalese mission was sent to China in 1894 after a span of more than seven years, and no explanation was given for this delay. The 1894 Nepalese quinquennial mission has not been mentioned in the Chinese Imperial records[1]. But the Nepalese and Indian archival documents clearly state of Nepal's sending of five-yearly mission to China in 1894. As usual, the Chinese *Amban* instructed the Nepalese government to send the name of the leader and deputy leader of the mission, the list of the presents and the draft of the *arji* beforehand for confirmation.[2] The 1894 Nepalese mission was led by *Kazi* Major Indra Bikram Rana, a grandson of Late Prime Minister Bam Bahadur Rana.[3] The delegation also included *Sardar* Juddhabir Khadka, deputy leader of the mission, seven headmen, four headmen of inferior rank, twenty two soldiers and eleven servants.[4] The mission left Kathmandu for Peking on 10 August, 1894[5] (1951 B.S., Ashad 31)[6] carrying presents[7] and an

---

1. J.K. Fairbank and S.Y. Teng, " On the Ch'ing Tributary System", *Harvard Journal of Asiatic Studies*, Vol. VI, 1941, pp. 195-198.
2. Chinese *Amban* to King Prithvi Bir Bikram, Kwang-hsu 20th year 6th month 9th day (1951 B.S.), Ministry of Foreign Affairs, Kathmandu (hereafter referred as MFA), *Poka* No. Pa 64. See Appendix E.
3. H. Wylie, Resident in Nepal to Secretary, Govt. of India, 9 July 1894, Foreign Dept. Sec. E, July 1894, No 184, National Archives of India, New Delhi (hereafter mentioned as NAI). See Appendix A.
4. N.R.O.' Conor, Her Majesty's Minister in Peking to Kimberley, Foreign Secretary, 30 April 1895, Foreign Dept. Sec. E, September 1895, No. 117, NAI.
5. *Peking Gazette*, 24 April 1895, cited in Foreign Dept. Sec. E, September 1895, No. 118, NAI. See Appendix B.
6. Commander-in-Chief to *Dhewas* (Tibetan Officials) of Kuti, 1951 B.S. Jestha Ṣudi 8 Roj 2 (11 June 1894), MFA, *Poka* No. Pa 64. See Appendix F. Basing on this Nepalese document, Manandhar and Mishra have stated that the Nepalese mission left Kathmandu for Peking in June 1894, instead of the correct date of 10 August, 1894 being mentioned in *Peking Gazette*, 24 April 1895. See Tri Ratna Manandhar and Tirtha Prasad Mishra, *Nepal's Quinquennial Missions to China*, Kathmandu: Purna Devi Manandhar and Puspa Mishra, 1986, p. 30. Likewise Sever has wrongly stated that the Nepalese mission left Kathmandu on 18 June 1894.

arji from Nepalese King Prithvi Bir Bikram Shah Dev to Ch'ing Emperor Kwang Hsu.[8] It was reported that the Nepalese mission was stopped at Kuti (a chief town of Tibet, situated two hundred and fifty miles from Lhasa and seventy two miles from Kathmandu) pending further orders from the Imperial Throne, and that no carriage had been collected, or any other arrangement made, for their onward journey[9]. Afterwards the Nepalese mission arrived at Lhasa on 25 November 1894. On 22 February, 1895, the Nepalese mission left Lhasa for Peking. The then Chinese *Amban* K'uei-huan dispatched Lieutenant Chou Tzu-Kuei along with a guard of nineteen soldiers and a number of linguists and students versed in the Nepali language to escort the Nepalese mission as far as Szechuan. The *Amban* also notified the various postal stations *en route* to make suitable preparations for the arrival of the Nepalese delegates, and he likewise wrote in to the Viceroy of Szechuan and to the high authorities of Shensi, Shansi, Honan and Chihli.[10]

It seems that by 10 July 1896, the Nepalese mission had

See Adrian Sever, *Aspects of Modern Nepalese History*, New Delhi: Vikas Publishing House Pvt. Ltd., 1996, p. 170.

7. The presents were as follows:

i) A string of 109 coral beads
ii) A piece of silk brocade
iii) 24 rolls of satin
iv) 13 pieces of felt cloth
v) 2 Rhinoceros horns
vi) 4 Tusks of ivory
vii) 1000 Nutmegs
viii) 360 oz. of Cloves
ix) 300 oz. of Cinnamon
x) 360 oz. of betel nut (round)
xi) 6000 oz. of betel nut (flat)
xii) 3 Fowling-pieces (all complete)
xiii) 12 Swords of different kinds.

See List of articles of Tribute, cited in Foreign Department Sec. E., September 1895, No. 117, NAI.

8. Letter from the King of Nepal to the Emperor of China, cited in Foreign Department, Sec. E., September 1895, No. 119, NAI. See Appendix C.
9. H.Wylie to H. Daly, Assistant Secratory to the Govt. of India, 9 October, 1894, Foreign Dept. Sec. E, March 1895, No. 69, NAI.
10. *Peking Gazette*, 24 April 1895, cited in Foreign Dept. Sec. E, September 1895, No. 118, NAI.

arrived at Peking.[11] After their arrival in Peking, it appears that the Nepalese envoy *Kazi* Indra Bikram Rana met W. Beauclerk, the British Minister at Peking. The Nepalese envoy probably asked the British Minister at Peking to send a telegram to the British Resident in Nepal to convey the message of the safe arrival of the Nepalese delegation at Peking to the Nepalese Prime Minister Bir Shamsher[12]. The Nepalese Prime Minister in his turn requested H. Wylie, the British Resident in Nepal to convey his thanks to the government of India and the British Minister at Peking for the information regarding the safe arrival of the Nepalese mission at Peking.[13] According to the paper *The Times* dated 25 December, 1896, the Nepalese mission of 1894 consisted of thirty two members, with a following of over twenty Nepalese traders.[14] It was also reported that *Sardar* Juddhabir Khadka, the deputy leader of the mission, died in Peking, where he was creamated with Nepalese rites.[15] The paper also published the report that special officials from the Mongolian Superintendency had taken the members of the Nepalese mission about to the sights of Peking. The return presents from the Ch'ing Emperor Kwang Hsu were placed in the southern Lake Palace outside the west gate of Peking, and the occasion of the visit to this palace to receive them was one of great ceremony. The surviving Nepalese envoy, *Kazi* Indra Bikram Rana, was carried there in a green Sedan-chair, and the other Nepalese on

---

11. Telegram of Her Brittanic Majesty's Minister at Peking to Resident in Nepal, 10 July-11 July, 1896, Foreign Dept. External 'B', August 1896, Nos. 15-18, NAI. But the English paper *The Times* dated 25 December, 1896 has given the incorrect date of the arrival of the Nepalese mission in Peking in mid-September 1896. See Adrian Sever, *Nepal Under the Ranas*, New Delhi: Oxford and IBH Publishing Co. Pvt. Ltd., 1993, p. 205.
12. Telegram of Her Brittanic Majesty's Minister at Peking to Resident in Nepal, 10 July-11 July, 1896, Foreign Dept. External 'B', August 1896, Nos. 15-18, NAI.
13. Telegram of the Resident in Nepal to British Minister in China, 24 July 1896, Foreign Dept. External 'B', August 1896, Nos. 15-18, NAI.
14. Sever, f.n. no. 11, p. 205. But the Indian Archival document has mentioned that the 1894 Nepalese mission consisted of forty-six persons. See List of members of Mission, cited in Foreign Dept. Sec.E, September 1895, No. 117, NAI.
15. Draft letter from Nepalese King to Chinese *Amban*, 1953 B.S. Magh Sudi 3 Roj 5 (1897), MFA, *Poka* No. Pa. 64. See Appendix G and Sever, f.n. no. 11, p. 205.

horseback or in mule carts, the starting from the Nepalese Envoy's Hall, where the whole party was lodged at the expense of the Chinese government from the moment of their arrival. The trading members were kept outside the sacred precincts, while the official members were conveyed to the great halls of the palace, where they prostrated themselves before the eunuch commissioned to read the Imperial edict authorising the Nepalese to return to their own country[16]. The paper also mentioned that the Chinese presents consisted of a thousand *taels* of silver (about £ 180), four complete suits of fur, robes of wadded cotton and gauze for each member of the mission, in addition to silk pongees and gauze, Peking curios and the like, according to the ranks of the recipients. Those presents were ultimately conveyed to the residence of the Nepalese mission in special carts, and the members were taken to another part of the palace, about a quarter of a mile from the place where the Emperor was supposed to be seated --- for he was quite invisible --- and there they went through the regulation three prostrations and nine *Kowtows* in recognition of the Imperial generous gifts. In fact, only the Chief envoy ever saw the Emperor, and this was on his arrival, when he presented the letter from his own sovereign avowing allegiance to China. When the ceremony of giving presents was over, the Nepalese mission was informed that it could begin its return journey as soon as the necessary conveyances for so large a party could be prepared by the Mongolian Superintendency. The journey from Kathmandu to Peking took six months.[17]

Finally the 1894 Nepalese mission returned to Kathmandu along with a *Parwana* and presents from the Ch'ing Emperor Kwang Hsui[18] in 1958 B.S. Baisakh Badi 2 Roj 7[19] (1 March, 1901)[20] after the lapse of nearly six and half years. It seems that it

---

16. Sever, f.n.no. 11, p. 205.
17. *Ibid.*
18. Translation of a *Kharita* from His Highness the *Maharajadhiraja* to His Majesty the Emperor of China, Foreign Dept. Sec. E, November 1910, No. 15, NAI. See Appendix D.
19. Draft letter from Commander-in-Chief to Chinese *Talloye* (Official), 1958 B.S. Baisakh Badi 2 Roj 7 (1901), MFA, *Poka* No. Pa 64. See Appendix H.
20. Resident in Nepal to Secretary, Govt. of India, 15 March, 1901, Foreign Dept. External B, April 1901, No. 31, NAI. But Manandhar and Mishra have wrongly stated that the 1894 Nepalese mission returned home after

was due to its commercial nature that the mission of 1894 took nearly six and half years to complete the journey. The Nepalese sources clearly state that, like the previous mission, this mission of 1894 too was involved in opium trading in China. Upon reading the instructions from *Maharaja* Bir Shamsher to *Kazi* Indra Bikram Rana, it appears that the 1894 mission, too, could not dispose of the opium in China[21]. Furthermore, it was mainly due to the commercial character of this very mission, that the newspaper *The Times* dated 25th December, 1896 even referred to twenty members of 1894 Nepalese mission as traders. *The Times* further reported that those twenty delegates seemed to have taken their wares to Peking for sale[22].

This seventeenth quinquennial mission of 1894 was important due to the following reasons: Firstly, it was the first five-yearly Nepalese mission to Peking which had taken the longest time to complete the journey since 1792. Secondly, this happened to be the second mission sent to China during the sixteen year Premiership of Bir Shamsher (1885-1901). Thirdly, it was the third mission led continuously by a member of the ruling Rana family. Above all, the Nepalese Prime Minister Chandra Shamsher (1901-1929) had made the travel diary of *Kazi* Indra Bikram Rana, the leader of the 1894 Nepalese mission to China, available to the British Resident Leiutenant-Colonel C.W. Ravenshaw in 1904.[23]

Appendix A

No. 47P-30-896, dated Nepal, the 9th July 1894

From - Lieutenant-Colonel H. Wylie, C.S.I., Resident in Nepal,

To - The Secretary to the Government of India, Foreign Department.

I have the honour to report, for the information of the Government

---

seven years. See Manandhar and Mishra, f.n.no. 6, p. 40. Similarly Sever has wrongly stated that the 1894 Nepalese mission returned home on 18 March 1901 after six years. See Sever, f.n.no. 6, pp. 167-170.

21. Prem R. Uprety, *Nepal- Tibet Relations 1850-1930*, Kathmandu: Puga Nara, 1980, p. 165.
22. Sever, f.n. no. 11, p. 205.
23. C.W. Ravenshaw to Secretary, Govt. of India, 16 June 1904, Foreign Dept. Sec. E, September 1904, No. 91, NAI.

of India, that the Nepalese Minister tells me that his Darbar intends to despatch the usual mission to Peking in about three weeks time. The mission will be under the Charge of Major Indra Bikram Jung Rana, a grandson of Sir Jung Bahadur's brother, Bam Bahadur.

2. It appears that the last Nepalese mission to China left this in September 1886, and returned in June 1891.

Source : Foreign Dept. Sec. E, July 1894, No. 184, National Archives of India, New Delhi (NAI) .

Appendix B

[Translation] Peking Gazette (M.S.) 24th April 1895. (K.H.XXI - 3 - 30)

The Imperial Resident in Tibet, K'uei-huan, reports that the Tribute Mission from the Erdeni Prince of Nepal has started from Tibet and has been forwarded under proper escorts as for as Szechuan.

Some time ago, as already reported to the Throne, the memorialist received a petition from the Erdeni Prince of the Gurkhas, Pi-je-t'i-pi-pi-k'a-erh-ma-sheng-hsieh-je-tseng-k'a-pa-ha-tu-je-sa-ha, stating that the time for forwarding the tribute for the 13th year of Kuang Hsu (1887) having now arrived, he had prepared the full complement of offerings which were being entrusted to a principal and assistant *Ko-chi* for transmission to their high destination in Peking. The Mission was met by an escort at Nilam and on their arrival in Anterior Tibet on the 25th November last, they submitted a petition from the Prince of their country which was translated into Chinese and was to the following effect. The Prince stated that he had deputed a principal and assistant *Ko-chi* named respectively Ying-ta-je-pi-ka-erh-ma-je-na-pa-ha-tu-je and Sa-erh-ta-erh-tsu-ta-pi-je-ch'ia-cha-k'a-ch'ieh-ti-je who had started from Katmandu for Peking on the 10th August 1894, and he asked that on their arrival in Tibet they might be furnished with instructions for their guidance. A translation was likewise made of the Prince's letter to the Emperor, the language of which evinced feelings of the deepest sincerity.

On a day fixed for the purpose the memorialist carefully examined the articles of tribute and invited the members of the Mission to the customary' banquet, bestowing upon the *Ko-chi* and headmen presents of silks, satins, silver badges, purses, pocket knives, tea, sheep, rice, flour, &c. The memorialist made them a further donation of Tls. 100 for travelling expenses and gave them money to procure for clothing, fur boots and other articles required for the journey. He likewise instructed them in the etiquette of the Imperial Court in the matters of audiences.

The memorialist felt that the Mission being a special one from a feudatory state, it was most important that an officer of experience should be detached to escort it so as to ensure its receiving proper care and respect. A Lieutenant of the name of Chou Tzu-Kuei, whose period of service in Tibet has expired, has accordingly been deputed to escort the Mission as far as Szechuan. He has with him a guard of 19 soldiers and a number of linguists and students versed in the Gurkha language. The whole party started from Tibet on the 22nd February 1895.

The memorialist notified the various postal stations *en route* to make suitable preparations for their arrival, and he wrote in a similar sense to the Viceroy of Szechuan and to the High authorities of Shensi, Shansi, Honan and Chihli.

Rescript. Let the Yamen concerned take note and let the three enclosures in this memorial be furnished to it.

Source: Foreign Dept. Sec. E, September 1895, No. 118, NAI.

Appendix C

[Translation] Letter from the King of Nepal to the Emperor of China

The Erdeni Prince of the Gurkhas, P'i-je-t'i-pi-pi-k'a-erh-ma-sheng-hsieh-je-tseng-k'a-pa-ha-tu-je-sa-ha, in his attitude of an humble vassal, makes nine prostrations before the Throne of the Emperor of China and presents his respectful prayer for the health of His most noble and mighty Majesty, the Wenchu P'usa or Manjusri, whose fostering kindness is as the overspreading vault of Heaven, whose brilliancy is as the rays of the Sun and Moon, whose care extends to the myriad Kindoms, and whose length of years shall be as enduring as the Hsu Mi Mountain.

In accordance with the custom which prescribes the payment of tribute once every five years, it becomes your vassal's duty to despatch special *Ko-chi* to take it and deliver it to its High Destination. The full complement of offerings has been duly prepared, and is being despatched to Peking by the hands of a Principal and Assistant Envoy named respectively *Ko-chi* Ying-ta-je-pi-k'a-erh-ma-je-na-pa-ha-tu-je and the *Ko-chi* Sa-erh-ta-erh-tsu-ta-pi-je-ch'ia-cha-k'a-ch'ieh-ti-je, accompanied by a number of headmen and secretaries who started from Katmandu on the 10th August 1894.

In accordance with the custom which has always prevailed in the past when anything occurred in your vassal's State of submitting petitions to the Throne through the Imperial Resident in Tibet, he has duly petitioned the present Resident and begged His Excellency to graciously bear in mind the distance which separates Nepal from Peking, and make allowances for his unfamiliarity with the usages of the Court of the Heavenly Dynasty. His Excellency was also asked to take into consideration the earnestness of purpose with which your vassal turned towards the civilisation of China and to place His Majesty the Emperor in full possession of the facts of the case.

Ever since your vassal's state in the days of his ancestors yielded fealty to the Celestial Court, its conduct has been characterised by the most complete respect and submission. Your vassal's whole heart and mind are imbued with feelings of circumspection and reverential obedience. He would humbly implore your Majesty graciously to regard him as a person who has tendered his allegiance and done some service. Should he hereafter fall into any errors, he trusts Your Majesty will look upon him as a slave and extend to him your kindness, so that he may continue for ever to be the recipient of the Celestial favours, for which he will be inexpressibly grateful.

He indites this memorial at Katmandu on the 14th August 1894 and accompanies it with a respectful offering of gold satin brocade.

Imperial Rescript. Perused.

Source : Foreign Dept. Sec. E, September 1895, No. 119, NAI.

Appendix D

Translation of a Kharita from His Highness the Maharajadhiraja to His Majesty the Emperor of China.

As soon as the information of the expected arrival of the Parwana graciously vouchsafed by His Celestial Majesty the Emperor of China was received, Sardars and gentries of the place accompanied by soldiers, elephants, horses, dancing parties and "tamashas" (show) went out far from here to offer welcome and having respectfully saluted the Imperial Parwana, and brought it up in procession to the Kantipur palace with incense and lighted tapers, sealtering vermillion and firing *feu de joie*, and placing it on a throne with bended knees and reverential mien we saw it opened. With wrapt attention I listened to the contents of the said Parwana addressed to me on the day of the month of the 22nd year of Shri Kwangsui. Your Majesty has been pleased to state" I am very glad to see that, since you were granted the throne of your father, you have acted in accordance with the advice of the Ambas at Lhasa with a sincere and true heart, living under our protection. Kazi Indra Bikram Rana, deputed by you, was here to pay his respects to me. The petition and presents, sent by you, arrived here and were laid before me. Appreciating your sincere devotion I granted audience to the said Kazi Indra Bikram Rana and his party, and I have sent by his hands for being taken on his return to you one golden "Parwana", 24 pieces of Kochin known as Tachiang Pastung, 4 pieces of Tangtwang Kochin, 4 pieces of blue Mantwang Kochin, 4 pieces of Yanfaichin Kochin, 4 pieces of Chintwang Kochin of Bakkha class, 4 pieces of Tangrung, 8 pieces Tangrung sheets or carpets, 2 silver tea-pots, 2 silver dishes, 2 Phalachhis, 2 Polis, 4 cups of "usay" colour, 4 cups of uchhai colour, 1 Rui, studded with Sangisan, 2 articles of Sangisan, 1 Rosary of sootoo beads, 2 Tiaochhi fur, 2 Malouchhi fur, 2 yellow dishes, 2 Hundochhis, 2 pairs of large purse, 4 pairs of small purse, and 8 packets of tea, which please take delivery of on arrival. Continue to follow as before the advice of the Ambas at Lhasa, bearing in mind our kindness. Keep those under you well in hand. Make yourself comfortable and happy. Cherish our kindness towards you. Don't fail or be lazy in your duty." Hearing these advice and instructions so graciously vouchsafed and also hearing in detail that the Kazi and his party, having arrived at Peking and presented the customary quinquennial presents to Your Imperial Majesty, and that they, after having had many opportunities to pay their profound respects to Your Majesty and having received gifts and Khillats, had returned bidding farewell to Your Majesty, and regarding all these as marks of Your Majesty's high favour, myself, my Prime Minister, Kazis, Bhardars, gentries and all others of my people have been delighted. Your Imperial gifts have all arrived, and I have respectfully accepted them with pleasure. My ancestors had respected and enjoyed the protection of Your Majesty, and I, for my part, have also been truly and sincerely respecting you according to the direction of the Ambas at Lhasa. Formerly, too, the Ambas were the mediums for the representation of our grievances or troubles, and now, too, with the hope that our troubles, brought to Your Majesty's notice by the said Ambas, would come to an end, it is my desire to remain faithful forages to come and secure Your Majesty's good-will by my services. I pray that Your Majesty will be graciously pleased, taking me, as a ward or child, to overlook the faults of commission or omission in this petition of me who living in a far off country serves Your Majesty and is ignorant of manners and customs.

Dated the 15th Jestha Sudi, Sunday, Sambat 1958

Source: Foreign Dept. Sec. E., November 1910, No. 15, NAI.

Appendix E

चीन जाने अफिसको नाम, संख्या, अर्जिको नक्कल, सौगातका चीजको तपसील स्मेत चाडो लेखी पठाउनु भन्यां क्काङस्यूई २० साल ६ मैन्हा ९ दिन जादा १९५१ साल्मा श्री ५ पृथ्वीका हजुरमा श्री धुङ तारीन अम्वाले लेखेको..............
(Chinese *Amban* to King Prithvi instructing to send soon the names of the members of the forthcoming Nepalese mission, draft of the *arji* and the detailed list of the presents to be carried by the mission.)

Source : Ministry of Foreign Affairs, Kathmandu (MFA), *Poka* No. Pa. 64.

Appendix F

मामुली सौगात चढाउन काजी इन्द्र विक्रम राणा सर्दार जुद्धवीर खडकालाई आषाढ ३१ जादा ज्राहावाट पठायौं भन्या ५१ साल ज्येष्ठ सुदी ८ रोज २ मा कम्मांडर इन चीफवाट कुतिका २ ढेवालाई लेषी पठाउन जाहेर गरेको साधक...

(Draft letter from Commander-in-Chief to *Dhewas* of Kuti informing about the departure of the Nepalese mission from Kathmandu under the leadership of *Kazi* Indra Bikram Rana and *Sardar* Juddha Bir Khadka.)

Source : MFA, *Poka* No. Pa. 64.

Appendix G

हाम्रा सर्दार जुद्धवीर षडका परलोकको षवर आउदा अप्सोच लाग्यो . नीज सर्दारलाई २०० टाक वकसीस भयाको र हामीलाई र हाम्रा काजी सवैलाई साविक वमोजीम वकसीस दिनु भंने हुकुमको षवर लेषी पठाउने काम वढिया भयेछ भन्या १९५३ साल माघ सुदी ३ रोज ५ मा श्री ५ सर्कारवाट अम्वालाई लेषी पठाउन जाहेर गरेको साधक ....

(Draft letter from Nepalese King to Chinese *Amban* expressing sadness at the sad demise of *Sardar* Juddhabir Khadka.)

Source : MFA, *Poka* No. Pa. 64

Appendix H

प्रमाना सौगाद ली निकानन्द साथ काजी इन्द्र विक्रम राणा फागुन शुदी ११ रोज ६ का दिन आई पुगे . षर्चले सिकिस्त भो भनेकालाई मोरु ९९॥ दावा भोटे हस्ते पठायाको छ. षर्च लि फर्की जाने काम गरे वेस होला भन्या ५८ साल वैशाष वदी २ रोज ७ मा श्री कम्माडर इन चीफवाट चीनीज्रा स्याउतालोयेलाई लेषी पठाउन जाहेर गरेको साधक ....

(Draft letter from Commander-in-Chief to Chinese *Talloye* informing about the arrival of *Kazi* Indra Bikram Rana in Nepal carrying *Parwana* and presents from the Ch'ing Emperor.)

Source : MFA, *Poka* No. Pa. 64

* * *

Kazi Bhairab Bahadur Gadhatola's Mission of 1906

Even before the return of the Nepalese mission of 1894 to Nepal, the Nepalese government had prepared to send another mission to China in 1901. But the Chinese *Amban* postponed it on the grounds of famine in the Chinese provinces of Shansi and Shensi.[1] Greatly appreciating the decision of the Chinese *Amban*, the Nepalese government expressed her readiness to send a mission to China as soon as the Ch'ing Emperor gave instructions.[2] Nepal sent her next mission to China in 1906 after a span of twelve years. The Chinese Imperial records have mentioned of Nepal's dispatching five-yearly mission to China in 1908.[3] But the Nepalese and Indian archival documents clearly state of Nepal's sending of quinquennial mission to China in 1906.

Leo E. Rose has referred to the leader of the 1906 Nepalese mission to China as Bharat Bahadur[4]. The Nepalese and Indian Archival documents prove that it was *Kazi* Bhairab Bahadur Gadhatola Chhetri who led the Nepalese mission of 1906 to China[5]. The deputy-leader of the mission was *Sardar* Kahar Singh Khadka Chhetri[6]. The other members of the mission were *Khardar* Bhim

1. Chinese *Amban* to King Prithvi, Kwang-hsu 29th year 12th month 26th day (1957 B.S.), Ministry of Foreign Affairs, Kathmandu (hereafter mentioned as MFA), *Poka* No. Pa 64. See Appendix M.
2. Draft letter from Nepalese King to Chinese *Amban*, 1958 B.S. Baisakh Badi 10 Roj 1 (14 April 1901), MFA, *Poka* No. Pa 64. See Appendix N.
3. J.K. Fairbank and S.Y. Teng, "On the Ch'ing Tributary System", *Harvard Journal of Asiatic Studies*, Vol. VI., 1941, pp. 195-198.
4. Leo E. Rose, *Nepal: Strategy For Survival*, Berkeley: University of California Press, 1971, p. 164, and Margaret W. Fisher and Leo E. Rose, *England, India, Nepal, Tibet, China, 1765-1958*, Berkeley: University of California, 1959, pp. 2-12.
5. MFA, *Poka* No Pa 64; J. Manners Smith to Secretary, Govt. of India, 17 August 1906, Foreign Department Sec. E, September 1906, No. 263, National Archives of India, New Delhi (hereafter referred as NAI).
6. Translation of a news-letter from *Kazi* Bhairab Bahadur, 15 February 1909, Foreign Department Sec. E, June 1909, No. 478, NAI; Jnanmani Nepal, *Nepal-Bhot Chin Sambandhaka Kehi Sanskritik Paksha* (Some Cultural Aspect of Nepal-Tibet China Relations), Kathmandu: Royal Nepal Academy, 2045 B.S., pp. 391-392.

Bahadur, *Subedar* Ran Gambhir Gharti, *Subedar* Debnath Upadhayaya.[7] According to one source, Bakhat Man Manandhar (Sayami) and Harkha Narsingh Manandhar (Sayami) were also included in the 1906 Nepalese mission.[8] Kazi Bhairab Bahadur Gadhatola was the son of Major Captain Mahavir Gadhatola Chhetri, a veteran of the Indian Mutiny, who had served as Nepal's *Vakil*(envoy) at Lhasa during the crucial period from 1882 to 1886[9]. Major Bhairab Bahadur was formerly Orderly Officer to the British Residency in Nepal for thirteen years. He had received the rank of *Kazi* for the purpose of the mission. A few days before his departure, the Nepalese Prime Minister Chandra Shamsher had sent Major Bhairab Bahadur to pay the British Resident in Nepal, Major J. Manners Smith, a formal call before leaving Kathmandu. During that call, Major Bhairab Bahadur had asked the British Resident to furnish him with a letter to the British representative in China to serve as an introduction on his arrival in Peking. The Nepalese quinquennial mission to Peking left Kathmandu on 10 August 1906[10]. It was well received by both the Chinese and Tibetan officials at the Nepal-Tibet border. As the Nepalese *Kazi* fell ill in Shigatse, he went to Gyantse, reaching there on 16 October 1906 to get medical help from the British. The other members of the mission went from Shigatse to Lhasa *via* the Rong valley. On 21 October 1906, Major Bhairab Bahadur called on Lieutenant F.M. Bailey, officiating British Trade Agent at Gyantse and expressed his gratitude for the British medical help which he had obtained there. He also told Lieutenant Bailey that he preferred to go by sea but Chinese government insisted on his coming by road follow like the earlier Nepalese missions. He also stated that the

7. Nepal, f.n. no. 6, p. 392 and p. 451.
8. An interview with Mr. Jit Bahadur Manandhar, a research scholar on Nepalese Culture and the Manandhars.
9. J. N. Jordan to Edward Grey, 5 June 1908, Foreign Department Sec. E, October 1908, No. 709, NAI. See Appendix F. The Crisis of 1883 placed both Nepal and Tibet in a war-like situation which ended only after a long negotiation in 1884.
10. J. Manners Smith to Secretary, Government of India, 17 August 1906, Foreign Department Sec. E, September 1906, No. 263, NAI. See Appendix A.

costs incurred by the Chinese government would be more than the value of the presents he was carrying for the Chinese Emperor, which were worth about twenty thousand rupees. Lieutenant Bailey had described the Nepalese envoy an "intelligent" man who spoke English fluently and read all the books in English available to him[11]. The Nepalese *Kazi* left Gyantse for Lhasa on 23 October 1906. It seems that he had arrived in Lhasa by January, 1907[12], from whence he wrote a letter in English to the Nepalese Prime Minister regarding the details of his arrival at Lhasa along with a brief account of the journey. The Nepalese mission left Lhasa for Peking on 6 February 1907[13].

Upon his arrival at Bathang, *Kazi* Bhairab Bahadur met an American named Henry Endemenilt, who after staying in Japan for two years came to China, where he was a school teacher in Peking and Tientsin. The Nepalese envoy's meeting and conversation with this American gentleman was friendly. The American teacher gave the Nepalese envoy a letter of introduction to the American Minister at Peking. Besides that, he also informed the Nepalese envoy about the edict prohibiting the use of opium by the Chinese government servants and the public, and thus the diminishing consumption of opium. The Nepalese court had also sent opium with this mission to be sold in China[14]. The Nepalese envoy left Bathang on 21 May 1907 and reached Lithang on 27 May 1907. Through a letter dated 17 August 1907 from Tarchindeo, the Nepalese *Kazi* informed Premier Chandra Shamsher that the opium which he had brought with him for sale on government account had not yet been sold and he believed that the opium could not be sold on the open market due to the Chinese government's policy of closing the smoking dens and the gradual restriction of the use of

---

11. Diary of Lieutenant F.M. Bailey, Officiating Trade Agent at Gyantse, 20 October- 27 October 1906, Foreign Dept. Sec. E, July 1907, Nos. 304-305, NAI.
12. Chinese *Ambans* to King Prithvi, Kwang-hsu 32nd year 12th month 18th day (1963 B.S.), MFA, *Poka* No. Pa 64. See Appendix O.
13. Translation of a letter from the Nepalese representative at Lhasa, 18 February 1907, Foreign Dept. Sec. E, June 1907, No. 88, NAI.
14. J. Manners Smith to Assistant Secretary, Govt. of India, 7 August 1907, Foreign Dept. Sec. E, September 1907, No. 98, NAI. See Appendix B.

opium among the people. He also stated that in the event that it was impossible to dispose of the opium stock by any means, he would be obliged to take the opium back to Nepal[15]. The Nepalese envoy reached Chengtu on 11 October 1907. According to H.H. Fox, the acting British Consul-General at Chengtu, the Chinese provincial authorities of Chengtu treated the Nepalese envoy with scant courtesy, for the Nepalese *Kazi* was lodged in miserable quarters outside the North Gate. Mr. H.H. Fox called on the Nepalese envoy soon after his arrival at Chengtu and supplied the Nepalese envoy with English newspapers[16]. While in Singafu, on 10 February 1908 *Kazi* Bhairab Bahadur met the Dalai Lama, who was also on his way to Peking. The Nepalese mission most likely arrived at Peking by April, 1908 and was given a warm welcome at Peking.[17] Here it should be mentioned that even before the arrival of the Nepalese mission in Peking, on 12 October 1907, through the British Resident J. Manners Smith, the Nepalese Prime Minister had sent to the British Legation in Peking a cover addressed to *Kazi* Bhairab Bahadur Gadhatola Chhetri, containing a draft for two thousand and twenty nine *Taels* equivalent to five thousand rupees in Indian currency[18]. Upon arrival of the Nepalese mission in Peking, Sir J.N. Jordan, the British Minister at Peking, delivered the draft to the Nepalese envoy. Besides that, the British Minister furnished the Nepalese envoy with newspapers from the British Legation and sent a number of his staff members to enquire about the Nepalese envoy's health. According to the British Minister, the Nepalese mission was lodged in the extreme north of the city of Peking, some four miles from the British Legation quarters, with somewhat inadequate accommodation, and guarded by an escort of Chinese

---

15. Translation of information received from *Kazi* Bhyrab Bahadur, 17 August 1907, Foreign Dept. Sec. E, March 1908, No. 1, NAI. The carrying of opium for trading purposes in China began with the Nepalese quinquennial mission of 1852.
16. H.H. Fox to J.Jordan, 25 November 1907, Foreign Dept. Sec. E, March 1908, No. 6, NAI.
17. *Kazi* Bhairab Bahadur's news-letter from Peking, MFA, *Poka* No. 64, No. 2 Ka Chi (51 Ka). See Appendix P.
18. J. Manners Smith to Secretary, Govt. of India, 12 October 1907, Foreign Dept. External B, January 1908, No. 92, NAI. See also Appendix C.

troops which kept a careful watch on all comings and goings. The Russian Military Attache, Colonel L. Korniloff had called upon the Nepalese delegation but was not received.[19] The Nepalese envoy had informed the British Minister that he had instructions from the Nepalese Prime Minister to turn to the British Minister for assistance, if required, and as such he did not propose to establish relations with any other Legations[20].

The Nepalese delegation had its first audience with the Chinese Emperor on 24 April 1908.[21] This took place in a courtyard of the Palace as *Kazi* Bhairab Bahadur and his suite (sixteen in number) were kneeling on one knee, while the Emperor was carried past them in his chair, apparently on his way to worship. The delegation was dressed in Nepalese uniforms. The presents which the delegates had brought for the Emperor were sent to the Palace on the following day. The Nepalese presents consisted of four elephant tusks, bales of cloth of gold, silk brocade and other stuffs, and spices. Two sets of official robes were subsequently presented to each member of the mission, one set for summer and the other for winter wear. *Kazi* Bhairab Bahadur's robes were of rich silk and the winter garments were lined with sable. The Nepalese envoy himself received the coral button of the first rank, and his suite the blue button[22].

The Nepalese mission's next audience with the Chinese Emperor took place early on the morning of 5 May 1908. On this occasion, the Empress Dowager was also present. The delegates did not enter the hall of audience in which the Imperial personages were seated, but advanced only as far as the foot of the steps leading up to the hall, and there knelt down on one knee, their eyes being, according to instructions, directed on the ground. The Emperor enquired about the health of His Highness the *Maharaja* and

---

19. *Kazi* Bhairab Bahadur's news-letter from Peking, MFA, *Poka* No. 64, No. 2 Ka Chi (51 Ka). See Appendix T.
20. J.N. Jordan to Edward Grey, 29 April 1908, Foreign Dept. Sec. E, October 1908, No. 705, NAI. See Appendix D.
21. *Kazi* Bhairab Bahadur's news-letter from Peking, MFA, *Poka* No. 64, No. 2 Ka Chi (51 Ka). See Appendix R.
22. Memorandum of P. Grant Jones, 5 July 1908, Foreign Dept. Sec. E, October 1908, No. 711, NAI. See Appendix G.

whether the mission had had a successful journey. *Kazi* Bhairab Bahadur, through his interpreter, returned favourable replies to His Majesty's queries, and the mission then withdrew. The ceremony of *Kowtow* was not performed and everything on this occasion was done strictly according to precedence. The Nepalese envoy complained to the British official, P. Grant Jones somewhat bitterly of Chinese conservatism, and seemed to imply that his exclusion from the actual presence was not entirely to his taste[23].

The Nepalese envoy *Kazi* Bhairab Bahadur called on British Minister Sir J. N. Jordan on 12 May 1908. A guard of honour of the 2nd Battalion Cameron Highlanders was called in to receive the Nepalese envoy at the main gate of the British Legation, and the British Minister received him in the drawing room with all the members of the Legation staff who were able to attend. According to the British Minister, *Kazi* Bhairab Bahadur was dressed in semi-European uniform and spoke fairly good English. During the course of the conversation, the Nepalese envoy described the principal incidents of his journey, his stay in Lhasa, his interview with the Dalai Lama at Singafu (His-An-Fu), and his halt at Chengtu in Szechuan, where, he said, he received much kindness at the hands of the Acting British Consul-General Mr. H.H. Fox. On 15 May 1908, Sir J.N. Jordan returned the Nepalese envoy's call. On 20 May 1908, at the invitation of Colonel J. H. Abbot Anderson, Commandant of the Legation Guard, the Nepalese envoy attended the International Legation guards Athletic Sports event which was held that year on the British Legation's grounds. This appeared to have been the Nepalese envoy's first meeting with other Europeans during his stay in Peking, as he had paid no calls, and did not propose to do so. On that occasion, the Nepalese envoy informed the British Minister that he had been commanded by the Nepalese Prime Minister to buy presents in Peking to be offered to the Nepalese King, and requested the British Minister's assistance in choosing them. According to Sir J.N. Jordan, as the Nepalese envoy was suffering from the effects of his long journey, he gratefully accepted the British Minister's offer that he should be attended to by the medical

23. *Ibid.*

officer of the Legation, Dr. Gray, who was to visit him on 21 May 1908[24].

Another meeting between the British Minister and the Nepalese envoy took place on 4 June 1908. During the conversation, *Kazi* Bhairab Bahadur stated that the question of continuing the Nepalese missions to China appeared to him to be of doubtful utility. Former missions had been largely in the nature of commercial speculations and had proved very successful in that respect. Little profit was now to be made by bringing Nepalese produce to China. The change, although the Nepalese envoy did not say so, was probably due to the restriction placed upon the sale of opium which was, the British Minister believed, in former years one of the articles in which the Nepalese mission traded. According to *Kazi* Bhairab Bahadur, the only advantage he saw in the continuance of the Nepalese missions to China was the opportunity it gave Nepal of gaining access to China and of acquiring some first-hand information of the great changes that were going on in China. The Nepalese envoy had utilized that opportunity to the best of his ability and had during his journey acquired a working knowledge of Chinese language[25] in order to enable him to gain a better insight into the conditions of Chinese life. But, on the whole, *Kazi* Bhairab Bahadur was inclined to think that the mission was a relic of the past which might be discontinued, although the process should be a gradual one. It seems that the relations between the Nepalese envoy and the British Legation had been particularly cordial, for the British Legation provided medical attendance for the Nepalese envoy and one of his staff also underwent a minor operation in the British Legation hospital. Besides that, the British Minister had frequently designated for one of his staff, Mr. P. Grant Jones, to enquire about the health and comfort of the Nepalese envoy. Interestingly, the British Minister had also mentioned that he found it difficult, in view of the Nepalese envoy's

---

24. J.N. Jordan to Edward Grey, 25 May 1908, Foreign Dept. Sec. E, October 1908, No. 707, NAI. See Appendix E.
25. *Kazi* Bhairab Bahadur's news-letter from Peking, MFA, *Poka* No. 64, No. 2 Ka Chi (51 Ka). See Appendix Q.

scruples, to show him as much attention as he could have wished[26].

According to Sir J. N. Jordan, during his other interview with *Kazi* Bhairab Bahadur in July 1908, he found the Nepalese envoy less disposed than on a previous occasion to advocate the discontinuance of the Nepalese missions to China. The Nepalese envoy spoke of them as a "harmless and friendly practice" and considered them of some use in promoting friendly relations between Nepal and China in Tibet. While in Peking, *Kazi* Bhairab Bahadur took lessons in surveying from one of the British Legation's Indian surveyors with the view of making a road map of his journey on his way back to Nepal. According to the memorandum drawn up by the British Legation's staff Mr. P. Grant Jones, the Nepalese *Kazi* was anxious to set out on his return journey, as he found that the summer climate of Peking did not suit his health or that of the members of his retinue. The Nepalese envoy told Mr. Jones that the servants who attended to the mission while in Peking were all paid by the Chinese government, and he feared it was in the interest of their pockets to detain him in Peking as long as possible. According to Mr. Jones, the Nepalese envoy intended, however, to make inquiries of the Chinese officials, who occasionally visited him, as to the probable date of his farewell audience and the issue of his passport. To Mr. Jones, the Nepalese envoy expressed his deep gratitude for the various acts of kindness which he had received from the British Legation[27].

Through *Kazi* Bhairab Bahadur's letter dated 6 August 1908, it seems that he had made an inquiry at the *Lifa Yamen* (an office) whether he could have two or three Chinese rifles on purchase, so that he might take them with him for the safety of himself and his party on the way during his return journey to Nepal. On 30 July 1908, some officials of the *Lifa Yamen* came to the Nepalese envoy's place, bringing with them four China-made magazine (five-Chambered) rifles, which, they said, were sent by the *Tunthan* of the *Yamen* by order of the Emperor as a present

26. J.N. Jordan to Edward Grey, 5 June 1908, Foreign Dept. Sec. E, October 1908, No. 709, NAI. See Appendix F.
27. Memorandum of P. Grant Jones, 5 July 1908, Foreign Dept. Sec. E, October 1908, No. 711, NAI. See Appendix G.

from His Majesty[28] for the Nepalese mission's safety during its return journey. Of the four rifles, two which had long barrels were intended for *Kazi* Bhairab Bahadur, and the two others, viz. one long barreled and another short barreled (cavalry carbine), for *Sardar* Kahar Singh, the deputy leader of the Nepalese delegation. Those Chinese officials also informed the Nepalese envoy that the following day, i.e. 31 July 1908 had been appointed as the day for the Nepalese mission's leave taking with the Emperor, and that conveyances with an escort of Chinese officials would be ready at the Nepalese envoy's residence very early in the morning. Accordingly they came a little before daybreak, while it was still dark, with two foreign-made and eight Chinese-made carriages and escorted the Nepalese mission to Wansausan Palace where the Emperor was residing. On arrival there the Nepalese delegates were taken to a waiting room where the *Tunthan* and other officials were present. The Nepalese mission rested for a while there and when His Majesty came to the audience chamber, *Kazi* Bhairab Bahadur and *Sardar* Kahar Singh were ushered into his presence. At that time, the Emperor was seated on his throne and approaching near as the Nepalese *Kazi* and *Sardar* paid their respects to him, he said : "Convey my enquiries about health to the *Maharaja*. Do your journey comfortably". Both the Nepalese *Kazi* and *Sardar* paid their farewell respects to His Majesty and returned. The members of *Kazi* Bhairab Bahadur's retinue, i.e., *Subedars, Jamadars* and others, were told that as His Majesty was unwell they should pay their respects from the door of the Chamber, and they did accordingly. At the time of audience, the Emperor looked very weak and emaciated. After taking leave of the Emperor, the Nepalese envoy urged the *Lifa Yamen* for an early completion of the arrangement of the Nepalese mission's return journey[29].

During their five months stay in Peking, the Nepalese mission had four audiences with the Ch'ing Emperor Kwang Hsu[30]

---

28. *Kazi* Bhairab Bahadur's news-letter from Peking, MFA, *Poka* No. 64, No. 2 Ka Chi (51 Ka). See Appendix S.
29. Translation of news received from *Kazi* Bhairab Bahadur, 6 August 1908, Foreign Dept. Sec. E, October 1908, No. 714, NAI. See Appendix H.
30. Translation of *Kazi* Bhairab Bahadur's letter, 15 September 1908, Foreign Dept. Sec. E, January 1909, No. 413, NAI. See Appendix J.

The Nepalese *Kazi* and *Sardar* also attended the birthday celebration function of the Ch'ing Emperor.[31] In addition to the British Minister, the Nepalese envoy Bhairab Bahadur also met the American Minister William Woodville Rockhill and *London Times* correspondent Dr. Morrison (G.E. Morrison ?).[32] *Kazi* Bhairab Bahadur had offered a Nepalese *Khukuri* (Knife) as a present to the British Minister J.N. Jordan.[33] While in Peking, the Nepalese delegation visited several places of interest, such as factories, schools, colleges, the zoo, botanical garden, agricultural farm and Wansausan Imperial Palace.[34]

On 11 September 1908, the Nepalese mission left Peking[35] for Tientsin by a special train. According to the head of the Nepalese mission, *Kazi* Bhairab Bahadur, at the time of his departure, a guard of honour composed of twenty five soldiers with two officers besides those that were on sentry duty, was dispatched to the gate of his residence, and saluted as he passed. Just outside the gate a body of twenty four mounted soldiers also with two officers were ready to escort him to the railway station. Twelve of them rode in front and twelve behind him. As the Nepalese envoy passed through the main street of the city, crowds of spectators, among whom there were some Europeans, gathered at the place. On arrival at the railway station, *Kazi* Bhairab Bahadur found a guard of honour composed of one company with officers in full dress uniform drawn up on the platform. As he approached the railway carriage, Dr. Morrison met him and bade him a hearty good-bye. He also informed the Nepalese envoy of the return of the British Minister from Peticho to Peking and his intention to come to see him. No sooner had Dr. Morrison left than Sir J.N. Jordan, the

---

31. *Kazi* Bhairab Bahadur's news-letter from Peking, MFA, *Poka* No. 64, No. 2 Ka Chi (51 Ka). See Appendix R.
32. Tirtha Prasad Mishra and Niranjan Sharma, "Chin Jane *Kazi* Bhairab Bahadur Ko Jaheri" (Reports of *Kazi* Bhairab Bahadur from China), *Rolamba*, Vol. 3, No. 3, July-September 1983, pp. 1-7.
33. *Kazi* Bhairab Bahadur's news-letter from Peking, MFA, *Poka* No. 64, No. 2 Ka Chi (51 Ka). See Appendix T.
34. Nepal, f.n. no. 6, pp. 368-370.
35. *Kazi* Bhairab Bahadur's news-letter from Peking, MFA, *Poka* No. 64, No. 2 Ka Chi (51 Ka). See Appendices U and V.

British Minister, accompanied by his Secretary, Mr. Campbell, arrived at the place. *Kazi* Bhairab Bahadur took the British Minister to his railway carriage which was clean and nicely furnished. The interview was of a most cordial nature. Sir J.N. Jordan asked the Nepalese envoy as to why he was in a hurry to leave Peking so soon and told him that he could have prolonged his stay there by a few days more. The Nepalese *Kazi* replied that his business at Peking was accomplished and that the earlier he started from the place the sooner he would reach home[36]. He also told the British Minister that he had obtained special permission from the Chinese government to pay a visit to Tientsin and to travel thence by train to Honan, whence he will proceed overland *via* Chengtu[37]. The Nepalese *Kazi* expressed to Sir J.N. Jordan his warm thanks for all his kindness to him which had added so much to his comfort during his stay at Peking. The British Minister wished the Nepalese envoy a comfortable journey. He also informed the Nepalese *Kazi* that he had written to the British Consuls at Tientsin and Thindafu (Chengtu), who would be pleased to afford the Nepalese envoy any necessary assistance. The Nepalese envoy thanked him saying that the British Minister's kindness will ever remain engraved in his mind. The British Minister looked quite cheerful and as it was time for the train to start he got up to take leave. *Kazi* Bhairab Bahadur got down to the platform and warmly shook hands with Sir J.N. Jordan. Soon after the train started and the guard of honour presented arms. It was half past one in the afternoon when the Nepalese mission departed for Tientsin[38]. According to the British Minister, at the time of leaving Peking, *Kazi* Bhairab Bahadur and the principal members of his staff were all dressed in Chinese official costume and wore the decorations which had been conferred upon them by the Emperor. Meanwhile, Sir J.N. Jordan had also remarked that a Chinese guard of honour was at the railway station, but no Chinese official of any standing was present and the

---

36. Translation of *Kazi* Bhairab Bahadur's letter, 15 September 1908, Foreign Dept. Sec. E, January 1909, No. 413, NAI. See Appendix J.
37. Jordan to Edward Grey, 14 September 1908, Foreign Dept. Sec. E, January 1909, No. 411, NAI. See Appendix I.
38. Translation of *Kazi* Bhairab Bahadur's letter, 15 September 1908, Foreign Dept. Sec. E, January 1909, No. 413, NAI. See Appendix J.

Nepalese envoy's departure, like his reception generally, was attended with scant ceremony[39].

From Peking it took the Nepalese mission four hours to reach Tientsin by train. Some Chinese officials sent by the local *Chundu* were present at the railway platform there to receive the Nepalese mission. The British Consul-General of Tientsin had also taken the trouble to come and meet the Nepalese envoy in his railway carriage. After he had some talk with the British Consul-General concerning mutual welfare, the Nepalese envoy along with his retinue proceeded to the Tientsin city. While in Tientsin, the Nepalese *Kazi* called on the *Chundu* of Paochinfu and the British Consul-General. Besides that, he did some sight seeing in Tientsin. On 15 September 1908, the Nepalese mission left Tientsin for Honan *en route* to Thindafu by train[40]. On their arrival at Fusiang after leaving Singafu, the Nepalese mission heard the news of the death of the Emperor Kuang-hsu and the Dowager Empress as well as the accession of the new Emperor[41]. While in Thindafu, the Nepalese envoy met the British Consul-General, visited various government factories, bought four horses for himself, ten horses and other goods for the Nepalese Prime Minister. Regarding *Sardar* Kahar Singh's purchasing of twenty three horses, the Nepalese envoy had remarked that the *Chundu* of Thindafu did not like it and passed some remarks on it. The Nepalese mission left Thindafu on 5 February 1909 and reached Yutoofu on 21 February 1909. From Yutoofu, the Nepalese mission left for Tarchindeo (Tachienlu) on 25 February 1909[42]. On 7 May 1909, the Nepalese mission left Tarchindeo. The Nepalese mission after leaving Tarchindeo proceeded on their journey without stopping anywhere except where horses and transportation for their use had to be changed. Travelling through Lithang and Bathang, the Nepalese mission finally reached Lhasa on 11

---

39. Jordan to Edward Grey, 14 September 1908, Foreign Dept. Sec. E., January 1909, No. 411, NAI. See Appendix I.
40. Translation of *Kazi* Bhairab Bahadur's letter, 15 September 1908, Foreign Dept. Sec. E, January 1909, No. 413, NAI. See Appendix J.
41. Translation of a news-letter from *Kazi* Bhairab Bahadur, 7 February 1909, Foreign Dept. Sec. E, June 1909, No. 478, NAI.
42. *Ibid.*

September 1909[43]. Here it should be pointed out that there were the reports on the alleged strange conduct of Nepalese envoy Bhairab Bahadur on his return journey to Nepal overland *via* Chengtu.[44] The Nepalese mission had brought with them about one hundred and eighty horses of different breeds known as *Chianta*, *Pony*, and *Siling*. While in Lhasa, the Nepalese envoy met the Dalai Lama as well as the Chinese *Ambans*. The Nepalese mission seemed to have left Lhasa for Kathmandu around 21 January 1910[45]. Finally, the Nepalese delegation returned to the Nepalese capital by April, 1910. Thus, *Kazi* Bhairab Bahadur's mission of 1906 returned home after nearly four-years (nearly forty four months). Except with the death of one soldier, all the members of the 1906 Nepalese mission returned home safely.[46] As usual, at the time of the arrival of *Kazi* Bhairab Bahadur's mission at Kathmandu along with a *Parwana*[47] and presents, it was given a warm welcome.[48]

This eighteenth five-yearly mission of 1906 was significant due to the following reasons: Firstly, it was the last Nepalese quinquennial mission to go to the Imperial court of China. For the nearly one hundred and fifteen years old mission system was terminated with this very mission. Secondly, the Nepalese court had also sent opium with *Kazi* Bhairab Bahadur's mission to be sold in China.[49] The Nepalese envoy hinted the British Minister that the Nepalese missions suffered a monetary loss by the new Chinese law

---

43. Chandra Shamsher to J. Manners Smith, 5 October 1909, Foreign Dept. Sec. E, October 1909, No. 716, NAI.
44. For the details of the strange conduct of *Kazi* Bhairab Bahadur on his return journey to Nepal, see Vijay Kumar Manandhar, *Cultural and Political Aspects of Nepal-China Relations*, Delhi: Adroit Publishers, 1999, pp. 59-68. See also W.N. Fergusson, *Land and People of Tibet and China in the Early Twentieth Century*, Delhi: Sharda Prakashan, Reprint, 1989, pp. 334-338.
45. Translation of a letter from *Kazi* Bhairab Bahadur, 3 January 1910, Foreign Dept. Sec. E, March 1910, No. 431, NAI.
46. Nepal, f.n. no. 6, pp. 383-390.
47. *Parwana* from the Chinese Throne to the *Maharajadhiraja* of Nepal, Foreign Dept. Sec. E, November 1910, No. 15, NAI. See Appendix K.
48. Translation of a *Kharita* from His Highness the *Maharajadhiraja* to His Majesty the Emperor of China, Foreign Dept. Sec. E, November 1910, No. 15, NAI. See Appendix L.
49. Manandhar, f.n. no. 39, pp. 80-83.

of imposing severe restrictions on the sale of opium and as such, the future Nepalese missions would be of doubtful utility. This remark made by the head of the Nepalese mission was quite significant in that it soon resulted in the termination of the mission system itself. Thirdly, it also happened to be most probably the first Nepalese mission to use trains during their journey to China. Fourthly, compared to other Nepalese missions to China, the leader of this Nepalese mission of 1906, *Kazi* Bhairab Bahadur became a subject of controversy. For due to his strained relations with the Nepalese envoy, *Sardar* Kahar Singh had made the allegation that *Kazi* Bhairab Bahadur had misappropriated an amount of more than nineteen thousand and five hundred rupees. Upon the arrival of the Nepalese mission in Kathmandu, a case dealing with the misappropriation of money was even reported to have been filed against *Kazi* Bhairab Bahadur.[50] Finally, *Kazi* Bhairab Bahadur's mission of 1906 happened to be the first Nepalese mission which had made a very close rapport with Sir J.N. Jordan, the British Minister in Peking. The British Minister paid due attention to *Kazi* Bhairab Bahadur's mission to China on their return journey from Peking, for which the Nepalese Prime Minister Chandra Shamsher thanked Sir J.N. Jordan.[51]

---

50. Nepal, f.n. no. 6, pp. 392-394 and pp. 450-454.
51. Chandra Shamsher to J. Manners Smith, 4 July 1909, Foreign Dept. Sec. E, September 1909, No. 18, NAI.

Appendix A

No. 146, dated Nepal, the 17th (received 23rd) August 1906
From - Major J. Manners Smith, V.C., C.I.E., Resident in Nepal,
To - The Secretary to the Government of India in the Foreign Department.

I have the honour to report, for the information of the Government of India, that the Nepalese Quinquennial Mission to Peking started from Katmandu on the 10th instant.

2. The Mission is in charge of Major Bhairab Bahadur, formerly for 13 years orderly officer to the British Residency. He has received the rank of Kazi for the purposes of the Mission.

A few days before his departure His Excellency the Prime Minister sent Major Bhairab Bahadur to pay me a formal call before leaving Katmandu, a compliment which I duly acknowledged; and I was asked at the same time to furnish him with a letter to the address of the British Representative in China to serve as an introduction on his arrival in Peking.

Source : Foreign Department Sec. E, September 1906, No. 263, National Archives of India, New Delhi (NAI).

Appendix B

Translation of a memorandum from the Prime Minister to the Orderly Officer to the British Residency, Nepal.

On the arrival of the Nepalese Mission to China at Bathang, Kazi Bhairab Bahadur, who is in charge of the Mission, met there an American named Henry Endemenilt.

The American told the Kazi that he, after staying for two years in Japan, came to China where he was a Professor in the schools at Pekin and Tientsin for two years; that after that he went to Chingtu, from where he went to Tarchindeo, and that from there he came to Bathang. He had a mind to go to Lhassa from Bathang. As he could not understand the representations made by the local Chinese officials to him (that he cannot go to Lhassa), he asked *Kazi* Bhairab Bahadur to explain to him what the Chinese officials told him. On the instructions of the Chinese officials being explained to

Kazi Bhairab Bahadur Gadhatola
Leader of 1906 Nepalese Quinquennial Mission to China

Kazi Bhairab Bahadur Gadhatola and a Nepalese Companion

Kazi Bhairab Bahadur Gadhatola (sitting left) and other foreign dignitaries (?)

Kazi Bhairab Bahadur Gadhatola and his wife Ganesh Kumari
(grand daughter of Jang Bahadur Rana)

him by the Kazi, he said that he would not go to Lhassa, and that he would go to Yamchin, and from there he would proceed to Talif, on reaching which he would go to Bhamo in Burma, and from there he would go towards Darjiling to see Dewal-Pustaks (Books on Buddhism) and that he had a desire to visit Nepal also.

The meeting and conversation with the American was friendly. The American also gave the Kazi a letter of introduction to the American Minister at Pekin. The American also said that on account of an Edict having been passed in China about two months ago, prohibiting the use of opium by (Chinese) Government servants and the public, the former within six months and the latter within one year, the consumption of opium has greatly diminished. The (Chinese) Government servants do not touch it. It seems that China will improve much in seven or eight years.

The Darbar have also sent opium, etc. with the Mission to be sold in China. If what the American said about opium is correct, the opium sent by the Darbar will not sell which means a loss to the Darbar.

Give my compliments to the Resident and read him out the contents of this memorandum merely as a sort of news and tell me what the Resident says.

Source: Foreign Dept. Sec. E, September 1907, No. 98, NAI.

Appendix C

Peking, November 29, 1907

Sir,

I have the honour to acknowledge the receipt of your letter No. 4164 E.C. of October 22 enclosing a cover addressed to the Head of the Nepalese Mission to Peking, containing a draft for Tls. 2029, equal to Rupees 5,000 Indian Currency.

The cover will be delivered to the Head of the Mission on his arrival.

I have the honour to be,
Sir,
Your most obedient, humble servant
J.N. Jordan

Secretary to the Government of India
in the Foreign Department,
Simla

Source: Foreign Dept. Extl. B, January 1908, No. 94, NAI.

Appendix D

No. 189Peking,
(Confidential) 29th April 1908

Sir

I have the honour to report the arrival in Peking of the Quinquennial Mission from Nepal to the Emperor of China.

The head of the Mission is named Bhyrub Bahadur. Until his final audience has taken place it is not practicable for him to pay calls, and I consequently have not yet seen him; but he has been furnished with news-papers from the Legation and I have sent a member of my staff to enquire after his health, and to offer any civilities which could be rendered before the final audience takes place.

The Mission is lodged in the extreme north of the city, with somewhat inadequate accommodation, and guarded by an escort of Chinese troops which keep a careful watch on all comings and goings.

As soon as the court ceremonials have been completed, I hope to make the personal acquaintance of the representative, who brought with him a letter of introduction from the Resident in Nepal.

The Russian Military Attache, Colonel L. Korniloff, has called upon the Mission, but was not received; and the Nepalese Representative stated, for my information, that as he had instructions from the Maharaja to turn to me for assistance, if required, he did not propose to establish relations with any other Legations.

I have the honour to be, with the highest respect,
Sir,
Your most obedient, humble servant,
J.N. Jordan.

The Right Hon'ble Sir Edward Grey, Bart, M.P.,
etc., etc., etc.

Source: Foreign Dept. Sec.E, October 1908, No. 705, NAI.

Appendix E

No. 225Peking,

Confidential 25th May 1908.

Sir,

With reference to my despatch No. 189 of April 29th, I have the honour to report that the Nepalese Envoy called on me on the 12th instant.

A guard of honour of the 2nd Battalion Cameron Highlanders was drawn up to receive him at the Main Gate of the Legation, and I received him in the drawing room with all the members of the Legation staff who were able to attend.

The Envoy was dressed in semi-European uniform, and speaks fairly good English. In the course of conversation he described the principal incidents of his journey, his stay in Lhassa, where, he said, everything was quiet; his interview with the Dalai Lama at Hsi-An-Fu, an account of which appears in a letter from the Resident in Nepal of March last, copy of which has been transmitted to me by the Government of India; and his halt at Chengtu in Szechuan, where, he said, he received much kindness at the hands of His Majesty's Acting Consul- General Mr. H.H. Fox.

On May 15th I returned his call, and on the 20th, at the invitation of Colonel J.H. Abbot Anderson, Commandant of the Legation Guard, he attended the International Legation Guards athletic sports which were held this year in our grounds. This appears to have been his first meeting with other Europeans during his stay here, as he has paid no calls, and does not propose to do so.

He informed me on this occasion that he had been commanded by His Highness the Maharaja to buy presents here to be offered to His Majesty the King, and requested assistance in their choice. Steps are therefore being taken to help him in this matter.

As he is suffering from the effects of his long journey, he gratefully accepted my offer that he should be attended by the medical officer of the Legation, Dr. Gray, who is to visit him to-morrow.

It is improbable that he will be able to leave Peking for another month or more.

I have the honour to be, with the highest respect,

Sir

Your most obedient, humble servant,
J.N. Jordan.

The Right Hon'ble Sir Edward Grey, Bart.
etc., etc., etc.

Source: Foreign Dept. Sec. E, October 1908, No. 707, NAI.

Appendix F

No. 260 Peking
5th June 1908

Sir,

I have the honour to report the substance of a conversation which I had yesterday with the Nepalese Envoy, Kaji Bhyrub Bahadur, who is living in quarters provided for him by the Chinese Government at the extreme north of the city, some four miles from the Legation quarter. It is possible that the Chinese selected this locality with the view of removing the Envoy from foreign influence, but if so, the precaution was unnecessary as the latter has instructions from the Maharaja to enter into relations only with this Legation.

The Envoy is especially proud of the fact that his father, who is now eighty-three, is one of the two surviving Nepalese veterans of the Indian Mutiny. He was Nepalese Agent at Lhasa in 1883 when the attack was made upon the Gurkha traders there by the Tibetans, and, according to his son, was mainly instrumental in averting war between the two countries by his skilful diplomacy in securing suitable reparation for the outrage.

The Kaji does not seem to think that Chinese influence in Tibet is increasing or that her efforts at reform there have so far produced much effect. The relations between the Gurkha traders and the Chinese were, he said, only passably good, as the Chinese Resident rather grudged the Nepalese the enjoyment of the rights which they had acquired by the longstanding treaty with Tibet. The chinese viewed with especial disfavour the arrangement by which all male children born of a Gurkha father and a Tibetan mother assumed the nationality of the father.

On his journey across Tibet he had been passed on from one Chinese Commissariat station to another, and had found things made comparatively easy for him. It was only when he reached the borders of China Proper that his difficulties began. These had at no time been very serious, but they had constituted a constant worry and had been caused entirely by the malpractices of the smaller officials. When he appealed to the Governors and Viceroys he had universally received instant redress, but the difficulty was to reach the ears of the higher authorities. After resorting to a variety of other methods, he had found in the end that an appeal by letter sent through the Customs Post proved the most efficacious remedy.

His treatment in Peking the Envoy described as being of the stereotyped kind which had been meted out to previous Missions since the last years of the 18th century. He had presented the usual letter and articles of so-called tribute from his sovereign and had been twice received in audience by the Emperor and Empress Dowager.

The letter, of which he promised me an English translation, was not, he said, so obsequious in tone as the version usually published in the Peking Gazette represented it to be.

The question of continuing these Missions appeared to him to be of doubtful utility, and he was reporting on the subject. Former Missions had been largely in the nature of commercial speculations and had proved very successful in this respect. Little profit was now to be made by bringing Nepalese produce to China. The change, although the Envoy did not say so, is probably due to the restrictions placed upon the sale of opium which was, I believe, in former years one of the articles in which the Mission traded.

The only advantage he saw in the continuance of the Missions was the opportunity it gave Nepal of gaining access to China and of acquiring some first-hand in-formation of the great changes that were going on in the country. He had utilized this opportunity to the best of his ability and had during his journey acquired a working knowledge of Chinese in order to enable him to gain a better insight into the conditions of Chinese life. But, on the whole, he was inclined to think that the Mission was a relic of the past which might be discontinued, although the process should be a gradual one.

The relations between the Envoy and this Legation have been particularly cordial, but except providing medical attendance for himself and one of his staff, who is now undergoing a minor operation in the Legation hospital, we have found it difficult, in view of his religious scruples, in showing him as much attention as we could have wished.

I am sending a copy of this despatch to the Government of India.

I have the honour to be, with the highest respect,

Sir,

Your most obedient, humble servant,

J.N. Jordan.

The Right Hon'ble Sir Edward Grey, Bart, M.P., etc., etc., etc.

Source: Foreign Dept. Sec. E, October 1908, No. 709, NAI.

Appendix G

No. 308 Confidential Peking,
7th July 1908

Sir,

With reference to my despatch No. 260 of 5th June, I have the honour to transmit to you herewith copy of a memorandum, which has been drawn up by Mr. Jones, whom I frequently deputed to enquire after the health and comfort of the Nepalese Envoy, on the subject of a conversation which he had with the Kaji on the occasion of his last visit.

It had been my desire to ascertain, if possible, more definitely what form of ceremonial was employed at the Envoy's audience with the Emperor, and Mr. Jones informs me that he found the Kaji quite ready to impart full information on the subject, his remarks suggesting a mild ridicule of the rigid observance of formalities which he apparently considered to be hardly in keeping with the actual relations which at present exist between his native country and the Empire of China.

The ceremonial at the audience appears to have adhered strictly to the rules which have governed such interviews in the past, and the articles brought by the Mission for presentation to the Throne to have been of the same kind as those enumerated in the enclosure to Sir N. O' Connor's despatch No. 164 of 30th April 1895. The translation of the letter from the Maharaja to the Emperor, which was handed to me by the Envoy himself, is identical in wording with that furnished in 1895 by Colonel Wylie, then Resident in Nepal, which formed enclosure in despatch No. 179 of 10th September of that year from the Government of India to His Majesty's Secretary of State, and, according to the statement made at the time by the Minister of Nepal to the Resident, the terms of the document would appear to have been settled at the end of the previous century.

At a recent interview which I had with the Kaji I found him less disposed than on a previous occasion to advocate the discontinuance of these Missions. He spoke of them as "a harmless and friendly practice" and considered them of some use in promoting friendly relations between Nepal and China in Tibet.

I should mention that the Kaji is taking lessons in surveying from one of our Indian surveyors with the view of making a road map of his journey on his way back.

I have the honour to be, with the highest respect,

Sir

Your most obedient humble servant,

J.N. Jordan

The Right Hon'ble Sir E. Grey, Bart, M.P.,
etc., etc., etc.

Memorandum

I saw the Nepalese Envoy this afternoon and obtained form him the following information respecting his audience.

The Envoy first saw the Emperor on April 24th. This took place in a courtyard of the Palace when the Kaji and his suite (16 in number) kneeling on one knee, the Emperor was carried past them in his chair, apparently on his way to worship. The Mission were dressed in Nepalese uniform.

The presents which the Mission had brought for the Emperor were sent to the Palace on the following day. They consisted of four elephant tusks, bales of cloth of gold, silk brocade and other stuffs, and spices.

Two sets of official robes were subsequently presented to each member of the Mission, one set for summer and the other for winter wear. The Envoy's robes were of rich silk and the winter garments were lined with sable. The Kaji himself received the coral button of the first rank, his suite the blue button.

The audience took place early on the morning of May 5th, both the Emperor and the Empress Dowager being present. The Mission did not enter the hall of audience in which the Imperial Personages were seated, but advanced only as far as the foot of the steps leading up to the hall, and there knelt down on one knee, their eyes being, according to instructions, directed on the ground. The Emperor enquired after the health of His Highness the Maharaja and whether the Mission had had a successful journey. The Kaji, through his interpreter, returned favourable replies to His Majesty's questions, and the Mission then withdrew. The ceremony of kowtow was not performed, nor does it seem to have ever been the custom as far as these Missions are concerned, as the Envoy told me that everything on this occasion was done strictly according to precedent. In fact, he complained, somewhat bitterly, of Chinese conservatism, and seemed to imply that his exclusion from the actual presence was not entirely to his taste.

The Kaji is anxious to set out on his return journey, as he finds that the summer climate of Peking does not suit his health or that of the members of his retinue. He told me that the servants in attendance on the Mission while in Peking are all paid by the Chinese Government, and he feared it was to the interest of their pockets to detain him in the capital as long as possible. He intended, however, to make enquiries of the Chinese officials, who occasionally visit him, as to the probable date of his farewell audience and the issue of his passport.

The Envoy expressed his deep gratitude for the various services of kindness which he had received from this Legation.

P. Grant Jones

Peking;
The 5th July 1908

Source: Foreign Dept. Sec. E, October 1908, No. 711, NAI.

Appendix H

Translation of news received from Kazi Bhairab Bahadur, dated Peking, 23rd Sravan Thursday 1965 = the 6th August 1908.

Tang Tarin Amba, who was deputed by the Government of China to Tibet for the settlement of Tibetan questions, has arrived from Simla. The Potala Lama is still at Uthaisa. The Government of China has already prepared on a rather grand scale a house for him in Peking. But there is a talk here that he would come only after the summer heat has abated a little. I understand that after his arrival here he will be given necessary instructions about arrangements in Tibet and then will be sent back to Lhassa.

I had at the Lifa Yamen made an enquiry whether I could have 2 or 3 rifles of China on purchase, so that I may take them with me for the safety for myself and party on the way during my return journey. On Thursday the 16th Sravan some officials of the said Yamen came to my place, bringing with them four China-made magazine (five-Chambered) rifles, which they said were sent by the Tunthan of the Yamen by order of the Emperor as a present from His Majesty for our safety during our return journey. Of the four rifles, two which had long barrels were intended for me, and the other two, viz., one long barrelled and one short barrelled (cavalry carbine), for Sirdar Kaharsing. There were also 800 cartridges with the rifles at the rate of 200 each. The rifles are of the same kind with which the Chinese army here are armed.

The same officials who brought to us the above-mentioned rifles had also come with a message that the following day, viz., Friday, the 17th Sravan, had been appointed as the day for our leave taking with the Emperor, and that conveyances with an escort of Chinese officials would be ready at my residence very early in the morning. Accordingly they came a little before daybreak, while it was still dark, with two foreign-made and 8 China-made carriages and escorted us to Wansausan Palace where the Emperor then was. On arrival there we were taken to a waiting room where the Tun than and other officials were present. We rested a while there, and when His Majesty came to the audience chamber, myself and the Sirdar were ushered into his presence. His Majesty was seated on his throne and approaching near as we paid our respects to him, he said: "Convey my enquiries about health to the Maharaja. Do your journey comfortably". We then paid our farewell respects to His Majesty and returned. The members of my retinue, i.e., Subadars, Jamadars and others, were told that as His Majesty was unwell they should pay their respects from the door of the Chamber, and they did accordingly. The Emperor looked very weak and emaciated. Several noted physicians and doctors (Chinese) were in attendance in the palace, where His Majesty was confined owing to illness. From outside enquiry, I learned that he was suffering from urinal disease. He has no issue till now, nor is there any prospect of having any. Now that we have taken leave of the Emperor. I am urging the Lifa Yamen for an early completion of the arrangements of our journey, which as soon as ready we will start from here. I am sorry I have not been able to send the goods of your Highness's order. Some of them are not available here at all, others are in the course of preparation. I shall try to pick up those things not available here should I be able to get any en route.

At 9 O'clock on Sunday evening, the 10th Sravan, a serious fire broke out in the German Legation here. The British, French, Italian and Austrian soldiers were out to extinguish the fire, but in spite of all their united efforts, the fire extended to a magazine, causing tremendous explosions, which damaged the sorrounding buildings and the splinters of exploded balls killed two German and three French soldiers besides 3 German officers, while 57 more of various nationalities were wounded. I heard that the loud explosions suddenly in the darkness of night caused alarm in all the Foreign Legations and made them stand on their guard.

Source: Foreign Dept. Sec. E, October 1908, No. 714, NAI.

Appendix I

No. 413 Peking,
14 September 1908

Sir,

I have the honour to report that the Nepalese Envoy left Peking on the 11th instant by special train for Tientsin where he proposes to stay a few days before starting on his homeward journey. The Envoy, whom I saw off at the station, told me that he had obtained special permission from the Chinese Government to pay a visit to Tientsin and to travel thence by train to Honan, whence he will proceed overland *via* Chengtu.

The Envoy and the principal members of his staff were all dressed when leaving in Chinese official costume and wore the decorations which had been conferred upon them by the Emperor. A Chinese Guard of Honour was at the station, but no Chinese official of any standing was present and the Envoy's departure, like his reception generally, was attended with scant ceremony.

I furnished the Envoy with a letter of introduction to His Majesty's Consul-General at Tientsin, by whom he was met there on his arrival, and with similar letters of recommendation to His Majesty's Consul-General at Chengtu and to the members of the various British Missionary communities in the districts through which he will pass on his overland journey.

The relations between the Nepalese Mission and this Legation have been very friendly, and the Envoy expressed his appreciation of the attention that had been shown to him.

I am sending a copy of this despatch to the Government of India.

I have the honour to be, with the highest respect,

Sir

Your most obedient, humble servant,

J.N. Jordan

The Right Hon'ble
Sir Edward Grey, Bart, M.P.,
etc., etc., etc.

Source: Foreign Dept. Sec. E, January 1909, No. 411, NAI.

Appendix J

Translation of Kazi Bhairab Bahadur's letter, dated the 31st Bhadra 1965 = 15th September 1908.

On Friday, the 27th Bhadra, I, with all the members of my party, left Peking by train for Tientsin. At the time of my departure a guard of honour composed of 25 sepoys with two officers besides those that were on sentry duty, was drawn up at the gate of my residence, who saluted as I passed. Just outside the gate a body of 24 mounted sowars also with two officers was ready to escort me to the railway station. Twelve of them rode in front and twelve behind me. As I passed through the main street of the city, crowds of spectators, among whom there were some Europeans, gathered at the place. On arrival at the station I found a guard of honour composed of one company with officers in full dress uniform drawn up on the platform. As I approached the railway carriage, Dr. Morrison met me and bade me a hearty good-bye. He also kindly informed me of the return of the British Minister from Peticho to Peking and of his intention to come to see me. No sooner had Dr. Morrison left than Sir Jordan, the British Minister, accompanied by his Secretary, Mr. Campbell, arrived at the place. I took His Excellency to my railway carriage which was clean and nicely furnished. The interview was of a most cordial nature. His Excellency asked me why I was in a hurry to leave Peking so soon and told me that I could have prolonged my stay there by a few days more. I replied that my business at Peking was finished, and that the earlier I started from the place the sooner I would reach home. I then expressed to him my warm thanks for all his kindness to me which had added so much to my comfort during my stay at Peking. He said that he hoped I would have a comfortable journey and added that he would write to the British Consuls at Tientsin and Thindafu (Chengtu), who would be pleased to afford me any necessary assistance. I thanked him saying that his kindness will ever remain engraved in my mind. His Excellency looked quite cheerful, and as it was time for the train to start he got up to take leave. I got down to the platform and warmly shook hands with him. Soon after the train started and the guard of honour presented arms. It was half past one in the afternoon when we left. In four hours, i.e., at 5-30 P.M., we reached Tientsin. Some Chinese officials deputed by the local Chundu were present at the railway platform there to receive me. The British Consul-General of the place had also kindly taken the trouble to come and met me in my railway carriage. After I had some talk with him concerning mutual welfare, etc., I proceeded to the city.

It was customary to pay a visit to the Chundu of Paochinfu while passing through his place. I have not had occasion to see him on my way to Peking, and as he happened to be staying at Tientsin, he sent to me a Chinese officer the very evening of my arrival here with a message that he would be pleased to receive me at his Yamen the next day. Accordingly at 10 in the morning I went to him escorted by a deputation of Chinese officials. At the gate of the Yamen four sentries were mounting guard. In the first courtyard a guard of honour composed of one company was drawn up who saluted as I passed. I was then taken through the next courtyard where there were only four sentries mounting guard at the gates, who also saluted me. In the third courtyard, which was rather a big one, another guard of honour composed of two companies was drawn up in two lines and in a parlour there the Chundu with some 50 of his officers was present. He received me kindly, and after I had some friendly talk with him concerning news about Your Highness's welfare and the comforts of my journey, etc., he enquired whether I could speak English. On my replying in the affirmative, he pointed out to me two of his officers present, namely, a military officer, Captain Liu, and another, a civil officer, as those who knew English and said that I might speak with them in that language. These officers then acted as interpreters for the Chundu. He asked me the strength of the Nepalese army to which I replied that there were some fifty thousand efficient standing army. He next enquired how many audiences I have had with the Emperor. I replied, "four times". He next said that I had brought back with me a lot of things which could not be sold at Peking and kindly promised to help me in disposing of the things. I thanked him for his kindness and said that I had brought only a small quantity of things and that as the unsold things were not much I was taking them back with me. He then handed over to me two photographs of himself for presentation to Your Highness, another one for me and again one for the Sirdar, and said that he had deputed Captain Liu to take me to any place which I wished to see or visit. I thanked him for his kindness. After which I took leave. On arrival at the courtyard Captain Liu asked me to allow him to take a photograph of myself, and I gave him a sitting. The same ceremonial was observed at departure as on arrival.

As the Chundu had directed Captain Liu to take me out sight seeing on Monday, the 30th Bhadra, at half past nine in the morning, the Captain came to my place with a carriage and sowars. At 10 I went out with him for a drive through the principal market place and the street where the Foreign Consulates were situated. On arrival at the British Consulate I expressed a wish to get down there to meet the

British Consul-General. We sent in our cards, and were received by the Consul-General. We had a friendly talk and spent a pleasant hour at his place. I then took leave and drove thence to the Japanese Bazar. Captain Liu expressed a wish when we arrived in front of a photorapher's to have a photograph, which will serve as a memento, in which we both were seated together. I agreed and had a photo taken. At 1-30 P.M., I returned to my lodging. The same afternoon at 5 the Chinese Civil Officer on duty with me came to me with a carriage to acquire whether I would go out for a drive. I went out to see a large and beautiful park or garden. Thence I drove along the bank of the river and came to a police station with a nice building on it. I enquired what it was and was told that it was a police station, and was asked whether I would like, to look in. On my replying in the affirmative, I was taken in and shown to all the parts of the building. There was a German Officer, a Captain by rank, in the Chinese Government employ there, who explained to me everything concerning the police station. Everything seemed to be done there in the European style. There were also nine Sikhs in service there. I then drove along the river, saw the river wharfs and quays and returned to my lodging at 7-30 P.M.

To-day at nine in the morning I drove out and visited some of the Chinese institutions here. I am leaving Tientsin this evening by rail.

Source: Foreign Dept. Sec. E, January 1909, No. 413, NAI.

Appendix K

Parwana from the Chinese Throne to the Maharajadhiraja of Nepal

Command of the Emperor who being an incarnation of the Supreme Being exists for the protection of this world. To the Gorkha Erhteni Wang Raja Prithvi Bir Bikram Shumshere Jung Bahadur Shah Deva. I have meted out in this year to all living creatures impartial and equal treatment, and it is my wish that all countries may ever enjoy peace and happiness through my blessings. I am very glad to see that, since you were granted the throne of your father, you have acted in accordance with the advice of the Ambas at Lhasa with a sincere and true heart, living under our protection. Kazi Bhairab Bahadur Garhtora Chhetri deputed by you was here to pay his respects to me. The petition and presents sent by you arrived here and were laid before me. Appreciating your sincere devotion, I granted audience to the said Kazi Bhairab Bahadur Garhtora Chhetri and his party, and I have sent by his hands for being taken on his return to you 24 pieces of Kochin known as Tachien Ustwan, 4 pieces of Tangtwang Kochin, 4 pieces of Siantwang Kochin, 4 pieces of Mantwang Kochin, 4 pieces of Ching Kochin, 4 pieces of Tangrun, 8 pieces of Tangrun sheets or carpets, 2 silver tea-pots, weighing $17^1/_5$ Taks of silver, 2 silver dishes, weighing 18 Taks of silver, 2 Tamaphopatas, 2 Polisis, 2 pairs cups, 2 woolen articles, 2 pairs cups for milk, 1 Ean Rui, 1 Taotoo, 2 Yangtis, 2 Tiachhi fur, 2 Malochhi fur, 2 Maiyoos, 2 Wondusis, 2 pairs large purse, 4 pairs small purse, 8 packets of tea, which please take delivery of on arrival. Continue to follow as before the advice of the Ambas at Lhasa, bearing in mind our kindness. Keep those under you well in hand. Make yourself comfortable and happy. Cherish our kindness towards you. Don't fail or be lazy in your duty. These are my instructions.

Dated the 4th day of the 11th month of the 34th year of Shri Kwangsui.

Source: Foreign Dept. Sec. E, November 1910, No. 15, NAI.

Appendix L

Translation of a Kharita from His Highness the Maharajadhiraja to His Majesty the Emperor of China.

No sooner the information was received of the expected arrival of the Parwana graciously vouchsafed by His Celestial Majesty the Emperor of China, than, having consulted old records and having according to precedents, sent out far from here Sardars, gentries, soldiers, dancing parties, and tamashas (show) and brought the Imperial Parwana to the Kantipur palace with great honour and respect we received it with reverence. From the said Parwana favoured to my address on the 4th day of the 11th month of the 34th year of Shri Kwangsui, we were all delighted to learn that Kazi Bhairab Bahadur having approached Your Majesty's August presence had the high honour of paying his humble respects to Your Majesty and of submitting the petition and presents sent from here and that Your Merciful Majesty had sent by his hands tokens of your kindness consisting of one golden Parwana and other articles, all of which we regard as a mark of great favour and kindness of the high and great Celestial Majesty. I have respectfully and with pleasure accepted the gracious gifts so kindly sent. As a ward or child who respect Your Majesty with affection living in a far off country, I entertain the hope, with a true and sincere heart, for Your Imperial Majesty's favour and kindness, and pray that Your Majesty may be graciously pleased to overlook the faults of commission or omission that may have crept in this petition owing to ignorance of manners and customs.

Dated the 4th Sravan, Tuesday 1967.

Source: Foreign Dept. Sec. E., November 1910, No.15, NAI.

Appendix M

यो साल स्यान्सी स्यांसी सहरमा अनिकाल भएको हुनाले सौगात चढाउन पर्न्यालाई थामि दिनु भन्ने हुकुम भै आयो भन्या ककास्यूई २९ साल १२ मैन्हा २६ दिन जादा १९५७ सालमा श्री ५ पृथ्वीका हजुरमा युतारिन अंवाले पठाएको............................

(Chinese *Amban* to King Prithvi informing about the postponement of the forthcoming mission on the ground of famine at Shansi and Shensi towns.)

Source : Ministry of Foreign Affairs, Kathmandu (MFA), *Poka* No. Pa 64.

Appendix N

वढिया लेषी आयेछ. यो स्यास्यान २ अडामा अनिकाल भयाका सुविस्ता भै वाटो षुलेपछि जैले पठाउनु भनी आफुहरुवाट लेषी आउला उसै वषतमा पठाउला भंन्या १९५८ साल वैसाष वदी १० रोज १ मा श्री ५ वाट यूतारीन अंवालाई लेषी पठाउन् जाहेर गरेको साधक ....

(Draft letter from Nepalese King to Chinese *Amban* expressing Nepal's readiness to send mission to China at the Emperor's instruction.)

Source: MFA, *Poka* No. 64.

Appendix O

काजी भैरव गढतोला छेत्रीहरु अर्जि सौगात ली ल्हासा आइ पुगे माल विचार गर्दा मिल्दछ . अघिका रीत वमोजिम काजी भारदारलाई वक्स दि आफु वाङ वाट पठायाको सौगात लि हामी ताठिन वाट फ्रीस्त वमोजिमको माल थ्वानस्यान मार्फत पठायाको छ वुझि लिनु होला भन्ने श्री ५ पृथ्वीका हजुरमा काङ्स्यूई ३२ साल १२ मैन्हाका १८ दिन जादा ६३ सालमा भोट ल्हासाको अम्वा टुथान तान् र ल्यान तारीनले पठाएको.................

(Chinese *Ambans* to King Prithvi informing about the arrival of *Kazi* Bhairab Gadhatola Chhetri at Lhasa.)

Source: MFA, *Poka* No. Pa 64.

Appendix P

१९६५ साल वैशाख ९ गते रोज २ पेकीङवाट भैरव वहादुरले पठाएको विन्ती पत्र-

ठाउँ ठाउँमा राम्रो स्वागत, वास वास फापुनहरु आएको. ड्रेस लगाई सलाम गरेको -

टाङतेफुमा आई पुगेपछि सेवकलाई लिना निमित पेचीनवाट खटिएका अफिसरहरु आएको . त्याहावाट रेलमा ल्याएको . सजाइएको रेलवाट पालो पहारा राम्रो भएको . Station मा सलामी दिएको -

पेचीनमा नया ठाउमा वास दिएको . पालो पहरा दिएका -

पेचिन वदलिएको, कलकारखाना भएको. युरोपियनले जस्तै गर्न लागेको, जापानको influence वढेको -

फौजी अफिसरले स्वागत गरेको -

तोफाका माल जाच्न आउने-साविक अनुसार छ छैन भनी हेर्ने -

(*Kazi* Bhairab Bahadur's news-letter from Peking mentioning about his arrival in Peking.)

Source: MFA, *Poka* No. 64, No. 2 Ka Chi (51 Ka).

Appendix Q

१९६५ साल वैशाष २४ गते रोज ३ भैरवको विन्तीपत्र

Tibet तर्फ पनी सर्भेका कामहरु गराउन्या तजवीज गर्न लागेको वुझियाको हालखवर जाहेर गऱ्याको छ -

Tibet पनि China proper मा include गरी लासामा Viceroy राषन्या तजवीज भयाको हाल सुनेको . अघि ठिंडफु वाट जाहर भयाका आई वुझदा

पनी सोही तजवीजको वन्दोवस्त गर्न लागन्या वुभ्दामा आउछ -
Anti opium regulations कढाईसाथ पालन गर्दै रहेको . अफिमको चलन हराएको . हाम्रो अफिम अहिले सम्म विक्री हुन नसकेका -
चीनीया पढन लागेको लेख्न पढन थालेको. माष्टर १ तलव दी राखेको -
तिब्वतमा १० हजार फौज तरफ राख्न लागेको -
अर्जिका विषयमा British मिनिष्टरले सोध्दा निर्देशन दिए वमोजिम अंग्रेजी उल्था दिएको -
(*Kazi* Bhairab Bahadur's news-letter from Peking mentioning about the strict implementation of anti-opium regulations in China, not yet selling of the Nepalese mission's opium, learning of Chinese language through a teacher and providing the translation of the Nepalese government's *arji* into English to the British Minister at Peking.)

Source : MFA, *Poka* No. 64, 2 Ka Chi (51 Ka).

Appendix R

१९६५ साल श्रावण गते १२ रोज १ मा पेचीनवाट भैरव वहादुर गडतौडा सहर घुमाएको -

आषाढ २२ गते British Minister का Private Secretary आई नेपालवाट के माल सामान ल्याएको हेरेको . श्री ५ चीन वादसाहको दर्शन कुन हिसावले गरेको सोधनी हुदा अधिको थिती अनुसार भएको जवाफ दिएको -
श्रावण १० गते चीन वादशाहको दर्शन गरेको. जन्म दिन भएको वादसाहको. १ रात दरवारमा नै वस्दै गरी आएको. नाच तमासा भएको -
गर्मी छ . गर्मी कम भएपछि मात्र विदा दिने -
(*Kazi* Bhairab Bahadur's news-letter from Peking mentioning about sightseeing in Peking, British Minister's Private Secretary inspecting the Nepalese Mission's presents to the Chinese Emperor, Chinese Emperor's audience to the Nepalese mission and the Nepalese mission's invitation to the Chinese Emperor's birthday celebration programme in the palace.)

Source : MFA, *Poka* No. 64, 2 Ka Chi (51 Ka).

Appendix S

१९६५ साल श्रावण २३ गते रोज ५ मा पेचीनवाट भैरव वहादुर

राम्रो वन्दुक किन्न खोजेको तर नपाइने. तर २/४ वन्दुक वक्स दिनु भन्ने हुकुं

भयाको छ -
विदाई दर्शण श्रावण १७ गते १९६५ सालमा वादशाहसंग -
(*Kazi* Bhairab Bahadur's news-letter from Peking mentioning about the Chinese Emperor's ordering of offering of guns as presents to the Nepalese mission and the Nepalese mission's farewell meeting with the Chinese Emperor.)

Source : MFA, *Poka* No. 64, 2 Ka Chi (51 Ka).

Appendix T

१९६५ साल भाद्र २ गते पेचीनवाट भैरव वहादुर

कुच हुने वन्दोवस्त गर्न अनुरोध गरेको- British Minister लाई खुकुरी presents दिएको- British legation मात्रै भेटघाट गरेको वर्णन -
पेकीङ आउदा रसीयन भेट माग्दा नदिएको. अव आयेमा दिन रसीयनसंग सेवकलाई शिक्षा वक्से अनुसार काम गर्ने -
प्रभु ञाहावाट हिडेका दिन देषी पेचीन सम्म जादा आउदा ठाउ ठाउमा यो यो दस्तुर भेट मुलाकाद गर्नु पर्न्यारहेछ यो यो दस्तुर येति येति दिदो रहेछ. येति कोस यति वास पर्दो रहेछ. उस तर्फवाट पायाका जम्मा येतिमा यो दरले फलाना फलानाले ज्मा येति पाया भन्या जवान जवानले पायाको फाँट षोली ज्मा येति भन्या र हाम्रा तर्फवाट येस येस ठाउमा येस येसलाई येती येती दस्तुर ...... दिनु पर्ने रहेछ भनी सवै देषिने गरी कीताव षडा गरी ल्याउनु भन्या सिक्षा मोतािवक आउदाको ञाहासम्मको वास कोस समेतको कीताव तयार गराउदैछु फर्कदा पनि जो होला सवाल र शिक्षा मोताविकको किताव षडा गरी सर्कारमा नजर गराउन्यानैछु -
(*Kazi* Bhairab Bahadur's news-letter from Peking mentioning about offering a *Khukuri* as a present to British Minister, meeting only with the British legation, not meeting with Russian legation, preparing a detailed and systematic summary of the routes from Kathmandu to Peking and the details of the incomes and expenditures of the Nepalese mission.)

Source : MFA, *Poka* No. 64, 2 Ka Chi (51 Ka).

Appendix U

१९६५ साल भाद्र २३ गते पेचीनवाट भैरवले श्री ३ लाई

सर्कारको वेलायत सवारी भै वकस्याका विषयेमा कुरा चिनीञा अफिसरहरुले गऱ्याका भया सेवकलाई वक्स्याको सीक्षा वमोजिम कुरा गर्ने थिञा तर आज

सम्म सो कुरा चीन govt. का भारदारले नसोधेको -
चीनको स्थिति ठीक छैन . चाडै आउने भाद्रको २७ गते आउने छ -
रसियाको वादसाहवाट पनि credentials आउने -

(*Kazi* Bhairab Bahadur's news-letter from Peking to *Sri Tin* mentioning about the Chinese government officials not yet making any enquiries about Nepalese Prime Minister's visit to London, the Nepalese mission's departure from Peking in Bhadra 27, the arrival of Russian Emperor's credentials.)

Source: MFA, *Poka* No. 64, No. 2 Ka Chi (51 Ka).

Appendix V

१९६५ साल भाद्र २७ गते रोज ६ मा पेचीनवाट कुच भएको दिन पठाएको पत्र

Greeting exchange

(*Kazi* Bhairab Bahadur's news-letter from Peking mentioning about exchanging greetings on the eve of the Nepalese mission's departure from Peking.)

Source: MFA, *Poka* No. 64, No. 2 Ka Chi (51 Ka).

* * *

Conclusion

While tracing the nearly one hundred and fifteen year old history of Nepalese complimentary quinquennial missions to China, we see that Nepal sent altogether eighteen customary five-yearly missions to China. Out of them, only fifteen missions reached Peking and had an audience with the Chinese Emperor. As regards to the remaining three Nepalese missions, the five-yearly missions of 1802 and 1807 proceeded only up to the Nepal-Tibet border area and handed over the presents and *arji* meant for the Ch'ing Emperor to the Chinese officials there. The Nepalese mission of 1866 was not allowed to visit Peking by the Chinese authorities, and had to return from the Chinese border town of Chen-tu. For the first sixty years, the period from 1792 to 1852, Nepal was quite regular in sending quinquennial missions to China, and altogether thirteen missions were sent during this period. After the Nepal-Tibet war of 1855-56, the mission system moved slowly and irregularly, for during the fifty year period following the Nepal-Tibet war of 1855-56, from 1856 to 1906, only five missions were sent to China by Nepal.

Here it should be noted that *Kazi* Bhaktabir Thapa and *Kazi* Bir Keshar Pande led the missions continuously for two times whereas soon after his return from Peking as the leader of the Nepalese mission to China, *Chautariya Kazi* Pushkar Shah was appointed to the post of *Mukhtiyar. Kazi* Jagat Bam Pande, leader of the 1852 mission did not return to Nepal and escaped to India from Tibet due to the execution of prominent Pandes in Nepal. Both the leaders and deputy leaders of 1847 and 1852. Nepalese missions passed away while they were returning home. Likewise the deputy leader of 1894 mission died in Peking.

The Nepalese mission generally consisted of forty-five members comprising a leader, a deputy leader, *Subedars, Khardars, Jamadars, Nayaks,* interpreters, doctors and other junior staff. Next, the Nepalese envoy's retinue was not rigidly fixed. For sometimes the Chinese authorities permitted some more members to be enlisted in the Nepalese mission. The mission 1877 led by *Kazi* Tej Bahadur Rana consisted of forty-five members, whereas the mission of 1894 consisted of forty-six. As the journey of the

Nepalese mission was long, difficult and risky, the leader and the deputy leader of the mission used to include their sons. Regarding the list of general presents being carried by the Nepalese missions to the Ch'ing court, they varied from time to time,. Besides the Ch'ing Emperor, Nepal also sent presents to the Chinese and Tibetan authorities. On five occasions in 1795, 1822, 1852, 1866 and 1877, Nepal sent her delegates to China with the usual five-yearly presents and special presents for the new Ch'ing Emperors Chia Ch'ing, Tao Kwang, Hsien Feng, T'ung Chih and Kwang Hsu. Significantly enough, the presents sent by the Ch'ing Emperor to the Nepalese King were of more value than the Nepalese gifts meant for the Ch'ing Emperor. The Nepalese mission along with presents and *arji* generally started from Kathmandu on an auspicious day fixed by the astrologers and it set out from Kathmandu to Lhasa *en route* to Peking by the traditional route through Kuti, and while returning from Peking, they always entered Kathmandu *via* Kerung. The Chinese and Tibetan authorities provided all sorts of facilities of transportation, lodging and fooding to the Nepalese mission. They were warmly welcomed in China. During their stay at Peking, the Nepalese delegates had the audiences with the Ch'ing Emperor, delivered the presents and the *arji* they brought to him, and received awards, presents and a golden *Parwana* to give to the Nepalese king on behalf of the Ch'ing Emperor. The members of the Nepalese mission were also duly awarded by the Ch'ing Emperor. On their return to Nepal, the Nepalese delegates had to perform the ceremony of purification at Betravati river. Afterwards they were given a grand reception at Kathmandu. From 1792 to 1852, generally the journey of each Nepalese mission to China was completed in less than two years, but afterwards it seems that mainly due to the involvement of Nepalese missions in trading activities, the duration of the delegates' journey became much longer. It took about five years each for the Nepalese missions of 1877 and 1886 to finish their journey to China, whereas the missions of 1894 and 1906 returned home after a lapse of nearly seven and four years respectively. Likewise, as to the duration of the sojurn of mission at Peking, in the pre-Rana period, the Nepalese missions generally remained at Peking for forty-five days, but in the Rana period, due to their involvement in trading activities, the Nepalese missions started staying in Peking for a longer period. The Nepalese mission travelled about 2500 miles from Kathmandu to Peking. The length of the journey, the severity of the climate, and the bad roads from Kathmandu to Peking were a source of great anxiety for the Nepalese missions. The Nepalese delegates suffered a lot of hardships, physical as well as mental on account of the illness and even death of some of the members, manhandling by Tibetans, thieves and robbers, negligence by Chinese authorities, and great humiliation on the part of the Chinese government. Jang Bahadur seemed to have even used the issue of the mistreatment of the 1852 Nepalese mission as a pretext to declare war against Tibet in 1855.

With the appearance of the Ranas on the political scene of Nepal, especially with the mission of 1852, the purpose of the Nepalese mission to China became less political and more commercial for the personal profit of the Rana Prime Minister and his close relatives than for the national interest. From 1852 to 1906, all six Nepalese missions to China were engaged in the much profitable opium trade and other commercial activities.

Thus the quinquennial mission system truly formed an important integral part of Nepal-China relations. Remarkably enough even when the journey from Kathmandu to Peking was quite difficult, long and hazardous, Nepal continued to send missions to Ch'ing court from 1792 to 1906. In the pre-Rana period, the mission system was mainly guided by Nepal's political or national interests. But in the Rana period, it was guided more by Rana family's commercial interests rather than national interests. For the Rana rulers, it provided the only way to gain access to the markets of China and good business for many items including the much profitable opium. As Nepal always needed China's good-will for the protection of her greater interests in Tibet, Nepal continued to dispatch five-yearly mission to China up to 1906, long after China had ceased to be an effective power in the Himalayas. Significantly enough, throughout the eighteenth and nineteenth century, Nepal tended to look upon China as too distant to be real threat but close enough to serve as a possibly useful balance to its threat from the British India.

* * *

Chronology of Nepalese Quinquennial Missions To China 1792-1906

A

Year	Nepalese King	Chinese Emperor	Nepalese *Mukhtiyar*/ Prime Minister
1792	Ran Bahadur Shah	Ch'ien Lung	
1795	Ran Bahadur Shah	Chia Ch'ing	
1802	Girwan Yuddha Bikram Shah	Chia Ch'ing	
1807	Girwan Yuddha Bikram Shah	Chia Ch'ing	* Bhimsen Thapa
1812	Girwan Yuddha Bikram Shah	Chia Ch'ing	* Bhimsen Thapa
1817	Rajendra Bikram Shah	Chia Ch'ing	* Bhimsen Thapa
1822	Rajendra Bikram Shah	Tao Kwang	* Bhimsen Thapa
1827	Rajendra Bikram Shah	Tao Kwang	* Bhimsen Thapa
1832	Rajendra Bikram Shah	Tao Kwang	* Bhimsen Thapa
1837	Rajendra Bikram Shah	Tao Kwang	* Bhimsen Thapa/ Ranajung Pande
1842	Rajendra Bikram Shah	Tao Kwang	**Chautariya* Fateh Jang Shah
1847	Surendra Bikram Shah	Tao Kwang	Jang Bahadur Rana
1852	Surendra Bikram Shah	Hsien Feng	Jang Bahadur Rana
1866	Surendra Bikram Shah	T'ung-Chih	Jang Bahadur Rana
1877	Surendra Bikram Shah	Kwang Hsu	Ranauddip Singh
1886	Prithvi Bir Bikram Shah	Kwang Hsu	Bir Shamsher
1894	Prithvi Bir Bikram Shah	Kwang Hsu	Bir Shamsher
1906	Prithvi Bir Bikram Shah	Kwang Hsu	Chandra Shamsher

* *Mukhtiyar*

B

Year	Departed	Returned	Leader and Deputy Leader	Remarks
1792	16 September, 1792 (from Kathmandu) 6 October, 1792 (from Dhaibung)		a. *Kazi* Dev Dutta Thapa b. *Subba* (*Sardar*) Pratiman Rana	It was the first Nepalese customary quinquennial mission to the Imperial Court of China.
1795	July 1795	August 1796	a. *Kazi* Narsingh Gurung b. *Jetha Budha* Madho Sahi	It was the first Nepalese mission carrying at a time the usual five-yearly presents as well as special presents on the occasion of the Ch'ing Emperor Chia Ch'ing ascending the throne
1802	August 1802		a. *Kazi* Sarvajit Pande b. *Sardar* Chamu Bhandari	It was the first Nepalese quinquennial mission not to go to Peking itself and went only up to Nepal-Tibet border area to hand over the usual five-yearly presents meant for the Ch'ing Emperor
1807	August 1807		a. *Kazi* Bhaktabir Thapa b. *Subedar* (*Sardar*) Dambar Thapa	The 1807 Nepalese mission did not go to Peking itself and delivered the presents to the Chinese officials at the border area of Kuti.
1812	June 1812	September 1813	a. *Kazi* Bhaktabir Thapa b. *Sardar* Dambar Thapa	
1817	June 1817	September 1818	a. *Kazi* Ranajoor Thapa b. (?)	
1822	June 1822	August 1823	a. *Kazi* Dalbhanjan Pande b. *Sardar* Devi Bhagat Khatri	It was the second Nepalese mission carrying the usual five-yearly presents and special presents on the occasion of the new Ch'ing Emperor Tao Kwang's ascending the throne in 1820
1827	June 1827	August 1828	a. *Kazi* Bir Keshar Pande b. *Sardar* Ranajung Karki	
1832	18 June 1832	22 October 1833	a. *Kazi* Bir Keshar Pande b. *Sardar* Lakshabir Sahi	
1837	14 July 1837	25 September 1838	a. *Chautariya* Pushkar Shah b. Captain (*Sardar*) Kirti Dhoj Pande	
1842	3 July 1842	October 1843	a. *Kazi* Jagat Bam Pande b. *Sardar* Bir Bhadra Karki	The leader of the 1842 Nepalese mission did not return to Nepal and escaped to India from Tibet as the prominent Pandes were executed in Nepal even

				before the appointment of Mathabar Singh Thapa as *Mukhtiyar* in December 1843.
1847	June 1847	March 1849	a. *Kazi* Surath Singh Pantha b. *Sardar* Ahibarna Basnyat	Both the leader and the deputy-leader of this mission died in Lhasa while they were on their way back to Nepal.
1852	August 1852	22-May 1854	a. *Kazi* Gambhir Singh Adhikari b. *Sardar* Samsher Jang Thapa	Both the leader and deputy-leader of the 1852 mission also passed away while they were returning home from Peking. This mission happened to be the third such Nepalese mission which had carried the usual five-yearly presents as well as the special presents to the new Ch'ing Emperor Hsien Feng who had ascended the throne in 1850
1866	2 August 1866	May 1869	a. *Kazi* Jagat Sher Sijapati b. *Sardar* Mullay Jung Pande	This mission was not allowed to visit Peking on the plea of a Muslim rebellion in western China and had to return from Ta-Chien-lu, about half way to Peking, near the China-Tibet border where the Nepalese mission waited for nearly two years for permission to proceed to Peking. Besides that it was the fourth Nepalese mission carrying the usual five-yearly presents and special presents to the new Ch'ing Emperor T'ung Chih.
1877	July 1877	18 June 1882	a. *Kazi* Tej Bahadur Rana b. Lieutenant (*Sardar*) Bal Bhadra Pande	This mission happened to be the fifth Nepalese mission which had carried the usual five-yearly presents and special presents on the occasion of the new Ch'ing Emperor Kwang Hsu's ascending the throne in 1875.
1886	13 September 1886	June 1891	a. *Kazi* Ran Bikram Rana b. *Sardar* Drigman (Dirgha Man) Singh Basniat.	
1894	10 August 1894	1 March, 1901	a. *Kazi* Indra Bikram Rana b. *Sardar* Juddhabir Khadka	The deputy-leader of this 1894 Nepalese mission died in Peking.
1906	10 August 1906	April 1910	a. *Kazi* Bhairab Bahadur Gadhatola Chhetri b. *Sardar* Kahar Singh Khadka	It was the last Nepalese customary quinquennial mission to the Imperial Court of China.

* * *

Selected Bibliography

PRIMARY SOURCES

Unpublished Documents

National Archives of India, New Delhi:

Acting Secretary to Secretary, Govt. Fort William, Foreign Dept. Ext., 4 June 1832, No. 33.

'Embassy to China', Foreign Political Consultation, 27 August 1832, No. 18

'Chinese Emperor's Epistle received by the Maharaja of Nepal', Foreign Political Consultation, 21 November 1833, No. 36.

'Mission to Pekin', Foreign Department Political, 19 December 1833, Nos. 11-12.

'Mission to Pekin', Foreign Department Secret, 13 June 1838, No. 10.

'Mission to China', Foreign Department Secret, 26 December 1839, No. 139.

'Mission to Pekin', Foreign Department Secret, 10 August 1842, No. 126.

'Embassy to Peking and Intelligence regarding the proceeding of the Nepalese Embassy to Peking', Foreign Department Secret, 19 October 1842, No. 70

'Nepalese Embassy to China', Foreign Secret Consultation, 26 May 1854, Nos. 50-53.

'Nepal and China', Foreign Secret Consultation, 30 June 1854, Nos. 42-43.

'Intention of Nipalese Government to resume diplomatic relations with Court of Pekin', Foreign Political A, June 1866, Nos. 163-164.

'Reports the Starting of the Mission to Pekin with presents for the Emperor', Foreign Political A, August 1866, No. 104.

'Nepalese Embassy to China', Foreign Political A, August 1867, Nos. 53-54.

'Nepalese Mission to China', Foreign Political A, March 1869, Nos. 208-214.

'Countries traversed by the late Nepalese Mission to China', Foreign Secret I, September 1870, Nos. 400-404.

'Alleged Illicit traffic in opium through Nepal', Foreign Political A, May 1875, Nos. 104-104 A.

'Embassy from Nipal to China', Foreign Secret, September 1876, Nos. 129-133.

'Nepalese "tribute" mission to China', Foreign Secret, October 1877, Nos. 149-150.

'Nepalese Mission to China', Foreign Secret, December 1878, Nos. 23-28.

'Nipalese Mission to China', Foreign Secret, January 1879, Nos. 88-91.

'Nipalese Mission to China', Foreign Secret, June 1879, Nos. 22-25.

'Nipalese Envoy to China', Foreign Secret, July 1879, Nos. 7-8.

'Arrival in Peking of a Mission from Nipal', Foreign Political A, April 1880, Nos. 98-99.

'Departure of the Nipalese Mission', Foreign Political A, January 1881, Nos. 83-84.

'Return of the Nipalese Mission to Pekin', Foreign Political B, July 1881, Nos. 156-157.

'Return to Nipal of the Mission sent thence to China', Foreign Secret, July 1882, Nos. 155-157.

'Departure of the usual Complimentary Nepalese Mission to Pekin', Foreign Secret E. October 1886, Nos. 1-2.

'Presentation of tribute by Maharaj Adhiraj of Nepal to Emperor of China', Foreign Secret E, February 1894, Nos. 461-464.

'Intention of the Nepal Darbar to despatch the usual Complimentary Mission to Peking', Foreign Secret E, July 1894, Nos. 184-185.

'Information regarding Nepalese Affairs', Foreign Secret E, March 1895, Nos. 69-70.

'Tribute Mission from Nepal to China and Question of the Subordination of Nepal to China', Foreign Secret E, September 1895, Nos. 116-130.

'Safe arrival at Peking of the Nepalese Mission to China', Foreign External B, August 1896, Nos. 15-18.

'Return to Nepal of the Quinquennial Mission to China', Foreign External B, April 1901, No. 31.

'Itinerary of Kazi Indra Bikram Rana from Kathmandu to Peking in Samvat 1951', Foreign Secret E, September 1904, Nos. 88-97.

'Nepalese Commercial Mission to China', Foreign Secret E, September 1906, Nos. 262-265.

'News-Letters from the Nepalese Representative at Lhasa regarding Tibet Affairs', Foreign Secret E, June 1907, Nos. 76-102.

'Nepalese Commercial Mission to China', Foreign Secret E, July 1907, Nos. 304-305.

'Nepalese Commercial Mission to China', Foreign Secret E, September 1907, Nos. 98-99.

'Transmission through H.B.M.'s Minister Peking of a cover containing a draft for 2029 Taels for delivery to Her Officer in charge of the Nepalese Mission to Peking', Foreign External B, January 1908, Nos. 92-95.

'Nepalese Commercial Mission to Peking', Foreign Secret E, March 1908, Nos. 1-7.

'Nepalese Commercial Mission to China', Foreign Secret E, October 1908, Nos. 696-717.

'Departure of the Nepalese Commercial Mission from Peking', Foreign Secret E, January 1909, Nos. 411-413.

'Reports regarding the Nepalese Commercial Mission to China', Foreign Secret E, June 1909, Nos. 478-482.

'Nepalese Mission to China and Thanks of the Nepal Durbar to British Consuls for their Kindness and Courtesy to the Mission', Foreign Secret E, September 1909, Nos. 16-21,

'Nepalese Commercial Mission to China', Foreign Secret E, October 1909, Nos. 713-716.

'Action of the Chinese in Tibet and the Flight of the Dalai Lama to India', Foreign Secret E, March 1910. Nos. 385-510.

'Question of new treaty with Nepal', Foreign Secret E, November 1910, Nos. 15-17.

'Rejection of Chinese Claims to Suzerainty over Nepal and Bhutan', Foreign Secret E, July 1911, Nos. 248-280.

Ministry of Foreign Affairs, Kathmandu:

'Documents dealing with Nepalese Quinquennial Missions to China', *Poka* No. 64.

'Documents relating to Nepal-Tibet and China Relations', Unnumbered *Poka*.

National Archives of Nepal, Kathmandu:

'Correspondence between Chinese Amban and Nepal Govt.', *Poka* No. 2, Letter No. 81.

'Documents dealing with Surath Singh Pantha's mission to China', *Poka* No. 2, Letter No. 158.

'Document relating to Jagat Bam Pande's mission to China', *Poka* No. 5, Letter No. 44.

Royal Nepal Army Head-Quarters, Kathmandu:

'Documents relating to presents sent to the Chinese and Tibetan authorities through the Nepalese missions', Part 3, Serial No. 63 (53).

Unpublished Dissertation:

Sharma, Kunjar M. *The Economic Theme in Nepali Foreign Policy: An Historical Analysis Up to the end of the Anglo-Nepal War,* Ph.D. Dissertation, University of Kansas, 1973.

Published Documents (Nepali):

"Nepal Desh Ko Itihas" (History of Nepal), A Manuscript in the National Archives of Nepal, Kathmandu, Published in *Ancient Nepal*, No. 27 (April, 1974).

Vajracharya, Dhanavajra and Nepal, Jnanmani, (eds.) *Aitihasik Patra Sangraha* (Collection of Historical Letters) Vol. I, Kathmandu: Nepal Sanskritik Parishad, 2014 B.S..

Vajracharya, Dhanavajra and Nepal, Jnanmani, (eds.) *Tri-Ratna Saundarya Gatha* (An Account of the Beauty of the Three Jewels), Kathmandu: Nepal Sanskritik Parishad, 2019 B.S.

SECONDARY SOURCES

Books in English

Fergusson, W.N. *Land and People of Tibet and China in the Early Twentieth Century,* Delhi: Sharda Prakashan, Reprint, 1989.

Fisher, Margaret W. and Rose, Leo E. *England, India, Nepal, Tibet, China 1765-1958,* Berkeley: University of California, 1959.

Hasrat, Bikram Jit (ed.). *History of Nepal: As Told By Its Own and Contemporary Chronicles,* Hoshiarpur, Punjab: V.V. Research Institute Book Agency, 1970.

Hunter, William Wilson. *Life of Brian Houghton Hodgson,* New Delhi: Asian Educational Services, Reprint, 1991.

Manandhar, Tri Ratna. *Nepal: The Years of Trouble (1877-85),* Kathmandu: Purna Devi Manandhar, 1986.

Manandhar, Tri Ratna and Mishra, Tirtha Prasad. *Nepal's Quinquennial Missions To China,* Kathmandu: Mrs. Purna Devi Manandhar and Mrs. Puspa Mishra, 1986.

Manandhar, Vijay Kumar. *Cultural and Political Aspects of Nepal-China Relations,* Delhi: Adroit Publishers, 1999.

Oldfield, H. Ambrose. *Sketches from Nepal*, Vol. I, Delhi: Cosmos Publications, Reprint, 1981.

Rana, Pudma Jung Bahadur. *Life of Maharaja Sir Jung Bahadur,* Kathmandu: Ratna Pustak Bhandar, Reprint, 1980.

Rana, Purushottam Sham Shere J.B.. *Jung Bahadur Rana: The Story of His Rise and Glory*, Delhi: Book Faith India, 1998.

Regmi, D.R. *Modern Nepal.* Vol. I, Calcutta: Firma K.L. Mukhopadhayay, 1975.

Rockhill, William Woodville. *The Land of the Lamas,* New Delhi: Asian Publication Services, Reprint, 1975.

Rose, Leo E. and Fisher, Margaret W. *The Politics of Nepal: Persistence and Change in an Asian Monarchy*, Ithaca and London: Cornell University Press, 1970.

Rose, Leo E. *Nepal: Strategy For Survival,* Berkeley: University of California Press, 1971.

Sever, Adrian. *Nepal Under the Ranas*, New Delhi: Oxford and IBH Publishing Co. Pvt. Ltd., 1993.

Sever, Adrian. *Aspects of Modern Nepalese History*, New Delhi: Vikas Publishing House Pvt. Ltd., 1996.

Shakabpa, Tsepon W.D. *Tibet: A Political History,* New Heaven: Yale University Press, 1967.

Stiller, Ludwig F. *The Silent Cry: The People of Nepal, 1816-1839*, Kathmandu: Sahayogi Prakashan, 1976.

Tucci, Giuseppe. *Nepal: The Discovery of the Malla*, London: George Allen and Unwin, 1962.

Twitchett, Dennis and Fairbank, John K., (eds.). *The Cambridge History of China*, Vol. 10, Late Ch'ing 1800-1911, Part I, Cambridge: Cambridge University Press, 1978.

Uprety, Prem R. *Nepal-Tibet Relations 1850-1930*, Kathmandu: Puga Nara, 1980.

Books in Nepali:

Bhattarai, Niranjan. *Chin Ra Tyasasita Nepal Ko Sambandha* (China and Her Relations with Nepal), Kathmandu: Nepal Academy, 2018 B.S..

Dixit, Kamal. *Mahachin* (Greatr China). Lalitpur: Jagdamba Prakashan, 2055 B.S.

Gurung, Jagman. *Nepalko Ekikaranma Gurungharuko Bhumika* (Role of The Gurungs in the Unification of Nepal), Pokhara: Sri Bauddha Arghaun Sadana, 2041 B.S.

Nepal, Jnanmani. *Nepal-Bhot Chin Sambandhaka Kehi Sanskritik Paksha* (Some Cultural Aspect of Nepal-Tibet China Relations), Kathmandu: Royal Nepal Academy, 2045 B.S..

Nepali, Chitta Ranjan. *Shree Panch Ran Bahadur Shah* (King Ran Bahadur Shah), Kathmandu: Mrs. Mary Rajbhandari, 2020. B.S..

Nepali, Chitta Ranjan. *General Bhimsen Thapa Ra Tatakalin Nepal* (General Bhimsen Thapa and Contemporary Nepal), Kathmandu: Ratna Pustak Bhandar, Third Edition, 2035 B.S..

Pande Chhetri, Bhim Bahadur. *Rastra Bhakti Ko Jhalak: Pande Bamsa Ko Bhumika, 1594-1904* (A Glimpse of Loyalty to the Nation: Role of the Pande Dynasty), 1539-1847, Kathmandu: Ratna Pustak Bhandar, 2034 B.S..

Rana, Purushottam Shamsher Jang Bahadur. *Sri Tin Haruko Tathya Brittanta* (Factual Description of *Sri Tins)*, Banaras: Parambir Shamsher J.B.R., 2047 B.S.

Upadhyaya, Ramji. *Nepal Ko Itihas Arthat Digdarshan* (History of Nepal or Survey), Banaras: *Subba* Homnath Kedarnath, 2007 B.S..

Articles (English):

Hodgson, B.H. "Route of two Nepalese Embassies to Pekin with remarks on the water-shed and plateau of Tibet", *Journal of the Asiatic Society*, No. VI, 1856.

Manandhar, Tri Ratna and Mishra, Tirtha Prasad. "Cavenagh and Rose on Nepal's Mission to China", *Rolamba,* Vol. 3, No. 1, January-March 1983.

Manandhar, Vijay Kumar."*Sahu* Dharma Narayan Manandhar: A Financier And Member of the Bereaucratic Elite of the Nineteenth Century", *Voice of History*, Vol. XIV, No. 1 (June 1999).

Articles (Nepali):

Mishra, Tirtha Prasad. "Shree Panch Surendra Ko Chinia Badshah Lai Upahar" (King Surendra's presents to the Chinese Emperor), *Garima*, Year 8 No. 1, Vol. No. 93, Bhadra 2047 B.S.

Mishra, Tirtha Prasad and Sharma, Niranjan. "Chin Jane Kazi Bhairab Bahadur Ko Jaheri" (Reports of Kazi Bhairab Bahadur from China), *Rolamba*, Vol. 3, No. 3. July-September 1983.

Nepal, Jnanmani. "Jang Bahadur Ko Bidesh Niti Ra Sambat 1904 Ko Pechin Jane Pratinidhi Mandal" (Jang Bahadur's Foreign Policy and Mission to Peking of 1904 B.S.), *Contributions to Nepalese Studies*, Journal of Centre for Nepal and Asian Studies, Tribhuvan University, Kathmandu, Vol. VIII No. 2, June 1981.

Published Book and Article (Oriental):

Fairbank, John K. and Teng, S.Y., "On the Ch'ing Tributary System", *Harvard Journal of Asiatic Studies*, Vol. VI, 1941.

Tikhvinsky, S.L. (ed.). *China and Her Neighbours: From Ancient Times to the Middle Ages*, Moscow: Progress Publishers, 1981.

Interview:

Manandhar, Jit Bahadur. Ex-Secretary, His Majesty's Government and a Research Scholar on Nepalese Culture and the Manandhars.

* * *

Index

A

Ahibarna Basnyat, *Sardar* 107-108, 239

Ambans, Chinese 8-10, 18, 22-26, 28, 32, 35, 37-40, 44, 48-53, 57, 59-61, 64, 66-67, 76-78, 80, 82-83, 86, 88-99, 106-111, 117-118, 120, 137, 155-156, 161-163, 166, 175-180, 183, 202, 212, 230

Arji 1, 61, 87-88, 101, 137

B

Bahadur Shah, Regent 1, 3, 5, 7, 9, 17, 19, 22, 228, 246

Bal Bahadur Pande, Lt. 162, 169, 177

Bhairab Bahadur Gadhatola Chhetri, *Kazi* 200, 203, 240

Bhaktabir Thapa, *Kazi* 31, 37-39, 44-45, 235, 239

Bhariya Nayak 38, 49, 60, 65, 76, 86, 107, 120

Bhimsen Rana, Lt. 120-121, 135

Bhimsen Thapa, *Mukhtiyar* 31, 38, 44, 46, 51, 58, 77, 238, 246

Bir Bhadra Karki, *Sardar* 86, 88, 99, 239

Bir Keshar Pande, *Kazi* 60-61, 64-65, 67, 69-70, 235, 239

Bir Man Thapa, *Sardar* 119, 126

Bir Shamsher, *Maharaja* 180, 182-183, 191, 193, 238

British Legation 164, 203, 205-207

C

C.W. Ravenshaw, Lt. Colonel 193

Chamu Bhandari, *Sardar* 23, 239

Chandra Shamsher, *Maharaja* 193, 201-202, 211, 213, 238

Chauvean, Bishop 139, 141, 148

Chia Ch'ing, *Emperor* 6, 10, 22, 31, 46, 48, 236, 238, 239

Chou Tzu-Kuei, Lt. 190, 195

D

D.R. Regmi 1, 3

Dalbhanjan Pande, *Kazi* 48, 50, 52-53, 56-59, 239

Dambar Thapa, *Sardar* 31, 38, 44, 76, 239

Dambar Thapa, *Subedar* 31, 38, 44, 76, 239

Devi Bhagat Khatri, *Sardar* 49, 239

Dharma Narayan Manandhar, *Sahu* 140, 247

F

F.M. Bailey, Lt. 201-202

Fu K'ang-an, General 1

G

Gambhir Singh Adhikari, *Kazi* 60, 119, 121, 126, 134, 239

Girwan Yuddha Bikram Shah, King 22, 29, 238

Gorkha Ko Geet 2

Gray, Dr. 205, 217

H
H.H. Fox 203, 205, 217
H.Wylie 190
Henry Endemenilt, Prof. 202, 214
Hsien Feng, Emperor 119, 122, 137, 236, 238-239
I
Indra Bikram Rana, *Kazi* Major 189, 191, 193, 197, 199, 240, 243
J
J.H. Abbot Anderson, Colonel 217
J.N. Jordan, Sir 203-206, 209, 213, 215-217, 219, 221, 225
Jagat Bam Pande, *Kazi* 77, 85-86, 88-89, 93, 98-101, 235, 239, 244
Jagat Sher Sijapati, *Kazi* 137-138, 160, 239
Jang Bahadur 88, 105, 108-109, 117, 119, 121, 135, 137, 140, 142-143, 161-162, 167, 175, 237-238, 246-247
Jnanmani Nepal 1, 6, 49, 77, 105, 119, 200
Juddhabir Khadka, *Sardar* 189, 191, 199, 240
K
Kahar Singh Khadka, *Sardar* 200, 240
Kirti Dhoj Pande, *Sardar* Captain 76, 79, 239
Kowtow 204
Kwang Hsu, Emperor 163, 165, 167, 180-181, 183, 190, 192, 208, 236, 238-239
L
Lakshabir Sahi, Sardar 65, 67, 70, 239
Leo E. Rose 3, 6, 46, 76, 78, 85, 105-106, 139, 162, 180, 200
Lhasa 1, 7-9, 17-19, 32, 38, 48, 52, 57-60, 66, 75-77, 83, 86-87, 98, 107, 109, 117-118, 120, 125, 137-138, 140, 143, 158, 163, 180, 183, 187, 190, 197, 201-202, 205, 211, 218, 228, 230, 236, 239, 243
Lifa Yamen 207, 222-223
M
Madho Sahi, *Jetha Budha* 7, 18, 239
Mahout 2, 4
Meng-pao, *Amban* 87
Morrison, Dr. 209, 225
Mullay Jung Pande, *Sardar* 138-239
N
Narsingh Gurung, *Kazi* 6-8, 17, 22, 239
O
Opium 88, 105
P
P. Grant Jones 204-207, 222
Parwana 8-9, 19, 24, 28-30, 32, 35, 38, 44, 46, 50-51, 58-59, 67, 78, 83, 88, 100-101, 108, 122, 137, 157, 187-188, 192, 197, 199, 212, 228-229, 236

Peking Gazette 162-164, 167, 170, 180, 184, 189, 191, 194, 219
Pratiman Rana, *Subba* 1, 239
Prithvi Bir Bikram Shah, King 180, 190, 238
Pudma Jung 121, 245
Pushkar Shah, *Chautariya Kazi* 76-79, 82-83, 235, 239
R
R.C. Lawrence, Colonel 141, 143
Rajendra Bikram Shah, King 47, 65, 85, 238
Ran Bahadur Shah, King 1-10, 18-19, 22-23, 25, 31, 238, 246
Ran Bikram Rana, *Kazi* 180-182, 188, 239
Ran Mehar Singh Adhikari, *Kazi* 119, 126
Ranajoor Thapa, *Kazi* 46-47, 239
Ranajung Karki, *Sardar* 60-61, 239
Ranajung Pande 77, 80, 238
Ranauddip Singh 162-163, 167, 180, 238
S
Sarvajit Pande, *Kazi* 22-23, 25, 28, 30, 239
Shakabpa, Tsepon W.D. 3, 245
Subarna Prabha, Queen 23, 28, 30
Surath Singh Pantha, *Kazi* 105-106, 108-110, 117-118, 239, 244
Surendra Bikram Shah, King 105, 238
T
T.F. Wade, Sir 164-166, 173
T.T. Cooper 141
Ta Chien-lu 139, 141, 143, 161, 164-166
Tej Bahadur Rana, *Kazi* Colonel 161-162, 164-165, 169, 177, 181, 235, 239
The Times 191, 193
Tientsin 202, 209, 210, 214, 224-226, 228
Tirtha Prasad Mishra 6, 31, 49, 86, 106, 109, 120, 141, 163, 180, 190, 209
Tri Ratna Manandhar 6, 31, 49, 86, 106, 109, 120, 141, 163, 180, 190
W
W. Beauclerk 191
Wang 3, 5, 32, 34, 167, 183, 228
Wansausan Palace 208, 223
William Woodville Rockhill 182-183, 208

***